PENGUIN CLASSICS

THE INTERESTING NARRATIVE
AND OTHER WRITNGS

By his own account, OLAUDAH EQUIANO was born in 1745 in what is now
southeastern Nigeria, enslaved at the age of eleven, and sold to English
slave traders, who transported him to the West Indies. Within a few days,
he was taken to Virginia and sold to a local planter. He was resold after
about a month to Michael Henry Pascal, an officer in the British navy, who
brought him to London and gave him the name he always used thereafter:
Gustavus Vassa.

With Pascal, Equiano saw military action during the Seven Years' War,
but at the end of the war in 1762, Pascal reneged on his promise to free
Equiano, instead selling him into the horrors of West Indian slavery.
Equiano, a clever businessman, managed to save enough money to buy his
own freedom in 1766.

Once free, Equiano set off on voyages of commerce and adventure to
North America, the Mediterranean, the West Indies, and the North Pole.
Returning to London, he became concerned with spiritual and social reform. He converted to Methodism and became an outspoken opponent of
the slave trade, first in letters to newspapers and then in *The Interesting Narrative,* published in 1789. He married an Englishwoman in 1792, and one
of their two daughters lived to inherit the sizeable estate he left at his death
on March 31, 1797.

VINCENT CARRETTA is a professor of English at the University of Maryland.
His publications include *"The Snarling Muse": Verbal and Visual Political
Satire from Pope to Churchill* (1983); *George III and the Satirists from Hogarth
to Byron* (1990); and *Unchained Voices: An Anthology of Black Authors in the
English-Speaking World of the Eighteenth Century* (1996). He has also published separate Penguin editions of the complete works of Ignatius Sancho
(1998), Quobna Ottobah Cugoano (1999), and Phillis Wheatley (2001).
Most recently, Carretta has co-edited, with Philip Gould, *Genius in Bondage*
(2001), a collection of essays on early English-speaking transatlantic writers of African descent.

OLAUDAH EQUIANO

The Interesting Narrative
and Other Writings

*Edited with an Introduction and
Notes by* VINCENT CARRETTA

PENGUIN BOOKS

To
Pat, Nat, Maude,
and the guys on the porch

PENGUIN BOOKS
Published by the Penguin Group
Penguin Group (USA) Inc., 375 Hudson Street, New York, New York 10014, U.S.A.
Penguin Group (Canada), 90 Eglinton Avenue East, Suite 700, Toronto, Ontario,
Canada M4P 2Y3 (a division of Pearson Penguin Canada Inc.)
Penguin Books Ltd, 80 Strand, London WC2R 0RL, England
Penguin Ireland, 25 St. Stephen's Green, Dublin 2, Ireland (a division of Penguin Books Ltd)
Penguin Group (Australia), 250 Camberwell Road, Camberwell, Victoria 3124, Australia
(a division of Pearson Australia Group Pty Ltd)
Penguin Books India Pvt Ltd, 11 Community Centre, Panchsheel Park,
New Delhi – 110 017, India
Penguin Group (NZ), 67 Apollo Drive, Rosedale, North Shore 0632, New Zealand
(a division of Pearson New Zealand Ltd)
Penguin Books (South Africa) (Pty) Ltd, 24 Sturdee Avenue, Rosebank,
Johannesburg 2196, South Africa

Penguin Books Ltd, Registered Offices: 80 Strand, London WC2R 0RL, England

The Interesting Narrative of the Life of Olaudah Equiano, or Gustavus Vassa, the African
first published in Great Britain by the author 1789
Published in the United States of America by W. Durell 1791
Volume edited and with an introduction and notes by Vincent Carretta published in Penguin Books 1995
This revised edition published 2003

30

Copyright © Vincent Carretta, 1995, 2003
All rights reserved

LIBRARY OF CONGRESS CATALOGING IN PUBLICATION DATA
Equiano, Olaudah, b. 1745.
The interesting narrative and other writings/Olaudah Equiano;
edited with an introduction and notes by Vincent Carretta.
p. cm.
ISBN 978-0-14-243716-2
l. Equiano,Olaudah, b.1745. 2. Slaves—Great Britain—Biography. 3. Slaves—United States—Biography.
I. Carretta, Vincent. II.Title.
HT869.E6A3 1996
305.5'67'092—dc20   95-23577
[B]

Printed in the United States of America
Set in Bembo

ACKNOWLEDGMENTS

I AM very grateful to Timothy D. Pyatt, curator of the Marylandia and Rare Books Collection of the University of Maryland, College Park, for his aid in making the text of the ninth edition available for publication. I thank, as well, Dr. Sidney E. Berger, head of Special Collections at the University of California at Riverside, for enabling me to reproduce the frontispiece of the 1794 edition.

My greatest debts are to the staffs and collections of the following institutions: the McKeldin Library of the University of Maryland; the John Carter Brown Library; the Folger Shakespeare Library; the British Library; the British Museum; the Public Record Offices (PRO) in Kew and London; Dr. Williams's Library, London; the Library of the Society of Friends House, London; the Greater London Record Office; the Goldsmiths' Library of the University of London Library; the City of Westminster Libraries; the Guildhall Library of the City of London; the Rhodes House Library, Oxford; the Cambridgeshire County Record Office; the University of Glasgow Library; the Gloucestershire County Record Office; the Hornby Collection of the Liverpool Libraries and Information Services; the Shropshire County Record Office; the Trustees of the Wedgwood Museum, Barlaston, Staffordshire; the Wisbech and Fenland Museum, Cambridgeshire; the Banks Archive Project (the Natural History Museum, London); the Van Pelt Library of the University of Pennsylvania; and the Library of Congress. I also owe thanks for help in my research to John Barrell, Christopher L. Brown, Brycchan Carey, Neil Chambers, Malcolm Dick, Kenneth Donovan, Mark Jones, Reyahn King, Lynn Miller, Stephen Price, Nini Rodgers, Erin Sadlack, Philip Saunders, J. V. Thorpe, James Walvin, and Iain Whyte.

An abridged version of the Penguin text of *The Interesting Narrative*, some of its notes, and parts of its Introduction appear, by permission of both presses, in *Unchained Voices: An Anthology of Black Authors in the English-Speaking World of the Eighteenth Century* (The University Press of Kentucky, 1996).

CONTENTS

THE INTERESTING NARRATIVE OF THE LIFE OF OLAUDAH EQUIANO, OR GUSTAVUS VASSA, THE AFRICAN. WRITTEN BY HIMSELF

INTRODUCTION

MOST of what we know about Olaudah Equiano (or Gustavus Vassa, as he almost always referred to himself in public and private) is found in his *Interesting Narrative*. External evidence enables us to supplement and correct his own account. He tells us that he was born an Igbo in 1745 in the part of Africa that is now southeastern Nigeria, kidnapped from there at the age of eleven, and taken to Barbados, in the West Indies. After a few days there, he says, he was brought to Virginia and sold to a local planter. A month or so later, Michael Henry Pascal, an officer in the British navy, purchased him from the planter. Pascal renamed him Gustavus Vassa, and took him to London, and then into service in the Royal Navy during the Seven Years' War (known in North America as the French and Indian Wars). Vassa/Equiano writes that he first reached England "about the beginning of the spring 1757," and that he entered naval service with Pascal during that summer. Pascal, reneging on his promise to free Vassa after the war, sold him at the end of 1762 to a merchant captain who returned him to the West Indies, where Vassa eventually purchased himself, and thus his freedom, in 1766. As he points out in his *Narrative*, Vassa chose to gain his freedom by purchase, a process called at the time "redemption," rather than by escape. In effect, Vassa implicitly acknowledged the legitimacy of slavery.

As a free man, he remained for a while in the employ of his former master, the Quaker Robert King, making several trading trips to Savannah, Georgia, and Philadelphia, Pennsylvania. Between 1767 and 1773, Vassa, based in London, worked on commercial vessels sailing to the Mediterranean and the West Indies. After joining an expedition to the Arctic seeking the Northeast Passage in 1773, he returned to London, where his spiritual needs led him to embrace Methodism. Soon again growing restless, in 1775–76 he helped his friend and former employer, Dr. Charles

Irving, in Irving's plan to develop a plantation in Central America, with Vassa acting as the buyer and driver (overseer) of their black slaves. Disgusted by the immorality of his fellow workers, Vassa resigned in 1776, and returned to London at the beginning of 1777. There he became increasingly involved with efforts to help other blacks, with the project to resettle the black poor in Sierra Leone, and with the drive to abolish the African slave trade. He published the first edition of his *Narrative* in March 1789, establishing his dual identity as Olaudah Equiano/Gustavus Vassa. The ninth edition, the last published in English in his lifetime, appeared in 1794.

Using his legal name, Gustavus Vassa, Equiano married an Englishwoman, Susanna Cullen (1762–1796), on 7 April 1792. Gustavus and Susanna Vassa had two daughters: Ann Mary (or Maria), born 16 October 1793, and Joanna, born 11 April 1795. Ann Maria died on 21 July 1797, exactly a year and a half after her mother's death and four months after her father's death on 31 March 1797. The demands of supporting two daughters alone may help account for Equiano's apparent public silence after 1794. Certainly by then he had earned enough from sales of his book to permit him to live on its proceeds, his inheritance, and his investments, which together were ample enough to justify Equiano's calling himself a gentleman in his will. Unlike the vast majority of his fellow Britons, Equiano was wealthy enough to require a will, and he was one of very few Afro-Britons in the eighteenth century in this position. Granville Sharp, the well-known philanthropist and abolitionist, attended him on his deathbed, and his death was noted in *The Gentleman's Magazine*. On her twenty-first birthday, in 1816, Joanna inherited £950 from her father's estate, a sum roughly equivalent to £80,000 or $120,000 today. Equiano achieved the fame and wealth he sought and deserved.

Recently discovered evidence sheds additional light on Equiano's early life. For example, commercial and military records suggest that he may have been much younger when he entered Pascal's service than he claims in his *Narrative*. Equiano reached England in early December 1754, more than two years sooner than recounted in the *Narrative*. The name "Gust. Vasa" appears on the muster book of the ship *Roebuck* as of 6 August 1755. More surprisingly, his baptismal record in 1759 and naval records from his Arctic voyage in 1773 suggest that he may well have been born in South Carolina, not Africa. External contradictions are especially intriguing because Equiano's account of his life is generally remarkably verifiable when tested against documentary and historical evidence, so much so that deviations from the truth seem more likely to have been the result of artistic premeditation than absentmindedness. From the available evidence, one could argue that the author of *The Interesting Narrative* invented an African identity rather than reclaimed one. If so, Equiano's literary achievements have been underestimated.

In 1789 the *Narrative* became the latest of a series of works published in England since 1772 by Afro-British authors, writers of African birth or descent who were subjects of the British king. At the end of 1772, James Albert Ukawsaw Gronniosaw's *A Narrative of the Most Remarkable Particulars in the Life of . . . an African Prince, as Related by Himself* was published in Bath, capitalizing on the attention brought to the condition of Afro-Britons by the Mansfield decision in June of that year. Lord Chief Justice of the King's Bench, Lord Mansfield, in a judicial ruling that was taken to be an emancipation proclamation for blacks in England, determined in the case of James Somerset that a slave could not legally be compelled by a master to return to the colonies from England. Although the ruling was narrowly restricted to the question of forcing the return of a slave, in practice it was widely perceived to have declared slavery illegal on English soil.

Phillis Wheatley's *Poems on Various Subjects, Religious and Moral* was published in London in 1773, sharing Gronniosaw's patron, the Methodist Countess of Huntingdon. Wheatley appears to acknowledge Gronniosaw's work in a letter to the Countess. Edward Long, a defender of slavery, published a poem by Francis Williams, a free black Jamaican, in his *History of Jamaica* (London, 1774). *Letters of the Late Ignatius Sancho* was published posthumously in London in 1782, and the London edition of John

Marrant's *A Narrative of the Lord's Wonderful Dealings with John Marrant, a Black* was published in 1785, the latter also with the patronage of the Countess of Huntingdon. Although none of these works very directly addresses the issues of the abolition of the slave trade or of slavery itself, all to some extent became involved in the arguments of the 1780s and later about the literary and intellectual capacities of Africans. For example, in his *Letter to the Treasurer of the Society Instituted for the Purpose of Effecting the Abolition of the Slave Trade* (London, 1788), the Reverend Robert Boucher Nikkols (Nichols), a future subscriber to Equiano's *Narrative*, writes,

> The stupidity of negroes is . . . urged by the friends of slavery as a plea for using them as brutes; for they represent the negroes as little removed above the monkey, or the oran-outang, with regard to intellects. But I am very certain, nothing has been written by the late defenders of slavery, that discovers [displays] half the literary merit or ability of two negroe writers. Phillis Wheatley wrote correct English poetry within a few years after her arrival in Boston from Africa; and there is a Latin ode of considerable length written in classic language by Francis Williams. . . . I never heard of poems by a monkey, or of Latin odes by an oran-outang. (46)

The context of Afro-British writers changed markedly after 1783, when loyalist blacks, freed by their masters, or self-emancipated by having joined the British forces against the colonial rebels, emigrated to Canada and London in large numbers. In 1786 the Committee for the Relief of the Black Poor, created to improve the conditions of the new immigrants, promoted the plan for resettlement in Sierra Leone that eventually included Equiano as the only person of African descent directly involved in the organization of the project. As "Commissary on the part of the Government," he was to act as the official representative of the British government in its dealings with the local African authorities in Sierra Leone. The Committee for Effecting the

Abolition of the Slave Trade, composed mainly of Quakers, formed in London in 1787 and soon was distributing anti-slave trade tracts throughout Britain. It should be noted that "abolition" in the eighteenth-century British context almost always refers to abolition of the trade in slaves from Africa to the remaining British colonies in the West Indies, not to the abolition of the institution of slavery itself, though many of the slave-trade abolitionists no doubt saw slavery as the ultimate target. Typical of the abolitionists' public position was that expressed by Equiano's friend the Reverend James Ramsay, writing in 1786 of his *An Essay on the Treatment and Conversion of African Slaves in the Sugar Colonies* (London, 1784), which can justly be called the opening salvo in the war over the slave trade: "Though I sincerely hope, that *some* plan will be devised for the future gradual abolition of slavery; and though I am convinced that this may, without any prejudice to the planter, or injury to commerce, be brought about by some such progressive method as is pointed out in the Essay; yet this was not the first, or immediate object of that book." Such circumspection also appears in Equiano's *Narrative*, where he concentrates on the evils of the slave trade, though in some of his letters to the newspapers his opinion of slavery is more directly and forcefully stated. Opponents of the trade hoped that its eradication would ameliorate the conditions of slavery because masters in West India, no longer being able to rely on inexpensive imports to maintain their stock, would have to create improved conditions that would enhance the natural rate of increase of their present slaves. And slavery itself would eventually wither away, eroded by the need for increasingly improved treatment of the slaves. Unfortunately, as the situation in the former British colonies in North America was already demonstrating, replacement by natural increase did not necessarily result from—or lead to—better conditions, and as the practical suspension of the trade during the rebellion showed, the end of the trade need not mean the end of slavery.

The most overt challenge to slavery by an Afro-Briton was made in 1787 by Equiano's friend and sometime collaborator, Ot-

tobah Cugoano (who also went by the name John Stewart or Stu-
art), in *Thoughts and Sentiments on the Evil and Wicked Traffic of the
Slavery and Commerce of the Human Species, Humbly Submitted to the
Inhabitants of Great-Britain, by Ottobah Cugoano, a Native of Africa*.
The title of his book, which may have been revised for publication by Equiano, clearly alludes to the work of another friend
of Equiano, Thomas Clarkson's *An Essay on the Slavery and Commerce of the Human Species, Particularly the African* (London, 1786).
The body of Cugoano's work, full of acknowledged and unacknowledged debts to the writings of others, like his title,
demonstrates that he saw the struggle against the trade as a kind
of group project.

Cugoano, however, did not seize the opportunity to describe
the horrors of the Middle Passage—the transatlantic voyage into
New World slavery—he had experienced because he believed that
"it would be needless to give a description of all the horrible
scenes which we saw, and the base treatment which we met with
in this dreadful captive situation, as the similar cases of thousands,
which suffer by this infernal traffic, are well known." Similarly,
Equiano's *Narrative* often relies on the evidence, examples, and arguments of others (usually acknowledged) but, unlike Cugoano,
Equiano recognized that what the opposition to the slave trade
needed in 1789 was not another account of the Middle Passage
by a white observer, but rather testimony from an enslaved African
survivor of it. As a professional author committed to the abolitionist cause, Equiano must have known that an African author-
ial identity would enhance the *Narrative's* credibility, raise its
market value, and serve the cause.

Even if Equiano played no role in the creation of Cugoano's
text, the *Narrative* was not Equiano's first publication. Quite a
master of the commercial book market, Equiano had promoted
himself and implicitly his forthcoming book in a number of letters, including book reviews, printed in the London newspapers.
And he publicly made the right enemies, like the pseudonymous
"Civis," who wrote defenses of slavery and the trade in *The Morning Chronicle and London Advertiser*, beginning with an essay "On

the Slavery of the Blacks" in the 5 February 1788 issue. In his letter to the newspaper printed on 19 August 1788, "Civis" remarks,
"If I were even to allow some share of merit to Gustavus Vasa
[sic], Ignatius Sancho, &c. it would not prove equality more, than
a pig having been taught to fetch a card, letters, &c. would shew
it not to be a pig, but some other animal. . . ." As "Civis"'s comment indicates, Equiano was already known to his future reading
public not only through his correspondence with the daily press
but also through profiles printed in the press, including the one
published in *The Morning Chronicle* (1 July 1788) itself:

> *Gustavus Vasa*, who addressed a letter in the name of his oppressed
> countrymen [in *The Morning Chronicle*, 27 June 1788], to the au-
> thor [Samuel Jackson Pratt] of the popular poem on Humanity
> [*Humanity, or the Rights of Nature*], which devotes several pages to
> that now universal subject of discussion, the Slave Trade, is,
> notwithstanding its romantick sound[,] the real name of an
> Ethiopian [that is, African] now resident in this metropolis, a na-
> tive of Eboe, who was himself twice kidnapped by the English,
> and twice sold to slavery. He has since been appointed the King's
> Commissary for the African settlement, and besides having an ir-
> reproachable moral character, has frequently distinguished himself
> by occasional essays in the different papers, which manifest a strong
> and sound understanding.

Despite his bad intentions, "Civis"'s comment could only help
to increase interest in the imminent publication of the *Narrative*,
the first purportedly firsthand account in the slave-trade debate
by a native African, former slave, and demonstrably loyal British
subject. The notice given him by "Civis" acknowledges Equiano's
prominence as the leading black abolitionist. In 1787 he had defended himself in *The Public Advertiser* against charges of misconduct as Commissary for the Sierra Leone project for resettling the
black poor in Africa; he had written scathing attacks on the publications of James Tobin, Gordon Turnbull, and the Reverend
Raymund Harris; and he had hinted in print that he might soon
"enumerate even my own sufferings in the West Indies, which

perhaps I may one day offer to the public. . . ." Even earlier, Equiano had actively intervened in the fight against the injustices of slavery: in 1774, as he tells us in the *Narrative*, he tried but failed to save John Annis from being kidnapped from London into West Indian slavery, and in 1783 he brought to Granville Sharp's attention the shocking story of how a cargo of 132 Africans were drowned to collect the insurance money on them. As Gustavus Vassa, Equiano was already well known to his audience when his *Narrative* first appeared in 1789.

Equiano published his book by subscription, that is, by convincing buyers to commit themselves to purchasing copies of his book prior to its publication, requiring partial payment in advance to cover his living and production costs. The first edition of Sancho's *Letters* had been published in the same way. Every edition of Equiano's *Narrative* added more subscribers, whose names were listed in the front of the book. By the ninth edition (1794), the original 311 names had increased to 894, with lists of English, Irish, and Scottish buyers. But the actual total was even higher: the names of 1,132 new subscribers, many for multiple copies, were added after the first edition, although obviously not all of them appear in the last edition.

To protect his copyright, Equiano registered the two-volume first edition of his *Narrative* with the Stationers' Company, delivering the requisite nine copies of the book to Stationers' Hall on 24 March 1789. When the one-volume third edition was published, he registered it on 30 October 1790. The six subsequent editions were all single volumes. He distributed the book widely, as the title page of the first edition shows, through booksellers, including two of the most noteworthy, Thomas Lackington and Joseph Johnson, the publisher of William Blake, Thomas Paine, and Mary Wollstonecraft, among many others. For later editions, Equiano conducted eighteenth-century anticipations of the modern book promotion tour throughout England, Ireland, and Scotland, and as one of his few extant manuscript letters attests, he was a very successful salesman. His letters also show that he worked for the cause of abolition during his book tours, distributing abolitionist works written by others, as well as his own, and even courageously venturing into the hostile territory of Bristol, a center of the British slave trade.

Publication by subscription, with its attendant lists, was itself a form of self-promotion. An increasing number of people clearly wanted to be publicly associated with the *Narrative* and its author. Equiano's credibility and stature were enhanced by the presence of the names of members of the royal family, the aristocracy, and other socially and politically prominent figures, such as men prominent in trade and the arts like the painter Richard Cosway or the potter Josiah Wedgwood. Elizabeth Montague and Hannah More, the leading bluestocking writers, were among the 11 percent of the original subscribers who were women. Furthermore, the list served to link Equiano to the larger movement against the slave trade by including names of others, like Thomas Clarkson, Thomas Cooper, William Dickson, James Ramsay, and Granville Sharp, who had already attacked the invidious practice in print or from the pulpit. Moreover, the lists connected Equiano explicitly and implicitly with the Afro-British writers of the preceding fifteen years: Cugoano's name appears; Sancho appears via his son William; Gronniosaw and Wheatley by association with the Countess of Huntingdon; and Marrant by association with his editor, Reverend William Aldridge. Less directly, the presence of the name of his patron's offspring, the Duke of Montague, recalls the poem by Williams. By 1789, a recognized tradition of Afro-British authors had been established, with new writers aware of the work of their predecessors, and an Afro-British canon was being created by the commentators, who argued about which were the most representative authors and works.

The subscription lists also played a structural role in the *Narrative*, which is presented as a petition, one of the hundreds submitted to Parliament between 1789 and 1792, containing thousands of names of people asking the members to outlaw the slave trade. The *Narrative* is formally framed by a petition to the Houses of Parliament that immediately follows the list, and the book virtually closes with an appeal to Queen Charlotte. By placement and implication, the subscribers are Equiano's co-petitioners. Although, like many of his subscribers, not qualified to vote, Equiano thus declares himself a loyal member of the larger British polity, which can still effect change within the walls of Westminster. He effectively aligns himself politically with subscribing members of Parliament like William Dolben, George Pitt, George Rose, and Samuel Whitbread, all of whom opposed the trade.

Calling attention to one's loyalty to Britain was conventional in the works by almost all the Afro-British writers. As Briton Hammon had earlier done in *A Narrative of the Most Uncommon Sufferings and Surprizing Deliverance of Briton Hammon, a Negro Man* (Boston, 1760), Gronniosaw and Marrant do so by speaking of their military service in the British army and navy; Sancho does so by his comments on the conduct of the war against the North American colonists; Williams and Wheatley write poems praising, respectively, the governor of Jamaica and the king of Great Britain. The military careers of most of the Afro-British men should not be surprising, given that the British army and navy were open to all talents in ways that most occupations were not. Competence mattered more than color, as Equiano's own service record demonstrates. Almost all the Afro-British writers whose religious beliefs we know were Methodist members of the Church of England, embracing the predestinarian Calvinism preached by George Whitefield and the clergymen associated with his aristocratic patron, the Countess of Huntingdon.

None of his predecessors asserts his or her identity as a Briton more fully than the way Equiano represents himself in his *Narrative*. African by birth, he is British by acculturation and choice. He can, of course, never be *English*, in the ethnic sense in which that word was used during the period, as his wife is *English*. But he adopts the cultural, political, religious, and social values that enable him to be accepted as *British*. Yet he always retains the perspective of an African who has been deracinated and thus has the advantage of knowing his adopted British culture from both the inside and the outside, a perspective that W.E.B. Du Bois calls the double consciousness of the black person in a predominantly white society.

Readers of any of the first nine editions of Equiano's book were immediately confronted by the author's dual identity: the frontispiece presents an indisputably African body in European dress; and the title page offers us "Olaudah Equiano, or Gustavus Vassa, the African." To call him consistently by either the one name or the other is to oversimplify his identity, and one should point out that to choose to use the name Equiano rather than Vassa, as I and most contemporary scholars and critics do, is to go against the author's own practice. As far as we know, he did not use the name Equiano before November 1788, when he was soliciting subscribers for his *Narrative*. Moreover, as the phrase "the African" in the title reminds us, the author is very aware that his readers will assess him not just as an individual but as the representative of his race, as a type as well as a person. Periodically in the *Narrative*, the author reminds his readers that he exists on the boundary between African and British identities. For example, at the beginning of Chapter IV, he tells us, "From the various scenes I had beheld on ship-board, I soon grew a stranger to terror of every kind, and was in that respect, at least, almost an Englishman." Several lines later he adds, "I now not only felt myself quite easy with these new countrymen, but relished their society and manners. I no longer looked upon them as spirits, but as men superior to us; and therefore I had the stronger desire to resemble them; to imbibe their spirit, and imitate their manners; I therefore embraced every occasion of improvement; and every new thing that I observed I treasured up in my memory."

His encounter with a black boy later in Chapter IV indicates to the reader, if not to the author either at the time of the event or at the time of recalling it, that Equiano is not fully comfortable in his position on the border between African and European identities. Although he calls the encounter "a trifling incident," it is a telling example of how quickly he has been acculturated into his new self and at the same time readily defined by others as still African. Confronted by the black boy, in effect his own mirror image, he at first turns away but then embraces his African side:

> I was one day in a field belonging to a gentleman who had a black boy about my own size; this boy having observed me from his master's house, was transported at the sight of one of his own countrymen, and ran to meet me with the utmost haste. I not knowing what he was about, turned a little out of his way at first, but to no purpose; he soon came close to me, and caught hold of me in his arms as if I had been his brother, though we had never seen each other before.

At the beginning of Chapter VIII, referring to the western hemisphere, Equiano remarks, "I began to think of leaving this part of the world, of which I had been long tired, and of returning to England, where my heart had always been. . . ." Later in this chapter, the behavior of whites in Georgia remind him that adoption of a British identity can never be fully achieved. But a question asked in Chapter XI by the prince of the Musquito Indians subtly reminds the author (although he does not seem to notice) and his readers just how far Equiano has come in the process of his British acculturation: "At last he asked me, 'How comes it that *all the white men on board*, who can read and write, observe the sun, and know all things, yet swear, lie, and get drunk, *only excepting yourself* ?' " (my emphasis). In the eyes of another non-European who has encountered the Old World, Equiano appears to be morally whiter than whites. Like Moses in the Book of Exodus, Equiano is a stranger in a strange land, but so too is the Indian, and though Equiano employs this perspective throughout the *Narrative*, it is for once turned on him, with significant but understated effect. Like the Indian, when Equiano uses this perspective it enables him to comment ironically on the behavior, especially the religious behavior, of those fellow Britons who falsely and foolishly suppose themselves his superiors. He can, at times, directly assume the stance of the satirist, who traditionally views his own or another society from a vantage point on the margin of or from outside that society, as he does in the last five editions, when he appropriates the voice and words of the great Roman satirist Juvenal in his address "To the Reader."

The way the *Narrative* is told also reflects the double vision of someone with a dual identity speaking from both within and from outside his society. Equiano addresses his audience from two positions at once. On a narrative level, he speaks of the past both as he experienced it at the time and as he reinterprets past events from the perspective of the time in which he is recalling them. Thus he can write from the perspective of an innocent African boy terrified by his first sight of white men, as well as interpret the religious significance of past events not noted at the time but now, from the perspective of the time of recounting them, fully recognized.

A dual perspective is inherent in retrospective autobiography and even more pronounced in a spiritual autobiography, the dominant generic influence on the *Narrative*. Protestant spiritual autobiographies, which include John Bunyan's nonfiction *Grace Abounding to the Chief of Sinners* (London, 1666) and Daniel Defoe's fictional *Robinson Crusoe* (London, 1719), typically recount a life that follows a pattern of sin, repentance, spiritual backsliding, and a new birth through true faith. Consequently, the protagonist is normally offered as an Everyman figure, neither extraordinarily good nor bad: as Equiano says at the opening of the first chapter, "I own I offer here the history of neither a saint, a hero, nor a tyrant" (though his decision to use the name of Gustavus Vassa, the Swedish patriot king who overthrew a tyrannical usurper, certainly gives him a heroic cast). Equiano uses the conventions of the genre, particularly the metaphor of being enslaved to sin, to contrast temporal and spiritual slavery. Although he buys his freedom halfway through the book (and almost halfway through his life), he is literally and spiritually still a slave, albeit his own, until he surrenders himself to Christ, and thus true, spiritual freedom.

The genre of the spiritual autobiography assumes that the spir-

itual life of an individual Christian, no matter how minutely detailed and seemingly singular his or her temporal existence,
reflects the paradigm of progress any true believer repeats. This
implicit invocation of the paradigm shared by the author and his
overwhelmingly Christian audience serves as the most powerful
argument in the *Narrative* for their common humanity. Equiano
couples it with a secular argument based on the philosophical
premise that the human heart, uncorrupted by poor nurturing,
has naturally benevolent feelings for others because it can empathize with their sufferings. Consequently, people of feeling, or
sentiment, will share the sufferings of others, and by so doing,
demonstrate their shared humanity, a humanity denied to people
of African descent by the racist supporters of slavery and the trade.

More subtly, perhaps, Equiano appears to offer the transfor-
mation of his own attitude toward the varieties of eighteenth-
century slavery as a model for the moral progress of his readers
as individuals and of the society he now shares with them. By
claiming personal experience and observation, Equiano becomes
an expert on the institution of slavery as well as on the effects of
the African slave trade. Many twentieth-first-century readers are
surprised to discover that eighteenth-century slavery was not a
monolithic institution simply divided into white owners and black
chattel. Equiano's initial encounter with slavery is reportedly in
Africa, where, in its native African form, it is domestic and the
slaves are treated almost like members of their owners' families
because of close personal contact. Thus it seems benign, and not
obviously dehumanizing. Slavery is neither racially based nor
hereditary; his description of African slavery would have reminded
his readers of ancient classical slavery. Slavery is simply one of the
many levels that constitute the apparently healthy social order in
which Equiano finds himself near the top. But, like an infectious
disease, the European slave trade with Africa has gradually spread
further inland until it destroys even the tranquility of Equiano's
homeland. He tells us that his first owners are fellow Africans,
and his treatment becomes increasingly more dehumanizing as he
approaches the English ships on the coast. He observes that his

successive African owners become more inhumane the closer they are located to the source of the infection, and when he finally encounters the financial cause of the disease, he remarks, "the white people looked and acted, as I thought, in so savage a manner; for I had never seen among any people such instances of brutal cruelty; and this not only shewn towards us blacks, but also to some of the whites themselves." Everyone becomes contaminated by the corruption of the trade.

Once he arrives in the Americas and travels to England and the Mediterranean, Equiano can identify and qualify different types of slavery, from the most brutal to the least. If one has to be a slave, the worst places to be one are in the West Indies and Georgia, where slaves are forced to labor in gangs in large-scale agricultural economies; the best are Africa, Philadelphia, and England, where slaves are domestic or artisanal workers in small-scale agricultural economies or urban societies. Somewhere in the middle lie Italy and the Levant, where whites enslave whites. The French, operating under the regulations of the *Code Noir* (1685), or Black Code, treat their slaves better in Martinique than the British do theirs in Barbados. Slavery is so pervasive and multiform that he knows of a free black woman in Saint Kitts who owns slaves, and he hears of Portuguese white men being sold (under false pretenses) as slaves in the West Indies. He does not, however, condemn slavery; he condemns some kinds of slavery. In fact, he experiences the other side of slavery when, as a free man, he effectively supports the African slave trade, buying his fellow countrymen and becoming their overseer for Dr. Irving's Central American plantation. Priding himself on being an exemplary slave driver, he resigns because of the immoral behavior of his associates, not because he rejects slavery. Only after he returns to England, the land of liberty, "where [his] heart had always been," does he come to see that the trade must be abolished because it cannot be ameliorated.

He does, maybe unintentionally, offer us a vision of what seems to be an almost utopian, microcosmic alternative to the slavery-infested greater world, in the little worlds of the ships of the British

Royal Navy and the merchant marine. As archival research proves, his memory of events and details of thirty years earlier is remarkably accurate, perhaps because he may be recalling the happiest period of his life. The demands of the seafaring life permit him to transcend the barriers imposed by race, forcing even whites to acknowledge him as having the responsibilities and capabilities, if not the rank itself, of the captain of a ship. He experiences a world in which artificially imposed racial limitations would have destroyed everyone, white and black. But, perhaps because he does not want to distance himself too far from his audience, by the end of the *Narrative*, like most of his readers, he has not quite reached the position of absolutely rejecting slavery itself. Readers can reasonably extrapolate from the progress he has made that the next logical step is such total rejection. If he can carry his audience as far as he has come in his autobiography, he will bring them a great way toward his probable ultimate goal. Unlike Cugoano in his jeremiad-like *Thoughts and Sentiments*, or Equiano himself in some of his letters to the newspapers, in the *Narrative*, Equiano neither engages in lengthy lamentations and exhortations, nor does he lecture to his readers; he invites them to emulate him.

Conciliatory as he is in the main, Equiano does not refrain from intimating a more combative and individualistic side to his nature. This side is most pronounced in the first few editions at the end of the *Narrative*, where the genre of the *apologia*, or justification and vindication of one's life, shows its influence. Having been accused in the newspapers by powerful opponents of having mismanaged his position as Commissary for the Sierra Leone project, Equiano defends himself with witnesses and evidence. As he adds prefatory letters attesting to his character and credibility in later editions, the *apologia* begins to replace the petition as the *Narrative*'s generic frame. And with the fifth edition, the new "To the Reader," designed to counter newspaper attacks on his true identity, suggests that his primary audience has shifted from the members of Parliament to the public at large.

From the first edition, he had indicated throughout the book that he is willing and able to resist whites in childhood boxing

matches or when mistreated by them as an adult. This willingness to resist is almost always limited, however, to threat, and not
carried into action, probably lest he alienate his overwhelmingly
white readership. He is certainly not reluctant to affront some of
his white audience directly: surely he knew that his inclusion in
the fifth and later editions of the news of his marriage to a white
woman would appall racist readers like James Tobin, whom he
had previously attacked in the newspaper *The Public Advertiser*
(28 January 1788), where Equiano recommends racial intermarriage. Sometimes his intimations of resistance are quite subtle, as
when he quotes John Milton, one of the most esteemed icons of
his shared British culture, at the end of Chapter V. By quoting
lines spoken in *Paradise Lost* by Beelzebub, one of Satan's follow-
ers, Equiano appropriates a voice of alienation and resistance from
within the very culture he is demonstrating that he has assimi-
lated. Shakespeare is similarly used from the fifth edition on, when
Equiano appropriates Othello's words in his initial address to the
reader in all the editions that include the announcement of his
marriage to a white woman. Surely he had bigots like Tobin in
mind when he invoked the image of Britain's most famous literary instance of intermarriage in the tragic figure of African sex-
uality and power. Even the most venerated icon of British culture,
the King James version of the Bible, becomes a means of self-
expression. At first glance, the image of the author in the frontispiece to the *Narrative* seems to be a representation of humble
fidelity to the text of the sacred book, but as we discover at the
end of his "Miscellaneous Verses," which conclude Chapter X,
Equiano appropriates Acts 4:12 by paraphrasing the original in
his own words, an interactive relationship with the sacred text
that may have been influenced by Cugoano's example.

Other generic influences serve to distance the author from his
audience. The form of the *Narrative* lies somewhere between the
future nineteenth-century North American slave narrative such as
Frederick Douglass's *Narrative of the Life of Frederick Douglass, an
American Slave, Written by Himself* (Boston, 1845) and the contemporaneous captivity narrative, frequently of European whites

abducted into alien cultures. Examples of the latter include Mary
Rowlandson's often republished *The Sovereignty and Goodness of
God, Together with the Faithfulness of His Promises Displayed; Being
a Narrative of the Captivity and Restauration of Mrs. Mary Rowlandson* (Cambridge [Massachusetts], 1682); Hammon's *Narrative*; or
the many fictional (Penelope Aubin's *The Noble Slaves* [Dublin,
1736]) and nonfictional (John Kingdon's *Redeemed Slaves* [Bris-
tol, 1780?]) eighteenth-century accounts of being enslaved by Bar-
bary pirates. Like the protagonists in the captivity narratives,
Equiano is taken from his native culture and freedom, but like
the protagonists of the later slave narratives, he does not return
to the conditions from which he started. His is not, however, a
fugitive slave narrative because he buys his freedom.

Because Equiano offers himself as a native African, unlike the
Creole (a person of nonindigenous American descent but born in
the Americas) protagonists of the later slave narratives, the *Narrative* is also a travel book and an adventure story. It introduces its
readers to the exotic worlds of the pastoral Africa of Equiano's
childhood and the unknown frontier of the North Pole. Equiano's
acknowledged reliance on the descriptions of his homeland by sec-
ondary sources like Anthony Benezet render his own account at
once both remotely familiar and familiarly remote. Like his use of
the Judaic analogy, his traditional description of Africa keeps the
foreign from being too alien. And as a native-born African, his
authority derived from personal experience and the authority of
European commentators derived from disinterested observation
seem to reinforce each other. Equiano's own later measured and
fairly objective and circumstantial descriptions of places remote
from both Europe and Africa suggest that his descriptions and eval-
uations of Africa, America, the West Indies, and England are
reliable.

Equiano places his original African culture within a Judeo-
Christian context, both by a kind of comparative anthropological drawing of analogies between Judaic and African traditions and
by invoking the authority of biblical scholarship. In so doing, he
implies that his own personal progress from pre-Christian to

Christian can be paralleled by the potential development of Africa from its present spiritual condition to that of a fully Christian culture, a progress that would be as natural and preordained on a societal level as his has demonstrably already been on an individual level. Later in the *Narrative*, when it briefly becomes an economic treatise, Equiano explicitly argues that Africa can be brought into the European commercial world, as he has been. Spiritual, cultural, and economic progress are intertwined, on the public as well as the personal levels.

Spiritual autobiography, captivity narrative, travel book, adventure tale, narrative of slavery, economic treatise, *apologia*, and perhaps historical fiction, among other things, Equiano's *Narrative* was generally well received, and the author, saying he did so in self-defense, quickly employed the eighteenth-century version of the modern publisher's blurb by prefacing later editions of his book with favorable reviews from *The Monthly Review* and *The General Magazine and Impartial Review*, as well as with letters of introduction and support. Understandably, he omits Richard Gough's less favorable review in the June 1789 issue of *The Gentleman's Magazine*:

Among other contrivances (and perhaps one of the most innocent) to interest the national humanity in favour of the Negro slaves, one of them here writes his own history, as formerly another [Sancho] of them published his correspondence. . . . —These memoirs, written in a very unequal style, place the writer on a par with the general mass of men in the subordinate stations of civilized society, and prove that there is no general rule without an exception. The first volume treats of the manners of his countrymen, and his own adventures till he obtained his freedom; the second, from that period to the present, is uninteresting; and his conversion to Methodism oversets the whole.

Nor does Equiano reprint the extensive and influential review Mary Wollstonecraft wrote for *The Analytical Review* (May 1789), published by Joseph Johnson, whose name is first among the booksellers listed on the title page as distributors of *The Interesting Narrative*. Wollstonecraft's judgments and phrasing obviously were appropriated by the reviewer in *The Gentleman's Magazine*:

The life of an African, written by himself, is certainly a curiosity, as it has been a favourite philosophic whim to degrade the numerous nations, on whom the sun-beams more directly dart, below the common level of humanity, and hastily to conclude that nature, by making them inferior to the rest of the human race, designed to stamp them with a mark of slavery. How they are shaded down, from the fresh colour of northern rustics, to the sable hue seen on the African sands, is not our task to inquire, nor do we intend to draw a parallel between the abilities of a negro and European mechanic; we shall only observe, that if these volumes do not exhibit extraordinary intellectual powers, sufficient to wipe off the stigma, yet the activity and ingenuity, which conspicuously appear in the character of Gustavus, place him on a par with the general mass of men, who fill the subordinate stations in a more civilized society than that which he was thrown into at his birth.

The first volume contains, with a variety of other matter, a short description of the manners of his native country, an account of his family, his being kidnapped with his sister, his journey to the sea coast, and terror when carried on shipboard. Many anecdotes are simply told, relative to the treatment of male and female slaves, on the voyage, and in the West Indies, which makes the blood turn its course; and the whole account of his unwearied endeavours to obtain his freedom, is very interesting. The narrative should have closed when he once more became his own master. The latter part of the second volume appears flat; and he is entangled in many, comparatively speaking, insignificant cares, which almost efface the lively impression made by the miseries of the slave. The long account of his religious sentiments and conversion to methodism, is rather tiresome.

Throughout, a kind of contradiction is apparent: many childish stories and puerile remarks, do not agree with some more solid reflections, which occur in the first pages. In the style also we observed a striking contrast: a few well written periods do not smoothly unite with the general tenor of the language.

An extract from the part descriptive of the national manners, we think will not be unacceptable to our readers. [A quotation describing African customs of singing and dancing follows.]

From his *Journal* and *Correspondence*, we know that one of the fathers of Methodism, John Wesley, another of Equiano's original subscribers, was reading his copy of the *Narrative* just before his death in February 1791 and recommended it to William Wilberforce, the leader in Parliament of the movement to abolish the African slave trade. In 1808 (the original French text was published in English in 1810), Henri Grégoire, the first historian of black literature, said of the *Narrative*, "[t]he work is written with that *naivete*, I had almost said, that roughness of a man of nature. His manner is that of Daniel de Foe, in his *Robinson Crusoe*."

Equiano's earliest reviewers also recognized the *Narrative* as testimony by an expert witness on the evils of slavery and the slave trade. In response to the growing public interest in the subject, by the order of King George III in February 1788, the Privy Council Committee for Trade and Plantations began an investigation of British commercial relations with Africa and the nature of the slave trade, which was transporting to European Colonies in the Americas approximately 80,000 Africans a year, more than half of them in British ships based in Bristol, Liverpool, and London. From 1789 to 1792 the House of Commons heard evidence for and against the slave trade, and in 1792 an abolition bill passed in Commons only to be defeated in the House of Lords. For the next few years the bill failed in the Commons by narrow margins.

The outbreak of the French Revolution and the consequent Terror in France during 1789–1794 made Britons reluctant to pursue any major social reforms lest they lead to revolutionary results. In November 1794 the British government prosecuted Thomas Hardy, Secretary of the London Corresponding Society, for high treason. Even though his trial, like those of his fellow reformers John Horne Tooke and John Thelwall, ended in acquittal, the government's willingness to prosecute discouraged the publication of radical or reformist sentiments in general, and may help explain Equiano's apparent public silence after 1794. Among the papers seized by the government when Hardy was arrested in May 1794 was a letter Equiano had sent to Hardy from Edinburgh on 28 May 1792. Equiano had been living with his friend Hardy and his wife, Lydia, while he was revising what would become the fifth edition of his *Interesting Narrative*, and he apparently acted as a representative of the London Corresponding Society during his book tours. By the close of 1794 Equiano could afford to retire from writing for money, and thus he had earned the right to refer to himself as a gentleman. By the end of the decade, the threat posed by Napoleon to national survival eclipsed all other issues until 1804. Although Equiano's offers in the press to give evidence in the parliamentary hearings were never accepted, his *Narrative* gave him a vehicle for making his testimony known. But despite the popularity and power of his *Narrative* and the cause it promoted, Equiano did not live to see the abolition of the African slave trade, which was not legislated until 1807, ten years after his death on 31 March 1797. Slavery was abolished by law in all the British colonies in the Americas in 1838.

A NOTE ON THE TEXT

NINE British editions were published during Equiano's lifetime, and he made substantive changes in each: 1st 1789 (London, 2 vols.); 2nd 1789 (London, 2 vols.); 3rd 1790 (London, 1 vol.); 4th 1791 (Dublin, 1 vol.); 5th 1792 (Edinburgh, 1 vol.); 6th 1793 (London, 1 vol.); 7th 1793 (London, 1 vol.); 8th 1794 (Norwich, 1 vol.); 9th 1794 (London, 1 vol.). For Equiano, his *Narrative*, like his life itself, continued to be a work in progress. Subscribers to the first edition are included in Appendix C. Although the names of additional subscribers appear in each of the following eight editions, the subscription lists were not strictly cumulative. Appendix G lists alphabetically the names of subscribers added in editions 2–8 by the edition in which their names first appeared.

An unauthorized two-volume edition, based on the second London edition, was published in New York City in 1791, without the address to the members of the Houses of Parliament, and with a new subscription list. The New York subscription list is included in Appendix D. Dutch, German, and Russian translations of the *Narrative* were published, respectively, in 1790, 1792, and 1794.

None of the posthumous editions has any testamentary authority, and all are untrustworthy. For example, the 1814 Leeds edition reparagraphs the text, imports substantive errors, moves large portions of the text out of context, and contains unidentified nonauthorial annotations, including one long religiously correcting footnote.

Anyone who writes on Equiano or his *Narrative* is indebted to Paul Edwards for his facsimile reproduction of the first edition (London: Dawsons of Pall Mall, 1969), with its magisterial introduction, as well as to his later related scholarly publications.

Since Equiano made substantive alterations in every one of the nine editions now known to have been published during his lifetime, I have chosen the ninth edition as the copy text of the Penguin edition. The rare ninth edition, which was unknown to Edwards, contains Equiano's final changes (only four copies are known to exist: the imperfect one at the University of Maryland, and the complete ones at the University of California, Riverside, the Bayerische Staatsbibliothek München, and Howard University). Except for the replacement of the long "s" used in the eighteenth century, spelling (including the various spellings of proper names) and punctuation have not been modernized, and all substantive changes are recorded in the notes. Obvious errors, such as inverted or dropped letters, have been silently corrected.

A NOTE ON MONEY

BEFORE 1971, when the British monetary system was decimal-tized, British money was counted in pounds sterling (£), shillings (s.), pence, or pennies (d.), and farthings. One pound sterling = 20 shillings; 5 shillings = 1 crown; 1 shilling = 12 pennies; 1 far-thing = ¼ pence. One guinea = 21 shillings. (The coin was so named because the gold from which it was made came from the Guinea coast of Africa and because the coin was first struck to celebrate the founding in 1663 of the slave-trading monopoly the Royal Adventurers into Africa.)

Each colony issued its own local paper currency. A colonial pound was worth less than a pound sterling, with the conversion rates for the currencies of the various colonies fluctuating throughout the century. Because of restrictions on the export of coins from England, the colonies relied on foreign coins, partic-ularly Spanish, for local transactions. The basic Spanish denomi-nation for silver coinage was the real ("royal"), with the peso (piece of eight reales), or pieces of eight, known in British Amer-ica as the dollar. Hence, two reales, or bits, became known as a quarter. Spanish reals were preferred as specie because their face value was equivalent to their intrinsic silver value. The Spanish pistareen, on the other hand, had a face value of two reales, but an intrinsic value of only ⅕ of a Spanish dollar. The Spanish dou-bloon was an 8 escudo gold coin worth, in 1759 pounds sterling, 3£ 6s. 0d. At the same time, a Spanish dollar was worth, in lo-cal currency, 0£ 7s. 6d. in Philadelphia, and 0£ 8s. 0d. in New York. Conversion charts showing the value of foreign money in Colonial currency and pounds sterling were frequently published throughout the eighteenth century. Also in circulation were coins like the copper ones paid to Equiano that lacked either face or intrinsic value.

To arrive at a rough modern equivalent of eighteenth-century

A NOTE ON THE MONEY

money, multiply by about 80. In mid-eighteenth-century urban England a family of four could live modestly on £40 sterling a year, and a gentleman could support his standard of living on £300 sterling a year. A maid might be paid (in addition to room, board, cast-off clothes, and tips) around 6 guineas per year; a manservant, around £10 per year; and an able seaman, after deductions, received 14£ 12s. 6d. per year, in addition to room and board. The price of a four-pound loaf of bread ranged from 5.1 d. to 6.6 d. between 1750 and 1794, when Equiano was charging 5s. for a copy of his *Interesting Narrative*. Samuel Johnson left his black servant, Francis Barber, an annuity of £70 sterling a year; the Duchess of Montagu left Sancho a sum of £70 sterling and £30 sterling a year; Sancho's widow received more than £500 sterling from the sales of his *Letters*; and Equiano's daughter inherited £950 sterling from her father's estate.

SUGGESTIONS FOR FURTHER READING

EDITION

The Interesting Narrative of the Life of Olaudah Equiano, or Gustavus Vassa, the African. Written by Himself. (2 vols. London, 1789); facsimile of the first edition, with an Introduction and Notes by Paul Edwards. London: Dawsons of Pall Mall, 1969.

CRITICISM AND SCHOLARSHIP

Acholonu, Catherine O. "The Home of Olaudah Equiano—A Linguistic and Anthropological Survey." *The Journal of Commonwealth Literature* 22 (1987).

Andrews, William L. *To Tell a Free Story: The First Century of Afro-American Autobiography.* Bloomington: University of Illinois Press, 1986.

Aravamudan, Srinivas. *Tropicopolitans: Colonialism and Agency, 1688–1804.* Durham and London: Duke University Press, 1999.

Baker, Houston A. *Blues, Ideology and Afro-American Literature: A Vernacular Theory.* Chicago: University of Chicago Press, 1984.

Braidwood, Stephen J. *Black Poor and White Philanthropists: London's Blacks and the Foundation of the Sierra Leone Settlement 1786–1791.* Liverpool: Liverpool University Press, 1994.

Brown, Christopher L. "Empire without Slaves: British Concepts of Emanicipation in the Age of the American Revolution." *William and Mary Quarterly* 56 (1999).

Caldwell, Tanya. " 'Talking Too Much English': Languages of Economy and Politics in Equiano's *The Interesting Narrative.*" *Early American Literature* 34 (1999).

Carretta, Vincent. *Unchained Voices: An Anthology of Black Authors in the English-Speaking World of the Eighteenth Century.* Lexington: University Press of Kentucky Press, 1996.

———. "Olaudah Equiano or Gustavus Vassa? New Light on an Eighteenth-Century Question of Identity." *Slavery and Abolition* 20 (1999).

————. "Defining a Gentleman: the Status of Olaudah Equiano or Gustavus Vassa." *Language Sciences* 22 (2000).

————. " 'Property of Author': Olaudah Equiano's Place in the History of the Book," in *"Genius in Bondage": A Critical Anthology of the Literature of the Early Black Atlantic*, edited by Vincent Carretta and Philip Gould. Lexington: University Press of Kentucky, 2001.

————. "Possible Gustavus Vassa/Olaudah Equiano Attributions," in *Faces of Anonymity: Anonymous and Pseudonymous Publications, 1600–2000*, edited by Robert Griffin. New York: Palgrave, 2003.

————. "More New Light on the Identity of Olaudah Equiano or Gustavus Vassa," in *The Global Eighteenth Century*, edited by Felicity Nussbaum. Baltimore: Johns Hopkins University Press, 2003.

Costanzo, Angelo. *Surprizing Narrative: Olaudah Equiano and the Beginnings of Black Autobiography.* New York: Greenwood Press, 1987.

Davis, Charles T., and Henry L. Gates, Jr. *The Slave's Narrative.* New York: Oxford University Press, 1985.

Davis, David Brion. *The Problem of Slavery in Western Culture.* New York: Oxford University Press, 1966.

————. *The Problem of Slavery in the Age of Revolution 1770–1823*. Ithaca: Cornell University Press, 1975.

Doherty, Thomas. "Olaudah Equiano's Journeys: The Geography of a Slave Narrative." *Partisan Review* 64 (1997).

Drescher, Seymour. *Capitalism and Antislavery: British Mobilization in Comparative Perspective.* London: Macmillan, 1986.

Edwards, Paul, and James Walvin. *Black Personalities in the Era of the Slave Trade.* Baton Rouge: University of Louisiana Press, 1983.

Edwards, Paul. "A Descriptive List of Manuscripts in the Cambridgeshire Record Office Relating to the Will of Gustavus Vassa (Olaudah Equiano)." *Research in African Literatures* 20 (1989).

————. "Equiano's Lost Family: 'Master' and 'Father' in *The Interesting Narrative.*" *Slavery and Abolition* 11 (1990).

Fichtelberg, Joseph. "Word between Worlds: The Economy of Equiano's Narrative." *American Literary History* 5 (1993).

Fryer, Peter. *Staying Power: The History of Black People in Britain*. London: Pluto Press, 1984.

Gates, Henry L., Jr. *The Signifying Monkey: A Theory of African-American Literary Criticism*. New York: Oxford University Press, 1988.

Green, James. "The Publishing History of Olaudah Equiano's *Interesting Narrative*." *Slavery and Abolition* 16 (1995).

Hinds, Elizabeth Jane Wall. "The Spirit of Trade: Olaudah Equiano's Conversion, Legalism, and the Merchant's Life." *African American Review* 32 (1998).

Hogg, Peter C. *The African Slave Trade and Its Suppression: A Classified and Annotated Bibliography of Books, Pamphlets and Periodical Articles*. London: Frank Cass, 1973.

Ito, Akiyo. "Olaudah Equiano and the New York Artisans: The First American Edition of *The Interesting Narrative of Olaudah Equiano, or Gustavus Vassa, The African*." *Early American Literature* 32 (1997).

Jennings, Judith. *The Business of Abolishing the Slave Trade 1783–1807*. London: Frank Cass, 1997.

Marren, Susan M. "Between Slavery and Freedom: The Transgressive Self in Olaudah Equiano's Autobiography." *Publications of the Modern Language Association* 108 (1993).

Murphy, Geraldine. "Olaudah Equiano, Accidental Tourist." *Eighteenth-Century Studies* 27 (1994).

Myers, Norma. *Reconstructing the Past: Blacks in Britain 1780–1830*. London: Frank Cass, 1996.

Nussbaum, Felicity. "Being a Man: Olaudah Equiano and Ignatius Sancho," in *"Genius in Bondage": A Critical Anthology of the Literature of the Early Black Atlantic*, edited by Vincent Carretta and Philip Gould. Lexington: University Press of Kentucky, 2001.

Ogude, S.E. *Genius in Bondage: A Study of the Origins of African Literature in English*. Ile-Ife, Nigeria: University of Ife Press, 1983.

Oldfield, J. R. *Popular Politics and British Anti-Slavery: The Mobilisation of Public Opinion against the Slave Trade, 1787–1807*. London: Frank Cass, 1998.

Orban, Katalin. "Dominant and Submerged Discourses in the Life of Olaudah Equiano." *African American Review* 27 (1993).

Potkay, Adam. "Olaudah Equiano and the Art of Spiritual Autobiography." *Eighteenth-Century Studies* 27 (1994).

Rodgers, Nini. "Equiano in Belfast: A Study of the Anti-Slavery Ethos in a Northern Town." *Slavery and Abolition* 18 (1997).

Samuels, Wilfred D. "The Disguised Voice in *The Interesting Narrative of Olaudah Equiano.*" *Black American Literature Forum* 19 (1985).

Sandiford, Keith. *Measuring the Moment: Strategies of Protest in Eighteenth-Century Afro-English Writing.* London: Associated Universities Press, 1988.

Shyllon, Folarin. *Black People in Britain 1555–1833.* London: Oxford University Press, 1977.

———. "Olaudah Equiano: Nigerian Abolitionist and First National Leader of Africans in Britain." *Journal of African Studies* 4 (1977).

Walvin, James. *Black Ivory: A History of British Slavery.* London: Fontana Press, 1992.

———. *An African's Life: The Life and Times of Olaudah Equiano, 1745–1797.* London: Cassell, 1998.

Wheeler, Roxann. *The Complexion of Race: Categories of Difference in Eighteenth-Century British Culture.* Philadelphia: University of Pennsylvania Press, 2000.

Zafar, Rafia. *We Wear the Mask: African Americans Write American Literature, 1760–1870.* New York: Columbia University Press, 1997.

THE INTERESTING NARRATIVE OF
THE LIFE OF OLAUDAH EQUIANO,
or
GUSTAVUS VASSA, THE AFRICAN.
WRITTEN BY HIMSELF.

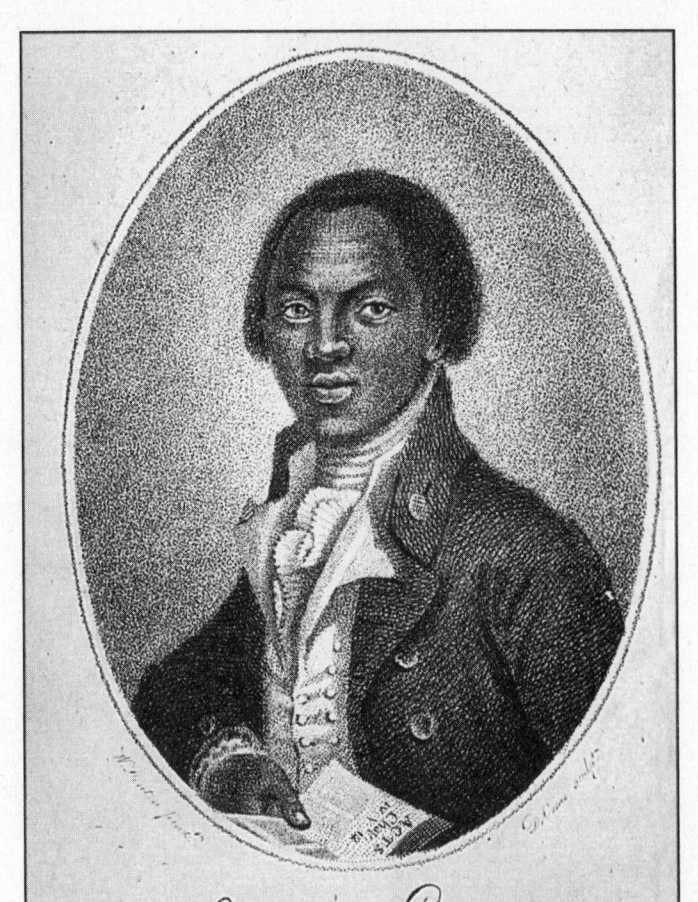

Olaudah Equiano,
or
GUSTAVUS VASSA,
the African?

Published March 1 1789 by G. Vassa

THE
INTERESTING NARRATIVE
OF
THE LIFE
OF
OLAUDAH EQUIANO,
OR
GUSTAVUS VASSA,
THE AFRICAN.

WRITTEN BY HIMSELF.

Behold, God is my salvation; I will trust, and not be afraid, for the Lord Jehovah is my strength and my song; he also is become my salvation.

And in that day shall ye say, Praise the Lord, call upon his name, declare his doings among the people. Isa. xii. 2. 4.

NINTH EDITION ENLARGED.

LONDON:

PRINTED FOR, AND SOLD BY THE AUTHOR.

1794.

PRICE FIVE SHILLINGS,
Formerly sold for 7s.
[*Entered at Stationers' Hall.*]

To the Reader[1]

AN invidious falsehood having appeared in the Oracle of the 25th,[2] and the Star of the 27th of April 1792,[3] with a view to hurt my character,[4] and to discredit and prevent the sale of my Narrative, asserting, that I was born in the Danish island of Santa Cruz, in the West Indies,[5] it is necessary that, in this edition, I should take notice thereof, and it is only needful of me to appeal to those numerous and respectable persons of character who knew me when I first arrived in England, and could speak no language but that of Africa.[6]

Under this appeal, I now offer this edition of my Narrative to the candid[7] reader, and to the friends of humanity, hoping it may still be the means, in its measure, of showing the enormous cruelties practiced on my sable brethren, and strengthening the generous emulation now prevailing in this country, to put a speedy end to a traffic both cruel and unjust.

Edinburgh, June 1792.[8]

Letter,
of
Alexander Tillock to John Montieth, Esq.
Glasgow.[9]

DEAR SIR,

YOUR note of the 30th ult.[10] I would have answered in course; but wished first to inform you what paper we had taken the article from which respected GUSTAVUS VASSA. By this day's post, have sent you a copy of the Oracle of Wednesday the 25th—in the last column of the 3rd page, you will find the article from which we inserted the one in the Star of the 27th ult.—If it be erroneous, you will see it had not its origin with us. As to G.V. I know nothing about him.

After examining the paragraph in the Oracle which immediately follows the one in question, I am inclined to believe that the one respecting G.V. may have been fabricated by some of the advocates for continuing the Slave Trade, for the purpose of weakening the force of the evidence brought against that trade; for, I believe, if they could, they would stifle the evidence altogether.

Having sent you the Oracle, we have sent all that we can say about the business. I am,

DEAR SIR,
Your most humble Servant,
ALEX. TILLOCH.

Star Office, 5th May, 1792.

LETTER
FROM THE REV. DR. J. BAKER, OF MAY FAIR
CHAPEL, LONDON, TO MR. GUSTAVUS
VASSA, AT DAVID DALE'S ESQ.
GLASGOW.[11]

DEAR SIR,

I went after Mr. [Buchanan] Millan (the printer of the Oracle), but he was not at home. I understood that an apology would be made to you, and I desired it might be a proper one, such as would give fair satisfaction, and take off any disadvantageous impressions which the paragraph alluded to may have made. Whether the matter will bear an action or not, I do not know, and have not inquired whether you can punish by law; because I think it is not worth while to go to the expence of a law-suit, especially if a proper apology is made; for, can any man that reads your Narrative believe that you are not a native of Africa? I see therefore no good reason for not printing a fifth edition, on account of a scandalous paragraph in a newspaper.

I remain,

DEAR SIR,

Your sincere Friend,

J. BAKER.

Grosvenor-street, May 14, 1792.

TO the Lords Spiritual and Temporal, and the Commons of the Parliament of Great Britain.[12]

My Lords and Gentlemen,

PERMIT me with the greatest deference and respect, to lay at your feet the following genuine Narrative; the chief design of which is to excite in your august assemblies a sense of compassion for the miseries which the Slave Trade has entailed on my unfortunate countrymen. By the horrors of that trade I was first torn away from all the tender connexions that were dear to my heart; but these, through the mysterious ways of Providence, I ought to regard as infinitely more than compensated by the introduction I have thence obtained to the knowledge of the Christian religion, and of a nation which, by its liberal sentiments, its humanity, the glorious freedom of its government, and its proficiency in arts and sciences, has exalted the dignity of human nature.

I am sensible I ought to entreat your pardon for addressing to you a work so wholly devoid of literary merit; but, as the production of an unlettered African, who is actuated by the hope of becoming an instrument towards the relief of his suffering countrymen. I trust that *such a man,* pleading in *such a cause,* will be acquitted of boldness and presumption.[13]

May the god of Heaven inspire your hearts with peculiar benevolence on that important day when the question of Abolition

is to be discussed, when thousands, in consequence of your determination, are to look for Happiness or Misery!

. I am,

My LORDS and GENTLEMEN,

Your most obedient,

And devoted humble servant,

OLAUDAH EQUIANO,

OR

GUSTAVUS VASSA.

March 1789.[14]

To the CHAIRMEN of the COMMITTEE for the ABOLITION of the SLAVE TRADE.[15]

Magdalen College, Cambridge, May 26 1790.

GENTLEMEN,

I TAKE the liberty, as being joined with you in the same
laudable endeavours to support the cause of humanity in the Abolition of the Slave Trade, to recommend to your protection the
bearer of this note GUSTAVUS VASSA, an African; and to beg
the favour of your assistance to him in the sale of his book.

I am, with great respect,

GENTLEMEN,

Your most obedient servant,

P. PECKARD.

Manchester, July 23, 1790.[16]

THOMAS WALKER has great pleasure in recommending the
sale of the NARRATIVE of GUSTAVUS VASSA to the friends
of justice and humanity, he being well entitled to their protection

and support, from the united testimonies of the Rev. T. Clarkson, of London; Dr. Peckard, of Cambridge; and Sampson and Charles Lloyd, Esqrs. of Birmingham.

Sheffield, August 20 1790.[17]

In consequence of the recommendation of Dr. Peckard, of Cambridge; Messrs. Lloyd, of Birmingham; the Rev. T. Clarkson, of London; Thomas Walker, Thomas Cooper, and Isaac Moss, Esqrs. of Manchester, we beg leave also to recommend the sale of the NARRATIVE of GUSTAVUS VASSA to the friends of humanity in the town and neighbourhood of Sheffield.

Dr. Brown,
Wm. Shore, Esq,
Samuel Marshall,

Rev. Ja. Wilkinson,
Rev. Edw. Goodwin,
John Barlow.

Nottingham, January 17, 1791.[18]

IN consequence of the respectable recommendation of several gentlemen of the first character, who have born testimony to the good sense, intellectual improvements, and integrity of GUSTAVUS VASSA, lately of that injured and oppressed class of men, the injured Africans; and further convinced of the justice of his recommendations, from our own personal interviews with him, we take the liberty also to recommend the said GUSTAVUS VASSA to the protection and assistance of the friends of humanity.

Rev. G. Walker,
John Morris,
Joseph Rigsby, Rector, St. Peter's,
Samuel Smith,
John Wright,

F. Wakefield,
T. Bolton,

Thomas Hawksley,
S. White, M.D.
J. Hancock.

LETTER
TO MR. O'BRIEN, CARRICKFERGUS,
(*PER FAVOUR OF* MR. GUSTAVUS VASSA.)[19]

Belfast, December 25, 1791.

DEAR SIR,

The bearer of this, Mr. GUSTAVUS VASSA, an enlightened
African, of good sense, agreeable manners, and of an excellent character, and who comes well recommended to this place, and noticed
by the first people here, goes to-morrow for your town, for the purpose of vending some books, written by himself, which is a Narrative
of his own Life and Sufferings, with some account of his native country and its inhabitants. He was torn from his relatives and country
(by the more savage white men of England) at an early period in life;
and during his residence in England, at which time I have seen him,
during my agency for the American prisoners, with Sir William Dolben, Mr. Granville Sharp, Mr. Wilkes, and many other distinguished
characters; he supported an irreproachable character, and was a principal instrument in bringing about the motion for the repeal of the
Slave-Act. I beg leave to introduce him to your notice and civility;
and if you can spare the time, your introduction of him personally
to your neighbours may be of essential benefit to him.

I am,

SIR,

Your obedient servant,

THOS. DIGGES.

LETTER
TO ROWLAND WEBSTER, ESQ. STOCKTON.
(*PER FAVOUR OF* MR. GUSTAVUS VASSA.)[20]

DEAR SIR,

I TAKE the liberty to introduce to your knowledge Mr. GUS-
TAVUS VASSA, an African of distinguished merit. He has rec-

ommendations to Stockton, and I am happy in adding to the number. To the principal supporters of the Bill for the Abolition of the Slave Trade he is well known; and he has, himself, been very instrumental in promoting a plan so truly conducive to the interests of religion and humanity. Mr. VASSA has published a Narrative which clearly delineates the iniquity of that unnatural and destructive commerce; and I am able to assert, from my own experience, that he has not exaggerated in a single particular. This work has been mentioned in very favourable terms by the Reviewers, and fully demonstrates that genius and worth are not limited to country or complexion. He has with him some copies for sale, and if you can conveniently assist him in the disposal thereof, you will greatly oblige,

DEAR SIR,

Your friend and servant,

WILLIAM EDDIS.

Durham, October 25, 1792.

Hull, November 12, 1792.[21]

THE bearer hereof, Mr. GUSTAVUS VASSA, an African, is recommended to us by the Rev. Dr. Peckard, Dean of Peterborough, and by many other very respectable characters, as an intelligent and upright man; and as we have no doubt but the accounts we have received are grounded on the best authority, we recommend him to the assistance of the friends of humanity in this town, in promoting subscriptions to an interesting Narrative of his Life.

John Sykes, Mayor,   R.A. Harrison, Esq.

Thomas Clarke, Vicar,   Jos. R. Pease, Esq.

William Hornby, Esq. of Gainsborough.

LETTER

TO WILLIAM HUGHES, ESQ. *DEVIZES.*[22]

DEAR SIR,

WHETHER you will consider my introducing to your acquaintance the bearer of this letter, OLAUDAH EQUIANO, the enlightened African, (or GUSTAVUS VASSA) as a liberty or favour, I shall not anticipate.

He came recommended to me by men of distinguished talents and exemplary virtue, as an honest and benevolent man; and his conversation and manners as well as his book do more than justice to the recommendation.

The active part he took in bringing about the motion for a repeal of the Slave Act, has given him much celebrity as a public man; and, in all the varied scenes of chequered life, through which he has passed, his private character and conduct have been irreproachable.

His *business* in your part of the world is to promote the sale of his book, and [it] is a part of *my business*, as a friend to the cause of humanity, to do all the little service that is in my poor power to a man who is engaged in so noble a cause as the freedom and salvation of his enslaved and unenlightened countrymen.

The simplicity that runs through his Narrative is singularly beautiful, and that beauty is heightened by the idea that it is *true*; this is all I shall say about this book, save only that I am sure those who buy it will not regret that they have laid out the price of it in the purchase.

Your notice, civility, and personal introduction of this fair minded black man, to your friends in Devizes, will be gratifying to your own feelings, and laying a considerable weight of obligation on,

DEAR SIR,
Your most obedient and obliged servant,
WILLIAM LANGWORTHY.

Bath, October 10, 1793.

MONTHLY REVIEW FOR JUNE 1789. PAGE 551.[23]

WE entertain no doubt of the authenticity of this very intelligent African's story; though it is not improbable that some English writer has assisted him in the compilement, or, at least, the correction of his book; for it is sufficiently well-written. The Narrative wears an honest face; and we have conceived a good opinion of the man, from the artless manner in which he has detailed the variety of adventures and vicissitudes which have fallen to his lot. His publication appears very seasonable, at a time when negro-slavery is the subject of public investigation; and it seems calculated to increase the odium that has been excited against the West-India planters, on account of the cruelties that some are said to have exercised on their slaves, many instances of which are here detailed.

The sable author of this volume appears to be a very sensible man; and he is, surely, not the less worthy of credit from being a convert to Christianity. He is a Methodist, and has filled many pages towards the end of his work, with accounts of his dreams, visions, and divine influences; but all this, supposing him to have been under any delusive influence, only serves to convince us that he is guided by principle, and that he is not one of those poor converts, who, having undergone the ceremony of baptism, have remained content with that portion only of the christian religion; instances of which are said to be almost innumerable in America and the West Indies.

GUSTAVUS VASSA appears to possess a very different character; and, therefore, we heartily wish success to his publication, which we are glad to see has been encouraged by a very respectable subscription.

THE GENERAL MAGAZINE and IMPARTIAL REVIEW for JULY 1789, CHARACTERIZES THIS WORK IN THE FOLLOWING TERMS:[24]

"This is 'a round unvarnished tale'[25] of the chequered adventures of an African, who early in life, was torn from his native country, by those savage dealers in a traffic disgraceful to humanity, and which has fixed a stain on the legislature of Britain. The Narrative appears to be written with much truth and simplicity.

The Author's account of the manners of the natives of his own province (Eboe) is interesting and pleasing; and the reader, unless, perchance he is either a West-India planter, or Liverpool merchant, will find his humanity often severely wounded by the shameless barbarity practised towards the author's hapless countrymen in all our colonies: if he feels, as he ought, the oppressed and the oppressors will equally excite his pity and indignation. That so unjust, so iniquitous a commerce may be abolished, is our ardent wish; and we heartily join in our author's prayer, 'That the God of Heaven may inspire the hearts of our Representatives in Parliament, with peculiar benevolence on that important day when so interesting a question is to be discussed; when thousands, in consequence of their determination, are to look for happiness or misery!' "

N.B.[26] These letters, and the Reviewers' remarks would not have appeared in the Narrative, were it not on the account of the false assertions of my enemies to prevent its circulation.

THE kind reception which this work has met with from many hundred persons, of all denominations, demand the Author's most sincere thanks to his numerous friends; and he most respectfully solicits the favour and encouragement of the candid and unprejudiced friends of the Africans.[27]

His Royal Highness the Prince of Wales.
His Royal Highness the Duke of York.
His Royal Highness the Duke of Cumberland.

A

The Earl of Ailesbury
Admiral Affleck
Mr. William Abingdon
James Adair, Esq.
Rev. Mr. Charles Adams
John Ady
Rev. Mr. Aldridge
Mr. Law Atkinson, of Huddersfield
Rev. Mr. Atkinson of Leeds
Mr. Audley
————Atkinson, Esq.
Rev. Mr. Astley, of Chesterfield

B

The Duke of Bedford
The Duchess of Buccleugh
The Lord Bishop of Bangor
Lord Belgrade
Rev. Dr. Baker
Mrs. Baker
Matthew Baillie, M.D.
Mrs. Baillie
Miss Baillie
Miss J. Baillie
Wm. Bliss, of Birmingham
David Barclay, Esq.
Mrs. Baynes
Mr. Thomas Bellamy
Admiral Geo. Balfour
Mr. J. Benjafield
Mr. Bensley
Rev. Mr. Bentley

Mr. Thomas Bently
Sir John Berney, Bart.
Alexander Blair, Esq.
Sir Brooke Boothby, of Ashborne
Mrs. E. Boverie
Alderman Boydell
Mr. Beanson, of Doncaster
F.J. Brown, Esq. M.P.
Dr. Brown, of Sheffield
Rev. Mr. Burgess, of Durham
Edward Burch, Esq. R.A.
————Buxton, Esq. of Leicester

C

Rt. Hon. Lord Cathcart
Lord Bishop of Chester
Hon. H.S. Conway
Lady Almiria Carpenter
Captain John Clarkson of the Royal Navy
Rev. Tho. Clarkson
Rev. Mr. Carlow of Mansfield
Mrs. Chambers of Derby
Tho. Clark of Northampton
Thomas Cooper, Esq. of Manchester
Richard Cosway, Esq.
William B. Crafton, of Tewksbury
Alderman Curtis, M.P.

D

The Earl of Dartmouth
The Earl of Derby
Thomas Digges, Esq. of America

Sir William Dolben, Bart.
John English Dolben, Esq.
Mrs. Dolben
Rev. C.E. De Coetlogon
John Delemain, Esq.
Dr. William Dickson
Mr. Charles Dilly
Andrew Drummond, Esq.
Rev. Mr. William Dunn
Rev. Mr. James Dyer, Devizes

E
The Earl of Essex
The Countess of Essex
Sir Gilbert Elliot, Bart.
Wm. Eddis, Esq. of Durham
Lady Ann Erskine
G. Noel Edwards, Esq. M.P.
Rev. Mr. John Eyre

F
Mary Ann Fothergill of York
Rev. Mr. Foster
Richard Fishwick, Esq. of Newcastle

G
The Earl of Gainsborough
The Earl of Grosvenor
Rt. Hon. Visc. Gallway
Rt. Hon. Viscountess Gallway
Mrs. Garrick
W.P. Gilliess, Esq.
John Grove, Esq.
Sir Philip Gibbes, Bart.
Wm. Green, Esq. of Newcastle
Dr. Grieve, of ditto
Mrs. Guerin
Rev. Mr. Gwinnup

H
The Earl of Hopetoun
Rt. Hon. Lord Hawke
Rt. Hon. Countess of Harrington
Rt. Hon. Dowager Countess of
    Huntingdon
Dr. Hey, Leeds

Charles Hamilton, Esq.
Thomas Hammersley, Esq.
Capt. Hare, of Lincoln
Hugh Josiah Hansard, Esq.
Mr. Moses Hart
Sir Richard Hill, Bart.
Rev. Mr. Rowland Hill
Captain John Hill, Royal Navy
Edmund Hill, Esq.
Rev. Mr. Edward Hoare
Rev. Mr. John Holmes
William Hornsby, Esq. of
    Gainsborough
Rev. Mr. Houseman, of Leicester
Mr. Martin Hopkins
Mr. Philip Hurlock, sen.

I
Rev. Mr. James
Mr. Jefferys, Royal Navy
Rev. Dr. Jowett
Thomas Irving, Esq.
Edward Ind, Esq.
George Johnson, Esq. of Byker, 100
    copies

K
Rt. Hon. Lord Kinnaird
James Karr, Esq.
Rev. Dr. Kippis
Mr. Robert Kent, Soham
Rev. Mr. Kingsbury, Southampton

L
The Ld. Bishop of London
Bennet Langton, Esq.
Sir Egerton Leigh, of Northampton
Charles Loyd, Esq.
Edw. Lovedon, Lovedon, Esq. M.P.
Mr. William Loyd
Charles and Sampson Loyd, Esqs. of
    Birmingham
Mr. John Low, jun. of Manchester
William Langworth, Esq.

M

The Duke of Marlborough
The Duke of Montague
Sir Herbert Mackworth, Bart.
Rt. Hon. Lord Mulgrave
Sir Charles Middleton, Bt.
Lady Middleton
Morris Morgan, Esq.
Mr. Musgrove
James Martin, Esq. M.P.
Mr. Martin, of Hayesgrove, Kent
Paul Le Mesurier, Esq. M.P.
Miss Hannah More
Mr. Thomas Musgrove
Lindly Murry, of York

N

The Duke of Northumberland
Capt. Norman, Navy
Pim Nevins, of Leeds
Mr. Deputy Nichols
John Nelthorpe, Esq. of Lincoln
Rev. Robert Boucher Nichols, Dean
    of Middleham

O

Rev. Mr. J. Owen
Edward Ogle, Esq.

P

Rt. Hon. W. Pickett, Esq. Lord
    Mayor of London
Rev. Dr. Peckard, of Cambridge
The Hon. George Pitt, M.P.
Joseph Peas, of Darlington
J. Penn, Esq. of Philadelphia
David Priestman of Malton
Stanley Pumphrey, of Worcester
George Peters, Esq.
John Plowes, Esq. Mayor of Leeds
Rev. Mr. Edward Packer, of Durham

Q

The Duke of Queensberry
Robert Quarme, Esq.

R

Rt. Hon. Lord Rawdon
Rt. Hon. Lord Rivers
Geo. Rose, Esq. M.P.
Dan. Roberts of Painswick
Rev. Mr. Robinson, of Dewsbery
Rev. Mr. James Ramsay
Lieut. Gen. Rainsford
Admiral Roddam
Isaac Richardson, of Newcastle
Thomas Richardson, of Sunderland

S

The Duke of St. Alban's
The Duchess of St. Alban's
The Lord Bishop of St. David's
The Earl of Stanhope
The Earl of Scarborough
William, the son of Ignatius Sancho
Granville Sharp, Esq.
Mrs. M. Shaw
William Shore, Esq. of Sheffield
Sir Sidney Smith of the Royal Navy
General Smith
John Smith, Esq.
Colonel Simcoe
Rev. Mr. Southgate
Tho. Steel. Esq. M.P.
Rev. Mr. Sloper, Devizes

T

Hen. Thornton, Esq. M.P.
Alex. Thomson, M.D.
Rev. Mr. John Till
Dr. Thackery
Rev. Mr. Rob. Thornton
Clement Todway, Esq.
William Tuke, of York
Dr. Trotter, of Newcastle
Rev. Mr. Townshend, of Cockermouth
Rev. Mr. C. La Trobe
Thomas Talford, Esq. Shrewsbury

W

Hon. Earl of Warwick
The Bishop of Worcester

Hon. William Windham, Esq. M.P.
Mr. C.B. Wadstrom
Thomas Walker, Esq. of Manchester
Dr. White, Nottingham
Jonathan Walker, Esq. of Rotherham
Samuel Walker, Esq. of Rotherham
Joshua Walker, Esq. ditto
Joseph Walker, Esq. ditto
Rev. Mr. George Walker, of
    Nottingham
Josiah Wedgwood, Esq.
Rev. Mr. John Wesley

Samuel Whitbread, Esq. M.P.
Rev. Mr. Tho. Wigzell
Rev. James Wilkinson, of Sheffield
Rev. Mr. Wills
Rev. Mr. Ward
Rev. Elhanan Winchester
Rev. Mr. Wraith, of Wolverhampton

Y
Mr. Yeo, of Portsmouth
Mr. Samuel Yockney

LIST

OF

SUBSCRIBERS AT HULL.[29]

A
Mr. Robert Atkinson
Dr. Alderson
Mr. George Adams
Captain Antoine
Mr. Anthony Atkinson
Mr. Thomas Althorp

B
Mr. Charles Broadley
Mr. John Bayes
Mr. Richard Brigham
Mr. Harrison Briggs
The Rev. Mr. Barker
Mr. Isaac Burnett
Miss Bolton
Mr. Peter John Bulmer
Miss Bine
Captain Thomas Brown
Mr. Jonas Brown
Mr. Peter Buttery
Mrs. and Miss Burn
Mr. John Briggs
Dr. Baynes
William Johnson Bell
Mr. George Wm. Brown
Dr. Bertram
Mr. William Barnes

Mr. John Burstale
Mr. William Baker
Mr. Eldred Brown
Mr. John Boyd
Mr. John Brookes
Mr. William Brown
Miss Ann Bateman

C
Rev. Mr. Tho. Clark
Mr. J.N. Cross
Mr. Johnson Cotton
Mr. Henry Coates
Mr. Richard Capes
Mr. Joseph Chapman
Miss Rachael Ann Cook
Mr. Thomas Cutsworth
Mr. Edward Chapman
Mr. William Coslass
Mr. J.S. Crosley
Mr. Joseph Cockerill
Mess. Cook and Walmsley

D
The Rev. Mr. Thomas Dykes
Major Ditmas
Mr. James Delemain
Mr. Dodsworth

Ralph Darling, Esq.
Mr. Joseph Denton
Mr. John Delvitte
Mr. Joseph Dickinson
Mr. Robert Dear

E
Mr. Joseph Eglin
Mr. Gardiner Egginton
Mr. Joseph Egginton
Mr. Thomas Escrett

F
Mr. John Fox
Mr. George Fletcher
Mr. Edmund Foster
Mr. George Fowler
Mr. Thomas Fishwick
Mr. Thomas Fletcher
Mr. John Fearnley
Mr. Thomas Frost
Mr. Henry Feasherston
Captain James Frank

G
The Rev. Edmund Garwood
Mr. John Gilder
Mr. William Green

H
R.A. Harrison, Esq.
Miss Harrison
Mr. Francis Hall
Mr. John Hutchinson
Mr. John Hall
Mr. Richard Hirst
Mr. Joseph Howard, jun.
Mr. Thomas Hall
Mr. Richard Howard
Mr. Wm. Huntingdon
Miss Howard, 5 copies
Mr. John Harrap
Mr. Bachus Huntingdon
Mr. Samuel Hall
Mr. J.P. Hendry
Mr. John Hardy

J
Mr. Anthony Jones
Mr. John Jackson
Mr. Thomas Jackson
Mr. Joseph Jewett
John Jarret, Esq.
Mr. Robert Jackson
Mr. Wm. Johnson
Mr. Robert Jennings

K
Mr. Samuel King
Mr. William Kirby
Mr. George Knowsley
Mr. Robert Kinder

L
Mr. William Levett
The Rev. Mr. George
    Lambert
Mr. Thomas Lee
Mr. John Lawson
Mr. John B. Lambert

M
John Melling, Esq.
Mr. Samuel Martin
The Rev. Mr. Joseph
    Milner
Mr. Michael Metcalfe
Mr. Richard Matson
Mr. Bailey Marley
Mr. Godfrey Martin

N
Mr. John Newmarch
Mr. Norris

O
Mr. Benjamin Outram
Mr. Thomas Outram
Mr. Joseph Outram
Robert Osbourne, Esq.
Wm. Osbourne, Esq.
Mr. John Orton

P

Mr. Wm. Proud
Miss Ann Pead
Joseph R. Pearse, Esq.
Mr. William Parker
Mr. John Parker
Isaac Pleasance, Esq.
Mr. Peter Peasegood
Mr. Josiah Prickett
Mr. Robert C. Pease
Mr. John Pickerd
Mr. Benjamin Pullan
Mr. John Popplewell
Charles Pool, Esq.
Mr. Thomas Parkinson

R

Mr. Joseph Rennard
Miss Ann Ramsey
Mr. Joseph Randall
Mr. Richard Rennard
Mr. Thomas Robinson
Mr. Robinson
Rev. Mr. A. Robinson
Mr. Wm. Reest
Mr. Edward Riddle
Mr. Wm. Richmon
Mr. George Roberts
Mr. Josiah Rhodes
Mr. William Ramsden
Mr. Edward Roisbeck
Mr. John Robinson

S

John Sykes, Esq. Mayor
Mr. Richard Stainton
Mr. Charles Smith
Mr. Thomas Scratchard
Mr. Thoms Sanderson
Mrs. Smith
Mr. Samuel Steekney
Mr. John Simpson
Mr. Wm. Shackles
James Stoven, Esq.
Mr. Wm. Steeple

Mr. Wm. Sedgwick
Mr. John Spouncer
Mr. John Spence
Mr. Wm. Stickney
Mr. Thomas Sargent

T

Mr. Thomas Thompson
Mr. Richard Taylor
Mr. William Thorp
Mr. John Thompson
Mr. John Travis
Mr. John Todd
Doctor Tucker
Mr. Richard Terry
Mr. Edward Terry
Mr. Simon Teale
Mr. Charles Trevor
Miss H. Travis
Mr. Thomas Turner
Mr. Tho. A. Terrington
Mr. Wm. Terrington
Mr. Christ. Thorley
Mr. Edward Thompson
Mr. Stephen Thorpe

W

Mr. Thomas Wasney
Mr. William Wasney
Mr. Benjamin Wright
Will. Williamson, Esq.
Mr. William Wasney
Mr. John Wilson
Mr. Isaac Womersley
Mr. George Wallis
Mr. Edward West
Mr. William Waring
Mr. John Wilson
Mr. Jonathan Walker
Mr. John Wray
Mr. J. Watson

V

Mr. John Voare

LIST

OF

SUBSCRIBERS AT BRISTOL.[30]

A
Edward Ash
Sam. Atkins, 3 copies

B
Dan. Bailey
Mr. A. Barber
Mr. John Innes Baker
Joseph Baker
Thomas Bonville
John Bradley
Rev. Mr. Samuel Bradburn,
  2 copies
Mr. Robert Bruce
John Burt
Mr. Geo. Bush
Mr. Tho. Baynton
Mr. Dan. Baynton

C
Robert Charlton
Fred. Cockworthy

E
George Eaton

F
Anthony Fletcher
Dr. Fox, 5 copies
Charles Fox, 2 ditto
Arnee Frank
Robert Fry
Cornelius Fry
Joseph Storrs Fry

G
Mess. Granger and Cropper
Mr. Joseph Green
John Godwin, 2 copies

H
Love Hammond
Henry Hale
Edward Harwood
James Harford
Richard S. Harford
Mr. Job Harril
Mr. Robert Hazel
Rev. Mr. Hey
Joseph Hughes

I
Mr. William James
William Impey
Rev. Mr. Robt. Jacomb, 2 copies

L
Robert Lawson
Alice Ludlow
Mr. Wm. Peter Lunall
John Lury, 6 copies
John Lury, jun.

M
Mr. Tho. Morgan
Mr. Joseph Maurice, 2 copies
Jacob Merchant
Mrs. Moore, of Minehead,
  2 copies
Mr. Wm. Moore, ditto
Cath. Morgan

N
George Napper
John Newman

P
Mr. Wm. Painter, 2 cop.
Henry Parson

D.P. Pearce
William Pink

R
Rev. Mr. Richardson, Bradford

S
William Stansell
W.T. Simpson
William Smith

T
Miss M. Thatcher
John Thomas, 2 copies
John Tuckett, ditto
P.D. Tuckett, ditto

W
John Waring, 3 copies
Edward Welmat
John Wills
Matthew Wright, 3 cop.

LIST
OF
SUBSCRIBERS AT NORWICH.[31]

A
Mr. Wm. Atthill
Miss Amelia Alderson
James Alderson, M.D.
Mrs. Aggs
Mr. E. Amond, Wyndham
Mr. Atkins
Rev. L. Adkin
J. Addey, Esq.
Mr. Hugh Alcock
Joseph Ainges, Yarmouth

B
John Buckle, Esq. Mayor
J.G. Baseley, Esq.
Mr. William Barnard
Mr. Wm. Barnard, jun.
Mrs. Barnard
Sam. Barnard, Esq.
Mr. Thomas Barnard
Mr. John Barnard
Mr. S.C. Barnard
Mr. John Corsbie Barnard
Master Joseph Barnard
Augustus Brevor, Esq.
Mr. John Bidwell
Miles Branthwaite, Esq.
Mr. Samuel Bond

Mr. Blunderfield
Mr. Edward Barrow, Esq.
Mr. Edward Booth
Mr. John Beckwith
Mr. Robert Bowen
Mr. Isaac Barnes, Bungay
Mr. Browne, Coltishall
Mr. William Burt
Wm. Buck, Esq. Bury
Miss Buck, Bury
Rev. C.R. Bond
Mr. James Back
Edward Bridgeman, Esq. Botesdale
Mr. Henry Brown, Diss
Mr. Tho. Bidwell, ditto
Mr. B. Boardman
Mr. Henry Baker
Mr. John Bouzell

C
Mr. Cubitt, Ludham
Mr. John Coleman
Mr. Bernard Church
Mr. Crouse
Miss E.B. Crouse
Miss Coe
Mr. Cully, Taverham
Mr. Crickmore, Seething

Mr. Cozens
Mr. Crane
Mr. Sam. Cole, sen.
Mr. Coke
Mr. H. Catton, Elmham
Mr. Christian
Mr. John Cully
Mr. Wright Coldham
Mr. Joseph Clarke
Mr. T. Cattermoul, jun.
Miss Crisp, Ipswich

D
B.G. Dillingham, Esq.
Mrs. Dillingham
Mr. E. De Hague
Mr. Danser
Rev. Tho. Drake, Shelton
Mr. Benjamin Dowson
Mr. Daveney
Mr. Ditchell, Cromer
Mr. Dairy
Mr. Dalrymple
Mr. Tho. Dyson, Diss

E
Wm. Enfield, LL.D.
Mr. Joseph English
Miss Eliza Errington, of Yarmouth
Miss Everett, Wyndham
Mr. J. Ebbets, Hellesdon

F
Rev. Sam. Forster, D.D.
Miss Frost
Travel Fuller, Yarmouth
Miss Firth
Mr. Firth
Mr. D. Fromanteel
Wm. Foster, jun. Esq.
Mr. Freshfield, sen.
Miss Fellows

G
J. Grigby, Esq. Drinkstone, Suffolk
Mrs. Gainsborough

Bartlett Gurney, Esq.
Miss Gurney
Miss H. Gurney
Mrs Gray
Mrs. Goddard
Mr. Thomas Goff
Mr. H. Gurney
Mr. John Graves
Mr. Gardiner
Mr. F. Gostling, jun.

H
James Hudson, Esq.
Miss Hart
Rev. Peter Hansel
John Harvey, Esq.
William Herring, Esq.
Robert Herring, Esq.
Mr. Samuel Harmer
Mr. Hawkins
Mr. James Hayward
Miss Headley
Rev. P. Houghton
Mr. John Herring
J. Harvey, Esq.
Miss Ann Harvey, Catton
Miss Hagon
Mr. William Hankes
Miss Hammond
Mr. James Herring

I
J. Ives, Esq.
Mr. J.L. Johnson
Miss Jackson
Miss Jarrold

K
Henry Kett, Esq.

L
Mr. Leyson Lewis
Mr. J. Langley, Long Melford
Miss Lay
Mr. John Lovick
Mr. J. Landy
Rev. Mr. Lindley
Mr. Robert Larke

M
Mr. Edward Marsh
Mr. Muskett
Mr. James Moore
Mr. J. March
Mr. Matchett, printer
Rev. Mr. Millard
Mr. David Martineau
Miss Mildred, Diss
Mr. R. Mindham of Wells
Mr. Thomas Martineau
Miss Maling, Bury

N
Rev. Samuel Newton
Mr. William Newson

O
Mr. Olier
Mr. Edward Ollett
Mr. John Oxley
Miss Olier

P
Mr. Pitchford, jun.
Mr. Plowman, Bungay
Mr. J. Paul, Mettingham
Mr. Prentice, Bungay
Miss Plumtree
Joseph Parker, Esq. of Mettingham
Mr. E. Peckover
Mr. Thomas Paul
Mr. Robert Pearson
Robert Partridge, Esq.
Mr. Robert Paul, Starston
Mrs. Pullyn, Beccles
Mr. Parkinson, Hellesdon

R
Mr. John Reymes
Rev. Mr. Ray, Sudbury
Mr. Wm. Rye
Rev. H. Robinson, Diss
H. Raven, Esq. Bramerton
Mr. James Rump

S
Miss E. Smith
Miss F. Smith
Mr. Edward Sparshall
Rev. J.G. Smith
Mr. Stevenson
Miss Stevenson
Mr. Simpson
N. Styleman, Esq.
Mr. J. Simpson
Robert Suffield, Esq.
Mr. Jacob Shalders
Mr. John Scott, jun.
Mr. Charles Starkey

T
Mr. John Taylor
Mr. J.S. Taylor
Mr. Thomas Theobald
Mr. Taylor, Ipswich
Mr. John Toll, sen.
Mr. Taylor, jun.
Mr. John Tuthill, jun.
Mr. M. Taylor, Diss
Mr. Charles Tuthill
Rev. Dr. Temple, near [Beccles]

U
Mr. Unthank

W
Mr. R. Woodhouse
Mr. George Watson
Rev. John Walker
Mr. S. Wilkin
Mr. John Wright, Buxton
Mr. William Wilkins
Mr. John Webb
Mr. Robert Ward
Rev. S. Westby, Diss
Mr. B. Wiseman, ditto
Rev. Mr. Willins

Y
Mess. Yarington and Bacon
Mr. Wm. Youngman

SUBSCRIBERS AT LYNN.[32]

Mr. Thomas Ayre
Mr. James Ayre
Mr. Samuel Baker
Mr. Birkboek
Mr. William Currie
Mr. William Cooper
Mr. James Coulton
Mr. Wm. Dunn, Docking
Mr. G. Edwards, 4 cop.
Rev. Mr. E. Edwards
Mr. John Egleton
Mr. John Benson Friend
Mr. Gamble
Mr. T. Gales, 2 copies
Mr. Harry Goodwin

Mr. Michael Gage
Mr. Samuel Hadley
Rev. Mr. W. Hardyman
Mr. J. Hedley, 4 copies
Mr. Michael Jackson
John Marshall, M.D.
Mr. Samuel Newham
Mr. Richard Newman
Mr. George Peeke
J. Packwood, M.D.
Mr. Henry Reggester
Rev. W. Richards, M.A. 2 copies
Mr. W.C. Tooke
Mr. R. Whincop

AT WISBEACH.[33]

Mr. John Cockett
Mrs. Clarkson
Mrs. John Clarkson
Mr. J. Clark, Gosberton

Mr. William Fallows
Mr. William Friend
Elizabeth Heightholme
Mr. J. Peckover, 2 cop.

LIST
OF
SUBSCRIBERS IN IRELAND.
DUBLIN.[34]

His Grace the Archbishop of Dublin

A
Richard Abel, of Cork
William Adamson
William Armstrong
John Allen, Esq.

B
Right Hon. the Earl of Belvedere
Mr. Mark Blair
Oliver Bond, Esq.

C
Right Rev. the Lord Bishop of Cork
James Christy, of Lurgan
Rev. Mr. Adam Clarke

D
Capt. Drough, of Mote
Robert Dudley of Clonmel
Mr. Frederick Darley
James Dale, Esq.

E

Rev. Dr. Ellison, of Kilkenny

F

Fisher and Hervey of Limerick
Mr. Samuel Forbes
Mr. Samuel Fayle
Capt. William Fitch

G

Dr. William Gray

H

The Right Hon. Henry Howson,
    Lord Mayor
Thomas Hancocks, of Lisborn
Sir Henry Hays of Cork
Joseph Henry, Esq.
John Hill, Esq.
Henry Hornton, of Carlow

I

Dr. Irving, of Lisborn

K

Alex. Kirkpatrick, Esq.
Fran. Kirkpatrick, Esq.
Wm. Kirkpatrick, Esq.
Mr. Wm. Kidd, of Mulingar
Rev. Walter B. Kirwan

L

His Grace the Duke of Leinster
Mr. Michael Lewis
———— Le Strange, Esq.
Lady Louth, of Drogheda

M

The Rt. Hon. the Earl of Miltown
Lady Miltown
The Rt. Rev. Lord Bishop of Meath
Lady Moira
Colin M'Kay, Esq. Belfast

Rev. Mr. W. Mann
S. M'Guire, Esq.
Rev. Dean Morgan

N

Samuel Neal, of Corke
Sam Neilson, Esq. Belfast

O

Rt. Hon. Earl of Ormond
Right Hon. John O'Neal

P

Wm. Penrose, Esq. Waterford
Mr. Thomas Prentice of Armaugh
Dr. Patten, of Tandragee
Richard Purcell, Esq. of Cork

R

Sir Samuel Rowland, Cork
Rev. Thomas Rutherford

S

Dr. F. Skelton, Drogheda
Mr. W. Sproule, Athlone
Mr. Joseph Sandwich
William Smyth, Esq.
James Stewart, Esq.
Mr. William Sleater

T

Right Hon. David La Touche, Esq.,
    jun.
Lady Celia La Touche
Rev. Dr. Trail of Lisborn
Jas. Napper Tandy, Esq.

W

Robert Waller, Esq.
Joseph Williams
Joseph C. Walker, Esq.
John Walker

LIST

OF

SUBSCRIBERS IN SCOTLAND.

EDINBURGH.[35]

A
Hon. Lord Ankerville
Professor Anderson, of Glasgow
Mr. J. Anderson, Leith
Dr. J. Anderson, Leith

B
Rev. Mr. Buchanan
Mr. James Bonar
Mr. Elphinston Balfour
Bailie Brown, Esq. Paisley
Rev. Mr. Balfour Glasgow
Messrs. Bogle & Scott, do.
Rev. Mr. Bogg, of Paisley

C
Mr. John Campbell, W.S.
Mr. Cathcart, Advocate
William Creech, Esq.
Misses Chancellors
Mr. J. Cochrane, Paisley
Rev. Mr. Colquhoun, Leith
James Christie, Esq.

D
David Dale, Esq. Glasgow
Mr. Donaldson
Mr. Wm. Dallas, W.S.
Mr. Wm. Dalziell, W.S.
Mr. Dickson

E
Hon. Hen. Erskine, D.F.
Col. Francis Erskine
Rev. Dr. Erskine

F
Sir William Forbes

G
Lord Adam Gordon
Capt. Gallia, of Greenock

Rev. Mr. Greenfield
Mr. Robert Graham of Glasgow
Wm. Gillespie, Esq. of do.
Rev. Dr. Gilles, of ditto

H
Rev. Mr. Hall
Rev. Dr. Andrew Hunter
Sir James Hall
Rev. Mr. Headrick

I
Dr. Jaffray, of Glasgow
Mrs. Irving

K
Rev. Mr. John Kemp
William Ker, Esq.

L
Mr. Laing, Advocate
J. Love, Esq. of Paisley

M
The Hon. Ld. Monboddo
R. Scott-Moncrief, Esq. of Glasgow
Mr. Wm. Mayne, do.
John Monteith, Esq. do.
Rev. Mr. Moyse
Mr. Andrew M'Kenzie
Mr. Christ. Moubray
Mr. Kenneth M'Kenzie
Mr. Colin M'Donald
Rev. Mr. Moodie
Rev. Sir H. Moncrieff-Welwood,
  Bart. D.D.

N
Mr. Alexander Nairne, of Paisley
Mr. Adam Neal, of Glasgow

O
Mr. Oswald, Advocate
Mr. W. Orhart, Glasgow

P
Mr. Richard Prentice
Mr. Robert Plenderleath
John Pattison, Esq. of Glasgow

R
Rev. Mr. Thos. Randall
Mr. Rolland, Advocate
Mr. Ross, ditto
Mr. Rae, ditto
Mr. David Ramsay
George Ramsay, Esq.

S
Hon. Lord Swinton
Mr. Swinton
Mr. Robertson Scott, Advocate
David Stewart, Esq.
Francis Scott, Esq.
Mr. C. Stewart, W.S.
Dr. Charles Stewart

Sir John Sinclair, M.P.
Professor Dugald Stewart
Dr. Somerville, Edinburgh
Mr. John Swanston, of Glasgow
Mr. G. Stewart, W.S.

T
Mr. Crawford Tait, W.S.
Mr. John Tawse, ditto
Mr. Todd
Jn. Trotter, Esq. of Glasgow
Wm. Turnbull, printer

W
Mr. Wauchop, Advocate
Mr. Williamson, ditto
Mr. J. Watson, Writer
Mr. Kirkpatrick Williamson
Mr. Wardlow, Glasgow

Y
Mr. Charles Young
Mr. Robert Young
Alexander Young, Esq.
Dr. Yuile

CONTENTS

THE LIFE OF GUSTAVUS VASSA

CHAPTER I.

The Author's account of his country, and their manners and customs—Admin-
istration of justice—Embrenché—Marriage ceremony, and public entertaiments—
Mode of living—Dress—Manufactures—Buildings—Commerce—Agriculture
—War and Religion—Superstition of the natives—Funeral ceremonies of the
priests or magicians—Curious mode of discovering poison—Some hints con-
cerning the origin of the Author's countrymen, with the opinions of
different writers on that subject.

I BELIEVE it is difficult for those who publish their own memoirs
to escape the imputation of vanity; nor is this the only disadvan-
tage under which they labour; it is also their misfortune, that
whatever is uncommon is rarely, if ever, believed; and what is
obvious we are apt to turn from with disgust, and to charge the
writer with impertinence. People generally think those memoirs
only worthy to be read or remembered which abound in great or
striking events; those, in short, which in a high degree excite
either admiration or pity: all others they consign to contempt and
oblivion. It is, therefore, I confess, not a little hazardous, in a
private and obscure individual, and a stranger too, thus to solicit
the indulgent attention of the public; especially when I own I
offer here the history of neither a saint, a hero, nor a tyrant.[36] I
believe there are a few events in my life which have not happened
to many; it is true the incidents of it are numerous; and, did I
consider myself an European, I might say my sufferings were great;
but, when I compare my lot with that of most of my countrymen,[37] I regard myself as a *particular favourite of Heaven,* and
acknowledge the mercies of Providence in every occurrence of
my life.[38] If, then, the following narrative does not appear sufficiently interesting to engage general attention, let my motive be
some excuse for its publication. I am not so foolishly vain as to

expect from it either immortality or literary reputation. If it affords any satisfaction to my numerous friends, at whose request it has been written, or in the smallest degree promotes the interest of humanity, the ends for which it was undertaken will be fully attained, and every wish of my heart gratified. Let it therefore be remembered that, in wishing to avoid censure, I do not aspire to praise.

That part of Africa, known by the name of Guinea, to which the trade for slaves is carried on, extends along the coast above 3400 miles, from Senegal to Angola, and includes a variety of kingdoms. Of these the most considerable is the kingdom of Benin, both as to extent and wealth, the richness and cultivation of the soil, the power of its king, and the number and warlike disposition of the inhabitants. It is situated nearly under the line[39] and extends along the coast about 170 miles, but runs back into the interior part of Africa to a distance hitherto I believe unexplored by any traveller; and seems only terminated at length by the empire of Abyssinia,[40] near 1500 miles from its beginning. This kingdom is divided into many provinces or districts: in one of the most remote and fertile of which [, called Eboe,][41] I was born, in the year 1745, in a charming fruitful vale, named Essaka.[42] The distance of this province from the capital of Benin and the sea coast must be very considerable; for I had never heard of white men or Europeans, nor of the sea; and our subjection to the king of Benin was little more than nominal; for every transaction of the government, as far as my slender observation extended, was conducted by the chiefs or elders of the place. The manners and government of a people who have little commerce with other countries are generally very simple; and the history of what passes in one family or village may serve as a specimen of the whole nation. My father was one of those elders or chiefs I have spoken of, and was styled Embrenché; a term, as I remember, importing the highest distinction, and signifying in our language a mark of grandeur. This mark is conferred on the person entitled to it, by cutting the skin across at the top of the forehead, and drawing it down to the eye-brows; and, while it is in this situation, applying a warm hand, and rubbing it until it shrinks up into a thick *weal* across the lower part of the forehead. Most of the judges and senators were thus marked; my father had long borne it: I had seen it conferred on one of my brothers, and I was also *destined* to receive it by my parents. Those Embrenché, or chief men, decided disputes and punished crimes; for which purpose they always assembled together. The proceedings were generally short; and in most cases the law of retaliation prevailed. I remember a man was brought before my father, and the other judges, for kidnapping a boy; and, although he was the son of a chief or senator, he was condemned to make recompense by a man or woman slave. Adultery, however, was sometimes punished with slavery or death; a punishment which I believe is inflicted on it throughout most of the nations of Africa:[43] so sacred among them is the honour of the marriage bed, and so jealous are they of the fidelity of their wives. Of this I recollect an instance.—A woman was convicted before the judges of adultery, and delivered over, as the custom was, to her husband to be punished. Accordingly he determined to put her to death: but it being found, just before her execution, that she had an infant at her breast; and no woman being prevailed on to perform the part of a nurse, she was spared on account of the child. The men, however, do not preserve the same constancy to their wives, which they expect from them; for they indulge in a plurality, though seldom in more than two. Their mode of marriage is thus:—both parties are usually betrothed when young by their parents (though I have known the males to betroth themselves). On this occasion a feast is prepared, and the bride and bridegroom stand up in the midst of all their friends, who are assembled for the purpose, while he declares she is thenceforth to be looked upon as his wife, and that no other person is to pay any addresses to her. This is also immediately proclaimed in the vicinity, on which the bride retires from the assembly. Some time after, she is brought home to her husband, and then another feast is made, to which the relations of both parties are invited: her parents then deliver her to the bridegroom, accompanied with a number of blessings, and at the same time they tie round her waist a cotton string of the thickness of a goose-quill, which none but married women are permitted to wear: she is now considered as completely his wife; and at this time the dowry is given to the new married pair, which generally consists of portions of land, slaves, and cattle, household goods, and implements of husbandry. These are offered by the friends of both parties; besides which the parents of the bridegroom present gifts to those of the bride, whose property she is looked upon before marriage; but after it she is esteemed the sole property of her husband. The ceremony being now ended, the festival begins, which is celebrated with bonfires, and loud acclamations of joy, accompanied with music and dancing.

We are almost a nation of dancers, musicians, and poets. Thus every great event, such as a triumphant return from battle, or other cause of public rejoicing, is celebrated in public dances, which are accompanied with songs and music suited to the occasion. The assembly is separated into four divisions, which dance either apart or in succession, and each with a character peculiar to itself. The first division contains the married men, who in their dances frequently exhibit feats of arms, and the representation of a battle. To these succeed the married women, who dance in the second division. The young men occupy the third; and the maidens the fourth. Each represents some interesting scene of real life, such as a great achievement, domestic employment, a pathetic story, or some rural sport; and as the subject is generally founded on some recent event, it is therefore ever new. This gives our dances a spirit and variety which I have scarcely seen elsewhere.[44] We have many musical instruments, particularly drums of different kinds, a piece of music which resembles a guitar,[45] and another much like a stickado.[46] These last are chiefly used by betrothed virgins, who play on them on all grand festivals.

As our manners are simple, our luxuries are few. The dress of both sexes is nearly the same. It generally consists of a long piece of calico, or muslin,[47] wrapped loosely round the body, somewhat in the form of a Highland plaid.[48] This is usually dyed blue, which is our favourite colour. It is extracted from a berry, and is brighter and richer than any I have seen in Europe. Besides this, our women of distinction wear golden ornaments, which they dispose with some profusion on their arms and legs. When our women are not employed with the men in tillage, their usual occupation is spinning and weaving cotton, which they afterwards dye, and make into garments. They also manufacture earthen vessels, of which we have many kinds. Among the rest tobacco pipes, made after the same fashion, and used in the same manner, as those in Turkey.[49]

Our manner of living is entirely plain; for as yet the natives are unacquainted with those refinements in cookery which debauch the taste:[50] bullocks, goats, and poultry supply the greatest part of their food. These constitute likewise the principal wealth of the country, and the chief articles of its commerce. The flesh is usually stewed in a pan. To make it savory, we sometimes use also pepper, and other spices, and we have salt made of wood ashes. Our vegetables are mostly plantains,[51] eadas,[52] yams, beans, and Indian corn.[53] The head of the family usually eats alone; his wives and slaves have also their separate tables. Before we taste food, we always wash our hands: indeed our cleanliness on all occasions is extreme; but on this it is an indispensable ceremony. After washing, libation is made, by pouring out a small portion of the drink on the floor, and tossing a small quantity of the food in a certain place,[54] for the spirits of departed relations, which the natives suppose to preside over their conduct, and guard them from evil. They are totally unacquainted with strong or spiritous liquours; and their principal beverage is palm wine. This is got[55] from a tree of that name, by tapping it at the top, and fastening a large gourd to it; and sometimes one tree will yield three or four gallons in a night. When just drawn it is of a most delicious sweetness; but in a few days it acquires a tartish and more spirituous flavour: though I never saw any one intoxicated by it. The same tree also produces nuts and oil. Our principal luxury is in perfumes; one sort of these is an odoriferous wood of delicious fragrance: the other a kind of earth; a small portion of which thrown into the fire diffuses a most powerful odour.[56] We beat this wood into powder, and mix it with palm-oil; with which both men and women perfume themselves.

In our buildings we study convenience rather than ornament. Each master of a family has a large square piece of ground, surrounded with a moat or fence, or enclosed with a wall made of red earth tempered, which, when dry, is as hard as brick. Within this are his houses to accommodate his family and slaves; which, if numerous, frequently present the appearance of a village. In the middle stands the principal building, appropriated to the sole use of the master, and consisting of two apartments; in one of which he sits in the day with his family, the other is left apart for the reception of his friends. He has besides these a distinct apartment in which he sleeps, together with his male children. On each side are the apartments of his wives, who have also their separate day and night houses. The habitations of the slaves and their families are distributed throughout the rest of the enclosure. These houses never exceed one story in height; they are always built of wood, or stakes driven into the ground, crossed with wattles, and neatly plastered within, and without. The roof is thatched with reeds. Our dayhouses are left open at the sides; but those in which we sleep are always covered, and plastered in the inside, with a composition mixed with cow-dung, to keep off the different insects which annoy us during the night. The walls and floors also of these are generally covered with mats. Our beds consist of a platform, raised three or four feet from the ground, on which are laid skins, and different parts of a spungy tree called plaintain. Our covering is calico or muslin, the same as our dress. The usual seats are a few logs of wood; but we have benches, which are generally perfumed, to accommodate strangers; these compose the greater part of our household furniture. Houses so constructed and furnished require but little skill to erect them. Every man is a sufficient architect for the purpose. The whole neighbourhood afford their unanimous assistance in building them, and, in return, receive and expect no other recompense than a feast.

As we live in a country where nature is prodigal of her favours, our wants are few and easily supplied; of course we have few manufactures.[57] They consist for the most part of calicoes, earthen ware, ornaments, and instruments of war and husbandry. But these make no part of our commerce, the principal articles of which, as I have observed, are provisions. In such a state money is of little use; however we have some small pieces of coin, if I may call them such. They are made something like an anchor; but I do not remember either their value or denomination. We have also markets, at which I have been frequently with my mother. These are sometimes visited by stout,[58] mahogany-coloured men from the south west of us: we call them *Oye-Eboe,* which term signifies red men living at a distance. They generally bring us fire-arms, gun-powder, hats, beads, and dried fish. The last we esteemed a great rarity, as our waters were only brooks and springs. These articles they barter with us for odoriferous woods and earth, and our salt of wood-ashes. They always carry slaves through our land; but the strictest account is exacted of their manner of procuring them before they are suffered to pass. Sometimes indeed we sold slaves to them, but they were only prisoners of war, or such among us as had been convicted of kidnapping, or adultery, and some other crimes which we esteemed heinous. This practice of kidnapping induces me to think, that, notwithstanding all our strictness, their principal business among us was to trepan[59] our people. I remember too they carried great sacks along with them, which, not long after, I had an opportunity of fatally seeing applied to that infamous purpose.

Our land is uncommonly rich and fruitful, and produces all kinds of vegetables in great abundance. We have plenty of Indian corn, and vast quantities of cotton and tobacco. Our pine apples grow without culture; they are about the size of the largest sugar-loaf, and finely flavoured. We have also spices of different kinds, particularly pepper; and a variety of delicious fruits which I have never seen in Europe; together with gums of various kinds, and honey in abundance. All our industry is exerted to improve those blessings of nature. Agriculture is our chief employment; and every one, even the children and women, are engaged in it. Thus we are all habituated to labour from our earliest years. Every one

contributes something to the common stock; and as we are unacquainted with idleness, we have no beggars. The benefits of
such a mode of living are obvious. The West-India planters prefer
the slaves of Benin or Eboe to those of any other part of Guinea,
for their hardiness, intelligence, integrity, and zeal.[60] Those benefits are felt by us in the general healthiness of the people, and in
their vigour and activity; I might have added too in their come-
liness. Deformity is indeed unknown amongst us, I mean that of
shape. Numbers of the natives of Eboe now in London might be
brought in support of this assertion; for, in regard to complexion,
ideas of beauty are wholly relative.[61] I remember while in Africa
to have seen three negro children, who were tawny, and another
quite white, who were universally regarded by myself and the
natives in general, as far as related to their complexions, as de-
formed. Our women too were, in my eyes at least, uncommonly
graceful, alert, and modest to a degree of bashfulness; nor do I
remember to have ever heard of an instance of incontinence
amongst them before marriage. They are also remarkably cheerful.
Indeed cheerfulness and affability are two of the leading charac-
teristics of our nation.

Our tillage is exercised in a large plain or common, some hours
walk from our dwellings, and all the neighbours resort thither in
a body. They use no beasts of husbandry; and their only instruments are hoes, axes, shovels, and beaks, or pointed iron to dig
with. Sometimes we are visited by locusts, which come in large
clouds, so as to darken the air, and destroy our harvest. This however happens rarely, but when it does, a famine is produced by
it. I remember an instance or two wherein this happened. This
common is oftimes the theatre of war; and therefore when our
people go out to till their land, they not only go in a body, but
generally take their arms with them, for fear of a surprise; and
when they apprehend an invasion they guard the avenues to their
dwellings, by driving sticks into the ground, which are so sharp
at one end as to pierce the foot, and are generally dipt in poison.
From what I can recollect of these battles, they appear to have
been irruptions of one little state or district on the other, to obtain

prisoners or booty. Perhaps they were incited to this by those traders who brought the European goods I mentioned amongst us. Such mode of obtaining slaves in Africa is common; and I believe more are procured this way, and by kidnapping, than any other.[62] When a trader wants slaves, he applies to a chief for them, and tempts him with his wares. It is not extraordinary, if on this occasion he yields to the temptation with as little firmness, and accepts the price of his fellow creature's liberty with as little reluctance, as the enlightened merchant. Accordingly, he falls on his neighbours, and a desperate battle ensues. If he prevails, and takes prisoners, he gratifies his avarice by selling them; but, if his party be vanquished, and he falls into the hands of the enemy, he is put to death: for, as he has been known to foment their quarrels, it is thought dangerous to let him survive, and no ransom can save him, though all other prisoners may be redeemed.[63] We have fire-arms, bows and arrows, broad two-edged swords and javelins; we have shields also, which cover a man from head to foot. All are taught the use of the weapons. Even our women are warriors, and march boldly out to fight along with the men. Our whole district is a kind of militia: on a certain signal given, such as the firing of a gun at night, they all rise in arms and rush upon their enemy. It is perhaps something remarkable, that when our people march to the field, a red flag or banner is borne before them. I was once a witness to a battle in our common. We had been all at work in it one day as usual when our people were suddenly attacked. I climbed a tree at some distance, from which I beheld the fight. There were many women as well as men on both sides; among others my mother was there and armed with a broad sword. After fighting for a considerable time with great fury, and many had been killed, our people obtained the victory, and took their enemy's Chief prisoner. He was carried off in great triumph, and, though he offered a large ransom for his life, he was put to death. A virgin of note among our enemies had been slain in the battle, and her arm was exposed in our market-place, where our trophies were always exhibited. The spoils were divided according to the merit of the warriors. Those prisoners which were not sold or redeemed we kept as slaves: but how different was their condition from that of the slaves in the West-Indies! With us they do no more work than other members of the community, even their master. Their food, cloathing, and lodging were nearly the same as theirs, except that they were not permitted to eat with those who were free born and there was scarce any other difference between them, than a superior degree of importance which the head of a family possesses in our state, and that authority which, as such, he exercises over every part of his household. Some of these slaves have even slaves under them, as their own property, and for their own use.

As to religion, the natives believe that there is one Creator of all things, and that he lives in the sun, and is girded round with a belt, that he may never eat or drink; but, according to some, he smokes a pipe, which is our own favourite luxury. They believe he governs events, especially our deaths or captivity; but, as for the doctrine of eternity, I do not remember to have ever heard of it: some however believe in the transmigration of souls in a certain degree. Those spirits, which are not transmigrated, such as our dear friends or relations, they believe always attend them, and guard them from the bad spirits of their foes. For this reason, they always, before eating, as I have observed, put some small portion of the meat, and pour some of their drink, on the ground for them; and they often make oblations[64] of the blood of beasts or fowls at their graves. I was very fond of my mother, and almost constantly with her. When she went to make these oblations at her mother's tomb, which was a kind of small solitary thatched house, I sometimes attended her. There she made her libations, and spent most of the night in cries and lamentations. I have been often extremely terrified on these occasions. The loneliness of the place, the darkness of the night, and the ceremony of libation, naturally awful and gloomy, were heightened by my mother's lamentations; and these, concurring with the doleful cries of birds, by which these places were frequented, gave an inexpressible terror to the scene.

We compute the year from the day on which the sun crosses

the line, and, on its setting that evening, there is a general shout throughout the land; at least I can speak from my own knowledge throughout our vicinity. The people at the same time make a great noise with rattles, not unlike the basket rattles used by children here, though much larger, and hold up their hands to heaven for a blessing. It is then the greatest offerings are made; and those children whom our wise men foretell will be fortunate are then presented to different people. I remember many used to come to see me, and I was carried about to others for that purpose. They have many offerings, particularly at full moons; generally two at harvest, before the fruits are taken out of the ground: and, when any young animals are killed, sometimes they offer up part of them as a sacrifice. These offerings, when made by one of the heads of a family, serve for the whole. I remember we often had them at my father's and my uncle's, and their families have been present. Some of our offerings are eaten with bitter herbs. We had a saying among us to any one of a cross temper, "That if they were to be eaten, they should be eaten with bitter herbs."

We practised circumcision like the Jews, and made offerings and feasts on that occasion in the same manner as they did. Like them also, our children were named from some event, some circumstance, or fancied foreboding at the time of their birth. I was named *Olaudah,* which, in our language, signifies vicissitude, or fortunate also; one favoured, and having a loud voice and well spoken.[65] I remember we never polluted the name of the object of our adoration; on the contrary, it was always mentioned with the greatest reverence; and we were totally unacquainted with swearing, and all those terms of abuse and reproach which find the way so readily and copiously into the languages of more civilized people. The only expressions of that kind I remember were "May you rot, or may you swell, or may a beast take you."

I have before remarked, that the natives of this part of Africa are extremely cleanly. This necessary habit of decency was with us a part of religion, and therefore we had many purifications and washings; indeed almost as many, and used on the same occasions, if my recollection does not fail me, as the Jews. Those that touched the dead at any time were obliged to wash and purify themselves before they could enter a dwelling-house. Every woman too, at certain times,[66] was forbidden to come into a dwelling-house, or touch any person, or any thing we ate. I was so fond of my mother I could not keep from her, or avoid touching her at some of those periods, in consequence of which I was obliged to be kept out with her, in a little house made for that purpose, till offering was made, and then we were purified.

Though we had no places of public worship, we had priests and magicians, or wise men. I do not remember whether they had different offices, or whether they were united in the same persons but they were held in great reverence by the people. They calculated our time, and foretold events, as their name imported, for we called them Ah-affoe-way-cah, which signifies calculators, or yearly men, our year being called Ah-affoe. They wore their beards; and, when they died, they were succeeded by their sons. Most of their implements and things of value were interred along with them. Pipes and tobacco were also put into the grave with the corpse, which was always perfumed and ornamented; and animals were offered in sacrifice to them. None accompanied their funerals but those of the same profession or tribe. These buried them after sunset, and always returned from the grave by a different way from that which they went.

These magicians were also our doctors or physicians. They practised bleeding by cupping, and were very successful in healing wounds and expelling poisons. They had likewise some extraordinary method of discovering jealousy, theft, and poisoning; the success of which no doubt they derived from their unbounded influence over the credulity and superstition of the people. I do not remember what those methods were, except that as to poisoning. I recollect an instance or two, which I hope it will not be deemed impertinent here to insert, as it may serve as a kind of specimen of the rest, and is still used by the negroes in the West Indies. A young woman[67] had been poisoned, but it was not known by whom; the doctors ordered the corpse to be taken up by some persons, and carried to the grave. As soon as the bearers had raised it on their shoulders, they seemed seized with some[68] sudden impulse, and ran to and fro', unable to stop themselves. At last, after having passed through a number of thorns and prickly bushes unhurt, the corpse fell from them close to a house, and defaced it in the fall: and the owner being taken up, he immediately confessed the poisoning.[69]

The natives are extremely cautious about poison. When they buy any eatable the seller kisses it all round before the buyer, to shew him it is not poisoned; and the same is done when any meat or drink is presented, particularly to a stranger. We have serpents of different kinds, some of which are esteemed ominous when they appear in our houses, and these we never molest. I remember two of those ominous snakes, each of which was as thick as the calf of a man's leg, and in colour resembling a dolphin in the water, crept at different times into my mother's night-house, where I always lay with her, and coiled themselves into folds, and each time they crowed like a cock. I was desired by some of our wise men to touch these, that I might be interested in the good omens, which I did, for they were quite harmless, and would tamely suffer themselves to be handled; and then they were put into a large open earthen pan, and set on one side of the highway. Some of our snakes, however, were poisonous: one of them crossed the road one day when I was standing on it, and passed between my feet, without offering to touch me, to the great surprise of many who saw it; and these incidents were accounted by the wise men, and likewise by my mother and the rest of the people, as remarkable omens in my favour.

Such is the imperfect sketch my memory has furnished me with of the manners and customs of a people among whom I first drew my breath. And here I cannot forbear suggesting what has long struck me very forcibly, namely, the strong analogy which even by this sketch, imperfect as it is, appears to prevail in the manners and customs of my countrymen, and those of the Jews, before they reached the Land of Promise, and particularly the patriarchs, while they were yet in that pastoral state which is described in Genesis—an analogy, which alone would induce me to think that the one people had sprung from the other.[70] Indeed this is the opinion of Dr. Gill, who, in his commentary on Genesis, very ably deduces the pedigree of the Africans from Afer and Afra, the descendants of Abraham by Keturah his wife and concubine, (for both these titles are applied to her).[71] It is also conformable to the sentiments of Dr. John Clarke, formerly Dean of Sarum, in his Truth of the Christian Religion: both these authors concur in ascribing to us this original.[72] The reasonings of these gentlemen are still further confirmed by the Scripture Chronology of the Rev. Arthur Bedford;[73] and if any further corroboration were required, this resemblance in so many respects is a strong evidence in support of the opinion. Like the Israelites in their primitive state, our government was conducted by our chiefs, our judges, our wise men, and elders; and the head of a family with us enjoyed a similar authority over his household with that which is ascribed to Abraham and the other patriarchs. The law of retaliation[74] obtained almost universally with us as with them: and even their religion appeared to have shed upon us a ray of its glory, though broken and spent in its passage, or eclipsed by the cloud with which time, tradition, and ignorance might have enveloped it: for we had our circumcision (a rule I believe peculiar to that people): we had also our sacrifices and burnt-offerings, our washings and purifications, on the same occasions as they had.

As to the difference of colour between the Eboan Africans and the modern Jews, I shall not presume to account for it. It is a subject which has engaged the pens of men of both genius and learning, and is far above my strength. The most able and Reverend Mr. T. Clarkson, however, in his much-admired Essay on the Slavery and Commerce of the Human Species, has ascertained the cause, in a manner that at once solves every objection on that account, and, on my mind at least, has produced the fullest conviction. I shall therefore refer to that performance for the theory,[75] contenting myself with extracting a fact as related by Dr. Mitchel.[76] "The Spaniards, who have inhabited America, under the torrid zone, for any time, are become as dark coloured as our native Indians of Virginia, *of which I myself have been a witness.*

There is also another instance[77] of a Portuguese settlement at Mitomba, a river in Sierra Leona, where the inhabitants are bred from a mixture of the first Portuguese discoverers with the natives, and are now become, in their complexion, and in the woolly quality of their hair, *perfect negroes,* retaining however a smattering of the Portuguese language."

These instances, and a great many more which might be adduced, while they shew how the complexions of the same persons vary in different climates, it is hoped may tend also to remove the prejudice that some conceive against the natives of Africa on account of their colour. Surely the minds of the Spaniards did not change with their complexions! Are there not causes enough to which the apparent inferiority of an African may be ascribed, without limiting the goodness of God, and supposing he forbore to stamp understanding on certainly his own image, because "carved in ebony?"[78] Might it not naturally be ascribed to their situation? When they come among Europeans, they are ignorant of their language, religion, manners, and customs. Are any pains taken to teach them these? Are they treated as men? Does not slavery itself depress the mind, and extinguish all its fire, and every noble sentiment? But, above all, what advantages do not a refined people possess over those who are rude and uncultivated? Let the polished and haughty European recollect that *his* ancestors were once, like the Africans, uncivilized, and even barbarous. Did Nature make *them* inferior to their sons? and should *they too* have been made slaves? Every rational mind answers, No. Let such reflections as these melt the pride of their superiority into sympathy for the wants and miseries of their sable brethren, and compel them to acknowledge, that understanding is not confined to feature or colour. If, when they look round the world, they feel exultation, let it be tempered with benevolence to others, and gratitude to God, "who hath made of one blood all nations of men for to dwell on all the face of the earth;[79] and whose wisdom is not our wisdom, neither are our ways his ways."

CHAP. II.

I HOPE the reader will not think I have trespassed on his patience in introducing myself to him with some account of the manners and customs of my country. They had been implanted in me with great care, and made an impression on my mind, which time could not erase, and which all the adversity and variety of fortune I have since experienced served only to rivet and record: for, whether the love of one's country be real or imaginary, or a lesson of reason, or an instinct of nature, I still look back with pleasure on the first scenes of my life, though that pleasure has been for the most part mingled with sorrow.

I have already acquainted the reader with the time and place of my birth. My father, besides many slaves, had a numerous family, of which seven lived to grow up, including myself and a sister, who was the only daughter. As I was the youngest of the sons, I became, of course, the greatest favourite with my mother, and was always with her; and she used to take particular pains to form my mind. I was trained up from my earliest years in the arts of agriculture and war:[80] my daily exercise was shooting and throwing javelins; and my mother adorned me with emblems, after the manner of our greatest warriors. In this way I grew up till I was turned the age of eleven, when an end was put to my happiness in the following manner:—Generally, when the grown people in the neighbourhood were gone far in the fields to labour, the children assembled together in some of the neighbours' premises to play; and commonly some of us used to get up a tree to look out for any assailant, or kidnapper, that might come upon us; for they sometimes took those opportunities of our parents' absence, to attack and carry off as many as they could seize. One day, as I was watching at the top of a tree in our yard, I saw one of those people come into the yard of our next neighbour but one, to kidnap, there being many stout young people in it. Immediately, on this, I gave the alarm of the rogue, and he was surrounded by the stoutest of them, who entangled him with cords, so that he could not escape till some of the grown people came and secured him. But, alas! ere long it was my fate to be thus attacked, and to be carried off, when none of the grown people were nigh. One day, when all our people were gone out to their works as usual, and only I and my dear sister were left to mind the house, two men and a woman got over our walls, and in a moment seized us both; and, without giving us time to cry out, or make resistance, they stopped our mouths, tied our hands, and ran off with us into the nearest wood: and continued[81] to carry us as far as they could, till night came on, when we reached a small house, where the robbers halted for refreshment, and spent the night. We were then unbound, but were unable to take any food; and, being quite overpowered by fatigue and grief, our only relief was some sleep, which allayed our misfortune for a short time. The next morning we left the house, and continued travelling all the day. For a long time we had kept the woods, but at last we came into a road which I believed I knew. I had now some hopes of being delivered;[82] for we had advanced but a little way before I discovered some people at a distance, on which I began to cry out for their assistance; but my cries had no other effect than to make them tie me faster, and stop my mouth, and then they put me into a large sack. They also stopped my sister's mouth, and tied her hands; and in this manner we proceeded till we were out of the sight of these people.—When we went to rest the following night they offered us some victuals; but we refused them;[83] and the only comfort we had was in being in one another's arms all that night, and bathing each other with our tears. But, alas! we were soon deprived of even the smallest comfort[84] of weeping together. The next day proved a day of greater sorrow than I had yet experienced; for my sister and I were then separated, while we lay clasped in each other's arms. It was in vain that we besought them not to part us: she was torn from me, and immediately carried away, while I was left in a state of distraction not to be described. I cried and grieved continually; and for several days I did not eat any thing but what they forced into my mouth. At length, after many days travelling, during which I had often changed masters, I got into the hands of a chieftain, in a very pleasant country. This man had two wives and some children, and they all used me extremely well, and did all they could to comfort me; particularly the first wife, who was something like my mother. Although I was a great many days journey from my father's house, yet these people spoke exactly the same language with us. This first master of mine, as I may call him, was a smith,[85] and my principal employment was working his bellows, which were the same kind as I had seen in my vicinity. They were in some respects not unlike the stoves here in gentlemen's kitchens; and were covered over with leather; and in the middle of that leather a stick was fixed, and a person stood up, and worked it, in the same manner as is done to pump water out of a cask with a hand-pump. I believe it was gold he worked, for it was of a lovely bright yellow colour, and was worn by the women on their wrists and ancles. I was there I suppose about a month, and they at last used to trust me some little distance from the house. This liberty I used in embracing every opportunity to inquire the way to my own home: and I also sometimes, for the same purpose, went with the maidens, in the cool of the evenings, to bring pitchers of water from the springs for the use of the house. I had also remarked where the sun rose in the morning, and set in the evening, as I had travelled along; and I had observed that my father's house was towards the rising of the sun. I therefore determined to seize the first opportunity of making my escape, and to shape my course for that quarter; for I was quite oppressed and weighed down by grief after my mother and friends; and my love of liberty, ever great, was strengthened by the mortifying circumstance of not daring to eat with the free-born children, although I was mostly their companion.—While I was projecting my escape one day, an unlucky event happened, which quite disconcerted my plan, and put an end to my hopes. I used to be sometimes employed in assisting an elderly woman slave to cook and take care of the poultry; and one morning, while I was feeding some chickens, I happened to toss a small pebble at one of them, which hit it on the middle, and directly killed it. The old slave, having soon after missed the chicken, inquired after it; and on my relating the accident (for I told her the truth, because my mother would never suffer me to tell a lie) she flew into a violent passion, threatened that I should suffer for it; and, my master being out, she immediately went and told her mistress what I had done. This alarmed me very much, and I expected an instant correction,[86] which to me was uncommonly dreadful; for I had seldom been beaten at home. I therefore resolved to fly; and accordingly I ran into a thicket that was hard by, and hid myself in the bushes. Soon afterwards my mistress and the slave returned, and, not seeing me, they searched all the house, but, not finding me, and I not making answer when they called to me, they thought I had run away, and the whole neighbourhood was raised in the pursuit of me. In that part of the country (as well as ours)[87] the houses and villages were skirted with woods, or shrubberies, and the bushes were so thick, that a man could readily conceal himself in them, so as to elude the strictest search. The neighbours continued the whole day looking for me, and several times many of them came within a few yards of the place where I lay hid. I expected every moment,[88] when I heard a rustling among the trees, to be found out, and punished by my master; but they never discovered me, though they were often so near that I even heard their conjectures as they were looking about for me; and I now learned from them, that any attempt to return home would be hopeless. Most of them supposed I had fled towards home; but the distance was so great, and the way so intricate, that they thought I could never reach it, and that I should be lost in the woods. When I heard this I was seized with a violent panic, and abandoned myself to despair. Night too began to approach, and aggravated all my fears. I had before entertained hopes of getting home, and I had determined when it should be dark to make the attempt; but I was now convinced it was fruitless, and I began to consider that, if possibly I could escape all other animals, I could not those of the human kind; and that, not knowing the way, I must perish in the woods.—Thus was I like the hunted deer:

> Ev'ry leaf and ev'ry whisp'ring breath
> Convey'd a foe, and ev'ry foe a death.[89]

I heard frequent rustlings among the leaves; and, being pretty sure they were snakes, I expected every instant to be stung by them.—This increased my anguish, and the horror of my situation became now quite insupportable. I at length quitted the thicket, very faint and hungry, for I had not eaten or drank any thing all the day, and crept to my master's kitchen, from whence I set out at first, and which was an open shed, and laid myself down in the ashes, with an anxious wish for death to relieve me from all my pains. I was scarcely awake in the morning when the old woman slave, who was the first up, came to light the fire, and saw me in the fire-place. She was very much surprised to see me, and could scarcely believe her own eyes. She now promised to intercede for me, and went for her master, who soon after came, and, having slightly reprimanded me, ordered me to be taken care of, and not ill-treated.[90]

Soon after this my master's only daughter and child by his first wife sickened and died, which affected him so much that for some time he was almost frantic, and really would have killed himself had he not been watched and prevented. However, in a small time afterwards he recovered, and I was again sold. I was now carried to the left of the sun's rising, through many dreary wastes and dismal woods,[91] amidst the hideous roarings of wild beasts.— The people I was sold to used to carry me very often, when I was tired, either on their shoulders or on their backs. I saw many convenient well-built sheds along the roads, at proper distances, to accommodate the merchants and travellers, who lay in those buildings along with their wives, who often accompany them; and they always go well armed.

From the time I left my own nation I always found somebody that understood me till I came to the sea coast. The languages of different nations did not totally differ, nor were they so copious as those of the Europeans, particularly the English.[92] They were therefore easily learned; and, while I was journeying thus through Africa, I acquired two or three different tongues. In this manner I had been travelling for a considerable time, when one evening, to my great surprise, whom should I see brought to the house where I was but my dear sister. As soon as she saw me she gave a loud shriek, and ran into my arms.—I was quite overpowered; neither of us could speak, but, for a considerable time, clung to each other in mutual embraces, unable to do any thing but weep. Our meeting affected all who saw us; and indeed I must acknowledge, in honour of those sable destroyers of human rights, that I never met with any ill treatment, or saw any offered to their slaves, except tying them, when necessary, to keep them from running away. When these people knew we were brother and sister they indulged us to be together;[93] and the man, to whom I supposed we belonged, lay with us, he in the middle, while she and I held one another by the hands across his breast all night; and thus for a while we forgot our misfortunes in the joy of being together: but even this small comfort was soon to have an end; for scarcely had the fatal morning appeared, when she was again torn from me for ever! I was now more miserable, if possible, than before. The small relief which her presence gave me from pain was gone, and the wretchedness of my situation was redoubled by my anxiety after her fate, and my apprehensions lest her sufferings should be greater than mine, when I could not be with her to alleviate them. Yes, thou dear partner of all my childish sports! thou sharer of my joys and sorrows! happy should I have ever esteemed myself to encounter every misery for you, and to procure your freedom by the sacrifice of my own. Though you were early forced from my arms, your image has been always rivetted in my heart, from which neither *time nor fortune* have been able to remove it: so that, while the thoughts of your sufferings have damped my prosperity, they have mingled with adversity, and increased its bitterness.— To that heaven which protects the weak from the strong, I commit the care of your innocence and virtues, if they have not already received their full reward; and if your youth and delicacy have not long since fallen victims to the violence of the African trader, the pestilential stench of a Guinea ship, the seasoning in the European colonies, or the lash and lust of a brutal and unrelenting overseer.[94]

I did not long remain after my sister. I was again sold, and carried through a number of places, till, after travelling a considerable time, I came to a town called Tinmah, in the most beautiful country I had yet seen in Africa. It was extremely rich, and there were many rivulets which flowed through it; and supplied a large pond in the center of the town, where the people washed. Here I first saw and tasted cocoa nuts, which I thought superior to any nuts I had ever tasted before; and the trees, which were loaded, were also interspersed amongst the houses, which had commodious shades adjoining, and were in the same manner as ours, the insides being neatly plastered and whitewashed. Here I also saw and tasted for the first time sugar-cane.[95] Their money consisted of little white shells, the size of the finger nail: they are known in this country by the name of *core*.[96] I was sold here for one hundred and seventy-two of them by a merchant who lived and brought me there.[97] I had been about two or three days at his house, when a wealthy widow, a neighbour of his, came there one evening, and brought with her an only son, a young gentleman about my own age and size. Here they saw me; and, having taken a fancy to me, I was bought of the merchant, and went home with them. Her house and premises were situated close to one of those rivulets I have mentioned, and were the finest I ever saw in Africa: they were very extensive, and she had a number of slaves to attend her. The next day I was washed and perfumed, and when meal-time came, I was led into the presence of my mistress, and ate and drank before her with her son. This filled me with astonishment: and I could scarce help expressing my surprise that the young gentleman should suffer me,[98] who was bound,[99] to eat with him who was free; and not only so, but that he would not at any time either eat or drink till I had taken first, because I was the eldest, which was agreeable to our custom. Indeed every thing here, and all their treatment of me, made me forget that I was a slave. The language of these people resembled ours so nearly, that we understood each other perfectly. They had also the very same customs as we. There were likewise slaves daily to attend us, while my young master and I, with other boys, sported with our darts and bows and arrows, as I had been used to do at home. In this resemblance to my former happy state I passed about two months, and I now began to think I was to be adopted into the family, and was beginning to be reconciled to my situation, and to forget by degrees my misfortunes, when all at once the delusion vanished; for, without the least previous knowledge, one morning early, while my dear master and companion was still asleep, I was awakened out of my reverie to fresh sorrow, and hurried away even among the uncircumcised.[100]

Thus, at the very moment I dreamed of the greatest happiness, I found myself most miserable: and it seemed as if fortune wished to give me this taste of joy only to render the reverse more poignant.[101] The change I now experienced was as painful as it was sudden and unexpected. It was a change indeed from a state of bliss to a scene which is inexpressible by me, as it discovered[102] to me an element I had never before beheld, and till then had no idea of, and wherein such instances of hardship and cruelty continually occurred as I can never reflect on but with horror.

All the nations and people I had hitherto passed through resembled our own in their manners, customs and language: but I came at length to a country, the inhabitants of which differed from us in all those particulars. I was very much struck with this difference, especially when I came among a people who did not circumcise, and eat[103] without washing their hands. They cooked also in iron pots, and had European cutlasses and cross bows, which were unknown to us, and fought with their fists among themselves. Their women were not so modest as ours, for they eat, and drank, and slept with their men.[104] But, above all, I was amazed to see no sacrifices or offerings among them. In some of those places the people ornamented themselves with scars, and likewise filed their teeth very sharp. They wanted sometimes to ornament me in the same manner, but I would not suffer them; hoping that I might some time be among a people who did not thus disfigure themselves, as I thought they did. At last, I came to the banks of a large river, which was covered with canoes, in which the people appeared to live with their household utensils and provisions of all kinds. I was beyond measure astonished at this, as I had never before seen any water larger than a pond or a rivulet; and my surprise was mingled with no small fear when I was put into one of these canoes, and we began to paddle and move along the river. We continued going on thus till night; and when we came to land, and made fires on the banks, each family by themselves, some dragged their canoes on shore, others staid and cooked in theirs, and laid in them all night. Those on the land had mats, of which they made tents, some in the shape of little houses: In these we slept; and after the morning meal we embarked again, and proceeded as before. I was often very much astonished to see some of the women, as well as the men, jump into the water, dive to the bottom, come up again, and swim about. Thus I continued to travel, sometimes by land, sometimes by water, through different countries, and various nations, till, at the end of six or seven months after I had been kidnapped, I arrived at the sea coast. It would be tedious and uninteresting to relate all the incidents which befel me during this journey, and which I have not yet forgotten; of the various hands I passed through, and the manners and customs of all the different people among whom I lived: I shall therefore only observe, that, in all the places where I was, the soil was exceedingly rich; the pomkins, eadas, plantains, yams, &c. &c. were in great abundance, and of incredible size.[105] There were also vast quantities of different gums, though not used for any purpose; and every where a great deal of tobacco. The cotton even grew quite wild; and there was plenty of red wood. I saw no mechanics[106] whatever in all the way, except such as I have mentioned. The chief employment in all these countries was agriculture, and both the males and females, as with us, were brought up to it, and trained in the arts of war.

The first object which saluted my eyes when I arrived on the coast was the sea, and a slave-ship, which was then riding at anchor, and waiting for its cargo. These filled me with astonishment, which was soon converted into terror, which I am yet at a loss to describe, nor the then feelings of my mind. When I was carried on board I was immediately handled, and tossed up, to see if I were sound,[107] by some of the crew; and I was now persuaded that I had gotten into a world of bad spirits, and that they were going to kill me.[108] Their complexions too differing so much from ours, their long hair, and the language they spoke, which was very different from any I had ever heard, united to confirm me in this belief. Indeed, such were the horrors of my views and fears at the moment, that, if ten thousand worlds had been my own, I would have freely parted with them all to have exchanged my condition with that of the meanest slave in my own country. When I looked round the ship too, and saw a large furnace of copper boiling, and a multitude of black people of every description chained together, every one of their countenances expressing dejection and sorrow, I no longer doubted of my fate, and, quite overpowered with horror and anguish, I fell motionless on the deck and fainted. When I recovered a little, I found some black people about me, who I believed were some of those who brought me on board, and had been receiving their pay; they talked to me in order to cheer me, but all in vain. I asked them if we were not to be eaten by those white men with horrible looks, red faces, and long hair?[109] They told me I was not; and one of the crew brought me a small portion of spirituous liquor in a wine glass; but, being afraid of him, I would not take it out of his hand. One of the blacks therefore took it from him and gave it to me, and I took a little down my palate, which, instead of reviving me, as they thought it would, threw me into the greatest consternation at the

strange feeling it produced, having never tasted any such liquor
before. Soon after this, the blacks who brought me on board went
off, and left me abandoned to despair. I now saw myself deprived
of all chance of returning to my native country, or even the least
glimpse of hope of gaining the shore, which I now considered as
friendly: and I even wished for my former slavery in preference
to my present situation, which was filled with horrors of every
kind, still heightened by my ignorance of what I was to undergo.
I was not long suffered to indulge my grief; I was soon put down
under the decks, and there I received such a salutation in my
nostrils as I had never experienced in my life; so that with the
loathsomeness of the stench, and crying together, I became so sick
and low that I was not able to eat, nor had I the least desire to
taste any thing. I now wished for the last friend, Death, to relieve
me; but soon, to my grief, two of the white men offered me
eatables; and, on my refusing to eat, one of them held me fast by
the hands, and laid me across, I think, the windlass,[110] and tied
my feet, while the other flogged me severely. I had never experienced any thing of this kind before; and although, not being
used to the water, I naturally feared that element the first time I
saw it; yet, nevertheless, could I have got over the nettings,[111] I
would have jumped over the side, but I could not; and, besides,
the crew used to watch us very closely who were not chained
down to the decks, lest we should leap into the water; and I have
seen some of these poor African prisoners most severely cut for
attempting to do so, and hourly whipped for not eating. This
indeed was often the case with myself. In a little time after,
amongst the poor chained men, I found some of my own nation,
which in a small degree gave ease to my mind. I inquired of these
what was to be done with us? they gave me to understand we
were to be carried to these white people's country to work for
them. I then was a little revived, and thought, if it were no worse
than working, my situation was not so desperate: but still I feared
I should be put to death, the white people looked and acted, as
I thought, in so savage a manner; for I had never seen among any
people such instances of brutal cruelty; and this not only shewn

towards us blacks, but also to some of the whites themselves.[112] One white man in particular I saw, when we were permitted to be on deck, flogged so unmercifully with a large rope near the foremast,[113] that he died in consequence of it; and they tossed him over the side as they would have done a brute. This made me fear these people the more; and I expected nothing less than to be treated in the same manner. I could not help expressing my fears and apprehensions to some of my countrymen: I asked them if these people had no country, but lived in this hollow place the ship? they told me they did not, but came from a distant one. "Then," said I, "how comes it in all our country we never heard of them?" They told me, because they lived so very far off. I then asked where were their women? had they any like themselves! I was told they had: "And why," said I, "do we not see them?" they answered, because they were left behind. I asked how the vessel could go? they told me they could not tell; but that there were cloths put upon the masts by the help of the ropes I saw, and then the vessel went on; and the white men had some spell or magic they put in the water when they liked in order to stop the vessel.[114] I was exceedingly amazed at this account, and really thought they were spirits. I therefore wished much to be from amongst them, for I expected they would sacrifice me: but my wishes were vain; for we were so quartered that it was impossible for any of us to make our escape. While we staid on the coast I was mostly on deck; and one day, to my great astonishment, I saw one of these vessels coming in with the sails up. As soon as the whites saw it, they gave a great shout, at which we were amazed; and the more so as the vessel appeared larger by approaching nearer. At last she came to an anchor in my sight, and when the anchor was let go, I and my countrymen who saw it were lost in astonishment to observe the vessel stop; and were now convinced it was done by magic. Soon after this the other ship got her boats[115] out, and they came on board of us, and the people of both ships seemed very glad to see each other. Several of the strangers also shook hands with us black people, and made motions with their hands, signifying, I suppose, we were to go to

their country; but we did not understand them. At last, when the
ship we were in had got in all her cargo, they made ready with
many fearful noises, and we were all put under deck, so that we
could not see how they managed the vessel. But this disappointment was the least of my sorrow. The stench of the hold while
we were on the coast was so intolerably loathsome, that it was
dangerous to remain there for any time, and some of us had been
permitted to stay on the deck for the fresh air; but now that the
whole ship's cargo were confined together, it became absolutely
pestilential. The closeness of the place, and the heat of the climate,
added to the number in the ship, which was so crowded that each
had scarcely room to turn himself, almost suffocated us. This produced copious perspirations, so that the air soon became unfit for
respiration, from a variety of loathsome smells, and brought on a
sickness among the slaves, of which many died, thus falling victims
to the improvident avarice, as I may call it, of their purchasers.
This wretched situation was again aggravated by the galling of the
chains, now become insupportable; and the filth of the necessary
tubs, into which the children often fell, and were almost suffocated.[116] The shrieks of the women, and the groans of the dying,
rendered the whole a scene of horror almost inconceiveable. Happily perhaps for myself I was soon reduced so low here that it was
thought necessary to keep me almost always on deck; and from
my extreme youth I was not put in fetters. In this situation I
expected every hour to share the fate of my companions, some
of whom were almost daily brought upon deck at the point of
death, which I began to hope would soon put an end to my
miseries. Often did I think many of the inhabitants of the deep
much more happy than myself; I envied them the freedom they
enjoyed, and as often wished I could change my condition for
theirs. Every circumstance I met with served only to render my
state more painful, and heighten my apprehensions, and my opinion of the cruelty of the whites. One day they had taken a number
of fishes; and when they had killed and satisfied themselves with
as many as they thought fit, to our astonishment who were on
the deck, rather than give any of them to us to eat, as we ex-

pected, they tossed the remaining fish into the sea again, although we begged and prayed for some as well as we could, but in vain; and some of my countrymen, being pressed by hunger, took an opportunity, when they thought no one saw them, of trying to get a little privately; but they were discovered, and the attempt procured them some very severe floggings.

One day, when we had a smooth sea, and moderate wind, two of my wearied countrymen, who were chained together (I was near them at the time), preferring death to such a life of misery, somehow made through the nettings, and jumped into the sea: immediately another quite dejected fellow, who, on account of his illness, was suffered to be out of irons, also followed their example; and I believe many more would very soon have done the same, if they had not been prevented by the ship's crew, who were instantly alarmed. Those of us that were the most active were, in a moment, put down under the deck; and there was such a noise and confusion amongst the people of the ship as I never heard before, to stop her, and get the boat out to go after the slaves. However, two of the wretches were drowned, but they got the other, and afterwards flogged him unmercifully, for thus attempting to prefer death to slavery. In this manner we continued to undergo more hardships than I can now relate; hardships which are inseparable from this accursed trade.—Many a time we were near suffocation, from the want of fresh air, which we were often without for whole days together. This, and the stench of the necessary tubs, carried off many. During our passage I first saw flying fishes, which surprised me very much: they used frequently to fly across the ship, and many of them fell on the deck. I also now first saw the use of the quadrant.[117] I had often with astonishment seen the mariners make observations with it, and I could not think what it meant. They at last took notice of my surprise; and one of them, willing to increase it, as well as to gratify my curiosity, made me one day look through it. The clouds appeared to me to be land, which disappeared as they passed along. This heightened my wonder: and I was now more persuaded than ever that I was in another world, and that every thing about me was magic. At last we came in sight of the island of Barbadoes, at which the whites on board gave a great shout, and made many signs of joy to us. We did not know what to think of this; but as the vessel drew nearer we plainly saw the harbour, and other ships of different kinds and sizes: and we soon anchored amongst them off Bridge Town. Many merchants and planters now came on board, though it was in the evening. They put us in separate parcels,[118] and examined us attentively. They also made us jump,[119] and pointed to the land, signifying we were to go there. We thought by this we should be eaten by these ugly men, as they appeared to us; and, when soon after we were all put down under the deck again, there was much dread and trembling among us, and nothing but bitter cries to be heard all the night from these apprehensions, insomuch that at last the white people got some old slaves from the land to pacify us. They told us we were not to be eaten, but to work, and were soon to go on land, where we should see many of our country people. This report eased us much; and sure enough, soon after we were landed, there came to us Africans of all languages. We were conducted immediately to the merchant's yard, where we were all pent up together like so many sheep in a fold, without regard to sex or age. As every object was new to me, every thing I saw filled me with surprise. What struck me first was, that the houses were built with bricks, in stories,[120] and in every other respect different from those in I have seen in Africa:[121] but I was still more astonished on seeing people on horseback. I did not know what this could mean; and indeed I thought these people were full of nothing but magical arts. While I was in this astonishment, one of my fellow prisoners spoke to a countryman of his about the horses, who said they were the same kind they had in their country. I understood them, though they were from a distant part of Africa, and I thought it odd I had not seen any horses there; but afterwards, when I came to converse with different Africans, I found they had many horses amongst them, and much larger than those I then saw. We were not many days in the merchant's custody before we were sold after their usual manner, which is this:—On a signal given, (as the beat of a drum),

the buyers rush at once into the yard where the slaves are confined, and make choice of that parcel they like best.[122] The noise
and clamour with which this is attended, and the eagerness visible
in the countenances of the buyers, serve not a little to increase
the apprehensions of the terrified Africans, who may well be supposed to consider them as the ministers of that destruction to
which they think themselves devoted.[123] In this manner, without
scruple, are relations and friends separated, most of them never to
see each other again. I remember in the vessel in which I was
brought over, in the men's apartment, there were several brothers,
who, in the sale, were sold in different lots; and it was very moving on this occasion to see and hear their cries at parting. O, ye
nominal Christians! might not an African ask you, learned you
this from your God? who says unto you, Do unto all men as you
would men should do unto you? Is it not enough that we are
torn from our country and friends to toil for your luxury and lust
of gain? Must every tender feeling be likewise sacrificed to your
avarice? Are the dearest friends and relations, now rendered more
dear by their separation from their kindred, still to be parted from
each other, and thus prevented from cheering the gloom of slavery
with the small comfort of being together and mingling their sufferings and sorrows? Why are parents to lose their children, brothers their sisters, or husbands their wives? Surely this is a new
refinement in cruelty, which, while it has no advantage to atone
for it, thus aggravates distress, and adds fresh horrors even to the
wretchedness of slavery.

The Author is carried to Virginia—his distress—Surprise at seeing a picture and a watch—Is bought by Captain Pascal, and sets out for England—His terror during the voyage—Arrives in England—His wonder at a fall of snow—Is sent to Guernsey, and in some time goes on board a ship of war with his master—Some account of the expedition against Louisbourg, under the command of Admiral Boscawen, in 1758.

I NOW totally lost the small remains of comfort I had enjoyed in conversing with my countrymen; the women too, who used to wash and take care of me, were all gone different ways, and I never saw one of them afterwards.

I stayed in this island for a few days; I believe it could not be above a fortnight; when I and some few more slaves, that were not saleable among the rest, from very much fretting, were shipped off in a sloop for North America.[124] On the passage we were better treated than when we were coming from Africa, and we had plenty of rice and fat pork. We were landed up a river a good way from the sea, about Virginia county, where we saw few or none of our native Africans, and not one soul who could talk to me. I was a few weeks weeding grass, and gathering stones in a plantation; and at last all my companions were distributed different ways, and only myself was left. I was now exceedingly miserable, and thought myself worse off than any of the rest of my companions; for they could talk to each other, but I had no person to speak to that I could understand. In this state I was constantly grieving and pining, and wishing for death, rather than any thing else. While I was in this plantation, the gentleman, to whom I supposed the estate belonged, being unwell, I was one day sent for to his dwelling house to fan him: when I came into the room where he was, I was very much affrighted at some things I saw, and the more so as I had seen a black woman slave as I came through the house, who was cooking the dinner, and the poor creature was cruelly loaded with various kinds of iron machines; she had one particularly on her head, which locked her mouth so fast that she could scarcely speak; and could not eat nor drink. I was much astonished and shocked at this contrivance, which I afterwards learned was called the iron muzzle. Soon after I had a fan put into my hand, to fan the gentleman while he slept; and so I did indeed with great fear. While he was fast asleep I indulged myself a great deal in looking about the room, which to me appeared very fine and curious. The first object that engaged my attention was a watch which hung on the chimney, and was going. I was quite surprised at the noise it made, and was afraid it would tell the gentleman any thing I might do amiss: and when I immediately after observed a picture hanging in the room, which appeared constantly to look at me, I was still more affrighted, having never seen such things as these before. At one time I thought it was something relative to magic; and not seeing it move, I thought it might be some way the whites had to keep their great men when they died, and offer them libations as we used to do our friendly spirits. In this state of anxiety I remained till my master awoke, when I was dismissed out of the room, to my no small satisfaction and relief, for I thought that these people were all made of wonders. In this place I was called Jacob; but on board the African snow[125] I was called Michael. I had been some time in this miserable, forlorn, and much dejected state, without having any one to talk to, which made my life a burden, when the kind and unknown hand of the Creator (who in very deed leads the blind in a way they know not) now began to appear, to my comfort; for one day the captain of a merchant ship, called the Industrious Bee, came on some business to my master's house. This gentleman, whose name was Michael Henry Pascal, was a lieutenant in the royal navy,[126] but now commanded this trading ship, which was somewhere in the confines of the county many miles off. While he was at my master's house it happened that he saw me, and liked me so well that he made a purchase of me. I think I have often heard him say he gave thirty or forty pounds sterling for me; but I do not now remember which.[127] However, he meant me for a present to some of his friends in England; and I was sent accordingly from the house of my then master (one Mr. Campbell) to the place where the ship lay; I was conducted on horseback by an elderly black man (a mode of travelling which appeared very odd to me). When I arrived I was carried on board a fine large ship, loaded with tobacco, &c. and just ready to sail for England. I now thought my condition much mended; I had sails to lie on, and plenty of good victuals to eat; and every body on board used me very kindly, quite contrary to what I had seen of any white people before; I therefore began to think that they were not all of the same disposition. A few days after I was on board we sailed for England. I was still at a loss to conjecture my destiny. By this time, however, I could smatter a little imperfect English; and I wanted to know as well as I could where we were going. Some of the people of the ship used to tell me they were going to carry me back to my own country, and this made me very happy.[128] I was quite rejoiced at the idea[129] of going back; and thought if I should get home what wonders I should have to tell. But I was reserved for another fate, and was soon undeceived when we came within sight of the English coast. While I was on board this ship, my captain and master named me *Gustavus Vasa*.[130] I at that time began to understand him a little, and refused to be called so, and told him as well as I could that I would be called Jacob; but he said I should not, and still called me Gustavus; and when I refused to answer to my new name, which at first I did, it gained me many a cuff; so at length I submitted, and by which I have been known ever since.[131] The ship had a very long passage; and on that account we had very short allowance of provisions. Towards the last we had only one pound and a half of bread per week, and about the same quantity of meat, and one quart of water a day. We spoke with only one vessel the whole time we were at sea, and but once we caught a few fishes. In our extremities the captain and people told me in jest they would kill and eat me, but I thought them in earnest, and was depressed beyond measure, expecting every moment to be my last. While I was in this situation one evening they caught, with a good deal of trouble, a large shark, and got it on board. This gladdened my poor heart exceedingly, as I thought it would serve the people to eat instead of their eating me; but very soon, to my astonishment, they cut off a small part of the tail, and tossed the rest over the side.[132] This renewed my consternation; and I did not know what to think of these white people; I very much feared they would kill and eat me.[133] There was on board the ship a young lad who had never been at sea before, about four or five years older than myself: his name was Richard Baker.[134] He was a native of America,[135] had received an excellent education, and was of a most amiable temper. Soon after I went on board he shewed me a great deal of partiality and attention, and in return I grew extremely fond of him. We at length became inseparable; and for the space of two years, he was of very great use to me, and was my constant companion and instructor. Although this dear youth had many slaves of his own, yet he and I have gone through many sufferings together on shipboard; and we have many nights lain in each other's bosoms when we were in great distress. Thus such a friendship was cemented between us as we cherished till his death, which, to my very great sorrow, happened in the year 1759, when he was up the Archipelago,[136] on board his majesty's ship the Preston: an event which I have never ceased to regret, as I lost at once a kind interpreter, an agreeable companion, and a faithful friend; who, at the age of fifteen, discovered[137] a mind superior to prejudice; and who was not ashamed to notice, to associate with, and to be the friend and instructor of one who was ignorant, a stranger, of a different complexion, and a slave! My master had lodged in his mother's house in America: he respected him very much, and made him always eat with him in the cabin. He used often to tell him jocularly that he would kill and eat me.[138] Sometimes he would say to me—the black people were not good to eat, and would ask me if we did not eat people in my country. I said, No: then he said he would kill Dick (as he always called him) first, and afterwards me. Though this hearing relieved my mind a little as to myself, I was alarmed for Dick, and whenever he was called I used to be very much afraid he was to be killed; and I would peep and watch to see if they were going to kill him: nor was I free from this consternation till we made the land. One night we lost a man overboard; and the cries and noise were so great and confused, in stopping the ship, that I, who did not know what was the matter, began, as usual, to be very much afraid, and to think they were going to make an offering with me, and perform some magic; which I still believed they dealt in. As the waves were very high, I thought the Ruler of the seas was angry, and I expected to be offered up to appease him. This filled my mind with agony, and I could not any more that night close my eyes again to rest. However, when day-light appeared, I was a little eased in my mind; but still every time I was called I used to think it was to be killed. Some time after this we saw some very large fish, which I afterwards found were called grampusses.[139] They looked to me extremely terrible, and made their appearance just at dusk, and were so near as to blow the water on the ship's deck. I believed them to be the rulers of the sea; and, as the white people did not make any offerings at any time, I thought they were angry with them; and, at last, what confirmed my belief was, the wind just then died away, and a calm ensued, and in consequence of it the ship stopped going. I supposed that the fish had performed this, and I hid myself in the fore-part of the ship, through fear of being offered up to appease them, every minute peeping and quaking; but my good friend Dick came shortly towards me, and I took an opportunity to ask him, as well as I could, what these fish were? not being able to talk much English, I could but just make him understand my question; and not at all, when I asked him if any offerings were to be made to them? However, he told me these fish would swallow any body; which sufficiently alarmed me. Here he was called away by the captain, who was leaning over the quarter-deck[140] railing and looking at the fish; and most of the people were busied in getting a barrel of pitch to light, for them to play with.[141] The captain now called me to him, having learned some of my apprehensions from Dick;

and having diverted himself and others for some time with my fears, which appeared ludicrous enough in my crying and trembling, he dismissed me. The barrel of pitch was now lighted and put over the side into the water: by this time it was just dark, and the fish went after it; and, to my great joy, I saw them no more.

However, all my alarms began to subside when we got sight of land; and at last the ship arrived at Falmouth, after a passage of thirteen weeks.[142] Every heart on board seemed gladdened on our reaching the shore, and none more than mine. The captain immediately went on shore, and sent on board some fresh provisions, which we wanted very much: we made good use of them, and our famine was soon turned into feasting, almost without ending. It was about the beginning of the spring 1757 when I arrived in England, and I was near twelve years of age at that time.[143] I was very much struck with the buildings and the pavement of the streets in Falmouth; and, indeed, any object I saw filled me with new surprise. One morning, when I got upon deck, I saw it covered all over with the snow that fell over-night: as I had never seen any thing of the kind before, I thought it was salt; so I immediately ran down to the mate, and desired him, as well as I could, to come and see how somebody in the night had thrown salt all over the deck. He, knowing what it was, desired me to bring some of it down to him: accordingly I took up a handful of it, which I found very cold indeed; and when I brought it to him he desired me to taste it. I did so, and I was surprised beyond measure. I then asked him what it was? he told me it was snow: but I could not in any wise understand him. He asked me if we had no such thing in my country? and I told him, No. I then asked him the use of it, and who made it; he told me a great man in the heavens, called God: but here again I was to all intents and purposes at a loss to understand him; and the more so, when a little after I saw the air filled with it, in a heavy shower, which fell down on the same day. After this I went to church; and having never been at such a place before, I was again amazed at seeing and hearing the service. I asked all I could about it; and they gave me to understand it was worshipping God, who made us and all things. I was still at a great loss, and soon got into an endless field of inquiries, as well as I was able to speak and ask about things. However, my little friend Dick used to be my best interpreter; for I could make free with him, and he always instructed me with pleasure: and from what I could understand by him of this God, and in seeing these white people did not sell one another, as we did, I was much pleased; and in this I thought they were much happier than we Africans. I was astonished at the wisdom of the white people in all things I saw; but was amazed at their not sacrificing, or making any offerings, and eating with unwashed hands, and touching the dead. I likewise could not help remarking the particular slenderness of their women, which I did not at first like; and I thought they were not so modest and shamefaced as the African women.

I had often seen my master and Dick employed in reading; and I had a great curiosity to talk to the books, as I thought they did; and so to learn how all things had a beginning: for that purpose I have often taken up a book, and have talked to it, and then put my ears to it, when alone, in hopes it would answer me; and I have been very much concerned when I found it remained silent.[144]

My master lodged at the house of a gentleman in Falmouth, who had a fine little daughter about six or seven years of age, and she grew prodigiously fond of me; insomuch that we used to eat together, and had servants to wait on us. I was so much caressed by this family that it often reminded me of the treatment I had received from my little noble African master. After I had been here a few days, I was sent on board of the ship; but the child cried so much after me that nothing could pacify her till I was sent for again. It is ludicrous enough, that I began to fear I should be betrothed to this young lady; and when my master asked me if I would stay there with her behind him, as he was going away with the ship, which had taken in the tobacco again? I cried immediately, and said I would not leave him.[145] At last, by stealth, one night I was sent on board the ship again; and in a little time we sailed for Guernsey, where she was in part owned by a merchant, one Nicholas Doberry.[146] As I was now amongst a people who had not their faces scarred, like some of the African nations where I had been, I was very glad I did not let them ornament me in that manner when I was with them. When we arrived at Guernsey, my master placed me to board and lodge with one of his mates, who had a wife and family there; and some months afterwards he went to England, and left me in the care of this mate, together with my friend Dick. This mate had a little daughter aged about five or six years, with whom I used to be much delighted. I had often observed, that when her mother washed her face it looked very rosy; but when she washed mine it did not look so; I therefore tried oftentimes myself if I could not by washing make my face of the same colour as my little play-mate (Mary), but it was all in vain; and I now began to be mortified at the difference in our complexions. This woman behaved to me with great kindness and attention; and taught me every thing in the same manner as she did her own child, and indeed in every respect treated me as such. I remained here till the summer of the year 1757, when my master, being appointed first lieutenant of his Majesty's ship the Roebuck,[147] sent for Dick and me, and his old mate: on this we all left Guernsey, and set out for England in a sloop bound for London. As we were coming up towards the Nore,[148] where the Roebuck lay, a man of war's boat[149] came along-side to press our people; on which each man ran to hide himself.[150] I was very much frightened at this, though I did not know what it meant, or what to think or do. However, I went and hid myself also under a hencoop. Immediately the press-gang[151] came on board with their swords drawn, and searched all about, pulled the people out by force, and put them into the boat. At last I was found out also; the man that found me held me up by the heels while they all made their sport of me, I roaring and crying out all the time most lustily; but at last the mate, who was my conductor, seeing this, came to my assistance, and did all he could to pacify me; but all to very little purpose, till I had seen the boat go off. Soon afterwards we came to the Nore, where the Roebuck lay; and, to our great joy, my master came on board to us, and brought us to the ship. I was amazed indeed to see the quantity of men and the guns. However my surprise began to diminish, as my knowledge increased; and I ceased to feel those apprehensions and alarms which had taken such strong possession of me when I first came among the Europeans, and for some time after. I began now to pass to an opposite extreme; I was so far from being afraid of any thing new which I saw, that, after I had been some time in this ship, I even began to long for an engagement.[152] My griefs too, which in young minds are not perpetual, were now wearing away; and I soon enjoyed myself pretty well, and felt tolerably easy in my present situation. There was a number of boys on board, which still made it more agreeable; for we were always together, and a great part of our time was spent in play. I remained in this ship a considerable time, during which we made several cruises, and visited a variety of places: among others we were twice in Holland, and brought over several persons of distinction from it, whose names I do not now remember. On the passage, one day, for the diversion of those gentlemen, all the boys were called on the quarter-deck, and were paired proportionably, and then made to fight; after which the gentleman gave the combatants from five to nine shillings each. This was the first time I ever fought with a white boy; and I never knew what it was to have a bloody nose before. This made me fight most desperately; I suppose considerably more than an hour; and at last, both of us being weary, we were parted. I had a great deal of this kind of sport afterwards, in which the captain and the ship's company used very much to encourage me. Sometime afterwards the ship went to Leith, in Scotland, from thence to the Orkneys, where I was surprised in seeing scarcely any night; and from thence we sailed with a great fleet, full of soldiers, for England. All this time we had never come to an engagement, though we were frequently cruising off the coast of France; during which we chased many vessels, and took in all seventeen prizes.[153] I had been learning many of the manoeuvres of the ship during our cruise; and I was several times made to fire the guns.

One evening, off Havre de Grace, just as it was growing dark, we were standing off shore, and met with a fine large French-built frigate.[154] We got all things immediately ready for fighting; and I now expected I should be gratified in seeing an engagement, which I had so long wished for in vain. But the very moment the word of command was given to fire, we heard those on board the other ship cry "Haul down the jib";[155] and in that instant she hoisted English colours.[156] There was instantly with us an amazing cry of—"Avast!" or "stop firing!" and I think one or two guns had been let off, but happily they did no mischief. We had hailed them several times; but they not hearing, we received no answer, which was the cause of our firing. The boat was then sent on board of her, and she proved to be the Ambuscade man of war, to my no small disappointment. We returned to Portsmouth,[157] without having been in any action, just at the trial of Admiral Byng (whom I saw several times during it);[158] and my master, having left the ship, and gone to London for promotion, Dick and I were put on board the Savage sloop of war,[159] and we went in her to assist in bringing off the St. George man of war,[160] that had run ashore somewhere on the coast. After staying a few weeks on board the Savage, Dick and I were sent on shore at Deal, where we remained some short time, till my master sent for us to London, the place I had long desired exceedingly to see. We therefore both with great pleasure got into a waggon, and came to London, where we were received by a Mr. Guerin, a relation of my master. This gentleman had two sisters, very amiable ladies, who took much notice and great care of me.[161] Though I had desired so much to see London, when I arrived in it I was unfortunately unable to gratify my curiosity; for I had at this time the chilblains[162] to such a degree that I could not stand for several months, and I was obliged to be sent to St. George's Hospital. There I grew so ill, that the doctors wanted to cut my left leg off at different times, apprehending a mortification;[163] but I always said I would rather die than suffer it; and happily (I thank God) I recovered without the operation. After being there several weeks, and just as I had recovered, the small-pox broke out on me, so that I was again confined; and I thought myself now particularly unfortunate. However, I soon recovered again: and by this time my master having been promoted to be first lieutenant of the Preston man of war of fifty guns, then new at Deptford, Dick and I were sent on board her, and soon we went to Holland to bring over the late Duke of Cumberland to England.[164] While I was in this ship an incident happened, which though trifling, I beg leave to relate, as I could not help taking particular notice of it, and considering it then as a judgment of God. One morning a young man was looking up to the fore-top,[165] and in a wicked tone, common on shipboard, d——d[166] his eyes about something. Just at the moment some small particles of dirt fell into his left eye, and by the evening it was very much inflamed. The next day it grew worse; and within six or seven days he lost it. From this ship my master was appointed a lieutenant on board the Royal George.[167] When he was going he wished me to stay on board the Preston, to learn the French horn; but the ship being ordered for Turkey, I could not think of leaving my master, to whom I was very warmly attached; and I told him, if he left me behind it would break my heart. This prevailed on him to take me with him; but he left Dick on board the Preston, whom I embraced at parting for the last time. The Royal George was the largest ship I had ever seen; so that when I came on board of her I was surprised at the number of people, men, women, and children, of every denomination; and the largeness of the guns, many of them also of brass, which I had never seen before. Here were also shops or stalls of every kind of goods, and people crying their different commodities about the ship as in a town.[168] To me it appeared a little world, into which I was again cast without a friend, for I had no longer my dear companion Dick. We did not stay long here. My master was not many weeks on board before he got an appointment to be sixth lieutenant of the Namur,[169] which was then at Spithead, fitting up for Vice-Admiral Boscawen,[170] who was going with a large fleet on an expedition against Louis-bourgh.[171] The crew of the Royal George were turned over to her, and the flag of that gallant Admiral was hoisted on board, the blue at the maintop gallant-mast head.[172] There was a very great fleet of men of war of every description assembled together for this expedition, and I was in hopes soon to have an opportunity of being gratified with a sea-fight. All things being now in readiness, this mighty fleet (for there was also Admiral Cornish's fleet in company, destined for the East Indies) at last weighed anchor, and sailed. The two fleets continued in company for several days, and then parted; Admiral Cornish, in the Lenox, having first saluted our Admiral in the Namur, which he returned.[173] We then steered for America; but, by contrary winds, we were driven to Teneriffe,[174] where I was struck with its noted peak. Its prodigious height, and its form, resembling a sugar loaf,[175] filled me with wonder. We remained in sight of this island some days, and then proceeded for America, which we soon made, and got into a very commodious harbour called St. George, in Halifax,[176] where we had fish in great plenty, and all other fresh provisions. We were here joined by different men of war and transport ships with soldiers; after which, our fleet being increased to a prodigious number of ships of all kinds, we sailed for Cape Breton in Nova Scotia. We had the good and gallant General Wolfe on board our ship, whose affability made him highly esteemed and beloved by all the men.[177] He often honoured me, as well as other boys, with marks of his notice; and saved me once a flogging for fighting with a young gentleman. We arrived at Cape Breton in the summer of 1758: and here the soldiers were to be landed, in order to make an attack upon Louisbourgh. My master had some part in superintending the landing; and here I was in a small measure gratified in seeing an encounter between our men and the enemy. The French were posted on the shore to receive us, and disputed our landing for a long time: but at last they were driven from their trenches, and a complete landing was effected. Our troops pursued them as far as the town of Louisbourgh. In this action many were killed on both sides. One thing remarkable I saw this day;—A lieutenant of the Princess Amelia,[178] who, as well as my master, superintended the landing, was giving the word of command, and while his mouth was open a musket ball went through it, and passed out at his cheek. I had that day in my hand the scalp of an Indian king, who was killed in the engagement: the scalp had been taken off by an Highlander.[179] I saw this king's ornaments too, which were very curious, and made of feathers.

Our land forces laid siege to the town of Louisbourgh, while the French men of war were blocked up in the harbour by the fleet, the batteries at the same time playing upon them from the land.[180] This they did with such effect, that one day I saw some of the ships set on fire by the shells from the batteries, and I believe two or three of them were quite burnt. At another time, about fifty boats belonging to the English men of war, commanded by Captain George Balfour of the Aetna fireship,[181] and Mr. Laforey, another junior captain,[182] attacked and boarded the only two remaining French men of war in the harbour. They also set fire to a seventy-gun ship, but they brought off a sixty-four, called the Bienfaisant.[183] During my stay here I had often an opportunity of being near Captain Balfour, who was pleased to notice me, and liked me so much that he often asked my master to let him have me, but he would not part with me; and no consideration would[184] have induced me to leave him. At last Louisbourgh was taken,[185] and the English men of war came into the harbour before it, to my very great joy; for I had now more liberty of indulging myself, and I went often on shore. When the ships were in the harbour, we had the most beautiful procession on the water I ever saw. All the admirals and captains of the men of war, full dressed, and in their barges, well ornamented with pendants, came alongside of the Namur. The Vice-admiral then went on shore in his barge, followed by the other officers in order of seniority, to take possession, as I suppose, of the town and fort. Some time after this the French governor and his lady, and other persons of note, came on board our ship to dine. On this occasion our ships were dressed with colours of all kinds, from the topgallant-mast head to the deck; and this, with the firing of guns, formed a most grand and magnificent spectacle.

As soon as every thing here was settled, Admiral Boscawen sailed with part of the fleet for England, leaving some ships behind with Rear Admirals Sir Charles Hardy and Durell.[186] It was now winter; and one evening, during our passage home, about dusk, when we were in the channel, or near soundings,[187] and were beginning to look for land, we descried seven sail of large men of war, which stood off shore. Several people on board of our ship said, as the two fleets were (in forty minutes from the first sight) within hail of each other, that they were English men of war; and some of our people even began to name some of the ships. By this time both fleets began to mingle, and our admiral ordered his flag to be hoisted. At that instant, the other fleet, which were French, hoisted their ensigns,[188] and gave us a broadside[189] as they passed by. Nothing could create greater surprise and confusion among us than this. The wind was high, the sea rough, and we had our lower and middle deck guns housed in, so that not a single gun on board was ready to be fired at any of the French ships. However, the Royal William and the Somerset,[190] being our sternmost ships, became a little prepared, and each gave the French ships a broadside as they passed by. I afterwards heard this was a French squadron, commanded by Mons. Conflans;[191] and certainly had the Frenchman known our condition, and had a mind to fight us, they might have done us great mischief. But we were not long before we were prepared for an engagement. Immediately many things were tossed overboard; the ships were made ready for fighting as soon as possible; and about ten at night we had bent a new main sail,[192] the old one being split. Being now in readiness for fighting, we wore ship, and stood after the French fleet,[193] who were one or two ships in number more than we. However, we gave them chase, and continued pursuing them all night; and at day-light we saw six of them, all large ships of the line, and an English East-Indiaman,[194] a prize they had taken. We chased them all day till between three and four o'clock in the evening, when we came up with, and passed within a musquet shot of one seventy-four gun ship and the Indiaman also, who now hoisted her colours, but immediately hauled them down again. On this we made a signal for the other ships to take possession of her; and, supposing the man of war would likewise strike,[195] we cheered, but she did not; though if we had fired into her, from being so near, we must have taken her. To my utter

surprise the Somerset, who was the next ship a-stern of the Namur, made way likewise; and, thinking they were sure of this
French ship, they cheered in the same manner, but still continued
to follow us. The French Commodore was about a gun-shot
a-head of all, running from us with all speed; and about four
o'clock he carried his fore-top-mast overboard. This caused another loud cheer with us; and a little after the top-mast came close
by us; but, to our great surprise, instead of coming up with her,
we found she went as fast as ever, if not faster. The sea grew now
much smoother; and the wind lulling, the seventy-four gun ship
we had passed came again by us in the very same direction, and
so near, that we heard her people talk as she went by; yet not a
shot was fired on either side; and about five or six o'clock, just
as it grew dark, she joined her Commodore. We chased all night;
but the next day they were out of sight, so that we saw no more
of them; and we only had the old Indiaman (called Carnarvon I
think) for our trouble. After this, we stood in for the channel, and
soon made the land; and, about the close of the year 1758–9, we
got safe to St. Helen's. Here the Namur ran a-ground; and also
another large ship a-stern of us; but, by starting our water,[196] and
tossing many things overboard to lighten her, we got the ships
off without any damage. We stayed for a short time at Spithead,
and then went into Portsmouth harbour to refit; from whence
the Admiral went to London; and my master and I soon followed,
with a press-gang, as we wanted some hands to complete our
complement.

The Author is baptized—Narrowly escapes drowning—Goes on an expedition to the Mediterranean—Incidents he met with there—Is witness to an engagement between some English and French ships—A particular account of the celebrated engagement between Admiral Boscawen and Mons. Le Clue, off Cape Logas, in August 1759—Dreadful explosion of a French ship—The Author sails for England—His master appointed to the command of a fire-ship—meets a negro boy, from whom he experiences much benevolence—Prepares for an expedition against Belle-Isle—A remarkable story of a disaster which befel his ship—Arrives at Belle-Isle—Operations of the landing and siege—The Author's danger and distress, with his manner of extricating himself—Surrender of Belle-Isle—Transactions afterwards on the coast of France—Remarkable instance of kidnapping—The Author returns to England—Hears a talk of peace, and expects his freedom—His ship sails for Deptford to be paid off, and when he arrives there he is suddenly seized by his master, and carried forcibly on board a West India ship, and sold.

IT was now between three and four years[197] since I first came to England, a great part of which I had spent at sea; so that I became inured to that service, and began to consider myself as happily situated; for my master treated me always extremely well; and my attachment and gratitude to him were very great. From the various scenes I had beheld on ship-board, I soon grew a stranger to terror of every kind, and was, in that respect at least, almost an Englishman. I have often reflected with surprise that I never felt half the alarm at any of the numerous dangers I have been in, that I was filled with at the first sight of the Europeans, and at every act of theirs, even the most trifling, when I first came among them, and for some time afterwards. That fear, however, which was the effect of my ignorance, wore away as I began to know them. I could now speak English tolerably well, and I perfectly understood every thing that was said. I now not only felt myself quite easy with these new countrymen, but relished their society and manners. I no longer looked upon them as spirits, but as men superior to us; and therefore I had the stronger desire to resemble them; to imbibe their spirit, and imitate their manners; I therefore embraced every occasion of improvement; and every new thing that I observed I treasured up in my memory. I had long wished to be able to read and write; and for this purpose I took every opportunity to gain instruction, but had made as yet very little progress. However, when I went to London with my master, I had soon an opportunity of improving myself, which I gladly embraced. Shortly after my arrival, he sent me to wait upon the Miss Guerins, who had treated me with much kindness when I was there before; and they sent me to school.

While I was attending these ladies, their servants told me I could not go to heaven, unless I was baptized. This made me very uneasy; for I had now some faint idea of a future state: accordingly I communicated my anxiety to the eldest Miss Guerin, with whom I was become a favourite, and pressed her to have me baptized; when, to my great joy, she told me I should. She had formerly asked my master to let me be baptized, but he had refused; however, she now insisted on it; and he, being under some obligation to her brother, complied with her request; so I was baptized at St. Margaret's church, Westminster, in February 1759, by my present name.[198] The clergyman, at the same time, gave me a book, called a guide to the Indians, written by the Bishop of Sodor and Man.[199] On this occasion, Miss Guerin and her brother did me the honour to stand as godfather and godmother,[200] and afterwards gave me a treat. I used to attend these ladies about the town, in which service I was extremely happy; as I had thus very many opportunities of seeing London, which I desired of all things. I was sometimes, however, with my master at his rendezvous-house, which was at the foot of Westminster bridge.[201] Here I used to enjoy myself in playing about the bridge stairs, and often in the watermen's wherries with other boys.[202] On one of these occasions there was another boy with me in a wherry, and we went out into the current of the river; while there, two more stout boys came to us in another wherry, and, abusing us for taking the boat, desired me to get into the other wherry-boat. Accordingly I went to get out of the wherry I was in; but just as I had got one of my feet into the other boat, the boys shoved it off, so that I fell into the Thames and, not being able to swim, I should unavoidably have been drowned, but for the assistance of some watermen,[203] who providentially came to my relief.

The Namur being again got ready for sea, my master, with his gang, was ordered on board; and, to my no small grief, I was obliged to leave my school-master, whom I liked very much, and always attended while I stayed in London, to repair on board with my master. Nor did I leave my kind patronesses, the Miss Guerins, without uneasiness and regret. They often used to teach me to read, and took great pains to instruct me in the principles of religion, and the knowledge of God. I therefore parted from those amiable ladies with reluctance; after receiving from them many friendly cautions how to conduct myself, and some valuable presents.

When I came to Spithead, I found we were destined for the Mediterranean, with a large fleet, which was now ready to put to sea. We only waited for the arrival of the admiral, who soon came on board; and about the beginning of the spring 1759, having weighed anchor and got under way, sailed for the Mediterranean; and in eleven days from the Land's End,[204] we got to Gibraltar. While we were here I used to be often on shore, and got various fruits in great plenty, and very cheap.

I had frequently told several people, in my excursions on shore, the story of my being kidnapped with my sister, and of our being separated, as I have related before; and I had as often expressed my anxiety for her fate, and my sorrow at having never met her again. One day, when I was on shore, and mentioning these circumstances to some persons, one of them told me he knew where my sister was, and if I would accompany him, he would bring me to her. Improbable as this story was, I believed it immediately, and agreed to go with him, while my heart leaped for joy; and, indeed, he conducted me to a black young woman, who was so like my sister that, at first sight, I really thought it was she; but I was quickly undeceived; and, on talking to her, I found her to be of another nation.

While we lay here the Preston came in from the Levant.[205] As soon as she arrived, my master told me I should now see my old companion Dick, who was gone in her when she sailed for Turkey. I was much rejoiced at this information, and expected every minute to embrace him; and when the captain came on board of our ship, which he did immediately after, I ran to enquire about my friend; but, with inexpressible sorrow, I learned from the boat's crew that the dear youth was dead! and that they had brought his chest, and all his other things to my master: these he afterwards gave to me, and I regarded them as a memorial of my friend, whom I loved and grieved for as a brother.

While we were at Gibraltar I saw a soldier hanging by the heels at one of the moles.[206] I thought this a strange sight, as I had seen a man hanged in London by his neck. At another time I saw the master of a frigate towed to shore on a grating, by several of the men of war's boats, and discharged the fleet, which I understood was a mark of disgrace for cowardice. On board the same ship a sailor was also hung up at the main-yard-arm.

After lying at Gibraltar for some time, we sailed up the Mediterranean, a considerable way above the gulf of Lyons: where we were one night overtaken by a terrible gale of wind, much greater than any I had ever yet experienced. The sea ran so high that, though all the guns were well housed, there was great reason to fear their getting loose, the ship rolled so much; and if they had, it must have proved our destruction. After we had cruised here for a short time, we came to Barcelona, a Spanish sea-port, remarkable for its silk manufactories. Here the ships were all to be watered;[207] and my master, who spoke different languages, and used often to interpret for the admiral, superintended the watering of ours. For that purpose he and the officers of the other ships, who were on the same service, had tents pitched in the bay; and the Spanish soldiers were stationed along the shore, I suppose to see that no depredations were committed by our men.

I used constantly to attend my master, and I was charmed with this place. All the time of our stay it was like a fair with the natives, who brought us fruits of all kinds, and sold them to us much cheaper than I had got them in England. They used also to bring wine down to us in hog and sheep skins, which diverted me very much. The Spanish officers here treated our officers with great politeness and attention; and some of them, in particular, used to come often to my master's tent to visit him; where they did sometimes divert themselves by mounting me on the horses or mules, so that I could not fall, and setting them off at full gallop; my imperfect skill in horsemanship all the while affording them no small entertainment. After the ships were watered, we returned to our old station of cruizing off Toulon, for the purpose of intercepting a fleet of French men of war that lay there. One Sunday, in our cruize, we came off a place where there were two small French frigates lying in shore; and our admiral, thinking to take or destroy them, sent two ships in after them—the Culloden and the Conqueror.[208] They soon came up to the Frenchmen, and I saw a smart fight here, both by sea and land: for the frigates were covered by batteries, and they played upon our ships most furiously, which they as furiously returned, and for a long time a constant firing was kept up, on all sides, at an amazing rate. At last one frigate sunk; but the people escaped, though not without much difficulty: and a little after some of the people left the other frigate also, which was a mere wreck. However, our ships did not venture to bring her away, they were so much annoyed from the batteries, which raked them both in going and coming; their topmasts were shot away, and they were otherwise so much shattered, that the admiral was obliged to send in many boats to tow them back to the fleet. I afterwards sailed with a man who fought in one of the French batteries during the engagement, and he told me our ships had done considerable mischief that day on shore, and in the batteries.

After this we sailed for Gibraltar, and arrived there about August 1759. Here we remained with all our sails unbent, while the fleet was watering and doing other necessary things. While we

were in this situation, one day the admiral, with most of the principal officers, and many people of all stations, being on shore,
about seven o'clock in the evening we were alarmed by signals
from the frigates stationed for that purpose; and in an instant there
was a general cry that the French fleet was out, and just passing
through the streights. The admiral immediately came on board
with some other officers; and it is impossible to describe the noise,
hurry, and confusion, throughout the whole fleet, in bending their
sails, and slipping their cables;[209] many people and ship's boats
were left on shore in the bustle. We had two captains on board
of our ship, who came away in the hurry and left their ships to
follow. We shewed lights from the gun-wales[210] to the main-top-
mast-head; and all our lieutenants were employed amongst the
fleet to tell the ships not to wait for their captains, but to put the
sails to the yards, slip their cables and follow us; and in this confusion of making ready for fighting, we set out for sea in the dark
after the French fleet. Here I could have exclaimed with Ajax,

> Oh Jove! O father! if it be thy will
> That we must perish, we thy will obey,
> But let us perish by the light of day.[211]

They had got the start of us so far that we were not able to come
up with them during the night; but at day-light we saw seven sail
of ships of the line some miles a-head. We immediately chased
them till about four o'clock in the evening, when our ships came
up with them; and though we were about fifteen large ships, our
gallant admiral only fought them with his own division, which
consisted of seven; so that we were just ship for ship. We passed
by the whole of the enemy's fleet in order to come at their commander, Mons. La Clue,[212] who was in the Ocean, an eighty-four
gun ship: as we passed they all fired on us; and at one time three
of them fired together, continuing to do so for some time. Notwithstanding which our admiral would not suffer a gun to be fired
at any of them, to my astonishment; but made us lie on our bellies
on the deck till we came quite close to the Ocean, who was

a-head of them all; when we had orders to pour the whole three tiers into her at once.

The engagement now commenced with great fury on both sides: the Ocean immediately returned our fire, and we continued engaged with each other for some time; during which I was frequently stunned with the thundering of the great guns, whose dreadful contents hurried many of my companions into awful eternity. At last the French line was entirely broken, and we obtained the victory, which was immediately proclaimed with loud huzzas and acclamations. We took three prizes, La Modeste, of sixty-four guns, and Le Temeraire and Centaur, of seventy-four guns each. The rest of the French ships took to flight with all the sail they could crowd.[213] Our ship being very much damaged, and quite disabled from pursuing the enemy, the admiral immediately quitted her, and went in the broken, and only boat we had left, on board the Newark,[214] with which, and some other ships, he went after the French. The Ocean, and another large French ship, called the Redoutable,[215] endeavouring to escape, ran ashore at Cape Logas,[216] on the coast of Portugal; and the French admiral and some of the crew got ashore; but we, finding it impossible to get the ships off, set fire to them both. About midnight I saw the Ocean blow up, with a most dreadful explosion. I never beheld a more awful scene. About the space of a minute, the midnight seemed turned into day by the blaze,[217] which was attended with a noise louder and more terrible than thunder, that seemed to rend every element around us.

My station during the engagement was on the middle deck,[218] where I was quartered with another boy, to bring powder to the aftermost gun; and here I was a witness of the dreadful fate of many of my companions, who, in the twinkling of an eye, were dashed in pieces, and launched into eternity. Happily I escaped unhurt, though the shot and splinters flew thick about me during the whole fight. Towards the latter part of it my master was wounded, and I saw him carried down to the surgeon; but, though I was much alarmed for him, and wished to assist him, I dared not leave my post. At this station my gun-mate (a partner in bringing powder for the same gun) and I ran a very great risk for more than half an hour of blowing up the ship. For, when we had taken the cartridges out of the boxes, the bottoms of many of them proving rotten, the powder ran all about the deck, near the match-tub:[219] we scarcely had water enough at the last to throw on it. We were also, from our employment, very much exposed to the enemy's shots; for we had to go through nearly the whole length of the ship to bring the powder. I expected therefore every minute to be my last; especially when I saw our men fall so thick about me; but, wishing to guard as much against the dangers as possible, at first I thought it would be safest not to go for the powder till the Frenchmen had fired their broadside; and then, while they were charging, I could go and come with my powder: but immediately afterwards I thought this caution was fruitless; and, cheering myself with the reflection that there was a time allotted for me to die as well as to be born, I instantly cast off all fear or thought whatever of death, and went through the whole of my duty with alacrity; pleasing myself with the hope, if I survived the battle, of relating it and the dangers I had escaped to the Miss Guerins,[220] and others, when I should return to London.

Our ship suffered very much in this engagement; for, besides the number of our killed and wounded, she was almost torn to pieces, and our rigging so much shattered, that our mizen-mast, main-yard, &c. hung over the side of the ship; so that we were obliged to get many carpenters and others, from some of the ships of the fleet, to assist in setting us in some tolerable order; and, notwithstanding which, it took us some time before we were completely refitted; after which we left Admiral Broderick to command,[221] and we, with the prizes, steered for England. On the passage, and as soon as my master was something recovered of his wounds, the Admiral appointed him captain of the Aetna fire-ship, on which he and I left the Namur, and went on board of her at sea.[222] I liked this small ship very much. I now became the captain's steward, in which situation I was very happy, for I was extremely well treated by all on board, and I had leisure to improve myself in reading and writing. The latter I had learned a little before I left the Namur, as there was a school on board.[223] When we arrived at Spithead, the Aetna went into Portsmouth harbour to refit, which being done, we returned to Spithead, and joined a large fleet that was thought to be intended against the Havannah.[224] But about that time the king died;[225] whether that prevented the expedition I know not; but it caused our ship to be stationed at Cowes, in the Isle of Wight, till the beginning of the year sixty-one. Here I spent my time very pleasantly; I was much on shore all about this delightful island, and found the inhabitants very civil.

While I was here, I met with a trifling incident which surprised me agreeably. I was one day in a field belonging to a gentleman who had a black boy about my own size; this boy having observed me from his master's house, was transported at the sight of one of his own countrymen, and ran to meet me with the utmost haste. I not knowing what he was about, turned a little out of his way at first, but to no purpose; he soon came close to me, and caught hold of me in his arms as if I had been his brother, though we had never seen each other before. After we had talked together for some time, he took me to his master's house, where I was treated very kindly. This benevolent boy and I were very happy in frequently seeing each other, till about the month of March 1761, when our ship had orders to fit out again for another expedition. When we got ready, we joined a very large fleet at Spithead, commanded by Commodore Keppel, destined against Belle-Isle;[226] and having a number of transport ships in company, with troops on board, to make a descent on the place, we sailed once more in quest of fame. I longed to engage in new adventures, and to see fresh wonders.

I had a mind on which every thing uncommon made its full impression, and every event which I considered as marvellous. Every extraordinary escape, or signal deliverance, either of myself or others, I looked upon to be effected by the interposition of Providence. We had not been above ten days at sea before an incident of this kind happened; which, whatever credit it may obtain from the reader, made no small impression upon my mind.

We had on board a gunner, whose name was John Mondle, a man of very indifferent morals.[227] This man's cabin was between the decks, exactly over where I lay, a-breast of the quarter-deck ladder. One night, the 5th of April,[228] being terrified with a dream, he awoke in so great a fright that he could not rest in his bed any longer, nor even remain in his cabin; and he went upon deck about four o'clock in the morning extremely agitated. He immediately told those upon the deck of the agonies of his mind, and the dream which occasioned it; in which he said he had seen many things very awful, and had been warned by St. Peter to repent, who told him his time was short.[229] This he said had greatly alarmed him, and he was determined to alter his life. People generally mock the fears of others when they are themselves in safety; and some of his shipmates who heard him only laughed at him. However, he made a vow that he never would drink strong liquors again; and he immediately got a light, and gave away his sea-stores of liquor. After which, his agitation still continuing, he began to read the scriptures, hoping to find some relief; and soon afterwards he laid himself down again on his bed, and endeavoured to compose himself to sleep, but to no purpose; his mind still continuing in a state of agony. By this time it was exactly half after seven in the morning; I was then under the half deck[230] at the great cabin door; and all at once I heard the people in the waist[231] cry out most fearfully—"The Lord have mercy upon us! We are all lost! The Lord have mercy upon us!"—Mr. Mondle hearing the cries, immediately ran out of his cabin; and we were instantly struck by the Lynne, a forty-gun ship, Captain Clerk, which nearly ran us down.[232] This ship had just put about, and was by the wind, but had not got full head-way, or we must all have perished; for the wind was brisk. However, before Mr. Mondle had got four steps from his cabin door, she struck our ship, with her cutwater,[233] right in the middle of his bed and cabin, and ran it up to the combings of the quarter deck hatchway,[234] and above three feet below water, and in a minute there was not a bit of wood to be seen where Mr. Mondle's cabin stood; and he was so near being killed, that some of the splinters tore his face. As Mr. Mondle must inevitably have perished from this accident, had he not been alarmed in the very extraordinary way I have related, I could not help regarding this as an awful interposition of Providence for his preservation. The two ships for some time swinged alongside of each other; for ours being a fireship, our grappling-irons caught the Lynne every way, and the yards and rigging went at an astonishing rate. Our ship was in such a shocking condition that we all thought she would instantly go down, and every one ran for their lives, and got as well as they could on board the Lynne; but our lieutenant being the aggressor, he never quitted the ship.[235] However, when we found she did not sink, immediately, the captain came on board again and encouraged our people to return and try to save her. Many of them came back, but some would not venture. Some of the ships in the fleet, seeing our situation, immediately sent their boats to our assistance; but it took us the whole day to save the ship with all their help. And by using every possible means, particularly frapping her together with many hawsers,[236] and putting a great quantity of tallow below water where she was damaged, she was kept together; but it was well we did not meet with any gales of wind, or we must have gone to pieces; for we were in such a crazy[237] condition that we had ships to attend us till we arrived at Belle-Isle, the place of our destination; and then we had all things taken out of the ship, and she was properly repaired. This escape of Mr. Mondle, which he, as well as myself, always considered as a singular act of Providence, I believe had a great influence on his life and conduct ever afterwards.

Now that I am on this subject, I beg leave to relate another instance or two which strongly raised my belief of the particular interposition of Heaven, and which might not otherwise have found a place here, from their insignificance. I belonged for a few days, in the year 1758, to the Jason, of fifty-four guns, at Plymouth;[238] and one night, when I was on board, a woman, with a child at her breast, fell from the upper deck down into the hold, near the keel.[239] Every one thought that the mother and child must be both dashed to pieces; but, to our great surprise, neither of them was hurt. I myself one day fell headlong from the upper deck of the Aetna down the after-hold, when the ballast was out;²⁴⁰ and all who saw me fall called out I was killed; but I received not the least injury. And in the same ship a man fell from the mast-head on the deck without being hurt. In these, and in many more instances, I thought I could very plainly trace the hand of God, without whose permission a sparrow cannot fall. I began to raise my fear from man to him alone, and to call daily on his holy name with fear and reverence: and I trust he heard my supplications, and graciously condescended to answer me according to his holy word, and to implant the seeds of piety in me, even one of the meanest of his creatures.

When we had refitted our ship, and all things were in readiness for attacking the place, the troops on board the transports were ordered to disembark; and my master, as a junior captain, had a share in the command of the landing. This was on the 12th of April.²⁴¹ The French were drawn up on the shore, and had made every disposition to oppose the landing of our men, only a small part of them this day being able to effect it; most of them, after fighting with great bravery, were cut off, and General Crawford, with a number of others, were taken prisoners.²⁴² In this day's engagement we had also our lieutenant killed.

On the 21st of April we renewed our efforts to land the men, while all the men of war were stationed along the shore to cover it, and fired at the French batteries and breastworks,²⁴³ from early in the morning till about four o'clock in the evening, when our soldiers effected a safe landing. They immediately attacked the French; and, after a sharp encounter, forced them from the batteries. Before the enemy retreated, they blew up several of them, lest they should fall into our hands. Our men then proceeded to besiege the citadel,²⁴⁴ and my master was ordered on shore to superintend the landing of all the materials necessary for carrying on the siege; in this service I mostly attended him. While I was there I went about to different parts of the island; and one day, particularly, my curiosity almost cost me my life. I wanted very much to see the mode of charging the mortars, and letting off the shells, and for that purpose I went to an English battery that was but a very few yards from the walls of the citadel. There indeed I had an opportunity of completely gratifying myself in seeing the whole operation, and that not without running a very great risk, both from the English shells that burst while I was there, but likewise from those of the French. One of the largest of their shells bursted within nine or ten yards of me: there was a single rock close by, about the size of a butt;[245] and I got instant shelter under it in time to avoid the fury of the shell. Where it burst the earth was torn in such a manner that two or three butts might easily have gone into the hole it made, and it threw great quantities of stones and dirt to a considerable distance. Three shot were also fired at me, and another boy who was along with me, one of them in particular seemed

Wing'd with red lightning and impetuous rage;[246]

for, with a most dreadful sound, it hissed close by me, and struck a rock at a little distance, which it shattered to pieces. When I saw what perilous circumstances I was in, I attempted to return the nearest way I could find, and thereby I got between the English and the French centinels. An English serjeant, who commanded the outposts, seeing me, and surprised how I came there (which was by stealth along the sea-shore), reprimanded me very severely for it, and instantly took the centinel off his post into custody, for his negligence in suffering me to pass the lines. While I was in this situation I observed at a little distance a French horse belonging to some islanders, which I thought I would now mount, for the greater expedition of getting off. Accordingly, I took some cord which I had about me, and making a kind of bridle of it, I put it round the horse's head, and the tame beast very quietly suffered me[247] to tie him thus and mount him. As soon as I was on the horse's back I began to kick and beat him, and try every means to make him go quick, but all to very little purpose: I could not drive him out of a slow pace. While I was creeping along, still within reach of the enemy's shot, I met with a servant well mounted on an English horse. I immediately stopped; and, crying, told him my case; and begged of him to help me, and this he effectually did; for, having a fine large whip, he began to lash my horse with it so severely, that he set off full speed with me towards the sea, while I was quite unable to hold or manage him. In this manner I went along till I came to a craggy precipice. I now could not stop my horse; and my mind was filled with apprehensions of my deplorable fate, should he go down the precipice, which he appeared fully disposed to do: I therefore thought I had better throw myself off him at once, which I did immediately with a great deal of dexterity, and fortunately escaped unhurt. As soon as I found myself at liberty, I made the best of my way for the ship, determined I would not be so fool-hardy again in a hurry.

We continued to besiege the citadel till June, when it surrendered. During the siege I have counted above sixty shells and carcases[248] in the air at once. When this place was taken I went through the citadel, and in the bomb-proofs under it,[249] which were cut in the solid rock; and I thought it a surprising place, both for strength and building: notwithstanding which our shots and shells had made amazing devastation, and ruinous heaps all around it.

After the taking of this island, our ships, with some others commanded by Commodore Stanhope, in the Swiftsure, went to Basse-road, where we blocked up a French fleet.[250] Our ships were there from June till February following; and in that time I saw a great many scenes of war, and stratagems on both sides, to destroy each other's fleet. Sometimes we would attack the French with some ships of the line; at other times with boats; and frequently we made prizes. Once or twice the French attacked us, by throwing shells with their bomb-vessels;[251] and one day, as a French vessel was throwing shells at our ships, she broke from her springs[252] behind the Isle of Rhe: the tide being complicated, she came within a gun-shot of the Nassau;[253] but the Nassau could not bring a gun to bear upon her, and thereby the Frenchman got off. We were twice attacked by their fire-floats, which they chained together, and then let them float down with the tide; but each time we sent boats with grapplings,[254] and towed them safe out of the fleet.

We had different commanders while we were at this place, Commodores Stanhope, Dennis, Lord Howe, &c. From thence, before the Spanish war began, our ship and, the Wasp sloop, were sent to St. Sebastian, in Spain, by Commodore Stanhope;[255] and Commodore Dennis afterwards sent our ship as a cartel[256] to Bayonne in France;[257] after which we went in February 1762, to Belle-Isle, and there stayed till the summer, then[258] we left it, and returned to Portsmouth.

After our ship was fitted out again for service, in September she went to Guernsey, where I was very glad to see my old hostess, who was now a widow, and my former little charming companion her daughter. I spent some time here very happily with them, till October, when we had orders to repair to Portsmouth. We parted from each other with a great deal of affection, and I promised to return soon, and see them again, not knowing what all-powerful fate had determined for me. Our ship having arrived at Portsmouth, we went into the harbour, and remained there till the end of November, when we heard great talk about peace; and, to our very great joy, in the beginning of December we had orders to go up to London with our ship, to be paid off.[259] We received this news with loud huzzas, and every other demonstration of gladness; and nothing but mirth was to be seen through every part of the ship. I too was not without my share of the general joy on this occasion. I thought now of nothing but being freed, and working for myself, and thereby getting money to enable me to get a good education; for I always had a great desire to be able at least to read and write; and while I was on shipboard I had endeavoured to improve myself in both. While I was in the Aetna particularly, the captain's clerk taught me to write, and gave me a smattering of arithmetic as far as the rule of three.[260] There was also one Daniel Queen, about forty years of age, a man very well educated, who messed[261] with me on board this ship, and he likewise dressed and attended the captain. Fortunately this man soon became very much attached to me, and took very great pains to instruct me in many things. He taught me to shave and dress hair a little, and also to read in the Bible, explaining many passages to me, which I did not comprehend. I was wonderfully surprised to see the laws and rules of my country written almost exactly here; a circumstance which I believe tended to impress our manners and customs more deeply on my memory. I used to tell him of this resemblance; and many a time we had[262] sat up the whole night together at this employment. In short he was like a father to me; and some even used to call me after his name; they also styled me the black Christian. Indeed I almost loved him with the affection of a son. Many things I have denied myself that he might have them; and when I used to play at marbles, or any other game, and won a few halfpence, or got any little money, which I did sometimes, for shaving any one, I used to buy him a little sugar or tobacco, as far as my stock of money would go. He used to say, that he and I never should part; and that when our ship was paid off, as I was as free as himself or any other man on board, he would instruct me in his business, by which I might gain a good livelihood. This gave me new life and spirits, and my heart burned within me, while I thought the time long till I obtained my freedom: for though my master had not promised it to me, yet besides the assurances I had received that he had no right to detain me, he always treated me with the greatest kindness, and reposed in me an unbounded confidence; he even paid attention to my morals; and would never suffer me to deceive him, or tell lies, of which he used to tell me the consequences; and that if I did so, God would not love me; so that from all this tenderness, I had never once supposed, in all my dreams of freedom, that he would think of detaining me any longer than I wished.

In pursuance of our orders we sailed from Portsmouth for the Thames, and arrived at Deptford the 10th of December; where we cast anchor just as it was high water. The ship was up about half an hour, when my master ordered the barge to be manned;

and all in an instant, without having before given me the least
reason to suspect any thing of the matter, he forced me into the
barge, saying, I was going to leave him, but he would take care
I should not. I was so struck with the unexpectedness of this
proceeding, that for some time I could[263] not make a reply, only
I made an offer to go for my books and chest of clothes, but he
swore I should not move out of his sight; and if I did he would
cut my throat, at the same time taking his hanger.[264] I began,
however, to collect myself: and, plucking up courage, I told him
I was free, and he could not by law serve me so. But this only
enraged him the more; and he continued to swear, and said he
would soon let me know whether he would or not, and at that
instant sprung himself into the barge from the ship, to the astonishment and sorrow of all on board. The tide, rather unluckily for
me, had just turned downward, so that we quickly fell down the
river along with it, till we came among some outward-bound
West-Indiamen;[265] for he was resolved to put me on board the
first vessel he could get to receive me. The boat's crew, who
pulled against their will, became quite faint at different times,[266]
and would have gone ashore; but he would not let them. Some
of them strove then to cheer me, and told me he could not sell
me, and that they would stand by me, which revived me a little,
and encouraged my hopes;[267] for as they pulled along he asked
some vessels to receive me, and they would not.[268] But, just as we
had got a little below Gravesend, we came alongside of a ship
which was going away the next tide for the West Indies; her name
was the Charming Sally, Capt. James Doran; and my master went
on board and agreed with him for me; and in a little time I was
sent for into the cabin. When I came there, Captain Doran asked
me if I knew him. I answered that I did not; "Then," said he
"you are now my slave." I told him my master could not sell me
to him, nor to any one else. "Why," said he, "did not your master
buy you?" I confessed he did. But I have served him, said I, many
years, and he has taken all my wages and prize-money,[269] for I
only got one sixpence during the war; besides this I have been
baptized; and by the laws of the land no man has a right to sell

me: and I added, that I had heard a lawyer, and others at different times, tell my master so. They both then said that those people who told me so were not my friends: but I replied—It was very extraordinary that other people did not know the law as well as they.[270] Upon this Captain Doran said I talked too much English; and if I did not behave myself well, and be quiet, he had a method on board to make me. I was too well convinced of his power over me to doubt what he said: and my former sufferings in the slave-ship presenting themselves to my mind, the recollection of them made me shudder. However, before I retired, I told them that as I could not get any right among men here, I hoped I should hereafter in Heaven; and I immediately left the cabin, filled with resentment and sorrow. The only coat I had with me my master took away with him, and said, "If your prize-money had been 10,000£ I had a right to it all, and would have taken it."[271] I had about nine guineas, which during my long sea-faring life, I had scraped together from trifling perquisites and little ventures; and I hid it that instant, lest my master should take that from me likewise, still hoping that by some means or other I should make my escape to the shore, and indeed some of my old shipmates told me not to despair, for they would get me back again; and that, as soon as they could get their pay, they would immediately come to Portsmouth to me, where this ship was going: but, alas! all my hopes were baffled, and the hour of my deliverance was yet far off. My master, having soon concluded his bargain with the captain, came out of the cabin, and he and his people got into the boat, and put off; I followed them with aching eyes as long as I could, and when they were out of sight I threw myself on the deck, with a heart ready to burst with sorrow and anguish.[272]

CHAP. V.

THUS, at the moment I expected all my toils to end, was I plunged, as I supposed, in a new slavery: in comparison of which all my service hitherto had been perfect freedom; and whose horrors, always present to my mind, now rushed on it with tenfold aggravation. I wept very bitterly for some time: and began to think that I must have done something to displease the Lord, that he thus punished me so severely. This filled me with painful reflections on my past conduct; I recollected that on the morning of our arrival at Deptford I had rashly sworn that as soon as we reached London I would spend the day in rambling and sport. My conscience smote me for this unguarded expression: I felt that the Lord was able to disappoint me in all things, and immediately considered my present situation as a judgment of Heaven on account of my presumption in swearing: I therefore, with contrition of heart, acknowledged my transgression to God, and poured out my soul before him with unfeigned repentance, and with earnest supplications I besought him not to abandon me in my distress, nor cast me from his mercy for ever. In a little time my grief, spent with its own violence, began to subside; and after the first confusion of my thoughts was over, I reflected with more calmness on my present condition: I considered that trials and disappointments are sometimes for our good, and I thought God might perhaps have permitted this in order to teach me wisdom and resignation; for he had hitherto shadowed me with the wings of his mercy, and by his invisible but powerful hand brought me the way I knew not. These reflections gave me a little comfort, and I rose at last from the deck with dejection and sorrow in my countenance, yet mixed with some faint hope that the *Lord would appear* for my deliverance.

Soon afterwards, as my new master was going ashore, he called me to him, and told me to behave myself well, and do the business of the ship the same as any of the rest of the boys, and that I should fare the better for it; but I made him no answer. I was then asked if I could swim, and I said, No. However I was made to go under the deck, and was well watched. The next tide the ship got under way, and soon after arrived at the Mother Bank, Portsmouth; where she waited a few days for some of the West India convoy. While I was here I tried every means I could devise among the people of the ship to get me a boat from the shore, as there was none suffered to come along side of the ship; and their own, whenever it was used, was hoisted in again immediately. A sailor on board took a guinea[273] from me on pretence of getting me a boat; and promised me, time after time, that it was hourly to come off. When he had the watch upon deck I watched also; and looked long enough, but all in vain; I could never see either the boat or my guinea again. And what I thought was still the worst of all, the fellow gave information, as I afterwards found, all the while to the mates of my intention to go off, if I could in any way do it; but, rogue-like, he never told them he had got a guinea from me to procure my escape. However, after we had sailed, and his trick was made known to the ship's crew, I had some satisfaction in seeing him detested and despised by them all for his behaviour to me. I was still in hopes that my old ship-mates would not forget their promise to come for me to Portsmouth; and they did at last,[274] but not till the day before we sailed, some of them did come there, and sent me off some oranges, and other tokens of their regard. They also sent me word they would come off to me themselves the next day or the day after; and a lady also, who lived in Gosport, wrote to me that she would come and take me out of the ship at the same time. This lady had been once very intimate with my former master; I used to sell and take care of a great deal of property for her in different ships; and in return she always shewed great friendship for me; and used to tell my master that she would take me away to live with her: but unfortunately for me, a disagreement soon afterwards took place between them; and she was succeeded in my master's good graces by another lady, who appeared sole mistress of the Aetna, and mostly lodged on board. I was not so great a favourite with this lady as with the former; she had conceived a pique against me on some occasion when she was on board, and she did not fail to instigate my master to treat me in the manner he did.[275]

However the next morning, the 30th of December, the wind being brisk and easterly, the Aeolus frigate,[276] which was to escort the convoy, made a signal for sailing. All the ships then got up their anchors; and, before any of my friends had an opportunity to come off to my relief, to my inexpressible anguish, our ship had got under way. What tumultuous emotions agitated my soul when the convoy got under sail, and I, a prisoner on board, now without hope! I kept my swimming eyes upon the land in a state of unutterable grief; not knowing what to do, and despairing how to help myself. While my mind was in this situation, the fleet sailed on, and in one day's time I lost sight of the wished-for land. In the first expressions of my grief I reproached my fate, and wished I had never been born. I was ready to curse the tide that bore us, the gale that wafted my prison, and even the ship that conducted us; and I called on death to relieve me from the horrors I felt and dreaded, that I might be in that place

> Where slaves are free, and men oppress no more,
> Fool that I was, inur'd so long to pain,
> To trust to hope, or dream of joy again.
> . . . .
> Now dragg'd once more beyond the western main,
> To groan beneath some dastard planter's chain;
> Where my poor countrymen in bondage wait
> The long enfranchisement of a ling'ring fate:

Hard ling'ring fate! while, ere the dawn of day,
Rous'd by the lash, they go their cheerless way;
And as their souls with shame and anguish burn,
Salute with groans unwelcome morn's return,
And, chiding ev'ry hour the slow-pac'd sun,
Pursue their toils till all his race is run.
No eye to mark their suff'rings with a tear;
No friend to comfort, and no hope to cheer:
Then, like the dull unpity'd brutes, repair
To stalls as wretched, and as coarse a fare;
Thank heaven one day of mis'ry was o'er,
Then sink to sleep, and wish to wake no more.[277]

The turbulence of my emotions, however, naturally gave way to calmer thoughts, and I soon perceived what fate had decreed no mortal on earth could prevent. The convoy sailed on without any accident, with a pleasant gale and smooth sea, for six weeks, till February, when one morning the Aeolus ran down a brig, one of the convoy, and she instantly went down and was ingulfed in the dark recesses of the ocean. The convoy was immediately thrown into great confusion till it was day-light; and the Aeolus was il-luminated[278] with lights to prevent any farther mischief. On the 13th of February 1763, from the mast-head, we descried our des-tined island Montserrat; and soon after I beheld those

Regions of sorrow, doleful shades, where peace
And rest can rarely dwell. Hope never comes
That comes to all, but torture without end
Still urges.[279]

At the sight of this land of bondage, a fresh horror ran through all my frame, and chilled me to the heart. My former slavery now rose in dreadful review to my mind, and displayed nothing but misery, stripes, and chains; and, in the first paroxysm of my grief, I called upon God's thunder, and his avenging power, to direct the stroke of death to me, rather than permit me to become a slave, and to be sold from lord to lord.

In this state of my mind our ship came to an anchor, and soon after discharged her cargo. I now knew what it was to work hard; I was made to help to unload and load the ship. And, to comfort me in my distress in that time, two of the sailors robbed me of all my money, and ran away from the ship. I had been so long used to an European climate that at first I felt the scorching West-India sun very painful, while the dashing surf would toss the boat and the people in it frequently above high-water mark. Sometimes our limbs were broken with this, or even attended with instant death, and I was day by day mangled and torn.

About the middle of May, when the ship was got ready to sail for England, I all the time believing that Fate's blackest clouds were gathering over my head, and expecting their bursting would mix me with the dead, captain Doran sent for me ashore one morning, and I was told by the messenger that my fate was then determined. With trembling steps and fluttering heart I came to the captain, and found with him one Mr. Robert King, a quaker and the first merchant in the place.[280] The captain then told me my former master had sent me there to be sold; but that he had desired him to get me the best master he could, as he told him I was a very deserving boy, which Captain Doran said he found to be true, and if he were to stay in the West Indies he would be glad to keep me himself; but he could not venture to take me to London, for he was very sure that when I came there I would leave him.[281] I at that instant burst out a crying, and begged much of him to take me to England with him, but all to no purpose. He told me he had got me the very best master in the whole island, with whom I should be as happy as if I were in England, and for that reason he chose to let him have me, though he could sell me to his own brother-in-law for a great deal more money than what he got from this gentleman. Mr. King, my new master, then made a reply, and said the reason he had bought me was on account of my good character; and, as he had not the least doubt of my good behaviour, I should be very well off with him. He also told me he did not live in the West Indies, but at Philadelphia, where he was going soon; and, as I understood something of the rules of arithmetic, when we got there he would put me to school, and fit me for a clerk. This conversation relieved my mind a little, and I left those gentlemen considerably more at ease in myself than when I came to them; and I was very thankful[282] to Captain Doran, and even to my old master, for the character they had given me; a character which I afterwards found of infinite service to me. I went on board again, and took my[283] leave of all my shipmates; and the next day the ship sailed. When she weighed anchor I went to the waterside and looked at her with a very wishful and aching heart, and followed her with my eyes until she was totally out of sight.[284] I was so bowed down with grief that I could not hold up my head for many months; and if my new master had not been kind to me, I believe I should have died under it at last. And indeed I soon found that he fully deserved the good character which Captain Doran had given me of him; for he possessed a most amiable disposition and temper, and was very charitable and humane. If any of his slaves behaved amiss, he did not beat or use them ill, but parted with them. This made them afraid of disobliging him; and as he treated his slaves better than any other man on the island, so he was better and more faithfully served by them in return. By this kind treatment I did at last endeavour to compose myself; and with fortitude, though moneyless, determined to face whatever fate had decreed for me. Mr. King soon asked me what I could do; and at the same time said he did not mean to treat me as a common slave. I told him I knew something of seamanship, and could shave and dress hair pretty well; and I could refine wines,[285] which I had learned on shipboard, where I had often done it; and that I could write, and understood arithmetic tolerably well as far as the Rule of Three. He then asked me if I knew any thing of gauging; and, on my answering that I did not, he said one of his clerks should teach me to gauge.[286]

Mr. King dealt in all manner of merchandize, and kept from one to six clerks. He loaded many vessels in a year; particularly to Philadelphia, where he was born, and was connected with a great mercantile house in that city. He had besides many vessels

and droggers[287] of different sizes, which used to go about the island
and other places[288] to collect rum, sugar, and other goods. I understood pulling and managing those boats very well; and this hard
work, which was the first that he set me to, in the sugar seasons,
used to be my constant employment. I have rowed the boat, and
slaved at the oars, from one hour to sixteen in the twenty-four;
during which I had fifteen pence sterling per day to live on,
though sometimes only ten pence. However, this was considerably more than was allowed to other slaves that used to work often
with me, and belonged to other gentlemen on the island: these[289]
poor souls had never more than nine-pence a day,[290] and seldom
more than six-pence, from their masters or owners, though they
earned them three or four pisterines[291] a day: for it is a common
practice in the West Indies, for men to purchase slaves, though
they have not plantations themselves, in order to let them out to
planters and merchants, at so much a-piece by the day, and they
give what allowance they choose out of this produce of their daily
work to their slaves for subsistence; this allowance is often very
scanty. My master often gave the owners of those slaves two and
a half of these pieces per day, and found the poor fellows in
victuals himself, because he thought their owners did not feed
them well enough according to the work they did. The slaves
used to like this very well, and as they knew my master to be a
man of feeling,[292] they were always glad to work for him in preference to any other gentleman; some of whom, after they had
been paid for these poor people's labours, would not give them
their allowance out of it. Many times have I seen these unfortunate wretches beaten for asking for their pay; and often severely
flogged by their owners if they did not bring them their daily or
weekly money exactly to the time; though the poor creatures
were obliged to wait on the gentlemen they had worked for,
sometimes more than half the day, before they could get their
pay; and this generally on Sundays, when they wanted the time
for themselves. In particular, I knew a countryman of mine, who
once did not bring the weekly money directly that it was earned;
and though he brought it the same day to his master, yet he was

staked to the ground for his pretended negligence, and was just going to receive a hundred lashes, but for a gentleman who begged him off fifty. This poor man was very industrious, and by his frugality had saved so much money, by working on shipboard, that he had got a white man to buy him a boat, unknown to his master. Some time after he had this little estate, the governor wanted a boat to bring his sugar from different parts of the island; and, knowing this to be a negro-man's boat, he seized upon it for himself, and would not pay the owner a farthing.[293] The man on this went to his master, and complained to him of this act of the governor; but the only satisfaction he received was to be damned very heartily by his master, who asked him how dared any of his negroes to have a boat. If the justly-merited ruin of the governor's fortune could be any gratification to the poor man he had thus robbed, he was not without consolation. Extortion and rapine are poor providers; and some time after this, the governor died in the King's Bench, in England, as I was told, in great poverty.[294] The last war favoured this poor negro-man,[295] and he found some means to escape from his Christian master;[296] he came to England, where I saw him afterwards several times. Such treatment as this often drives these miserable wretches to despair, and they run away from their masters at the hazard of their lives. Many of them in this place, unable to get their pay when they have earned it, and fearing to be flogged as usual, if they return home without it, run away where they can for shelter, and a reward is often offered to bring them in dead or alive. My master used sometimes in these cases, to agree with their owners, and to settle with them himself; and thereby he saved many of them a flogging.

Once, for a few days, I was let out to fit a vessel, and I had no victuals allowed me by either party; at last I told my master of this treatment, and he took me away from him. In many of the estates, on the different islands where I used to be sent for rum or sugar, they would not deliver it to me, or to any other negro; he was therefore obliged to send a white man along with me to those places; and then he used to pay him from six to ten pisterines a day. From being thus employed, during the time I served Mr.

King, in going about the different estates on the island, I had all the opportunity I could wish for, to see the dreadful usage of the poor men; usage that reconciled me to my situation, and made me bless God for the hands into which I had fallen.

I had the good fortune to please my master in every department in which he employed me; and there was scarcely any part of his business, or household affairs, in which I was not occasionally engaged. I often supplied the place of a clerk, in receiving and delivering cargoes to the ships, in tending stores, and delivering goods; and, besides this, I used to shave and dress my master when convenient, and take care of his horse; and when it was necessary, which was very often, I worked likewise on board of different vessels of his. By these means I became very useful to my master, and saved him, as he used to acknowledge, above a hundred pounds a year. Nor did he scruple to say I was of more advantage to him than any of his clerks; though their usual wages in the West Indies are from sixty to a hundred pounds current a year.

I have sometimes heard it asserted, that a negro cannot earn his master the first cost;[297] but nothing can be further from the truth. I suppose nine tenths of the mechanics throughout the West Indies are negro slaves; and I well know the coopers among them earn two dollars a day;[298] the carpenters the same, and oftentimes more; also the masons, smiths, and fishermen, &c. and I have known many slaves whose masters would not take a thousand pounds current for them.[299] But surely this assertion refutes itself; for, if it be true, why do the planters and merchants pay such a price for slaves? And, above all, why do those, who make this assertion, exclaim the most loudly against the abolition of the slave trade? So much are we blinded,[300] and to such inconsistent arguments are they driven by mistaken interest! I grant, indeed, that slaves are sometimes, by half-feeding, half-cloathing, over-working, and stripes,[301] reduced so low, that they are turned out as unfit for service, and left to perish in the woods, or expire on a dunghill.

My master was several times offered by different gentlemen one hundred guineas for me; but he always told them he would not sell me, to my great joy: and I used to double my diligence and care for fear of getting into the hands of those men who did not allow a valuable slave the common support of life. Many of them used to find fault with my master for feeding his slaves so well as he did; although I often went hungry, and an Englishman might think my fare very indifferent; but he used to tell them he always would do it, because the slaves thereby looked better and did more work.

While I was thus employed by my master, I was often a witness to cruelties of every kind, which were exercised on my unhappy fellow slaves. I used frequently to have different cargoes of new negroes in my care for sale; and it was almost a constant practice with our clerks, and other whites, to commit violent depredations on the chastity of the female slaves; and these I was, though with reluctance, obliged to submit to at all times, being unable to help them. When we have had some of these slaves on board my master's vessels to carry them to other islands, or to America, I have known our mates to commit these acts most shamefully, to the disgrace, not of Christians only, but of men. I have even known them gratify their brutal passion with females not ten years old; and these abominations some of them practised to such scandalous excess, that one of our captains discharged the mate and others on that account. And yet in Montserrat I have seen a negro-man staked to the ground, and cut most shockingly,[302] and then his ears cut off bit by bit, because he had been connected with a white woman who was a common prostitute: as if it were no crime in the whites to rob an innocent African girl of her virtue; but most heinous in a black man only to gratify a passion of nature, where the temptation was offered by one of a different colour, though the most abandoned woman of her species.

[303]One Mr. Drummond told me that he had sold 41,000 negroes, and that he once cut off a negro-man's leg for running away.—I asked him, if the man had died in the operation? How he, as a Christian, could answer for the horrid act before God? And he told me, answering was a thing of another world; but what he thought and did were policy. I told him that the Christian

doctrine taught us to do unto others as we would that others should do unto us. He then said that his scheme had the desired effect—it cured that man and some others of running away.

[304]Another negro man was half hanged, and then burnt, for attempting to poison a cruel overseer. Thus by repeated cruelties are the wretched first urged to despair, and then murdered, because they still retain so much of human nature about them as to wish to put an end to their misery, and retaliate on their tyrants! These overseers are indeed for the most part persons of the worst character of any denomination of men in the West Indies. Unfortunately, many humane gentlemen, by not residing on their estates, are obliged to leave the management of them in the hands of these human butchers, who cut and mangle the slaves in a shocking manner on the most trifling occasions, and altogether treat them in every respect like brutes. They pay no regard to the situation of pregnant women, nor the least attention to the lodging of the field-negroes. Their huts, which ought to be well covered, and the place dry where they take their little repose, are often open sheds, built in damp places; so that, when the poor creatures return tired from the toils of the field, they contract many disorders, from being exposed to the damp air in this uncomfortable state, while they are heated, and their pores are open. This neglect certainly conspires with many others to cause a decrease in the births as well as in the lives of the grown negroes. I can quote many instances of gentlemen who reside on their estates in the West Indies, and then the scene is quite changed; the negroes are treated with lenity and proper care, by which their lives are prolonged, and their masters are profited. To the honour of humanity, I knew several gentlemen who managed their estates in this manner; and they found that benevolence was their true interest. And, among many I could mention in several of the islands, I knew one in Montserrat[305] whose slaves looked remarkably well, and never needed any fresh supplies of negroes; and there are many other estates, especially in Barbadoes, which, from such judicious treatment, need no fresh stock of negroes at any time. I have the honour of knowing a most worthy and humane gentle-

man, who is a native of Barbadoes, and has estates there.[306] This gentleman has written a treatise on the usage of his own slaves. He allows them two hours for refreshment at mid day; and many other indulgencies and comforts, particularly in their lying;[307] and, besides this, he raises more provisions on his estate than they can destroy; so that by these attentions he saves the lives of his negroes, and keeps them healthy, and as happy as the condition of slavery can admit. I myself, as shall appear in the sequel, managed an estate, where, by those attentions, the negroes were uncommonly cheerful and healthy, and did more work by half than by the common mode of treatment they usually do. "For want, therefore, of such care and attention to the poor negroes, and otherwise oppressed as they are, it is no wonder that the decrease should require 20,000 new negroes annually to fill up the vacant places of the dead.

"Even in Barbadoes, notwithstanding those humane exceptions which I have mentioned, and others I am acquainted with, which justly make it quoted as a place where slaves meet with the best treatment, and need fewest recruits of any in the West Indies, yet this island requires 1000 negroes annually to keep up the original stock, which is only 80,000. So that the whole term of a negro's life may be said to be there but sixteen years![308] and yet the climate here is in every respect the same as that from which they are taken, except in being more wholesome."[309] Do the British colonies decrease in this manner? And yet what a prodigious difference is there between an English and West India climate.

While I was in Montserrat, I knew a negro man, named Emanuel Sankey, who endeavoured to escape from his miserable bondage, by concealing himself on board of a London ship: but fate did not favour the poor oppressed man; for being discovered when the vessel was under sail, he was delivered up again to his master. This *Christian master* immediately pinned the wretch down to the ground at each wrist and ankle, and then took some sticks of sealing-wax, and lighted them, and dropped it all over his back.[309] There was another master who was noted for cruelty, and I believe he had not a slave but what had been cut, and had pieces fairly taken out of the flesh: and after they had been punished thus, he used to make them get into a long wooden box or case he had for that purpose, in which he shut them up during pleasure.[311] It was just about the height and breadth of a man; and the poor wretches had no room when in the case to move.

It was very common in several of the islands, particularly in St. Kitt's, for the slaves to be branded with the initial letters of their master's name, and a load of heavy iron hooks hung about their necks. Indeed, on the most trifling occasions they were loaded with chains, and often other[312] instruments of torture were added. The iron muzzle, thumb-screws, &c. are so well known, as not to need a description, and were sometimes applied for the slightest faults. I have seen a negro beaten till some of his bones were broken, for only letting a pot boil over. It is not uncommon, after a flogging, to make slaves go on their knees, and thank their owners, and pray, or rather say, God bless them. I have often asked many of the men slaves (who used to go several miles to their wives, and late in the night, after having been wearied with a hard day's labour) why they went so far for wives, and why they did not take them of their own master's negro women, and particularly those who lived together as household slaves? Their answers have ever been—"Because when the master or mistress choose to punish the women, they make the husbands flog their own wives, and that they could not bear to do."[313] Is it surprising that usage like this should drive the poor creatures to despair, and make them seek a refuge in death from those evils which render their lives intolerable—while,

> With shudd'ring horror pale, and eyes aghast,
> They view their lamentable lot, and find
> No rest![314]

This they frequently do. A negro man on board a vessel of my master's, while I belonged to her, having been put in irons for some trifling misdemeanor, and kept in that state for some days, being weary of life, took an opportunity of jumping overboard into the sea; however, he was picked up without being drowned. Another, whose life was also a burden to him, resolved to starve himself to death, and refused to eat any victuals: this procured him a severe flogging; and he also, on the first occasion which offered, jumped overboard at Charles Town,[315] but was saved.

Nor is there any greater regard shewn to the little property than there is to the persons and lives of the negroes. I have already related an instance or two of particular oppression out of many which I have witnessed; but the following is frequent in all the islands. The wretched field slaves, after toiling all the day for an unfeeling owner, who gives them but little victuals, steal sometimes a few moments from rest or refreshment to gather some small portion of grass, according as their time will admit. This they commonly tie up in a parcel; either a bit's worth (sixpence)[316] or half a bit's worth; and bring it to town, or to the market, to sell. Nothing is more common than for the white people on this occasion to take the grass from them without paying for it; and not only so, but too often also to my knowledge, our clerks, and many others, at the same time, have committed acts of violence on the poor, wretched, and helpless females, whom I have seen for hours stand crying to no purpose, and get no redress or pay of any kind. Is not this one common and crying sin, enough to bring down God's judgment on the islands? He tells us, the oppressor and the oppressed are both in his hands; and if these are not the poor, the broken-hearted, the blind, the captive, the bruised, which our Saviour speaks of, who are they? One of these depredators once, in St. Eustatia, came on board of our vessel, and bought some fowls and pigs of me; and a whole day after his departure with the things, he returned again and wanted his money back: I refused to give it, and, not seeing my captain on board, he began the common pranks with me; and swore he would even break open my chest and take my money. I therefore expected, as my captain was absent, that he would be as good as his word; and he was just proceeding to strike me, when fortunately a British seaman on board, whose heart had not been debauched by a West India climate, interposed and prevented him. But had the cruel man struck me, I certainly should have defended myself at the hazard of my life; for what is life to a man thus oppressed? He went away, however, swearing; and threatened that whenever he caught me on shore he would shoot me, and pay for me afterwards.

The small account in which the life of a negro is held in the West Indies is so universally known, that it might seem impertinent to quote the following extract, if some people had not been hardy enough of late to assert that negroes are on the same footing in that respect as Europeans. By the 329th Act, page 125, of the Assembly of Barbadoes, it is enacted, "That if any negro, or other slave, under punishment by his master, or his order, for running away, or any other crime or misdemeanor towards his said master, unfortunately shall suffer in life or member, no person whatsoever shall be liable to a fine; but if any man shall out of *wantonness, or only of bloody-mindedness, or cruel intention, wilfully kill a negro, or other slave, of his own, he shall pay into the public treasury fifteen pounds sterling.*"[317] And it is the same in most, if not all, of the West India islands. Is not this one of the many acts of the islands which call loudly for redress? And do not the assembly which enacted it, deserve the appellation of savages and brutes rather than of Christians and men? It is an act at once unmerciful, unjust, and unwise; which for cruelty would disgrace an assembly of those who are called barbarians; and for its injustice and *insanity* would shock the morality and common sense of a Samaide or a Hottentot.[318]

Shocking as this and many other acts of the bloody West India code at first view appear, how is the iniquity of it heightened when we consider to whom it may be extended. Mr. James Tobin, a zealous labourer in the vineyard of slavery, gives an account[319] of a French planter, of his acquaintance, in the island of Martinico, who shewed him many Mulattoes working in the fields like beasts of burden; and he told Mr. Tobin, these were all the produce of his own loins! And I myself have known similar instances. Pray, reader, are these sons and daughters of the French planter less his children by being begotten on black women![320] And what must be the virtue of those legislators, and the feelings of those fathers, who estimate the lives of their sons, however begotten, at no more than fifteen pounds, though they should be murdered, as the act says, *out of wantonness and bloody-mindedness?* But is not the slave trade entirely at war with the heart of man? And surely that which is begun, by breaking down the barriers of virtue, involves in its continuance destruction to every principle, and buries all sentiments in ruin!

I have often seen slaves, particularly those who were meagre, in different islands, put into scales and weighed, and then sold from three-pence to six-pence, or nine-pence a pound. My master, however, whose humanity was shocked at this mode, used to sell such by the lump. And at or after a sale, even those negroes born in the islands, it is not uncommon to see taken from their wives, wives taken from their husbands, and children from their parents, and sent off to other islands, and wherever else their merciless lords choose; and probably never more during life see each other! Oftentimes my heart has bled at these partings; when the friends of the departed have been at the water-side, and with sighs and tears have kept their eyes fixed on the vessel till it went out of sight.

A poor Creole negro I knew well, who, after having often been thus transported from island to island, at last resided in Montserrat. This man used to tell me many melancholy tales of himself. Generally, after he had done working for his master, he used to employ his few leisure moments to go a fishing. When he had caught any fish, his master would frequently take them from him without paying him; and at other times some other white people would serve him in the same manner. One day he said to me, very movingly, "Sometimes when a white man take away my fish, I go to my master, and he get me my right; and when my master, by strength, take away my fishes, what me must do? I can't go to any body to be righted"; then, said the poor man, looking up above, "I must look up to God Mighty in the top for right." This artless tale moved me much, and I could not help feeling the just cause Moses had in redressing his brother against the Egyptian.[321] I exhorted the man to look up still to the God on the top, since there was no redress below. Though I little thought then that I myself should more than once experience such imposition, and need[322] the same exhortation hereafter, in my own transactions in the islands; and that even this poor man and I should some time after suffer together in the same manner, as shall be related hereafter.

Nor was such usage as this confined to particular places or individuals; for, in all the different islands in which I have been (and I have visited no less than fifteen) the treatment of the slaves was nearly the same; so nearly indeed, that the history of an island, or even a plantation, with a few such exceptions as I have mentioned, might serve for a history of the whole. Such a tendency has the slave-trade to debauch men's minds, and harden them to every feeling of humanity! For I will not suppose that the dealers in slaves are born worse than other men—No! it is the fatality of this mistaken avarice, that it corrupts the milk of human kindness, and turns it into gall. And, had the pursuits of those men been different, they might have been as generous, as tender-hearted, and just, as they are unfeeling, rapacious, and cruel. Surely this traffic cannot be good, which spreads like a pestilence, and taints what it touches! Which violates that first natural right of mankind, equality and independency, and gives one man a dominion over his fellows which God could never intend! For it raises the owner to a state as far above man as it depresses the slave below it; and, with all the presumption of human pride, sets a distinction between them, immeasurable in extent, and endless in duration! Yet how mistaken is the avarice even of the planters. Are slaves more useful by being thus humbled to the condition of brutes, than they would be if suffered to enjoy the privileges of men? The freedom which diffuses health and prosperity throughout Britain answers you—No. When you make men slaves, you deprive them of half their virtue, you set them, in your own conduct, an example of fraud, rapine, and cruelty, and compel them to live with you in a state of war; and yet you complain that they are not honest or faithful! You stupify them with stripes, and think it necessary to keep them in a state of ignorance; and yet you assert that they are incapable of learning; that their minds are such a barren soil or moor, that culture would be lost on them; and that they came from a climate, where nature (though prodigal of her bounties in a degree unknown to yourselves) has left man alone scant and unfinished, and incapable of enjoying the treasures she has poured out for him! An assertion at once impious and absurd.[323] Why do you use those instruments of torture? Are they fit to be applied by one rational being to another? And are ye not struck with shame and mortification, to see the partakers of your nature reduced so low? But, above all, are there no dangers attending this mode of treatment? Are you not hourly in dread of an insurrection? Nor would it be surprising; for when

> . . . No peace is given
> To us enslav'd, but custody severe;
> And stripes and arbitrary punishment
> Inflicted—What peace can we return?
> But to our power, hostility and hate;
> Untam'd reluctance, and revenge, tho' slow,
> Yet ever plotting how the conqueror least
> May reap his conquest, and may least rejoice
> In doing what we most in suff'ring feel.[324]

But, by changing your conduct, and treating your slaves as men, every cause of fear would be banished. They would be faithful, honest, intelligent and vigorous; and peace, prosperity, and happiness would attend you.

Some account of Brimstone-hill in Montserrat—The Author surprised by two earthquakes—Favourable change in the Author's situation—He commences merchant with three-pence—His various success in dealing in the different islands, and America, and the impositions he meets with in his transactions with white people[325]—A curious imposition on human nature—Danger of the surfs in the West Indies—Remarkable instance of kidnapping a free mulatto—The author is nearly murdered by Dr. Perkins, in Savannah.

IN the preceding chapter I have set before the reader a few of those many instances of oppression, extortion and cruelty, to which I have been a witness in the West Indies; but, were I to enumerate them all, the catalogue would be tedious and disgusting. The punishments of the slaves, on every trifling occasion, are so frequent, and so well known, together with the different instruments with which they are tortured, that it cannot any longer afford novelty to recite them; and they are too shocking to yield delight either to the writer or the reader. I shall therefore hereafter only mention such as incidentally befel myself in the course of my adventures.

In the variety of departments in which I was employed by my master, I had an opportunity of seeing many curious scenes in different islands; but, above all, I was struck with a celebrated curiosity called Brimstone-Hill, which is a high and steep mountain, some few miles from the town of Plymouth, in Montserrat.[326] I had often heard of some wonders that were to be seen on this hill, and I went once with some white and black people to visit it. When we arrived at the top, I saw under different cliffs great flakes of brimstone, occasioned by the steams of various little ponds, which were then boiling naturally in the earth. Some of these ponds were as white as milk, some quite blue, and many others of different colours. I had taken some potatoes with me, and I put them into different ponds, and in a few minutes they were well boiled. I tasted some of them, but they were very sulphurous; and the silver shoe-buckles, and all the other things we had among us of that metal, were, in a little time, turned as black as lead.

[327]Whilst I was in the island, one night I felt a strange sensation, viz.[328] I was told that the house where I lived was haunted by spirits. And once, at midnight, as I was sleeping on a large chest, I felt the whole building shake in an uncommon and astonishing manner; so much so, that it shook me off the chest where I then lay; I was exceedingly frightened, and thought it was the visitation of the spirits. It threw me into such a tremor as is not to be described. I instantly covered my head all over as I lay, and did not know what to think or do; and in this consternation, a gentleman, who lay in the next room just by me came out, and I was glad to hear him, and made a sham cough, and he asked me, if I felt the earthquake. I told him I was shook off the chest where I lay, but did not know what occasioned it; and he told me it was an earthquake, and shook him out of his bed. At hearing this I became easy in my mind.

At another time a circumstance of this kind happened, when I was on board of a vessel in Montserrat-road, at midnight, as we were asleep, and it shook the vessel in the most unaccountable manner imaginable, and to me it seemed as when a vessel or a boat runs on gravel, as near as I can describe it. Many things on board were moved out of their places, but happily no damage was done.

About the end of the year 1763,[329] kind Providence seemed to be rather more favourable to me. One of my master's vessels, a Bermudas sloop, about sixty tons burthen,[330] was commanded by one Captain Thomas Farmer, an Englishman, a very alert and active man, who gained my master a great deal of money by his good management in carrying passengers from one island to another; but very often his sailors used to get drunk, and run away with the vessel's boat, which hindered him in his business very much. This man had taken a liking to me; and had many different times begged of my master to let me go a trip with him as a sailor: but he would tell him he could not spare me, though the vessel sometimes could not go for want of hands, for sailors were generally very scarce in the island. However, at last, from necessity, or force, my master was prevailed on, though very reluctantly, to let me go with this captain; but he gave him[331] great charge to take care that I did not run away; for, if I did, he would make him pay for me. This being the case, the captain had for some time a sharp eye upon me whenever the vessel anchored: and as soon as she returned I was sent for on shore again. Thus was I slaving, as it were for life, sometimes at one thing, and sometimes at another; so that the captain and I were nearly the most useful men in my master's employment. I also became so useful to the captain on ship board, that many times, when he used to ask for me to go with him, though it should be but twenty-four hours, to some of the islands near us, my master would answer he could not spare me; at which the captain would swear, and would not go the trip, and tell my master that I was better to him on board than any three white men he had; for they used to behave ill in many respects, particularly in getting drunk, and then they frequently got the boat stove,[332] so as to hinder the vessel from coming back so soon as she might have done. This my master knew very well; and, at last, by the captain's constant entreaties, after I had been several times with him, one day, to my great joy, told me[333] the captain would not let him rest, and asked whether I would go aboard as a sailor, or stay on shore and mind the stores, for he could not bear any longer to be plagued in this manner. I was very happy at this proposal, for I immediately thought I might in time stand a chance by being on board to get a little money, or possibly make my escape if I should be used ill: I also expected to get better food, and in greater abundance; for I had oftentimes felt much hunger,[334] though my master treated his slaves, as I have observed, uncommonly well; I therefore, without hesitation, answered him, that I would go and be a sailor if he pleased. Accordingly I was ordered on board directly. Nevertheless, between the vessel and the shore, when she was in port, I had little or no rest, as my master always wished to have me along with him. Indeed he was a very pleasant gentleman, and but for my expectations on shipboard I should not have thought of leaving him. But the captain liked me also very much, and I was entirely his right-hand man. I did all I could to deserve his favour, and in return I received better treatment from him than any other I believe ever met with in the West-Indies in my situation.

After I had been sailing for some time with this captain, I at length endeavoured to try my luck and commence merchant. I had but a very small capital to begin with; for one single half bit, which is equal to three pence in England, made up my whole stock. However I trusted to the Lord to be with me; and at one of our trips to *St. Eustatia*, a Dutch island, I bought a glass tumbler with my half bit, and when I came to Montserrat I sold it for a bit, or sixpence. Luckily we made several successive trips to St. Eustatia (which was a general mart for the West Indies, about twenty leagues from Montserrat), and in our next, finding my tumbler so profitable, with this one bit I bought two tumblers more; and when I came back I sold them for two bits, equal to a shilling sterling. When we went again, I bought with these two bits four more of these glasses, which I sold for four bits on our return to Montserrat; and in our next voyage to St. Eustatia, I bought two glasses with one bit, and with the other three I bought a jug of Geneva,[335] nearly about three pints in measure. When we came to Montserrat I sold the gin for eight bits, and the tumblers for two, so that my capital now amounted in all to a dollar, well husbanded and acquired in the space of a month or six weeks, when I blessed the Lord that I was so rich. As we sailed to different islands, I laid this money out in various things occasionally, and it used to turn out to very good account, especially when we went to Guadaloupe, Grenada, and the rest of the French islands. Thus was I going all about the islands upwards of four years, and ever trading as I went, during which I experienced many instances of ill usage, and have seen many injuries done to other negroes in our dealings with whites;[336] and, amidst our recreations, when we have been dancing and merry-making, they, without cause, have molested and insulted us. Indeed I was more than once obliged to look up to God on high, as I had advised the poor fisherman some time before. And I had not been long trading for myself in the manner I have related above, when I experienced the like trial in company with him as follows: This man being used to the water, was upon an emergency put on board of us by his master to work as another hand, on a voyage to Santa Cruz; and at our sailing he had brought his little all for a venture, which consisted of six bits worth of limes and oranges in a bag; I had also my whole stock; which was about twelve bits' worth of the same kind of goods, separate in two bags; for we had heard these fruits sold well in that island. When we came there, in some little convenient time, he and I went ashore with our fruits to sell them; but we had scarcely landed, when we were met by two white men, who presently[337] took our three bags from us. We could not at first guess what they meant to do, and for some time we thought they were jesting with us; but they too soon let us know otherwise; for they took our ventures immediately to a house hard by adjoining the fort, while we followed all the way begging of them to give us our fruits, but in vain. They not only refused to return them, but swore at us, and threatened if we did not immediately depart, they would flog us well. We told them these three bags were all we were worth in the world; and that we brought them with us to sell when we came from Montserrat, and shewed them the vessel. But this was rather against us, as they now saw we were strangers as well as slaves. They still therefore swore, and desired us to be gone; and even took sticks to beat us; while we, seeing they meant what they said, went off in the greatest confusion and despair. Thus, in the very minute of gaining more by three times than I ever did by any venture in my life before, was I deprived of every farthing I was worth. An insupportable misfortune! but how to help ourselves we knew not. In our consternation we went to the commanding officer of the fort, and told him how we had been served by some of his people; but we obtained not the least redress: he answered our complaints only by a volley of imprecations against us, and immediately took a horse-whip, in order to chastise us, so that we were obliged to turn out much faster than we came in. I now, in the agony of distress and indignation, wished that the ire of God, in his forked lightning, might transfix these cruel oppressors among the dead. Still, however, we persevered; went back again to the house, and begged and besought them again and again for our fruits, till at last some other people that were in the house asked if we would be contented if they kept one bag, and gave us the other two. We, seeing no remedy whatever, consented to this; and they, observing one bag to have both kinds of fruit in it, which belonged to my companion, kept that; and the other two, which were mine, they gave us back. As soon as I got them, I ran as fast as I could and got the first negro man I could to help me off; my companion, however, stayed a little longer to plead; he told them the bag they had was his, and likewise all that he was worth in the world; but this was of no avail, and he was obliged to return without it. The poor old man, wringing his hands, cried bitterly for his loss; and, indeed, he then did look up to God on high, which so moved me with pity for him, that I gave him nearly one third of my fruits. We then proceeded to the market to sell them; and Providence was more favourable to us than we could have expected, for we sold our fruits uncommonly well; I got for mine about thirty-seven bits. Such a surprising reverse of fortune in so short a space of time seemed like a dream to me, and proved no small encouragement for me to trust the Lord in any situation. My captain afterwards frequently used to take my part, and get me my right when I have been plundered or used ill by these tender Christian depredators; among whom I have shuddered to observe the unceasing blasphemous execrations which are wantonly thrown out by persons of all ages and conditions; not only without occasion, but even as if they were indulgencies and pleasures.

At one of our trips to St. Kitt's, I had eleven bits of my own; and my friendly captain lent me five bits more, with which I bought a Bible. I was very glad to get this book, which I scarcely could meet with any where. I think there was none sold in Montserrat;[338] and, much to my grief, from being forced out of the Aetna in the manner I have related, my Bible, and the Guide to the Indians, the two books I loved above all others, were left behind.

While I was in this place, St. Kitt's, a very curious imposition on human nature took place:—A white man wanted to marry in the church a free black woman that had land and slaves at Montserrat: but the clergyman told him it was against the law of the place to marry a white and a black in the church. The man then asked to be married on the water, to which the parson consented, and the two lovers went in one boat, and the parson and clerk in another, and thus the ceremony was performed. After this the loving pair came on board our vessel, and my captain treated them extremely well, and brought them safe to Montserrat.

The reader cannot but judge of the irksomeness of this situation to a mind like mine, in being daily exposed to new hardships and impositions, after having seen many better days, and been, as it were, in a state of freedom and plenty; added to which, every part of the world in which I had hitherto been seemed to me a paradise in comparison of the West-Indies. My mind was therefore hourly replete with inventions and thoughts of being freed, and, if possible, by honest and honourable means; for I always remembered the old adage, and I trust that it has ever been my ruling principle, "that Honesty is the best policy"; and likewise that other golden precept—"To do unto all men as I would they should do unto me." However, as I was from early years a predestinarian,[339] I thought whatever fate had determined must ever come to pass; and therefore, if ever it were my lot to be freed, nothing could prevent me, although I should at present see no means or hope to obtain my freedom; on the other hand, if it were my fate not to be freed, I never should be so, and all my endeavours for that purpose would be fruitless. In the midst of these thoughts I therefore looked up with prayers anxiously to God for my liberty; and at the same time used every honest means, and did all that was possible on my part to obtain it. In process of time I became master of a few pounds, and in a fair way of making more, which my friendly captain knew very well: this occasioned him sometimes to take liberties with me; but whenever he treated me waspishly, I used plainly to tell him my mind, and that I would die before I would be imposed upon as other negroes were, and that to me life had lost its relish when liberty was gone. This I said, although I foresaw my then well-being or future hopes of freedom (humanly speaking) depended on this man. However, as he could not bear the thoughts of my not sailing with him, he always became mild on my threats: I therefore continued with him; and, from my great attention to his orders and his business, I gained him credit, and, through his kindness to me, I at last procured my liberty. While I thus went on, filled with the thoughts of freedom, and resisting oppression as well as I was able, my life hung daily in suspense, particularly in the surfs I have formerly mentioned, as I could not swim. These are extremely violent throughout the West-Indies, and I was ever exposed to their howling rage and devouring fury in all the islands. I have seen them strike and toss a boat right up on end, and maim several on board. Once in the island of Grenada, when I and about eight others were pulling a large boat with two puncheons[340] of water in it, a surf struck us, and drove the boat and all in it about half a stone's throw among some trees, and above the high-water mark. We were obliged to get all the assistance we could from the nearest estate to mend the boat, and launch it into the water again. At Montserrat one night, in pressing hard to get off the shore on board, the punt[341] was overset with us four times; the first time I was very near being drowned; however, the jacket I had on kept me above water a little space of time, while I called on a man near me who was a good swimmer, and told him I could not swim; he then made haste to me, and, just as I was sinking, he caught hold of me and brought me to sounding,[342] and then he went and brought the punt also. As soon as we turned the water out of her, lest we should be used ill for being absent, we attempted again three times more, and as often the horrid surfs served us as at first; but at last, the fifth time we attempted, we gained our point, at the imminent hazard of our lives. One day

also, at Old Road, in Montserrat, our captain and three men besides myself, were going in a large canoe in quest of rum and
sugar, when a single surf tossed the canoe an amazing distance
from the water, and some of us near a stone's throw from each
other; most of us were very much bruised; so that I and many
more often said, and really thought, that there was not such another place under the heavens as this. I longed, therefore, much
to leave it, and daily wished to see my master's promise performed
of going to Philadelphia.

[343]While we lay in this place, a very cruel thing happened on
board of our sloop, which filled me with horror; though I found
afterwards such practices were frequent. There was a very clever
and decent free young mulatto-man who sailed a long time with
us; he had a free woman for his wife, by whom he had a child;
and she was then living on shore, and all very happy. Our captain
and mate, and other people on board, and several elsewhere, even
the natives of Bermudas, then with us,[344] all knew this young man
from a child that he was always free, and no one had ever claimed
him as their property: however, as might too often overcomes
right in these parts, it happened that a Bermudas captain, whose
vessel lay there for a few days in the road, came on board of us,
and seeing the mulatto-man, whose name was Joseph Clipson, he
told him he was not free, and that he had orders from his master
to bring him to Bermudas. The poor man could not believe the
captain to be in earnest; but he was very soon undeceived, his
men laying violent hands on him; and although he shewed a certificate of his being born free in St. Kitt's, and most people on
board knew that he served his time[345] to boat building and always
passed for a free man, yet he was forcibly taken out of our vessel.
He then asked to be carried ashore, before the secretary or mag-
istrates, and these infernal invaders of human rights promised him
he should; but, instead of that, they carried him on board of the
other vessel; and the next day, without giving the poor man any
hearing on shore, or suffering him even to see his wife or child,
he was carried away, and probably doomed never more in this
world to see them again. Nor was this the only instance of this

kind of barbarity I was a witness to. I have since often seen in Jamaica, and other islands, free men, whom I have known in America, thus villainously trepanned and held in bondage. I have heard of two similar practices even in Philadelphia: and were it not for the benevolence of the quakers in that city, many of the sable race, who now breathe the air of liberty, would, I believe, be groaning under some planter's chains. These things opened my mind to a new scene of horror, to which I had been before a stranger. Hitherto I had thought only slavery dreadful; but the state of a free negro appeared to me now equally so at least, and in some respects even worse, for they live in constant alarm for their liberty, which is but nominal,[346] for they are universally insulted and plundered without the possibility of redress; for such is the equity of the West Indian laws, that no free negro's evidence will be admitted in their courts of justice. In this situation, is it surprising that slaves, when mildly treated, should prefer even the misery of slavery to such a mockery of freedom? I was now completely disgusted with the West Indies, and thought I never should be entirely free till I had left them.

> With thoughts like these my anxious boding mind
> Recall'd those pleasing scenes I left behind;
> Scenes where fair Liberty, in bright array
> Makes darkness bright, and e'en illumines day;
> Where no complexion, wealth, or station can
> Protect the wretch who makes a slave of man.[347]

I determined to make every exertion to obtain my freedom, and to return to Old England. For this purpose, I thought a knowledge of navigation might be of use to me; for, though I did not intend to run away unless I should be ill used, yet, in such a case, if I understood navigation, I might attempt my escape in our sloop, which was one of the swiftest sailing vessels in the West Indies, and I could be at no loss for hands to join me: and, if I should make this attempt, I had intended to have gone for England; but this, as I said, was only to be in the event of my meeting with any ill usage. I therefore employed the mate of our vessel to teach me navigation, for which I agreed to give him twenty four dollars, and actually paid him part of the money down; though, when the captain, some time after, came to know that the mate was to have such a sum for teaching me, he rebuked him, and said it was a shame for him to take any money from me. However, my progress in this useful art was much retarded by the constancy of our work. Had I wished to run away, I did not want opportunities, which frequently presented themselves; and particularly at one time, soon after this. When we were at the island of Guadaloupe there was a large fleet of merchantmen bound for Old France; and, seamen then being very scarce, they gave from fifteen to twenty pounds a man for the run. Our mate, and all the white sailors, left our vessel on this account, and went on board of the French ships. They would have had me also gone with them, for they regarded me, and swore to protect me, if I would go; and, as the fleet was to sail the next day, I really believe I could have got safe to Europe at that time. However, as my master was kind, I would not attempt to leave him; still remembering[348] the old maxim, that "honesty is the best policy," I suffered them to go without me. Indeed my captain was much afraid of my leaving him and the vessel at that time, as I had so fair an opportunity: but I thank God, this fidelity of mine turned out much to my advantage hereafter, when I did not in the least think of it; and made me so much in favour with the captain, that he used now and then to teach me some parts of navigation himself. But some of our passengers, and others, seeing this, found much fault with him for it, saying, it was a very dangerous thing to let a negro know navigation; thus I was hindered again in my pursuits. About the latter end of the year 1764, my master bought a larger sloop, called the Prudence, about seventy or eighty tons, of which my captain had the command. I went with him into this vessel, and we took a load of new slaves for Georgia and Charles Town. My master now left me entirely to the captain, though he still wished me to be with him; but I, who always much wished to lose sight of the West Indies, was not a little rejoiced at the thoughts of seeing any other country. Therefore, relying on the goodness of my captain, I got ready all the little venture I could; and, when the vessel was ready, we sailed to my great joy. When we got to our destined places, Georgia and Charles Town, I expected I should have an opportunity of selling my little property to advantage; but here, particularly in Charles Town, I met with buyers, white men, who imposed on me as in other places. Notwithstanding, I was resolved to have fortitude: thinking no lot or trial too hard when kind Heaven is the rewarder.

We soon got loaded again, and returned to Montserrat; and there, among the rest of the islands, I sold my goods well; and in this manner I continued trading during the year 1764; meeting with various scenes of imposition, as usual. After this, my master fitted out his vessel for Philadelphia, in the year 1765; and during the time of loading her, and getting ready for the voyage, I worked with double alacrity, from the hope of getting money enough by these voyages to buy my freedom, if it should please God;[349] and also to see the city of Philadelphia, which I had heard a great deal about for some years past; besides which, I had always longed to prove[350] my master's promise the first day I came to him. In the midst of these elevated ideas, and while I was about getting my little merchandise in readiness, one Sunday my master sent for me to his house. When I came there I found him and the captain together; and, on my going in, I was struck with astonishment at his telling me he heard that I meant to run away from him when I got to Philadelphia: "And therefore," said he "I must sell you again: you cost me a great deal of money, no less than forty pounds sterling; and it will not do to lose so much. You are a valuable fellow," continued he, "and I can get any day for you one hundred guineas, from many gentlemen in this island." And then he told me of Captain Doran's brother-in-law, a severe master, who ever wanted to buy me to make me his overseer. My captain also said, he could get much more than a hundred guineas for me in Carolina. This I knew to be a fact: for the gentleman that wanted to buy me, came off several times on board of us, and spoke to me to live with him, and said he would use me well. When I asked what work he would put me to, he said, as I was a sailor, he would make me a captain of one of his rice vessels. But I refused; and fearing, at the same time, by a sudden turn I saw in the captain's temper, he might mean to sell me, I told the gentleman I would not live with him on any condition, and that I certainly would run away with his vessel: but he said he did not fear that, as he would catch me again: and then he told me how cruelly he would serve me if I should do so. My captain, however, gave him to understand that I knew something of navigation: so he thought better of it; and, to my great joy, he went away. I now told my master, I did not say I would run away in Philadelphia, neither did I mean it, as he did not use me ill, nor yet the captain: for if they did, I certainly would have made some attempts before now; but as I thought that if it were God's will I ever should be freed it would be so; and, on the contrary, if it was not his will it would not happen; so I hoped, if ever I were freed, whilst I was used well, it should be by honest means; but as I could not help myself, he must do as he please! I could only hope and trust in the God of heaven; and at that instant my mind was big with inventions, and full of schemes to escape. I then appealed to the captain, whether ever he saw[351] any sign of my making the least attempt to run away; and asked him if I did not always come on board according to the time for which he gave me liberty; and, more particularly, when all our men left us at Guadaloupe, and went on board the French fleet, and advised me to go with them, whether I might not, and that he could not have got me again. To my no small surprise, and very great joy, the captain confirmed every syllable I said, and even more; for he said he had tried different times to see if I would make any attempt of this kind, both at St. Eustatia and in America, and he never found that I made the smallest; but, on the contrary, I always came on board according to his orders; and he did really believe, if ever I meant to run away, that, as I could never have had a better opportunity, I would have done it the night the mate and all the people left our vessel at Guadaloupe. The captain then informed my master, who had been thus imposed on by our mate (though I did not know who was my enemy), the reason the mate had for imposing this lie upon him; which was, because I had acquainted the captain with the provisions the mate had given away, or taken out of the vessel. This speech of the captain was like life to the dead to me, and instantly my soul glorified God; and still more so on hearing my master immediately say that I was a sensible fellow, and he never did intend to use me as a common slave; and that, but for the entreaties of the captain, and his character of me, he would not have let me go from the stores about as I had done; that also, in so doing, he thought by carrying one little thing or other to different places to sell I might make money. That he also intended to encourage me in this, by crediting me with half a puncheon of rum and half a hogshead of sugar at a time; so that, from being careful, I might have money enough, in some time, to purchase my freedom: and, when that was the case, I might depend upon it he would let me have it for forty pounds sterling money, which was only the same price he gave for me. This soon gladdened my poor heart beyond measure; though indeed it was no more than the idea I had formed in my mind of my master long before; and I immediately made him this reply: "Sir, I always had that very thought of you, indeed I had, and that made me so diligent in serving you." He then gave me a large piece of silver coin, such as I had never seen or had before, and told me to get ready for the voyage, and he would credit me with a tierce[352] of sugar and another of rum; he also said that he had two amiable sisters in Philadelphia, from whom I might get some necessary things. Upon this my noble captain desired me to go aboard; and, knowing the African mettle,[353] he charged me not to say any thing of this matter to any body; and he promised that the lying mate should not go with him any more. This was a change indeed; in the same hour to feel the most exquisite pain, and in the turn of a moment, the fullest joy. It caused in me such sensations as I was only able to express in my looks; my heart was so overpowered with gratitude that I could have kissed both of their feet. When I left the room, I immediately went, or rather flew, to the vessel, which being loaded, my master, as good as his word, trusted me with a tierce of rum and another of sugar, when we sailed, and arrived safe at the elegant town of Philadelphia. I soon sold my goods here pretty well; and in this charming town I found every thing plentiful and cheap.

While I was in this place a very extraordinary occurrence befel me. I had been told one evening of a *wise* woman,[354] a Mrs. Davis, who revealed secrets, foretold events, &c. I put little faith in this story at first, as I could not conceive that any mortal could foresee the future disposals of Providence, nor did I believe in any other revelation than that of the holy Scriptures; however, I was greatly astonished at seeing this woman in a dream that night, though a person I never before beheld in my life; this made such an impression on me, that I could not get the idea the next day out of my mind, and I then became as anxious to see her as I was before indifferent; accordingly, in the evening, after we left off working, I enquired where she lived, and being directed to her, to my inexpressible surprise, beheld the very woman in the very same dress she appeared to me to wear in the vision. She immediately told me I had dreamed of her the preceding night; related to me many things that had happened with a correctness that astonished me; and finally told me I should not be long a slave. This was the more agreeable news, as I believed it the more readily from her having so faithfully related the past incidents of my life. She said I should be twice in very great danger of my life within eighteen months, which, if I escaped, I should afterwards go on well; so, giving me her blessing, we parted. After staying here some time till our vessel was loaded and I had bought in my little traffic, we sailed from this agreeable spot for Montserrat, once more to encounter the raging surfs.

We arrived safe at Montserrat, where we discharged our cargo, and I sold my things well.[355] Soon after that we took slaves on board for St. Eustatia, and from thence to Georgia. I had always exerted myself, and did double work, in order to make our voyage as short as possible; and from thus overworking myself while we were at Georgia I caught a fever and ague.[356] I was very ill for eleven days, and near dying; eternity was now exceedingly impressed on my mind, and I feared very much that awful event. I prayed the Lord therefore to spare me; and I made a promise in my mind to God, that I would be good if ever I should recover. At length, from having an eminent doctor to attend me, I was restored again to health: and soon after we got the vessel loaded, and set off for Montserrat. During the passage, as I was perfectly restored, and had much business of the vessel to mind, all my endeavours to keep up my integrity, and perform my promise to God, began to fail; and in spite of all I could do, as we drew nearer and nearer to the islands, my resolutions more and more declined, as if the very air of that country or climate seemed fatal to piety. When we were safe arrived at Montserrat, and I had got ashore, I forgot my former resolutions.—Alas! how prone is the heart to leave that God it wishes to love! And how strongly do the things of this world strike the senses and captivate the soul! —After our vessel was discharged, we soon got her ready, and took in, as usual, some of the poor oppressed natives of Africa, and other negroes; we then set off again for Georgia and Charles-town. We arrived at Georgia, and, having landed part of our cargo, proceeded to Charlestown with the remainder. While we were there I saw the town illuminated; the guns were fired, and bonfires and other demonstrations of joy shewn, on account of the repeal of the stamp-act.[357] Here I disposed of some goods on my own account; the white men buying them with smooth prom-ises and fair words, giving me, however, but very indifferent payment. There was one gentleman particularly who bought a puncheon of rum of me, which gave me a great deal of trouble; and although I used the interest of my friendly captain, I could not obtain any thing for it; for, being a negro man, I could not oblige him to pay me. This vexed me much, not knowing how to act; and I lost some time in seeking after this Christian; and though, when the sabbath came (which the negroes usually make their holiday) I was inclined to go to public worship, but, instead of that, I was obliged to hire some black men to help me[358] to pull a boat across the water to go in quest of this gentleman. When I found him, after much entreaty, both from myself and my worthy captain, he at last paid me in dollars, some of them, however, were copper, and of consequence of no value; but he took advantage of my being a negro man, and obliged me to put up with those or none, although I objected to them. Immediately after, as I was trying to pass them in the market amongst other white men, I was abused for offering to pass bad coin; and though I shewed them the man I had got them from, I was within one minute of being tied up and flogged without either judge or jury; however, by the help of a good pair of heels, I ran off and so escaped the bastinadoes[359] I should have received. I got on board as fast as I could, but still continued in fear of them until we sailed, which, I thank God, we did, not long after; and I have never been amongst them since.

We soon came to Georgia, where we were to complete our lading: and here worse fate than ever attended me: for one Sunday night, as I was with some negroes, in their master's yard, in the town of Savannah, it happened that their master, one Doctor Perkins, who was a very severe and cruel man, came in drunk; and not liking to see any strange negroes in his yard, he, and a ruffian of a white man he had in his service, beset me in an instant, and both of them struck me with the first weapons they could get hold of. I cried out as long as I could for help and mercy; but though I gave a good account of myself, and he knew my captain, who lodged hard by him, it was to no purpose. They beat and mangled me in a shameful manner, leaving me nearly dead. I lost so much blood from the wounds I received, that I lay quite motionless, and was so benumbed that I could not feel any thing for many hours. Early in the morning they took me away to the jail. As I did not return to the ship all night, my captain not knowing where I was, and being uneasy that I did not then make my appearance, he made inquiry after me; and, having found where I was, immediately came to me. As soon as the good man saw me so cut and mangled, he could not forbear weeping; he soon got me out of jail to his lodgings, and immediately sent for the best doctors in the place, who at first declared it as their opinion that I could not recover. My captain, on this, went to all the lawyers in the town for their advice, but they told him they could do nothing for me as I was a negro. He then went to Dr. Perkins, the hero who had vanquished me, and menaced him, swearing he would be revenged of him, and challenged him to fight. But cowardice is ever the companion of cruelty—and the Doctor refused. However, by the skilfulness of one Doctor Brady of that place, I began at last to amend; but, although I was so sore and bad, with the wounds I had all over me, that I could not rest in any posture, yet I was in more pain on account of the captain's uneasiness about me than I otherwise should have been. The worthy man nursed and watched me all the hours of the night and I was, through his attention, and that of the doctor, able to get out of bed in about sixteen or eighteen days. All this time I was very much wanted on board, as I used frequently to go up and down the river for rafts, and other parts of our cargo, and stow them, when the mate was sick or absent. In about four weeks I was able to go on duty; and in a fortnight after, having got in all our lading, our vessel set sail for Montserrat; and in less than three weeks we arrived there safe, towards the end of the year. This ended my adventures in 1765;[360] for I did not leave Montserrat again till the beginning of the following year.

The Author's disgust at the West Indies—Forms schemes to obtain his freedom —Ludicrous disappointment he and his Captain meet with in Georgia—At last, by several successful voyages, he acquires a sum of money sufficient to purchase it—Applies to his master, who accepts it, and grants his manumission, to his great joy—He afterwards enters as a freeman on board one of Mr. King's ships, and sails for Georgia—Impositions on free negroes as usual—His venture of turkies—Sails for Montserrat, and, on his passage, his friend, the Captain, falls ill and dies.

EVERY day now brought me nearer my freedom, and I was impatient till we proceeded again to sea, that I might have an opportunity of getting a sum large enough to purchase it. I was not long ungratified; for in the beginning of the year 1766, my master bought another sloop, named the Nancy, the largest I had ever seen. She was partly laden, and was to proceed to Philadelphia. Our captain had his choice of three, and I was well pleased he chose this, which was the largest, for, from his having a large vessel, I had more room, and could carry a larger quantity of goods with me. Accordingly, when we had delivered our old vessel, the Prudence, and completed the lading of the Nancy, having made near three hundred per cent. by four barrels of pork I brought from Charlestown, I laid in as large a cargo as I could, trusting to God's Providence to prosper my undertaking. With these views I sailed for Philadelphia. On our passage, when we drew near the land, I was for the first time surprised at the sight of some whales, having never seen any such large sea monsters before; and, as we sailed by the land, one morning I saw a puppy whale close by the vessel; it was about the length of a wherry boat, and it followed us all the day until we got within the Capes. We arrived safe and in good time at Philadelphia, and I sold my goods there chiefly to the Quakers. They always appeared to be a very honest discreet sort of people, and never attempted to impose on me; I therefore liked them, and ever after chose to deal with them in preference to any others.

[361]One Sunday morning, while I was here, as I was going to church, I chanced to pass a meeting house. The doors being open, and the house full of people, it excited my curiosity to go in. When I entered the house, to my great surprise, I saw a very tall woman standing in the midst of them, speaking in an audible voice something which I could not understand. Having never seen any thing of this kind before, I stood and stared about me for some time, wondering at this odd scene. As soon as it was over, I took an opportunity to make enquiry about the place and people, when I was informed they were called Quakers. I particularly asked what that woman I saw in the midst of them had said, but none of them were pleased to satisfy me;[362] so I quitted them, and soon after, as I was returning, I came to a church crowded with people; the church-yard was full likewise, and a number of people were even mounted on ladders, looking in at the windows. I thought this a strange sight, as I had never seen churches, either in England or the West Indies, crowded in this manner before. I therefore made bold to ask some people the meaning of all this, and they told me the Rev. George Whitfield was preaching.[363] I had often heard of this gentleman, and had wished to see and hear him; but I had never before had an opportunity. I now therefore resolved to gratify myself with the sight, and pressed in amidst the multitude. When I got into the church I saw this pious man exhorting the people with the greatest fervour and earnestness, and sweating as much as ever I did while in slavery on Montserrat beach. I was very much struck and impressed with this; I thought it strange I had never seen divines exert themselves in this manner before, and was no longer at a loss to account for the thin congregations they preached to.[364]

[365]When we had discharged our cargo here, and were loaded again, we left this fruitful land once more, and set sail for Montserrat. My traffic had hitherto succeeded so well with me, that I thought, by selling my goods when we arrived at Montserrat, I

should have enough to purchase my freedom. But as soon as our vessel arrived there, my master came on board, and gave orders for us to go to St. Eustatia, and discharge our cargo there, and from thence to proceed to Georgia. I was much disappointed at this; but thinking, as usual, it was of no use to murmur at[366] the decrees of fate, I submitted without repining, and we went to St. Eustatia. After we had discharged our cargo there, we took in a live cargo, (as we call a cargo of slaves.) Here I sold my goods tolerably well; but not being able to lay out all my money in this small island to as much advantage as in many other places, I laid out only part, and the remainder I brought away with me neat. We sailed from hence for Georgia, and I was glad when we got there, though I had not much reason to like the place from my last adventure in Savannah; but I longed to get back to Montserrat and procure my freedom, which I expected to be able to purchase when I returned. As soon as we had arrived here I waited on my careful doctor, Mr. Brady, to whom I made the most grateful acknowledgments in my power for his former kindness and attention during my illness.

[367]While we were here, an odd circumstance happened to the captain and me, which disappointed us both a good deal. A silversmith, whom we had brought to this place some voyages before, agreed with the captain to return to the West Indies, and promised at the same time to give the captain a great deal of money, having pretended to take a liking to him, and being as we thought very rich. But while we stayed to load our vessel this man was taken ill in a house where he worked, and in a week's time became very bad. The worse he grew, the more he used to speak of giving the captain what he had promised him, so that he expected something considerable from the death of this man, who had no wife or child, and he attended him day and night. I used also to go with the captain, at his own desire, to attend him; especially when we saw there was no appearance of his recovery; and in order to recompence me for my trouble, the captain promised me ten pounds, when he should get the man's property. I thought this would be of great service to me, although I had

nearly money enough to purchase my freedom, if I should get safe this voyage to Montserrat. In this expectation I laid out above eight pounds of my money for a suit of superfine cloathes to dance in at my freedom,[368] which I hoped was then at hand. We still continued to attend this man, and were with him even on the last day he lived, till very late at night, when we went on board. After we were got to bed, about one or two o'clock in the morning, the captain was sent for, and informed the man was dead. On this he came to my bed, and, waking me, informed me of it, and desired me to get up and procure a light, and immediately go with him.[369] I told him I was very sleepy, and wished he would take somebody else with him; or else, as the man was dead, and could want no farther attendance, to let all things remain as they were till the next morning. "No, no," said he, "we will have the money to-night, I cannot wait till to-morrow; so let us go." Accordingly I got up and struck a light, and away we both went and saw the man as dead as we could wish. The captain said he would give him a grand burial, in gratitude for the promised treasure; and desired that all the things belonging to the deceased might be brought forth. Among others, there was a nest of trunks of which he had kept the keys whilst the man was ill, and when they were produced we opened them with no small eagerness and expectation; and as there were a great number within one another, with much impatience we took them one out of the other. At last, when we came to the smallest, and had opened it, we saw it was full of papers, which we supposed to be notes;[370] at the sight of which our hearts leapt for joy; and that instant the captain, clapping his hands, cried out, "Thank God, here it is." But when we took up the trunk, and began to examine the supposed treasure and long-looked-for bounty (alas! alas! how uncertain and deceitful are all human affairs!) what had we found? While we thought we were embracing a substance, we grasped an empty nothing!![371] The whole amount that was in the nest of trunks was only one dollar and a half; and all that the man possessed would not pay for his coffin. Our sudden and exquisite joy was now succeeded by as sudden and exquisite pain; and my captain and I exhibited, for some time, most ridiculous figures—pictures of chagrin and disappointment! We went away greatly mortified, and left the deceased to do as well as he could for himself, as we had taken so good care of him when alive for nothing. We set sail once more for Montserrat, and arrived there safe, but much out of humour with our friend the silversmith. When we had unladen the vessel, and I had sold my venture, finding myself master of about forty-seven pounds—I consulted my true friend, the captain, how I should proceed in offering my master the money for my freedom. He told me to come on a certain morning, when he and my master would be at breakfast together. Accordingly, on that morning, I went, and met the captain there, as he had appointed. When I went in I made my obeisance to my master, and with my money in my hand, and many fears in my heart, I prayed him to be as good as his offer to me, when he was pleased to promise me my freedom as soon as I could purchase it. This speech seemed to confound him; he began to recoil; and my heart that instant sunk within me. "What!" said he, "give you your freedom? Why, where did you get the money; Have you got forty pounds sterling?" "Yes, sir," I answered. "How did you get it"; replied he; I told him, "Very honestly." The captain then said he knew I got the money very honestly, and with much industry, and that I was particularly careful. On which my master replied, I got money much faster than he did; and said he would not have made me the promise he did if he had thought I should have got money so soon. "Come, come," said my worthy captain, clapping my master on the back, "Come, Robert, (which was his name), I think you must let him have his freedom;—you have laid your money out very well; you have received good interest for it all this time, and here is now the principal at last. I know Gustavus has earned you more than an hundred a-year, and he will still save you money, as he will not leave you: Come, Robert, take the money." My master then said, he would not be worse than his promise; and, taking the money, told me to go to the Secretary at the Register Office, and get my manumission[372] drawn up. These words of my master were like a voice from heaven to me;

in an instant all my trepidation was turned into unutterable bliss; and I most reverently bowed myself with gratitude, unable to express my feelings, but by the overflowing of my eyes, and a heart replete with thanks to God;[373] while my true and worthy friend the captain congratulated us both with a peculiar degree of heartfelt pleasure. As soon as the first transports of my joy were over, and I had expressed my thanks[374] to these my worthy friends in the best manner I was able, I rose with a heart full of affection and reverence, and left the room in order to obey my master's joyful mandate of going to the Register Office. As I was leaving the house, I called to mind the words of the Psalmist, in the 126th Psalm, and like him, "I glorified God in my heart, in whom I trusted." These words had been impressed on my mind from the very day I was forced from Deptford to the present hour, and I now saw them, as I thought, fulfilled and verified. My imagination was all rapture as I flew to the Register Office: and, in this respect, like the apostle Peter,[375] (whose deliverance from prison was so sudden and extraordinary, that he thought he was in a vision), I could scarcely believe I was awake. Heavens! who could do justice to my feelings at this moment? Not conquering heroes themselves, in the midst of a triumph—Not the tender mother who has just regained her long-lost infant, and presses it to her heart—Not the weary hungry mariner, at the sight of the desired friendly port—Not the lover, when he once more embraces his beloved mistress, after she had been ravished from his arms!—All within my breast was tumult, wildness, and delirium! My feet scarcely touched the ground, for they were winged with joy, and, like Elijah, as he rose to Heaven, they "were with lightning sped as I went on."[376] Every one I met I told of my happiness, and blazed about the virtue of my amiable master and captain.

When I got to the office and acquainted the Register with my errand, he congratulated me on the occasion, and told me he would draw up my manumission for half price, which was a guinea. I thanked him for his kindness; and having received it, and paid him, I hastened to my master to get him to sign it, that I might fully be released. Accordingly he signed the manumission that day; so that, before night, I who had been a slave in the morning, trembling at the will of another, now became[377] my own master, and compleatly free. I thought this was the happiest day I had ever experienced; and my joy was still heightened by the blessings and prayers of the sable race, particularly the aged, to whom my heart had ever been attached with reverence.

As the form of my manumission has something peculiar in it, and expresses the absolute power and dominion one man claims over his fellow, I shall beg leave to present it before my readers at full length:

Montserrat.—To all men unto whom these presents shall come: I Robert King, of the parish of St. Anthony, in the said island, merchant, send greeting: Know ye, that I the aforesaid Robert King, for, and in consideration of the sum of seventy pounds current money of the said island,[378] to me in hand paid, and to the intent that a negro man slave, named Gustavus Vasa, shall and may become free, have manumitted, emancipated, enfranchised, and set free, and by these presents do manumit, emancipate, enfranchise, and set free, the aforesaid negro man-slave, named Gustavus Vasa, for ever; hereby giving, granting, and releasing unto him, the said Gustavus Vasa, all right, title, dominion, sovereignty, and property, which, as lord and master over the aforesaid Gustavus Vasa, I have had, or which I now have,[379] or by any means whatsoever I may or can hereafter possibly have over him the aforesaid Negro, for ever. In witness whereof, I the abovesaid Robert King, have unto these presents set my hand and seal, this tenth day of July, in the year of our Lord one thousand seven hundred and sixty-six.

ROBERT KING

Signed, sealed, and delivered in the presence of Terry Legay.

Montserrat,
    Registered the within manumission, at full length, this eleventh day of July, 1766, in liber D.[380] TERRY LEGAY, Register.

In short, the fair as well as black people immediately styled me by a new appellation, to me the most desirable in the world, which was freeman, and at the dances I gave, my Georgia super-fine blue cloathes made no indifferent appearance, as I thought. Some of the sable females, who formerly stood aloof, now began to relax, and appear less coy, but my heart was still fixed on London, where I hoped to be ere long. So that my worthy captain, and his owner my late master, finding that the bent of my mind was towards London, said to me, "We hope you won't leave us, but that you will still be with the vessels." Here gratitude bowed me down; and none but the generous mind can judge of my feelings, struggling between inclination and duty. However, not-withstanding my wish to be in London, I obediently answered my benefactors that I would go in the vessel, and not leave them; and from that day I was entered on board as an able-bodied sailor, at thirty-six shillings per month, besides what perquisites I could make. My intention was to make a voyage or two, entirely to please these my honoured patrons; but I determined that the year following, if it pleased God, I would see Old England once more, and surprise my old master, Capt. Pascal, who was hourly in my mind; for I still loved him, notwithstanding his usage of me, and I pleased myself with thinking of what he would say when he saw what the Lord had done for me in so short a time, instead of being, as he might perhaps suppose, under the cruel yoke of some planter. With these kind of reveries I often used to entertain my-self, and shorten the time till my return: and now, being as in my original free African state, I embarked on board the Nancy, after having got all things ready for our voyage. In this state of serenity we sailed for St. Eustatia; and having smooth seas and pleasant[381] weather, we soon arrived there: after taking our cargo on board, we proceeded to Savannah in Georgia, in August 1766. While we were there, as usual, I used to go for the cargo up the rivers in boats: and when on this business, I have been frequently beset by Alligators, which were very numerous on that coast and river.[382] I have shot many of them when they have been near getting into our boats; which we have with great difficulty sometimes prevented, and have been very much frightened at them. I have seen young ones sold alive in Georgia for six-pence.

[383]During our stay at this place, one evening a slave belonging to Mr. Read, a merchant of Savannah, came near to our vessel, and began to use me very ill. I entreated him, with all the patience I was master of, to desist, as I knew there was little or no law for a free negro here; but the fellow, instead of taking my advice, persevered in his insults, and even struck me. At this I lost all temper, and fell on him and beat him soundly. The next morning his master came to our vessel as we lay alongside the wharf, and desired me to come ashore that he might have me flogged all round the town, for beating his negro slave. I told him he had insulted me, and had given the provocation by first striking me. I had told my captain also the whole affair that morning, and desired him to go along with me to Mr. Read, to prevent bad consequences; but he said that it did not signify, and if Mr. Read said any thing he would make matters up, and desired me to go to work, which I accordingly did. The captain being on board when Mr. Read came and applied to him to deliver me up, he said he knew nothing of the matter, I was a free man.[384] I was astonished and frightened at this, and thought I had better keep where I was, than go ashore and be flogged round the town, without judge or jury. I therefore refused to stir; and Mr. Read went away, swearing he would bring all the constables in the town, for he would have me out of the vessel. When he was gone, I thought his threat might prove too true to my sorrow; and I was confirmed in this belief, as well by the many instances I had seen of the treatment of free negroes, as from a fact that had happened within my own knowledge here a short time before.

There was a free black man, a carpenter, that I knew, who for asking a gentleman that he had worked for, for the money he had earned, was put into gaol;[385] and afterwards this oppressed man was sent from Georgia, with false accusations, of an intention to set the gentleman's house on fire, and run away with his slaves. I was therefore much embarrassed, and very apprehensive of a flog-ging at least. I dreaded, of all things, the thoughts of being stripped, as I never in my life had the marks of any violence of that kind. At that instant a rage seized my soul, and for a while[386] I determined to resist the first man that should attempt to lay violent hands on me, or basely use me without a trial; for I would sooner die like a free man, than suffer myself to be scourged by the hands of ruffians, and my blood drawn like a slave. The captain and others, more cautious, advised me to make haste and conceal myself; for they said Mr. Read was a very spiteful man, and he would soon come on board with constables, and take me. At first I refused this council, being determined to stand my ground; but at length, by the prevailing entreaties of the Captain and Mr. Dixon, with whom we lodged, I went to Mr. Dixon's house, which was a little out of the town, at a place called *Yea-ma-chra*.[387] I was but just gone when Mr. Read, with the constables, came for me, and searched the vessel; but not finding me there he swore he would have me dead or alive. I was secreted about five days; however, the good character which my Captain always gave me, as well as some other gentlemen, who also knew me, procured me some friends. At last some of them told my Captain that he did not use me well, in suffering me thus to be imposed upon, and said they would see me redressed, and get me on board some other vessel. My captain, on this, immediately went to Mr. Read, and told him, that ever since I eloped from the vessel, his work had been neglected, and he could not go on with her loading, himself and mate not being well; and, as I had managed things on board for them, my absence must have retarded his voyage,[388] and consequently hurt the owner; he therefore begged of him to forgive me, as he said he never heard any complaint of me before, during the several years[389] I had been with him. After repeated entreaties, Mr. Read said I might go to hell, and that he would not meddle with me; on which my Captain came immediately to me at his lodging, and telling me how pleasantly matters had gone on, desired me to go on board.

[390]Some of my other friends then asked him if he had got the constable's warrant from them? the Captain said, No. On this I was desired by them to stay in the house; and they said they would

get me on board of some other vessel before the evening. When the Captain heard this, he became almost distracted. He went immediately for the warrants, and, after using every exertion in his power, he at last got them from my hunters; but I had all the expences to pay.

[391]After I had thanked all my friends for their kindness, I went on board again to my work, of which I had always plenty. We were in haste to complete our lading, and were to carry twenty head of cattle with us to the West Indies, where they are a very profitable article. In order to encourage me in working, and to make up for the time I had lost, my Captain promised me the privilege of carrying two bullocks of my own with me; and this made me work with redoubled ardour. As soon as I had got the vessel loaded, in doing which I was obliged to perform the duty of the mate as well as my own work, and when[392] the bullocks were near coming on board, I asked the captain leave to bring my two, according to his promise; but, to my great surprise, he told me there was no room for them. I then asked him to permit me to take one; but he said he could not. I was a good deal mortified at this usage, and told him I had no notion that he intended thus to impose on me: nor could I think well of any man that was so much worse than his word. On this we had some disagreement, and I gave him to understand that I intended to leave the vessel. At this he appeared to be very much dejected; and our mate, who had been very sickly, and whose duty had long devolved upon me, advised him to persuade me to stay: in consequence of which he spoke very kindly to me, making many fair promises, telling me that as the mate was so sickly, he could not do without me; and that as the safety of the vessel and cargo depended greatly upon me, he therefore hoped that I would not be offended at what had passed between us, and swore he would make up all matters when we arrived in the West Indies, so I consented to slave on as before. Soon after this, as the bullocks were coming on board, one of them ran at the captain, and butted him so furiously in the breast, that he never recovered of the blow. In order to make me some amends for this[393] treatment about the

bullocks, the captain now pressed me very much to take some turkies, and other fowls, with me, and gave me liberty to take as many as I could find room for; but I told him he knew very well I had never carried any turkies before, as I always thought they were such tender birds that they were not fit to cross the seas. However, he continued to press me to buy them for once: and, what seemed very surprising to me, the more I was against it, the more he urged my taking them, insomuch that he ensured me from all losses that might happen by them, and I was prevailed on to take them; but I thought this very strange, as he had never acted so with me before. This, and not being able to dispose of my paper money in any other way, induced me at length to take four dozen. The turkies, however, I was so dissatisfied about, that I determined to make no more voyages to this quarter, nor with this captain; and was very apprehensive that my free voyage would be the very worst I had ever made.[394]

[395]We set sail for Montserrat. The Captain and mate had been both complaining of sickness when we sailed, and as we proceeded on our voyage they grew worse. This was about November, and we had not been long at sea before we began to meet with strong northerly gales and rough seas; and in about seven or eight days all the bullocks were near being drowned, and four or five of them died. Our vessel, which had not been tight at first, was much less so now: and, though we were but nine in the whole, including five sailors and myself, yet we were obliged to attend to the pump, every half or three quarters of an hour. The captain and mate came on deck as often as they were able, which was now but seldom; for they declined so fast, that they were not well enough to make observations above four or five times the whole passage. The whole care of the vessel rested therefore upon me; and I was obliged to direct her by mere dint of reason,[396] not being able to work a traverse.[397] The Captain was now very sorry he had not taught me navigation, and protested, if ever he should get well again, he would not fail to do so: but in about seventeen days his illness increased so much, that he was obliged to keep his bed, continuing sensible, however, till the last, constantly having

the owner's interest at heart; for this just and benevolent man ever appeared much concerned about the welfare of what he was intrusted with. When this dear friend found the symptoms of death approaching, he called me by my name; and, when I came to him, he asked (with almost his last breath) if he had ever done me any harm? "God forbid I should think so," I replied, "I should then be the most ungrateful of wretches to the best of benefactors." While I was thus expressing my affection and sorrow by his bed-side, he expired without saying another word, and the day following we committed his body to the deep. Every man on board loved him, and regretted his death; but I was exceedingly affected at it, and found that I did not know, till he was gone, the strength of my regard for him. Indeed I had every reason in the world to be attached to him; for, besides that he was in general mild, affable, generous, faithful, benevolent, and just, he was to me a friend and father; and had it pleased Providence that he had died but five months before, I verily believe I should not have obtained my freedom when I did; and it is not improbable that I might not have been able to get it at any rate afterwards.

[398]The captain being dead, the mate came on the deck, and made such observations as he was able,[399] but to no purpose. In the course of a few days more, the few bullocks that remained were found dead; but the turkies I had, though on the deck, and exposed to so much wet and bad weather, did well, and I afterwards gained near three hundred per cent. on the sale of them; so that in the event it proved a happy circumstance for me that I had not bought the bullocks I intended, for they must have perished with the rest; I could not help looking upon this, otherwise trifling circumstance, as a particular providence of God, and was thankful accordingly. The care of the vessel took up all my time, and engaged my attention entirely. As we were now out of the variable winds, I thought I should not be much puzzled to hit the islands.[400] I was persuaded I steered right for Antigua, which I wished to reach, as the nearest to us; and in the course of nine or ten days we made that island, to our great joy; and the day after we came safe to Montserrat.

[401]Many were surprised when they heard of my conducting the sloop into the port, and I now obtained a new appellation, and was called captain. This elated me not a little, and it was quite flattering to my vanity to be thus styled by as high a title as any sable[402] freeman in this place possessed. When the death of the captain became known, he was much regretted by all who knew him; for he was a man universally respected. At the same time the sable captain lost no fame; for the success I had met with increased the affection of my friends in no small measure; and I was offered, by a gentleman of the place, the command of his sloop to go amongst the islands, but I refused.[403]

Facing page: *Bahama Banks*, 1767. "Thus God speaketh once, yea twice, yet Man perceiveth it not. In a Dream, in a Vision of the Night, when deep sleep falleth upon Men in slumbrings upon the Bed; Then he openeth the Ears of Men, & sealeth their instruction." (Job, chapter 33, verses 15, 16, 29, and 30.)

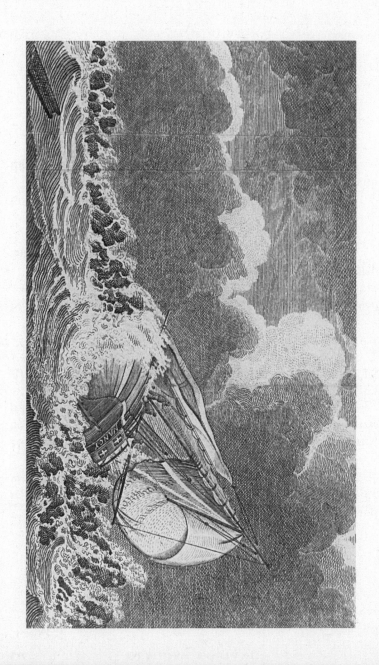

[404]They ran the ship aground, and the fore part stuck fast, and remained unmoveable, but the hinder part was broken by[405] the violence of the waves. ACTS xxvii. 41.

Howbeit we must be cast upon a certain island; Wherefore, sirs, be of good cheer; for I believe God, that it shall be even as it was told me. ACTS xxvii. 25, 26.[406]

And so it came to pass that they escaped all safe to the land. ACTS xxvii. 44.[407]

Now a thing was secretly brought to me, and mine ear received a little thereof.

In thoughts from the visions of the night, when dead sleep falleth on men. JOB iv. 12, 13.

Lo, all these *things* worketh God oftentimes with man.

To bring back his soul from the pit, to be enlightened with the light of the living. JOB xxxiii. 29, 30.

CHAP. VIII.

The Author, to oblige Mr. King, once more embarks for Georgia in the Nancy —A new captain is appointed—They sail, and steer a new course—Three remarkable dreams—The vessel is wrecked on Bahama Banks, but the crew are preserved, principally by means of the Author—He sets out from an island, with the captain, in a small boat, in quest of a ship—Their distress—Meet with a wrecker—Sail for Providence—Are overtaken again by a terrible storm, and are all near perishing—Arrive at New Providence—The Author, after some time, sails from thence to Georgia—Meets with another storm, and is obliged to put back and refit—Arrives at Georgia—Meets new impositions—Two white men attempt to kidnap him—Officiates as a parson at a funeral ceremony—Bids adieu to Georgia, and sails for Martinico.

AS I had now, by the death of my captain, lost my great bene-factor and friend, I had little inducement to remain longer in the West Indies, except my gratitude to Mr. King, which I thought I had pretty well discharged in bringing back his vessel safe, and delivering his cargo to his satisfaction. I began to think of leaving this part of the world, of which I had been long tired, and of returning to England, where my heart had always been; but Mr. King still pressed me very much to stay with his vessel; and he had done so much for me, that I found myself unable to refuse his requests, and consented to go another voyage to Georgia, as the mate from his ill state of health, was quite useless in the vessel. Accordingly, a new captain was appointed, whose name was William Phillips, an old acquaintance of mine; and, having refitted our vessel, and taken several slaves on board, we set sail for St. Eustatia, where we staid but a few days; and on the 30th of January, 1767, we steered for Georgia. Our new captain boasted strangely of his skill in navigating and conducting a vessel; and, in consequence of this, he steered a new course, several points more to the westward than we ever did before; this appeared to me very extraordinary.

On the 4th of February,[408] which was soon after we had got into our new course, I dreamt the ship was wrecked amidst the surfs and rocks, and that I was the means of saving every one on board; and on the night following I dreamed the very same dream. These dreams, however, made no impression on my mind; and the next evening, it being my watch below, I was pumping the vessel a little after eight o'clock, just before I went off the deck, as is the custom, and being weary with the duty of the day, and tired at the pump (for we made a good deal of water),[409] I began to express my impatience, and I uttered with an oath, "Damn the vessel's bottom out." But my conscience instantly smote me for the expression. When I left the deck I went to bed, and had scarcely fallen asleep when I dreamed the same dream again about the ship that I had dreamt the two preceding nights. At twelve o'clock the watch was changed; and, as I had always the charge of the captain's watch, I then went upon deck. At half after one in the morning, the man at the helm saw something under the lee-beam that the sea washed against,[410] and he immediately called to me that there was a grampus, and desired me to look at it. Accordingly I stood up and observed it for some time; but when I saw the sea wash up against it again and again, I said it was not a fish but a rock. Being soon certain of this, I went down to the captain, and, with some confusion, told him the danger we were in, and desired him to come upon deck immediately. He said it was very well, and I went up again. As soon as I was upon deck, the wind, which had been pretty high, having abated a little, the vessel began to be carried sideways towards the rock, by means of the current. Still the captain did not appear. I therefore went to him again and told him the vessel was then near a large rock, and desired he would come up with all speed. He said he would, and I returned on the deck. When I was upon the deck again I saw we were not above a pistol shot from the rock, and I heard the noise of the breakers all around us.[411] I was exceedingly alarmed at this; and the captain not having yet come on the deck, I lost all patience; and, growing quite enraged, I ran down to him again, and asked him, why he did not come up, and what he could mean by all this? "The breakers," said I, "are around us, and the vessel is almost on the rock." With that he came on the deck with me, and we tried to put the vessel about, and get her out of the current, but all to no purpose, the wind being very small. We then called all hands up immediately; and after a little we got up one end of a cable, and fastened it to the anchor. By this time the surf foamed round us, and made a dreadful noise on the breakers, and the very moment we let the anchor go, the vessel struck against the rocks. One swell now succeeded another, as it were one wave calling on its fellow. The roaring of the billows increased, and, with one single heave of the swells, the sloop was pierced and transfixed among the rocks! In a moment a scene of horror presented itself to my mind, such as I never had conceived or experienced before. All my sins stared me in the face; and especially I thought that God had hurled his direful vengeance on my guilty head for cursing the vessel on which my life depended. My spirits at this forsook me, and I expected every moment to go to the bottom: I determined if I should still be saved, that I would never swear again. And in the midst of my distress, while the dreadful surfs were dashing with unremitting fury among the rocks, I remembered the Lord, though fearful that I was undeserving of forgiveness, and I thought that as he had often delivered he might yet deliver; and, calling to mind the many mercies he had shewn me in times past, they gave me some small hope that he might still help me. I then began to think how we might be saved; and, I believe no mind was ever like mine so replete with inventions and confused with schemes, though how to escape death I knew not. The captain immediately ordered the hatches to be nailed down on the slaves in the hold, where there were above twenty, all of whom must unavoidably have perished if he had been obeyed. When he desired the men to nail down the hatches I thought that my sin was the cause of this, and that God would charge me with these people's blood. This thought rushed upon my mind that instant with such violence, that it quite overpowered me, and I fainted. I recovered just as the people were about to nail down the hatches; perceiving which, I desired them to stop. The captain then said it must be done; I asked him why? He said, that every one would endeavour to get into the boat, which was but small, and thereby we should be drowned; for it would not have carried above ten at the most. I could no longer restrain my emotion, and I told him he deserved drowning for not knowing how to navigate the vessel; and I believe the people would have tossed him overboard if I had given them the least hint of it. However, the hatches were not nailed down; and, as none of us could leave the vessel then on account of the darkness, and as we knew not where to go, and were convinced besides that the boat could not survive the surfs, and besides being broken,[412] we all said we would remain on the dry part of the vessel, and trust to God till day-light appeared, when we should know better what to do.

I then advised to get the boat prepared against morning, and some of us began to set about it; but some abandoned all care of the ship, and themselves, and fell to drinking. Our boat had a piece out of her bottom near two feet long, and we had no materials to mend her; however, necessity being the mother of invention, I took some pump leather and nailed it to the broken part, and plastered it over with tallow-grease. And, thus prepared, with the utmost anxiety of mind, we watched for day-light, and thought every minute an hour, till it appeared. At last it saluted our longing eyes, and kind Providence accompanied its approach with what was no small comfort to us; for the dreadful swell began to subside; and the next thing that we discovered to raise our drooping spirits, was a small key, or desolate island,[413] about five or six miles off; but a barrier soon presented itself; for there was not water enough for our boat to go over the reefs, and this threw us again into a sad consternation; but there was no alternative, we were therefore obliged to put but few things[414] in the boat at once; and, what was still worse, all of us were frequently under the necessity of getting out to drag and lift it over the reefs. This cost us much labour and fatigue; and, what was yet more distressing, we could not avoid having our legs cut and torn very much with the rocks. There were only four people that would work with me at the oars; and they consisted of three black men and a Dutch creole sailor;[415] and, though we went with the boat five times that day, we had no others to assist us. But, had we not worked in this manner, I really believe the people could not have been saved; for not one of the white men did any thing to preserve their lives; and indeed they soon got so drunk that they were not able, but lay about the deck like swine, so that we were at last obliged to lift them into the boat, and carry them on shore by force. This want[416] of assistance made our labour intolerably severe; insomuch that, by putting on shore so often that day, the skin was partly[417] stript off my hands.

However, we continued all the day to toil and strain our exertions, till we had brought all on board safe to the shore; so that out of thirty-two people we lost not one.

[418]My dream now returned upon my mind with all its force; it was fulfilled in every part; for our danger was the same I had dreamt of; and I could not help looking on myself as the principal instrument in effecting our deliverance: for, owing to some of our people getting drunk, the rest of us were obliged to double our exertions; and it was fortunate we did, for in a very little time longer the patch of leather on the boat would have been worn out, and she would have been no longer fit for service. Situated as we were, who could think that men should be so careless of the danger they were in? for, if the wind had but raised the swell as it was when the vessel struck, we must have bid a final farewell to all hopes of deliverance; and though I warned the people who were drinking, and entreated them to embrace the moment of deliverance, nevertheless they persisted, as if not possessed of the least spark of reason. I could not help thinking, that if any of these people had been lost, God would charge me with their lives, which, perhaps, was one cause of my labouring so hard for their preservation, and indeed every one of them afterwards seemed so sensible of the service I had rendered them, that while we were on the key, I was a kind of chieftain amongst them. I brought some limes, oranges, and lemons ashore; and, finding it to be a good soil where we were, I planted several of them as a token to

any one that might be cast away hereafter. This key, as we afterwards found, was one of the Bahama islands, which consist of a
cluster of large islands, with smaller ones or keys, as they are called,
interspersed among them. It was about a mile in circumference,
with a white sandy beach running in a regular order along it. On
that part of it where we first attempted to land, there stood some
very large birds, called flamingoes: these, from the reflection of
the sun, appeared to us, at a little distance, as large as men; and,
when they walked backwards and forwards, we could not conceive what they were: our captain swore they were cannibals. This
created a great panic among us; and we held a consultation how
to act. The captain wanted to go to a key that was within sight,
but a great way off; but I was against it, as in so doing we should
not be able to save all the people; "And therefore," said I, "let
us go on shore here, and perhaps these cannibals may take to the
water." Accordingly, we steered towards them; and when we approached them, to our very great joy and no less wonder, they
walked off one after the other very deliberately; and at last they
took flight, and relieved us entirely from our fears. About the key
there were turtles and several sorts of fish in such abundance that
we caught them without bait, which was a great relief to us after
the salt provisions on board.[419] There was also a large rock on the
beach, about ten feet high, which was in the form of a punch-
bowl at the top; this we could not help thinking Providence had
ordained to supply us with rain-water; and it was something singular, that, if we did not take the water when it rained, in some
little time after it would turn as salt as sea-water.

Our first care, after refreshment, was, to make ourselves tents
to lodge in, which we did as well as we could with some sails we
had brought from the ship. We then began to think how we
might get from this place, which was quite uninhabited; and
we determined to repair our boat, which was very much shattered,
and to put to sea in quest of a ship, or some inhabited island. It
took us up, however, eleven days before we could get the boat
ready for sea, in the manner we wanted it, with a sail and other
necessaries. When we had got all things prepared, the captain

wanted me to stay on shore, while he went to sea in quest of a vessel to take all the people off the key; but this I refused; and the captain and myself, with five more, set off in the boat towards New Providence.[420] We had no more than two musquet loads of gun-powder with us, if any thing should happen; and our stock of provisions consisted of three gallons of rum, four of water, some salt beef, some biscuit; and in this manner we proceeded to sea.

On the second day of our voyage, we came to an island called Abbico,[421] the largest of the Bahama islands. We were much in want of water; for by this time our water was expended, and we were exceedingly fatigued in pulling two days in the heat of the sun; and it being late in the evening, we hauled the boat ashore to try for water, and remain during the night: when we came ashore we searched for water, but could find none. When it was dark, we made a fire around us for fear of the wild beasts, as the place was an entire thick wood, and we took it by turns to watch. In this situation we found very little rest, and waited with impatience for the morning. As soon as the light appeared we set off again with our boat, in hopes of finding assistance during the day. We were now much dejected and weakened by pulling the boat; for our sail was of no use, and we were almost famished for want of fresh water to drink. We had nothing left to eat but salt beef, and that we could not use without water. In this situation we toiled all day in sight of the island, which was very long; in the evening, seeing no relief, we made shore again, and fastened our boat. We then went to look for fresh water, being quite faint for the want of it; and we dug and searched about for some all the remainder of the evening, but could not find one drop, so that our dejection at this period became excessive, and our terror so great, that we expected nothing but death to deliver us. We could not touch our beef, which was as salt as brine, without fresh water; and we were in the greatest terror from the apprehension of wild beasts. When unwelcome night came, we acted as on the night before; and the next morning we set off again from the island in hopes of seeing some vessel. In this manner we toiled as well as we were able till four o'clock, during which we passed several keys,[422] but could not meet with a ship; and, still famishing with thirst, went ashore on one of those keys again in hopes of finding some water. Here we found some leaves with a few drops of water on them, which we lapped with much eagerness; we then dug in several places, but without success. As we were digging holes in search of water, there came forth some very thick and black stuff; but none of us could touch it, except the poor Dutch Creole, who drank above a quart of it, as eagerly as if it had been wine. We tried to catch fish, but could not: and we now began to repine at our fate, and abandon ourselves to despair; when, in the midst of our murmuring, the captain, all at once cried out, "A sail! a sail! a sail!" This gladdening sound was like a reprieve to a convict, and we all instantly turned to look at it; but in a little time some of us began to be afraid it was not a sail. However, at a venture, we embarked, and steered after it; and, in half an hour, to our unspeakable joy, we plainly saw that it was a vessel. At this our drooping spirits revived, and we made towards her with all the speed imaginable. When we came near to her, we found she was a little sloop, about the size of a Gravesend hoy,[423] and quite full of people; a circumstance which we could not make out the meaning of. Our captain, who was a Welshman, swore that they were pirates, and would kill us. I said, be that as it might, we must board her if we were to die for it; and, if they should not receive us kindly, we must oppose them as well as we could: for there was no alternative between their perishing and ours. This counsel was immediately taken; and I really believe that the captain, myself, and the Dutchman, would then have faced twenty men. We had two cutlasses and a musquet, that I brought in the boat; and in this situation, we rowed alongside, and immediately boarded her. I believe there were about forty hands on board; but how great was our surprise, as soon as we got on board, to find that the major part of them were in the same predicament as ourselves.

They belonged to a whaling schooner[424] that was wrecked two days before us about nine miles to the north of our vessel. When she was wrecked, some of them had taken to their boats, and had left some of their people and property on a key, in the same manner as we had done; and were going, like us, to New Providence in quest of a ship, when they met with this little sloop, called a wrecker; their employment in those seas being to look after wrecks.[425] They were then going to take the remainder of the people belonging to the schooner; for which the wrecker was to have all things belonging to the vessel, and likewise their people's help to get what they could out of her, and were then to carry the crew to New Providence.

We told the people of the wrecker the condition of our vessel, and we made the same agreement with them as the schooner's people; and, on their complying, we begged of them to go to our key directly, because our people were in want of water. They agreed, therefore, to go along with us first; and in two days we arrived at the key, to the inexpressible joy of the people that we had left behind, as they had been reduced to great extremities for want of water in our absence. Luckily for us, the wrecker had now more people on board than she could carry or victual for any moderate length of time; they therefore hired the schooner's people to work on the wreck,[426] and we left them our boat, and embarked for New Providence.

Nothing could have been more fortunate than our meeting with this wrecker, for New Providence was at such a distance that we never could have reached it in our boat. The island of Abbico was much longer than we expected; and it was not till after sailing for three or four days that we got safe to the farther end of it, towards New Providence. When we arrived there we watered, and got a good many lobsters and other shell-fish, which proved a great relief to us, as our provisions and water were almost exhausted. We then proceeded on our voyage; but the day after we left the island, late in the evening and whilst we were yet amongst the Bahama keys, we were overtaken by a violent gale of wind, so that we were obliged to cut away the mast. The vessel was very near foundering;[427] for she parted from her anchors, and struck several times on the shoals. Here we expected every minute that she would have gone to pieces, and each moment to be our last; so much so, that my old captain and sickly useless mate, and several others, fainted; and death stared us in the face on every side. All the swearers on board now began to call on the God of Heaven to assist them: and sure enough beyond our comprehension he did assist us, and in a miraculous manner delivered us! In the very height of our extremity the wind lulled for a few minutes; and, although the swell was high beyond expression, two men, who were expert swimmers, attempted to go to the buoy of the anchor,[428] which we still saw in the water, at some distance, in a little punt that belonged to the wrecker, which was not large enough to carry more than two. She filled at[429] different times in their endeavours to get into her alongside of our vessel; and they saw nothing but death before them, as well as we; but they said they might as well die that way as any other. A coil of very small rope, with a little buoy, was put in along with them; and, at last, with great hazard they got the punt clear from the vessel; and these two intrepid water heroes paddled away for life towards the buoy of the anchor. Our eyes[430] were fixed on them all the time, expecting every minute to be their last; and the prayers of all those that remained in their senses were offered up to God, on their behalf, for a speedy deliverance, and for our own, which depended on them; and he heard and answered us! These two men at last reached the buoy; and having fastened the punt to it, they tied one end of their rope to the small buoy that they had in the punt, and sent it adrift towards the vessel. We on board observing this, threw out boat-hooks and leads fastened to lines,[431] in order to catch the buoy: at last we caught it, and fastened a hawser to the end of the small rope; we then gave them a sign to pull, and they pulled the hawser to them, and fastened it to the buoy: which being done, we hauled for our lives; and, through the mercy of God, we got again from the shoals into deep water, and the punt got safe to the vessel. It is impossible for any to conceive our heartfelt joy at this second deliverance from ruin, but those who have suffered the same hardships. Those whose strength and senses were gone, came to themselves, and were now as elated as they were before depressed. Two days after this the wind ceased, and the water became smooth. The punt then went on shore, and we cut down some trees; and having found our mast and mended it, we brought it on board, and fixed it up. As soon as we had done this we got up the anchor, and away we went once more for New Providence, which in three days more we reached safe, after having been above three weeks in a situation in which we did not expect to escape with life. The inhabitants here were very kind to us; and, when they learned our situation, shewed us a great deal of hospitality and friendship. Soon after this, every one of my old fellow-sufferers that were free, parted from us, and shaped their course where their inclination led them. One merchant, who had a large sloop, seeing our condition, and knowing we wanted to go to Georgia, told four of us that his vessel was going there; and, if we would work on board and load her, he would give us our passage free. As we could not get any wages whatever, and found it very hard to get off the place, we were obliged to consent to his proposal; and we went on board and helped to load the sloop, though we had only our victuals allowed us. When she was entirely loaded, he told us she was going to Jamaica first, where we must go if we went in her. This, however, I refused; but my fellow-sufferers not having any money to help themselves with, necessity obliged them to accept of the offer, and to steer that course, though they did not like it.

We stayed in New Providence about seventeen or eighteen days; during which time I met with many friends, who gave me encouragement to stay there with them, but I declined it; though, had not my heart been fixed on England, I should have stayed, as I liked the place extremely, and there were some free black people here who were very happy, and we passed our time pleasantly together, with the melodious sound of the catguts under the lime and lemon trees.[432] At length Capt. Phillips hired a sloop to carry him and some of the slaves that he could not sell here, to Georgia; and I agreed to go with him in this vessel, meaning now to take my farewell of that place. When the vessel was ready, we all embarked; and I took my leave of New Providence, not without regret. We sailed about four o'clock in the morning, with a

fair wind, for Georgia; and, about eleven o'clock the same morning, a sudden and short gale sprung up and blew away most of
our sails; and, as we were still among the keys, in a very few
minutes it dashed the sloop against the rocks. Luckily for us the
water was deep; and the sea was not so angry, but that, after
having for some time laboured hard, and being many in number,
we were saved through God's mercy: and, by using our greatest
exertions, we got the vessel off. The next day we returned to
[New] Providence, where we soon got her again refitted. Some
of the people swore that we had spells set upon us, by somebody
in Montserrat; and others said that we had witches and wizzards
amongst the poor helpless slaves; and that we never should arrive
safe at Georgia. But these things did not deter me; I said, "Let us
again face the winds and seas, and swear not, but trust to God,
and he will deliver us." We therefore once more set sail; and with
hard labour, in seven days time, arrived safe at Georgia.

After our arrival we went up to the town of Savannah; and the
same evening I went to a friend's house to lodge, whose name
was Mosa, a black man. We were very happy at meeting each
other; and, after supper, we had a light till between nine and ten
o'clock at night. About that time the watch or patrole came by,
and, discerning a light in the house, they knocked at the door;
we opened it, and they came in and sat down, and drank some
punch with us; they also begged some limes of me, as they understood I had some, which I readily gave them. A little after this,
they told me I must go to the watch-house with them; this surprised me a good deal after our kindness to them, and I asked
them, Why so? They said that all negroes, who had a light in their
houses after nine o'clock were to be taken into custody, and either
pay some dollars, or be flogged. Some of these people knew that
I was a free man; but, as the man of the house was not free, and
had his master to protect him, they did not take the same liberty
with him they did with me. I told them that I was a free man,
and just arrived from [New] Providence; that we were not making
any noise, and that I was not a stranger in that place, but was very
well known there: "Besides," said I, "what will you do with

me?"—"That you shall see," replied they; "but you must go to
the watch-house with us." Now, whether they meant to get
money from me or not, I was at a loss to know; but I thought
immediately of the oranges and limes at Santa Cruz: and seeing
that nothing would pacify them, I went with them to the watch-
house, where I remained during the night. Early the next morning
these imposing ruffians flogged a negro man and woman that they
had in the watch-house, and then they told me that I must be
flogged too; I asked why? and if there was no law for free men?
and told them if there was I would have it put in force against
them. But this only exasperated them the more, and they instantly
swore they would serve me as Doctor Perkins had done; and were
going to lay violent hands on me; when one of them, more humane than the rest, said, that as I was a free man they could not
justify stripping me by law. I then immediately sent for Dr. Brady,
who was known to be a honest and worthy man; and on his
coming to my assistance, they let me go.

This was not the only disagreeable incident I met with while
I was in this place; for, one day, while I was a little way out of
the town of Savannah, I was beset by two white men, who meant
to play their usual tricks with me in the way of kidnapping. As
soon as these men accosted me, one of them said to the other,
"This is the very fellow we are looking for, that you lost": and
the other swore immediately that I was the identical person. On
this they made up to me, and were about to handle me; but I
told them to be still and keep off, for I had seen those tricks played
upon other free blacks, and they must not think to serve me so.
At this they paused a little, and one said to the other—it will not
do; and the other answered that I talked too good English. I
replied, I believed I did; and I had also with me a revengeful stick
equal to the occasion; and my mind was likewise good. Happily,
however, it was not used; and, after we had talked together a little
in this manner, the rogues left me.

[433]I stayed in Savannah some time, anxiously trying to get to
Montserrat once more to see Mr. King, my old master, and then
to take a final farewell of the American quarter of the globe. At

last I met with a sloop called the Speedwell, Captain John Bunton, which belonged to Grenada, and was bound to Martinico, a French island, with a cargo of rice; and I shipped myself on board of her.

[434]Before I left Georgia, a black woman who had a child lying dead, being very tenacious of the church burial service, and not able to get any white person to perform it, applied to me for that purpose. I told her I was no parson; and, besides, that the service over the dead did not affect the soul. This however did not satisfy her; she still urged me very hard; I therefore complied with her entreaties, and at last consented to act the parson for the first time in my life. As she was much respected, there was a great company both of white and black people at the grave. I then accordingly assumed my new vocation, and performed the funeral ceremony to the satisfaction of all present; after which I bade adieu to Georgia, and sailed for Martinico.[435]

CHAP. IX.

The Author arrives at Martinico—Meets with new difficulties—Gets to Mont-serrat, where he takes leave of his old master, and sails for England—Meets Capt. Pascal—Learns the French horn—Hires himself with Doctor Irving, where he learns to freshen sea water—Leaves the Doctor and goes a voyage to Turkey and Portugal; & afterwards goes a voyage to Grenada, and another to Jamaica—Returns to the Doctor, and they embark together on a voyage to the North Pole, with the Hon. Capt. Phipps—Some account of that voyage, and the dangers the Author was in—He returns to England.

I THUS took a final leave of Georgia; for the treatment I had received in it disgusted me very much against the place; and when I left it and sailed for Martinico, I determined never more to revisit it. My new captain conducted his vessel safer than my former one; and, after an agreeable voyage, we got safe to our intended port. While I was on this island I went about a good deal, and found it very pleasant: in particular, I admired the town of St. Pierre, which is the principal one in the island, and built more like an European town than any I had seen in the West Indies. In general also, slaves were better treated, had more holidays, and looked better than those in the English islands.[436] After we had done our business here, I wanted my discharge, which was necessary; for it was then the month of May, and I wished much to be at Montserrat to bid farewell to Mr. King, and all my other friends there, in time to sail for Old England in the July fleet.[437] But, alas! I had put a great stumbling block in my own way, by which I was near losing my passage that season to England. I had lent my captain some money, which I now wanted, to enable me to prosecute my intentions. This I told him; but when I applied for it, though I urged the necessity of my occasion, I met with so much shuffling from him,[438] that I began at last to be afraid of losing my money, as I could not recover it by law; for I have already mentioned, that throughout the West Indies no black man's testimony is admitted, on any occasion, against any white person whatever, and therefore my own oath would have been of no use. I was obliged therefore, to remain with him till he might be disposed to return it to me. Thus we sailed from Martinico for the Grenades.[439] I frequently pressing the captain for my money, to no purpose; and, to render my condition worse, when we got there, the captain and his owners quarrelled; so that my situation became daily more irksome: for besides that we on board had little or no victuals allowed us, and I could not get my money nor wages, as I could then have gotten my passage free to Montserrat had I been able to accept it. The worst of all was, that it was growing late in July, and the ships in the islands must sail by the 26th of that month. At last, however, with a great many entreaties, I got my money from the captain, and took the first vessel I could meet with for St. Eustatia. From thence I went in another to Basseterre in St. Kitt's, where I arrived on the 19th of July. On the 22d, having met with a vessel bound to Montserrat, I wanted to go in her; but the captain and others would not take me on board until I should advertise myself, and give notice of my going off the island.[440] I told them of my haste to be in Montserrat; and that the time then would not admit of advertising, it being late in the evening, and the vessel about to sail; but he insisted it was necessary, and otherwise he said he would not take me. This reduced me to great perplexity; for if I should be compelled to submit to this degrading necessity, which every black freeman is under, of advertising himself like a slave, when he leaves an island, and which I thought a gross imposition upon any freedom,[441] I feared I should miss that opportunity of going to Montserrat, and then I could not get to England that year. The vessel was just going off, and no time could be lost; I immediately therefore set about with a heavy heart, to try who I could get to befriend me in complying with the demands of the captain. Luckily I found, in a few minutes, some gentlemen of Montserrat whom I knew; and having told them my situation, I requested their friendly assistance in helping me off the island. Some of them, on this, went with me to the captain, and satisfied him of my freedom; and, to my very great joy, he desired me to go on board. We then set sail, and the next day, the 23d, I arrived at the wished-for place, after an absence of six months, in which I had more than once experienced the delivering hand of Providence, when all human means of escaping destruction seemed hopeless. I saw my friends with a gladness of heart, which was increased by my absence, and the dangers I had escaped; and I was received with great friendship by them all, but particularly by Mr. King, to whom I related the fate of his sloop, the Nancy, and the causes of her being wrecked. I now learned, with extreme sorrow, that his house was washed away during my absence, by the bursting of a pond at the top of a mountain that was opposite the town of Plymouth. It swept great part of the town away, and Mr. King lost a great deal of property from the inundation, and nearly his life. When I told him I intended to go to London that season, and that I had come to visit him before my departure, the good man expressed a great deal of affection for me, and sorrow that I should leave him, and warmly advised me to stay there; insisting, as I was much respected by all the gentlemen in the place, that I might do very well, and in a short time have land and slaves of my own. I thanked him for this instance of his friendship; but, as I wished very much to be in London, I declined remaining any longer there, and begged he would excuse me. I then requested he would be kind enough to give me a certificate of my behaviour while in his service, which he very readily complied with, and gave me the following:

Montserrat, 26th of July, 1767.

The bearer hereof, Gustavus Vasa, was my slave for upwards of three years, during which he has always behaved himself well, and discharged his duty with honesty and assiduity.

ROBERT KING.

To all whom this may concern.

Having obtained this, I parted from my kind master, after many sincere professions of gratitude and regard, and prepared for my departure for London. I immediately agreed to go with one Capt. John Hamer, for seven guineas (the passage to London), on board a ship called the Andromache; and on the 24th and 25th, I had free dances, as they are called, with some of my friends and countrymen, previous to my setting off; after which I took leave of all my friends, and on the 26th I embarked for London, exceedingly glad to see myself once more on board of a ship, and still more so, in steering the course I had long wished for. With a light heart I bade Montserrat farewell, and never had my feet on it since; and with it I bade adieu to the sound of the cruel whip, and all other dreadful instruments of torture! adieu to the offensive sight of the violated chastity of the sable females, which has too often accosted my eyes! adieu to oppressions (although to me less severe than to most of my countrymen!) and adieu to the angry howling dashing surfs! I wished for a grateful and thankful heart to praise the Lord God on high for all his mercies! in this extacy I steered the ship all night.[442]

We had a most prosperous voyage, and, at the end of seven weeks, arrived at Cherry-garden stairs.[443] Thus were my longing eyes once more gratified with a sight of London, after having been absent from it above four years. I immediately received my wages, and I never had earned seven guineas so quick in my life before; I had thirty-seven guineas in all, when I got cleared of the ship. I now entered upon a scene quite new to me, but full of hope. In this situation my first thoughts were to look out for some of my former friends, and amongst the first of those were the Miss Guerins. As soon as I had regaled myself I went in quest of those kind ladies, whom I was very impatient to see; and, with some difficulty and perseverance, I found them at May's-hill, Greenwich. They were most agreeably surprised to see me, and I was[444] quite overjoyed at meeting with them. I told them my history, at which they expressed great wonder, and freely acknowledged it did their cousin, Capt. Pascal, no honour. He then visited there frequently; and I met him, four or five days after, in Greenwich-park. When he saw me, he appeared a good deal surprised, and asked me how I came back? I answered, "In a ship." To which he replied dryly, "I suppose you did not walk back to London on the water." As I saw, by his manner, that he did not seem to be sorry for his behaviour to me, and that I had not much reason to expect any favour from him, I told him that he had used me very ill, after I had been such a faithful servant to him for so many years; on which, without saying any more, he turned about and went away. A few days after this I met Capt. Pascal at Miss Guerin's house, and asked him for my prize-money. He said there was none due to me; for if my prize-money had been 10,000£ he had a right to it all. I told him I was informed otherwise, on which he bade me defiance, and, in a bantering tone, desired me to commence a law-suit against him for it: "There are lawyers enough," said he, "that will take the cause in hand, and you had better try it." I told him then that I would try it, which enraged him very much; however, out of regard to the ladies, I remained still, and never made any farther demand of my right. Some time afterwards, these friendly ladies asked me what I meant to do with myself, and how they could assist me. I thanked them, and said, if they pleased, I would be their servant; but if not I had thirty-seven guineas, which would support me for some time, and I would be much obliged to them to recommend me to some person who would teach me a business whereby I might earn my living. They answered me very politely, that they were sorry it did not suit them to take me as their servant, and asked me what business I should like to learn? I said, hair-dressing. They then promised to assist me in this; and soon after, they recommended me to a gentleman, whom I had known before, one Capt. O'Hara, who treated me with much kindness, and procured me a master,[445] a hair-dresser, in Coventry-court, Haymarket, with whom he placed me. I was with this man from September till the February following. In that time we had a neighbour in the same court, who taught the French-horn. He used to blow it so well that I was charmed with it, and agreed with him to teach me to blow it. Accordingly he took me in hand, and began to instruct

me, and I soon learned all the three parts.[446] I took great delight
in blowing on this instrument, the evenings being long; and besides that I was fond of it, I did not like to be idle, and it filled
up my vacant hours innocently. At this time also I agreed with
the Rev. Mr. Gregory, who lived in the same court, where he
kept an academy and an evening school, to improve me in arithmetic. This he did as far as Barter and Aligation; so that all the
time I was here I was entirely employed.[447] In February 1768, I
hired myself to Dr. Charles Irving, in Pall-mall, so celebrated for
his successful experiments in making sea-water fresh; and here
I had plenty of hair-dressing to improve my hand. This gentleman
was an excellent master; he was exceedingly kind and good-
tempered; and allowed me in the evenings to attend my schools,
which I esteemed a great blessing; therefore I thank[448] God and
him for it, and used all diligence to improve the opportunity. This
diligence and attention recommended me to the notice and care
of my three preceptors, who, on their parts, bestowed a great deal
of pains in my instruction, and besides were all very kind to me.
My wages, however, which were by two-thirds less than ever I
had in my life (for I had only 12£. per ann.) I soon found would
not be sufficient to defray this extraordinary expence of masters,
and my own necessary expences; my old thirty-seven guineas had
by this time worn all away to one. I thought it best, therefore, to
try the sea again in quest of more money, as I had been bred to
it, and had hitherto found the profession of it successful. I had
also a very great desire to see Turkey, and I now determined to
gratify it. Accordingly, in the month of May, 1768, I told the
Doctor of my wish to go to sea again, to which he made no
opposition; and we parted on friendly terms. The same day I went
into the city in quest of a master.[449] I was extremely fortunate in
my enquiry; for I soon heard of a gentleman who had a ship going
to Italy and Turkey, and he wanted a man who could dress hair
well. I was overjoyed at this, and went immediately on board of
his ship, as I had been directed, which I found to be fitted up
with great taste, and I already foreboded no small pleasure in sail-

ing in her. Not finding the gentleman on board, I was directed to his lodgings, where I met with him the next day, and gave him a specimen of my dressing. He liked it so well that he hired me immediately, so that I was perfectly happy, for the ship, master, and voyage, were entirely to my mind. The ship was called the Delaware, and my master's name was John Jolly, a neat, smart, good-humoured man, just such a one as I wished to serve. We sailed from England in July following, and our voyage was extremely pleasant. We went to Villa Franca, Nice, and Leghorn; and in all these places I was charmed with the richness and beauty of the countries, and struck with the elegant buildings with which they abound. We had always in them plenty of extraordinary good wines and rich fruits, which I was very fond of; and I had frequent occasions of gratifying both my taste and curiosity; for my captain always lodged on shore in those places, which afforded me opportunities to see the country around. I also learned navigation of the mate, which I was very fond of. When we left Italy, we had delightful sailing among the Archipelago islands, and from thence to Smyrna in Turkey. This is a very ancient city; the houses are built of stone, and most of them have graves adjoining to them; so that they sometimes present the appearance of church-yards. Provisions are very plentiful in this city, and good wine less than a penny a pint. The grapes, pomegranates, and many other fruits, were also the richest and largest I ever saw or tasted. The natives are well-looking and strong made, and treated me always with great civility. In general I believe they are fond of black people;[450] and several of them gave me pressing invitations to stay amongst them, although they keep the Franks, or Christians,[451] separate, and do not suffer them to dwell immediately amongst them. I was astonished in not seeing women in any of their shops, and very rarely any in the streets; and whenever I did they were covered with a veil from head to foot, so that I could not see their faces, except when any of them, out of curiosity, uncovered them to look at me, which they sometimes did. I was surprised to see how the Greeks are, in some measure, kept under by the Turks, as the negroes are in the West-Indies by the white people. The less refined Greeks, as I have already hinted, dance here in the same manner as we do in our nation.

[452]On the whole, during our stay here, which was about five months, I liked the place and the Turks extremely well. I could not help observing one remarkable circumstance there; the tails of the sheep are flat, and so very large, that I have known the tail even of a lamb to weigh from eleven to thirteen pounds. The fat of them is very white and rich, and is excellent in puddings, for which it is much used. Our ship being at length richly loaded with silk and other articles, we sailed for England.

In May 1769, soon after our return from Turkey, our ship made a delightful voyage to Oporto, in Portugal, where we arrived at the time of the carnival. On our arrival, there were sent on board of us thirty-six articles to be observed, with very heavy penalties if we should break any of them; and none of us even dared to go on board any other vessel, or on shore, till the Inquisition had sent on board and searched for every thing illegal, especially bibles.[453] All we had were produced, and certain other things were sent on shore till the ships were going away; and any person, in whose custody a bible was found concealed, was to be imprisoned and flogged, and sent into slavery for ten years. I saw here many magnificent sights, particularly the garden of Eden,[454] where many of the clergy and laity went in procession in their several orders with the host, and sung Te Deum.[455] I had a great curiosity to go into some of their churches, but could not gain admittance without using the necessary sprinkling of holy water at my entrance. From curiosity, and a wish to be holy, I therefore complied with this ceremony, but its virtues were lost upon me, for I found myself nothing the better for it. This place abounds with plenty of all kinds of provisions. The town is well built and pretty, and commands a fine prospect. Our ship having taken in a load of wine, and other commodities, we sailed for London, and arrived there in July following.

[456]Our next voyage was to the Mediterranean. The ship was again got ready, and we sailed in September for Genoa. This is

one of the finest cities I ever saw; some of the edifices were of beautiful marble, and made a most noble appearance; and many had very curious fountains before them. The churches were rich and magnificent, and curiously adorned both in the inside and out. But all this grandeur was, in my eyes, disgraced by the galley-slaves, whose condition, both there and in other parts of Italy, is truly piteous and wretched.[457] After we had staid there some weeks, during which we bought many different things we wanted, and got them very cheap, we sailed to Naples, a charming city, and remarkably clean. The bay is the most beautiful I ever saw; the moles for shipping are excellent. I thought it extraordinary to see grand operas acted here on Sunday nights, and even attended by their Majesties.[458] I too, like these great ones, went to those sights, and vainly served God in the day while I thus served mammon effectually at night.[459] While we remained here, there happened an eruption of Mount Vesuvius, of which I had a perfect view. It was extremely awful; and we were so near that the ashes from it used to be thick on our deck. After we had transacted our business at Naples, we sailed with a fair wind once more for Smyrna, where we arrived in December. A seraskier, or officer, took a liking to me here, and wanted me to stay, and offered me two wives; however I refused the temptation, thinking one was as much as some could manage, and more than others would venture on.[460] The merchants here travel in caravans or large companies. I have seen many caravans from India, with some hundreds of camels, laden with different goods. The people of these caravans are quite brown. Among other articles, they brought with them a great quantity of locusts, which are a kind of pulse, sweet and pleasant to the palate, and in shape resembling French beans, but longer.[461] Each kind of goods is sold in a street by itself, and I always found the Turks very honest in their dealings. They let no Christians into their mosques, or churches, for which I was very sorry; as I was always fond of going to see the different modes of worship of the people wherever I went. The plague broke out while we were in Smyrna, and we stopped taking goods into the ship till it was over. She was then richly laden, and we sailed in about March 1770 for England. One day in our passage we met with an accident which was near burning the ship. A black cook, in melting some fat, overset the pan into the fire under the deck, which immediately began to blaze, and the flame went up very high under the foretop. With the fright, the poor cook became almost white, and altogether speechless. Happily, however, we got the fire out without doing much mischief. After various delays in this passage, which was tedious, we arrived in Standgate-creek in July;[462] and at the latter end of the year, some new event occurred, so that my noble captain, the ship, and I, all separated.

In April 1771, I shipped myself as a steward with Capt. William Robertson, of the ship Grenada Planter, once more to try my fortune in the West-Indies; and we sailed from London for Madeira, Barbadoes, and the Grenadas. When we were at this last place, having some goods to sell, I met once more with my former kind of West-India customers.

[463]A white man, an islander, bought some goods of me to the amount of some pounds, and made me many fair promises as usual, but without any intention of paying me. He had likewise bought goods from some more of our people, whom he intended to serve in the same manner; but he still amused us with promises. However, when our ship was loaded and near sailing, this honest buyer discovered[464] no intention or sign of paying for any thing he had bought of us; but, on the contrary, when I asked him for my money, he threatened me and another black man he had bought goods of, so that we found we were like to get more blows than payment. On this we went to complain to one Mr. M'Intosh, a justice of the peace; we told his worship of the man's villainous tricks, and begged that he would be kind enough to see us redressed: but being negroes, although free, we could not get any remedy; and our ship being then just upon the point of sailing, we knew not how to help ourselves, though we thought it hard to lose our property in this manner. Luckily for us, however, this man was also indebted to three white sailors, who could not get a farthing from him; they therefore readily joined us, and we all went together in search of him. When we found where he was,

we[465] took him out of a house and threatened him with vengeance; on which, finding he was likely to be handled roughly, the rogue offered each of us some small allowance, but nothing near our demands. This exasperated us much; and some were for cutting his ears off; but he begged hard for mercy, which was at last granted him, after we had entirely stripped him. We then let him go, for which he thanked us, glad to get off so easily, and ran into the bushes, after having wished us a good voyage. We then repaired on board, and shortly after set sail for England. I cannot help remarking here a very narrow escape we had from being blown up, owing to a piece of negligence of mine. Just as our ship was under sail, I went down under the cabin to do some business, and had a lighted candle in my hand, which, in my hurry, without thinking, I held in a barrel of gunpowder. It remained in the powder until it was near catching fire, when fortunately I observed it, and snatched it out in time and providentially no harm happened; but I was so overcome with terror, that I immediately fainted at the deliverance.

In twenty-eight days time we arrived in England, and I got clear of this ship. But, being still of a roving disposition, and desirous of seeing as many different parts of the world as I could, I shipped myself soon after, in the same year, as steward on board of a fine large ship, called the Jamaica, Captain David Watt; and we sailed from England in December 1771, for Nevis and Jamaica. I found Jamaica to be a very fine, large island, well peopled, and the most considerable of the West-India islands. There were a vast number of negroes here,[466] whom I found, as usual, exceedingly imposed upon by the white people, and the slaves punished as in the other islands. There are negroes whose business it is to flog slaves; they go about to different people for employment, and the usual pay is from one to four bits. I saw many cruel punishments inflicted on the slaves in the short time I staid here. In particular I was present when a poor fellow was tied up and kept hanging by the wrists at some distance from the ground, and then some half hundred weights were fixed to his ancles, in which posture he was flogged most unmercifully. There were also, as I heard, two different masters noted for cruelty on the island, who had staked up two negroes naked, and in two hours the vermin stung them to death. I heard a gentleman, I well knew, tell my captain, that he passed sentence on a negro man to be burnt alive for attempting to poison an overseer. I pass over numerous instances, in order to relieve the reader by a milder scene of roguery. Before I had been long on the island, one Mr. Smith, at Port Morant, bought goods of me to the amount of twenty-five pounds sterling; but when I demanded payment from him, he was each time going to beat me, and threatened that he would put me in gaol. One time he would say I was going to set his house on fire; at another he would swear I was going to run away with his slaves. I was astonished at this usage from a person who was in the situation of a gentleman,[467] but I had no alternative, and was therefore obliged to submit. When I came to Kingston, I was surprised to see the number of Africans, who were assembled together on Sundays; particularly at a large commodious place called Spring Path. Here each different nation of Africa meet and dance, after the manner of their own country. They still retain most of their native customs: they bury their dead, and put victuals, pipes, and tobacco, and other things in the grave with the corpse, in the same manner as in Africa. Our ship having got her loading, we sailed for London, where we arrived in the August following. On my return to London, I waited on my old and good master, Dr. Irving, who made me an offer of his service again. Being now tired of the sea, I gladly accepted it. I was very happy in living with this gentleman once more; during which time we were daily employed in reducing old Neptune's dominions by purifying the briny element, and making it fresh.[468] Thus I went on till May 1773, when I was roused by the sound of fame to seek new adventures, and to find, towards the North Pole, what our Creator never intended we should, a passage to India. An expedition was now fitting out to explore a north-east passage, conducted by the Honourable Constantine John Phipps, late[469] Lord Mulgrave, in his Majesty's sloop of war the Race Horse.[470] My master being anxious for the reputation of this adventure, we therefore prepared

every thing for our voyage, and I attended him on board the Race
Horse, the 24th day of May 1773. We proceeded to Sheerness,
where we were joined by his Majesty's sloop the Carcass, commanded by Capt. Lutwidge.[471] On the 4th of June we sailed towards our destined place, the pole; and on the 15th of the same
month we were off Shetland. On this day I had a great and unexpected deliverance from an accident which was near blowing
up the ship and destroying the crew, which made me ever after
during the voyage uncommonly cautious. The ship was so filled
that there was very little room on board for any one, which placed
me in a very awkward situation. I had resolved to keep a journal
of this singular and interesting voyage; and I had no other place
for this purpose but a little cabin, or the doctor's store-room,
where I slept. This little place was stuffed with all manner of
combustibles, particularly with tow and aquafortis, and many
other dangerous things.[472] It happened[473] in the evening, as I was
writing my journal, that I had occasion to take the candle out of
the lanthorn, and a spark unfortunately[474] having touched a single
thread of the tow, all the rest caught the flame, and immediately
the whole was in a blaze. I saw nothing but present death before
me, and expected to be the first to perish in the flames. In a
moment the alarm was spread, and many people who were near
ran to assist in putting out the fire. All this time I was in the very
midst of the flames; my shirt, and the handkerchief on my neck,
were burnt, and I was almost smothered with the smoke. However, through God's mercy, as I was nearly giving up all hopes,
some people brought blankets and mattresses, and threw them on
the flames, by which means, in a short time, the fire was put out.
I was severely reprimanded and menaced by such of the officers
who knew it, and strictly charged never more to go there with a
light; and, indeed, even my own fears made me give heed to this
command for a little time; but at last, not being able to write my
journal in any other part of the ship, I was tempted again to
venture by stealth with a light in the same cabin, though not
without considerable fear and dread on my mind. On the 20th of
June we began to use Dr. Irving's apparatus for making salt water

fresh; I used to attend the distillery; I frequently purified from twenty-six to forty gallons a day.[475] The water thus distilled was perfectly pure, well tasted, and free from salt; and was used on various occasions on board the ship. On the 28th of June, being in lat[itude]. 78, we made Greenland, where I was surprised to see the sun did not set. The weather now became extremely cold; and as we sailed between north and east, which was our course, we saw many very high and curious mountains of ice; and also a great number of very large whales, which used to come close to our ship, and blow the water up to a very great height in the air. One morning we had vast quantities of sea-horses about the ship, which neighed exactly like any other horses.[476] We fired some harpoon guns amongst them in order to take some, but we could not get any. The 30th, the captain of a Greenland ship came on board, and told us of three ships that were lost in the ice; however we still held on our course till July the 11th, when we were stopt by one compact impenetrable body of ice.[477] We ran along it from east to west above ten degrees; and on the 27th we got as far north as 80, 37; and in 19 or 20 degrees east longitude from London. On the 29th and 30th of July we saw one continued plain of smooth unbroken ice, bounded only by the horizon, and we fastened to a piece of ice that was eight yards eleven inches thick. We had generally sunshine, and constant day-light; which gave cheerfulness and novelty to the whole of this striking, grand, and uncommon scene;[478] and, to heighten it still more, the reflection of the sun from the ice gave the clouds a most beautiful appearance. We killed many different animals at this time, and, among the rest, nine bears. Though they had nothing in their paunches but water yet they were all very fat. We used to decoy them to the ship sometimes by burning feathers or skins. I thought them coarse eating, but some of the ship's company relished them very much. Some of our people once, in a boat, fired at and wounded a sea-horse, which dived immediately; and in a little time after brought up with it a number of others. They all joined in an attack upon the boat, and were with difficulty prevented from staving or oversetting her; but a boat from the Carcass having come to assist ours, & joined it, they dispersed,[479] after having wrested an oar from one of the men. One of the ship's boats had before been attacked in the same manner, but happily no harm was done. Though we wounded several of these animals we never got but one. We remained hereabouts until the 1st of August; when the two ships got completely fastened in the ice, occasioned by the loose ice that set in from the sea. This made our situation very dreadful and alarming; so that on the 7th day we were in very great apprehension of having the ships squeezed to pieces. The officers now held a council to know what was best for us to do in order to save our lives; and it was determined that we should endeavour to escape by dragging our boats along the ice towards the sea; which, however, was farther off than any of us thought. This determination filled us with extreme dejection, and confounded us with despair; for we had very little prospect of escaping with life. However, we sawed some of the ice about the ships, to keep it from hurting them; and thus kept them in a kind of pond. We then began to drag the boats as well as we could towards the sea; but, after two or three days labour, we made very little progress; so that some of our hearts totally failed us, and I really began to give up myself for lost, when I saw our surrounding calamities. While we were at this hard labour I once fell into a pond we had made amongst some loose ice, and was very near being drowned; but providentially some people were near, who gave me immediate assistance, and thereby I escaped drowning. Our deplorable condition, which kept up the constant apprehension of our perishing in the ice, brought me gradually to think of eternity in such a manner as I never had done before. I had the fears of death hourly upon me, and shuddered at the thoughts of meeting the grim king of terrors in the *natural* state I then was in, and was exceedingly doubtful of a happy eternity if I should die in it.[480] I had no hopes of my life being prolonged for any time; for we saw that our existence could not be long on the ice after leaving the ships, which were now out of sight, and some miles from the boats. Our appearance now became truly lamentable; pale dejection seized every countenance; many, who had been before blasphemers, in this our distress began to call on the good God of heaven for his help; and in the time of our utter need he heard us, and against hope, or human probability, delivered us! It was the eleventh day of the ships being thus fastened, and the fourth of our drawing the boats in this manner, that the wind changed to the E. N. E.[481] The weather immediately became mild and the ice broke towards the sea, which was to the S. W.[482] of us. Many of us on this got on board again, and with all our might we hove the ships into every open water we could find, and made all the sail on them in our power: now, having a prospect of success,[483] we made signals for the boats and the remainder of the people. This seemed to us like a reprieve from death; and happy was the man who could first get on board of any ship, or the first boat he could meet. We then proceeded in this manner till we got into the open water again, which we accomplished in about thirty hours, to our infinite joy and gladness of heart. As soon as we were out of danger, we came to anchor and refitted; and on the 19th of August we sailed from this uninhabited extremity of the world, where the inhospitable climate affords neither food nor shelter, and not a tree or shrub of any kind grows amongst its barren rocks, but all is one desolate and expanded waste of ice, which even the constant beams of the sun, for six months in the year, cannot penetrate or dissolve. The sun now being on the decline, the days shortened as we sailed to the southward; and, on the 28th, in latitude 73, it was dark by ten o'clock at night. September the 10th, in latitude 58–59, we met a very severe gale of wind and high seas, and shipped a great deal of water in the space of ten hours. This made us work exceedingly hard at all our pumps a whole day; and one sea, which struck the ship with more force than any thing I ever met with of the kind before, laid her under water for some time, so that we thought she would have gone down. Two boats were washed from the booms, and the long-boat from the chucks;[484] all other moveable things on the deck were also washed away, among which were many curious things of different kinds, which we had brought from Greenland; and we were obliged, in order to lighten the ship, to toss some of our guns overboard. We saw a ship at the same time in very great distress, and her masts were gone; but we were unable to assist her. We now lost sight of the Carcass till the 26th, when we saw land about Orfordness,[485] off which place she joined us. From thence we sailed for London, and on the 30th came up to Deptford. And thus ended our Arctic voyage, to the no small joy of all on board, after having been absent four months; in which time, at the imminent hazard of our lives, we explored nearly as far towards the Pole as 81 degrees north, and 20 degrees east longitude; being much farther, by all accounts, than any navigator had ever ventured before; in which we fully proved the impracticability of finding a passage that way to India.[486]

The Author leaves Dr. Irving, and engages on board a Turkey ship—Account of a black man's being kidnapped on board, and sent to the West Indies, and the Author's fruitless endeavours to procure his freedom—Some account of the manner of the Author's conversion to the Faith of Jesus Christ.

OUR voyage to the North Pole being ended, I returned to London with Dr. Irving, with whom I continued for some time, during which I began seriously to reflect on the dangers I had escaped, particularly those of my last voyage, which made a lasting impression on my mind, and, by the grace of God, proved afterwards a mercy to me: it caused me to reflect deeply on my eternal state, and to seek the Lord with full purpose of heart ere it be too late.[487] I rejoiced greatly; and heartily thanked the Lord for directing me to London, where I was determined to work out my own salvation, and, in so doing, procure a title to heaven; being the result of a mind blinded by ignorance and sin.

In process of time I left my master, Doctor Irving, the purifier of waters. I lodged in Coventry-court, Haymarket, where I was continually oppressed and much concerned about the salvation of my soul, and was determined (in my own strength) to be a first-rate Christian.[488] I used every means for this purpose; and, not being able to find any person amongst those with whom I was then acquainted that acquiesced with me[489] in point of religion, or, in scripture language, that would shew me any good, I was much dejected, and knew not where to seek relief; however, I first frequented the neighbouring churches, St. James's and others, two or three times a day, for many weeks: still I came away dissatisfied: something was wanting that I could not obtain, and I really found more heart-felt relief in reading my bible at home than in attending the church; and, being resolved to be saved, I pursued other methods.[490] First I went among the people called

Quakers, whose meeting at times was held in silence, and I remained as much in the dark as ever.[491] I then searched into the Roman Catholic principles, but was not in the least edified.[492] I, at length,[493] had recourse to the Jews, which availed me nothing, as the fear of eternity daily harassed my mind and I knew not where to seek shelter from the wrath to come.[494] However, this was my conclusion, at all events, to read the Four Evangelists,[495] and whatever sect or party I found adhering thereto, such I would join. Thus I went on heavily without any guide to direct me the way that leadeth to eternal life. I asked different people questions about the manner of going to heaven, and was told different ways. Here I was much staggered, and could not find any at that time more righteous than myself, or indeed so much inclined to devotion. I thought we should not all be saved (this is agreeable to the holy scriptures), nor would all be damned. I found none among the circle of my acquaintance that kept holy the Ten Commandments. So righteous was I in my own eyes, that I was convinced I excelled many of them in that point, by keeping eight out of ten; and finding those, who in general termed themselves Christians, not so honest or so good in their morals as the Turks.[496] I really thought the Turks were in a safer way of salvation than my neighbours; so that between hopes and fears I went on, and the chief comforts I enjoyed were in the musical French-horn, which I then practised, and also dressing of hair. Such was my situation some months, experiencing the dishonesty of many people here. I determined at last to set out for Turkey, and there to end my days. It was now early in the spring 1774. I sought for a master, and found a Captain John Hughes, commander of a ship called Anglicania, fitting out in the river Thames, and bound to Smyrna in Turkey. I shipped myself with him as a steward; at the same time I recommended to him a very clever black man, John Annis, as a cook. This man was on board the ship near two months doing his duty; he had formerly lived many years with Mr. William Kirkpatrick, a gentleman of the island of St. Kitt's, from whom he parted by consent, though he afterwards tried many schemes to inveigle the poor man. He had applied to many

captains, who traded to St. Kitt's, to trepan him; and when all
their attempts and schemes of kidnapping proved abortive, Mr.
Kirkpatrick came to our ship at Union-stairs,[497] on Easter Monday, April the 4th,[498] with two wherry-boats and six men, having
learned that the man was on board; and tied, and forcibly took
him away from the ship, in the presence of the crew and the chief
mate, who had detained him after he had information to come
away.[499] I believe this was a combined piece of business;[500] but,
be that as it may, it certainly reflected great disgrace on the mate,
and captain also, who, although they had desired the oppressed
man to stay on board, yet notwithstanding this vile act on the
man who had served him, he did not in the least assist to recover
him, or pay me a farthing of his wages, which was about five
pounds. I proved the only friend he had, who attempted to regain
him his liberty, if possible, having known the want of liberty
myself. I sent, as soon as I could, to Gravesend, and got knowledge
of the ship in which he was; but unluckily she had sailed the first
tide after he was put on board. My intention was then immediately to apprehend Mr. Kirkpatrick, who was about setting off for
Scotland; and having obtained a *habeas corpus* for him,[501] and got
a tipstaff[502] to go with me to St. Paul's Church yard, where he
lived; he, suspecting something of this kind, set a watch to look
out. My being known to them obliged me to use the following
deception: I whitened my face, that they might not know me,
and this had the desired effect. He did not go out of his house
that night, and next morning I contrived a well-plotted stratagem,
notwithstanding he had a gentleman in his house to personate
him. My direction to the tipstaff had the desired effect; he got
admittance into the house, and conducted him to a judge, according to the writ. When he came there, his plea was, that he
had not the body in custody, on which he was admitted to bail.
I proceeded immediately to that well-known philanthropist,
Granville Sharp, Esq. who received me with the utmost kindness,
and gave me every instruction that was needful on the occasion.[503]
I left him in full hopes that I should gain the unhappy man his
liberty, with the warmest sense of gratitude towards Mr. Sharp for

his kindness. But, alas! my attorney proved unfaithful; he took my money, lost me many months employ, and did not the least good in the cause; and when the poor man arrived at St. Kitt's, he was, according to custom, staked to the ground with four pins through a cord, two on his wrists, and two on his ancles, was cut and flogged most unmercifully, and afterwards loaded cruelly with irons about his neck. I had two very moving letters from him while he was in this situation; and I made attempts to go after him at a great hazard, but was sadly disappointed: I also was told[504] of it by some very respectable families, now in London, who saw him in St. Kitt's, in the same state, in which he remained till kind death released him out of the hands of his tyrants.[505] During this disagreeable business, I was under strong convictions of sin, and thought that my state was worse than any man's; my mind was unaccountably disturbed; I often wished for death, though, at the same time, convinced I was altogether unprepared for that awful summons: suffering much by villains in the late cause, and being much concerned about the state of my soul, these things (but particularly the latter) brought me very low; so that I became a burden to myself, and viewed all things around me as emptiness and vanity, which could give no satisfaction to a troubled conscience. I was again determined to go to Turkey, and resolved, at that time, never more to return to England. I engaged as steward on board a Turkeyman (the Wester Hall, Capt. Lina), but was prevented by means of my late captain, Mr. Hughes, and others. All this appeared to be against me, and the only comfort I then experienced was in reading the Holy Scriptures, where I saw that "there is no new thing under the sun," Eccles.[iastes] i. 9. and what was appointed for me I must submit to. Thus I continued to travel in much heaviness, and frequently murmured against the Almighty, particularly in his providential dealings; and, awful to think! I began to blaspheme, and wished often to be any thing but a human being. In these severe conflicts the Lord answered me by awful "visions of the night, when deep sleep falleth upon men, in slumberings upon the bed," Job xxxiii. 15. He was pleased, in much mercy, to give me to see, and in some measure understand, the great and awful scene of the Judgment-day, that "no unclean person, no unholy thing, can enter into the kingdom of God," Eph[esians]. v. 5. I would then, if it had been possible, have changed my nature with the meanest worm on the earth, and was ready to say to the mountains and rocks, "fall on me," Rev[elation]. vi. 16. but all in vain. I then, in the greatest agony, requested the divine Creator, that he would grant me a small space of time to repent of my follies and vile iniquities, which I felt were grievous.[506] The Lord, in his manifold mercies, was pleased to grant my request, and being yet in a state of time, the sense of God's mercies was so great on my mind when I awoke, that my strength entirely failed me for many minutes, and I was exceedingly weak. This was the first spiritual mercy I ever was sensible of, and being on praying ground, as soon as I recovered a little strength, and got out of bed and dressed myself I invoked heaven from my inmost soul, and fervently begged that God would never again permit me to blaspheme his most holy name. The Lord, who is long-suffering, and full of compassion to such poor rebels as we are, condescended to hear and answer. I felt that I was altogether unholy, and saw clearly what a bad use I had made of the faculties I was endowed with: they were given me to glorify God with; I thought, therefore, I had better want them here, and enter into life eternal, than abuse them and be cast into hell fire. I prayed to be directed, if there were any holier persons than those with whom I was acquainted, that the Lord would point them out to me. I appealed to the searcher of hearts, whether I did not wish to love him more, and serve him better. Notwithstanding all this, the reader may easily discern, if a believer, that I was still in nature's darkness. At length I hated the house in which I lodged, because God's most holy name was blasphemed in it; then I saw the word of God verified, viz. "Before they call, I will answer; and while they are yet speaking, I will hear."[507]

I had a great desire to read the Bible the whole day at home; but not having a convenient place for retirement, I left the house in the day, rather than stay amongst the wicked ones; and that day, as I was walking, it pleased God to direct me to a house where there was an old sea-faring man, who experienced much of the love of God shed abroad in his heart. He began to discourse with me; and, as I desired to love the Lord, his conversation rejoiced me greatly; and indeed I had never heard before the love of Christ to believers set forth in such a manner, and in so clear a point of view. Here I had more questions to put to the man than his time would permit him to answer: and in that memorable hour there came in a Dissenting Minister;[508] he joined our discourse, and asked me some few questions; among others, where I heard the gospel preached? I knew not what he meant by hearing the gospel; I told him I had read the gospel: and he asked me where I went to church, or whether I went at all, or not? To which I replied, "I attended St. James's, St. Martin's, and St. Ann's, Soho."—"So," said he, "you are a churchman?" I answered, I was.[509] He then invited me to a love feast at his chapel that evening.[510] I accepted the offer, and thanked him; and soon after he went away. I had some further discourse with the old Christian, added to some profitable reading, which made me exceedingly happy. When I left him he reminded me of coming to the feast; I assured him I would be there. Thus we parted, and I weighed over the heavenly conversation that had passed between these two men, which cheered my then heavy and drooping spirit more than any thing I had met with for many months. However, I thought the time long in going to my supposed banquet. I also wished much for the company of these friendly men; their company pleased me much; and I thought the gentleman very kind in asking me, a stranger, to a feast; but how singular did it appear to me, to have it in a chapel! When the wished for hour came I went, and happily the old man was there, who kindly seated me, as he belonged to the place. I was much astonished to see the place filled with people, and no signs of eating and drinking. There were many ministers in the company. At last they began by giving out hymns, and between the singing, the ministers engaged in prayer: in short, I knew not what to make of this sight, having never seen any thing of the kind in my life before now. Some of the guests began to speak their experience, agreeable to what I read in the Scriptures: much was said by every speaker of the providence of God, and his unspeakable mercies to each of them. This I knew in a great measure, and could most heartily join them. But when they spoke of a future state, they seemed to be altogether certain of their calling and election of God;[511] and that no one could ever separate them from the love of Christ, or pluck them out of his hands. This filled me with utter consternation, intermingled with admiration. I was so amazed as not to know what to think of the company; my heart was attracted, and my affections were enlarged; I wished to be as happy as them, and was persuaded in my mind that they were different from the world "that lieth in wickedness," 1 John v. 19. Their language and singing, &c. did well harmonize; I was entirely overcome, and wished to live and die thus. Lastly, some persons produced some neat baskets full of buns, which they distributed about; and each person communicated with his neighbour, and sipped water out of different mugs, which they handed about to all who were present. This kind of Christian fellowship I had never seen, nor ever thought of seeing on earth; it fully reminded me of what I had read in the Holy Scriptures of the primitive Christians,[512] who loved each other and broke bread, in partaking of it, even from house to house. This entertainment (which lasted about four hours) ended in singing and prayer. It was the first soul-feast I ever was present at. These last twenty-four hours produced me things, spiritual and temporal, sleeping and waking, judgment and mercy, that I could not but admire the goodness of God, in directing the blind, blasphemous sinner in the path that he knew not of, even among the just; and instead of judgment he has shewed mercy, and will hear and answer the prayers and supplications of every returning prodigal;

> O! to grace how great a debtor
> Daily I'm constrain'd to be.[513]

After this I was resolved to win heaven, if possible; and if I perished, I thought it should be at the feet of Jesus, in praying to him for salvation. After having been an eye-witness to some of the happiness which attended those who feared God, I knew not how, with any propriety, to return to my lodgings, where the name of God was continually profaned, at which I felt the greatest horror; I paused in my mind for some time, not knowing what to do; whether to hire a bed elsewhere, or go home again. At last, fearing an evil report might arise, I went home, with a farewell to card-playing and vain-jesting, &c. I saw that time was very short, eternity long, and very near; and I viewed those persons alone blessed, who were found ready at midnight-call, or when the Judge of all, both quick[514] and dead, cometh.

The next day I took courage, and went to Holborn, to see my new and worthy acquaintance, the old man, Mr. C——; he, with his wife, a gracious woman, were at work at silk-weaving; they seemed mutually happy, and both quite glad to see me, and I more to see them. I sat down, and we conversed much about soul matters, &c. Their discourse was amazingly delightful, edifying, and pleasant. I knew not at last how to leave this agreeable pair, till time summoned me away. As I was departing, they lent me a little book, entitled "The Conversion of an Indian."[515] It was in questions and answers. The poor man came over the sea to London, to enquire after the Christian's God, who (through rich mercy) he found, and had not his journey in vain. The above book was of great use to me, and at that time was a means of strengthening my faith; however, in parting, they both invited me to call on them when I pleased. This delighted me, and I took care to make all the improvement from it I could: and so far I thanked God for such company and desires. I prayed that the many evils I felt within might be done away, and that I might be weaned from my former carnal acquaintances. This was quickly heard and answered, and I was soon connected with those whom the Scripture calls the excellent of the earth. I heard the gospel preached, and the thoughts of my heart and actions were laid open by the preachers, and the way of salvation by Christ alone was evidently set forth. Thus I went on happily for near two months; and I once heard, during this period, a reverend gentleman, Mr.

Green, speak of a man who had departed this life in full assurance of his going to glory.[516] I was much astonished at the assertion; and did very deliberately inquire how he could get at this knowledge. I was answered fully, agreeably[517] to what I read in the oracles of truth; and was told also, that if I did not experience the new birth, and the pardon of my sins, thro' the blood of Christ, before I died, I could not enter the kingdom of heaven. I knew not what to think of this report, as I thought I kept eight commandments out of ten; then my worthy interpreter told me I did not do it, nor could I; and he added, that no man ever did or could keep the commandments, without offending in one point. I thought this sounded very strange, and puzzled me much for many weeks; for I thought it a hard saying. I then asked my friend Mr. L——d, who was clerk in a chapel, why the commandments of God were given, if we could not be saved by them? To which he replied, "The law is a school-master to bring us to Christ," who alone could, and did keep the commandments, and fulfilled all their requirements for his elect people, even those to whom he had given a living faith, and the sins of those chosen vessels *were already* atoned for and forgiven them whilst living;[518] and if I did not experience the same before my exit, the Lord would say at that great day to me, "Go, ye cursed," &c. &c. for God would appear faithful in his judgments to the wicked, as he would be faithful in shewing mercy to those who were ordained to it before the world was; therefore Christ Jesus seemed to be all in all to that man's soul. I was much wounded at this discourse, and brought into such a dilemma as I never expected. I asked him, if *he* was to die that moment, whether he was sure to enter the kingdom of God; and added, "Do you *know* that your sins are forgiven you?" he answered in the affirmative. Then confusion, anger, and discontent seized me, and I staggered much at this sort of doctrine; it brought me to a stand, not knowing which to believe, whether salvation by works, or by faith only in Christ. I requested him to tell me how I might know when my sins were forgiven me. He assured me he could not, and that none but God alone could do this. I told him it was very mysterious; but he said it was really matter of fact, and quoted many portions of Scripture immediately to the point, to which I could make no reply. He then desired me to pray to God to shew me these things. I answered that I prayed to God every day. He said, "I perceive you are a churchman." I answered, I was. He then entreated me to beg of God, to shew me what I was, and the true state of my soul. I thought the prayer very short and odd; so we parted for that time. I weighed all these things over, and could not help thinking how it was possible for a man to know his sins were forgiven him in this life. I wished that God would reveal this self-same thing to me. In a short time after this, I went to Westminster chapel; the late Rev. Dr. Peckwell preached from Lam[entations]. iii 39.[519] It was a wonderful sermon; he clearly shewed that a living man had no cause to complain for the punishments of his sins; he evidently justified the Lord in all his dealings with the sons of men; he also shewed the justice of God in the eternal punishment of the wicked and impenitent. The discourse seemed to me like a two-edged sword cutting all ways; it afforded me[520] much joy, intermingled with many fears about my soul; and when it was ended, he gave it out that he intended, the ensuing week, to examine all those who meant to attend the Lord's table. Now I thought much of my good works, and, at the same time, was doubtful of my being a proper object to receive the sacrament: I was full of meditation till the day of examining. However, I went to the chapel, and, though much distressed, I addressed the reverend gentleman, thinking, if I was not right, he would endeavour to convince me of it. When I conversed with him, the first thing he asked me was, What I knew of Christ? I told him I believed in him, and had been baptized in his name. "Then," said he, "when were you brought to the knowledge of God; and how were you convinced of sin?" I knew not what he meant by these questions; I told him I kept eight commandments out of ten; but that I sometimes swore on board of ship, and sometimes when on shore, and broke the sabbath. He then asked me if I could read; I answered, "Yes."—"Then," said he, "do you read in the Bible, he that offends in one point is guilty of all?"[521] I said, "Yes."

Then he assured me, that one sin unattoned for was as sufficient
to damn a soul, as one leak was to sink a ship. Here I was struck
with awe; for the minister exhorted me much, and reminded me
of the shortness of time, and the length of eternity, and that no
unregenerate soul, or any thing unclean, could enter the kingdom
of Heaven.

[522]He did not admit me as a communicant;[523] but recommended
me to read the scriptures, and hear the word preached; not to
neglect fervent prayer to God, who has promised to hear the
supplications of those who seek him in godly sincerity; so I took
my leave of him, with many thanks, and resolved to follow his
advice, so far as the Lord would condescend to enable me. During
this time I was out of employ, nor was likely to get a situation
suitable for me, which obliged me to go once more to sea. I
engaged as steward of a ship called the Hope, Captain Richard
Strange, bound from London to Cadiz in Spain. In a short time
after I was on board, I heard the name of God much blasphemed,
and I feared greatly lest I should catch the horrible infection. I
thought if I sinned again, after having life and death set evidently
before me, I should certainly go to hell. My mind was uncommonly chagrined, and I murmured much at God's providential
dealings with me, and was discontented with the commandments,
that I could not be saved by what I had done; I hated all things,
and wished I had never been born; confusion seized me, and I
wished to be annihilated. One day I was standing on the very
edge of the stern of the ship, thinking to drown myself; but this
scripture was instantaneously impressed on my mind, "That no
murderer hath eternal life abiding in him," I John iii. 15. Then I
paused, and thought myself the unhappiest man living. Again, I
was convinced that the Lord was better to me than I deserved,
and I was better off in the world than many. After this I began
to fear death; I fretted, mourned, and prayed, till I became a
burden to others, but more so to myself. At length I concluded
to beg my bread on shore, rather than go again to sea amongst a
people who feared not God, and I entreated the captain three
different times to discharge me; he would not, but each time gave

me greater encouragement to continue with him, and all on board shewed me very great civility: notwithstanding all this, I was unwilling to embark again. At last some of my religious friends advised me, by saying it was my lawful calling, consequently it was my duty to obey, and that God was not confined to place, &c. particularly Mr. G. Smith,[524] the governor of Tothill-fields, Bridewell, who pitied my case, and read the eleventh chapter of the Hebrews to me, with exhortations. He prayed for me, and I believe that he prevailed on my behalf, as my burden was then greatly removed, and I found a heartfelt resignation to the will of God. The good man gave me a pocket Bible, and Alleine's Alarm to the Unconverted.[525] We parted, and the next day I went on board again. We sailed for Spain, and I found favour with the captain. It was the fourth of the month of September when we sailed from London, and we had a delightful voyage to Cadiz, where we arrived the twenty-third of the same month. The place is strong, commands a fine prospect, and is very rich. The Spanish galleons frequent that port, and some arrived whilst we were there. I had many opportunities of reading the Scriptures. I wrestled hard with God in fervent prayers, who had declared in his word that he would hear the groanings and deep sighs of the poor in spirit. I found this verified to my utter astonishment and comfort in the following manner:[526] On the morning of the 6th of October (I pray you to attend) all that day,[527] I thought I should see or hear something supernatural. I had a secret impulse on my mind of something that was to take place,[528] which drove me continually for that time to a throne of grace. It pleased God to enable me to wrestle with him, as Jacob did: I prayed that if sudden death were to happen, and I perished, it might be at Christ's feet.

In the evening of the same day, as I was reading and meditating on the fourth chapter of the Acts, twelfth verse,[529] under the solemn apprehensions of eternity, and reflecting on my past actions, I began to think I had lived a moral life, and that I had a proper ground to believe I had an interest in the divine favour; but still meditating on the subject, not knowing whether salvation was to be had partly for our own good deeds, or solely as the sovereign gift of God:—in this deep consternation the Lord was pleased to break in upon my soul with his bright beams of heavenly light; and in an instant, as it were, removing the veil, and letting light into a dark place, Isa[iah]. xxv. 7.[530] I saw clearly, with the eye of faith, the crucified Saviour bleeding on the cross on Mount Calvary: the Scriptures became an unsealed book, I saw myself a condemned criminal under the law, which came with its full force to my conscience, and when "the commandment came sin revived, and I died."[531] I saw the Lord Jesus Christ in his humiliation, loaded and bearing my reproach, sin, and shame. I then clearly perceived, that by the deed of the law no flesh living could be justified. I was then convinced, that by the first Adam sin came, and by the second Adam (the Lord Jesus Christ) all that are saved must be made alive. It was given me at that time to know what it was to be born again, John iii. 5.[532] I saw the eighth chapter to the Romans, and the doctrines of God's decrees verified, agreeable to his eternal, everlasting and unchangeable purposes. The word of God was sweet to my taste, yea sweeter than honey and the honey comb. Christ was revealed to my soul as the chiefest among ten thousand. These heavenly moments were really as life to the dead, and what John calls an earnest of the Spirit.[533] This was indeed unspeakable, and, I firmly believe, undeniable by many. Now every leading providential circumstance that happened to me, from the day I was taken from my parents to that hour, was then, in my view, as if it had but just then occurred. I was sensible of the invisible hand of God, which guided and protected me, when in truth I knew it not: still the Lord pursued me although I slighted and disregarded it; this mercy melted me down. When I considered my poor wretched state, I wept, seeing what a great debtor I was to sovereign free grace.[534] Now the Ethiopian was willing to be saved by Jesus Christ,[535] the sinner's only surety, and also to rely on none other person or thing for salvation. Self was obnoxious, and good works he had none; for it is God that worketh in us both to will and to do. Oh! the amazing things of that hour can never be told—it was joy in the Holy Ghost! I felt an astonishing change; the burden of sin, the gaping jaws of hell, and the fears of death, that weighed me down before, now lost their horror; indeed I thought death would now be the best earthly friend I ever had. Such were my grief and joy, as, I believe, are seldom experienced. I was bathed in tears, and said, What am I, that God should thus look on me, the vilest of sinners? I felt a deep concern for my mother and friends, which occasioned me to pray with fresh ardour; and, in the abyss of thought, I viewed the unconverted people of the world in a very awful state, being without God and without hope.

It pleased God to pour out on me the spirit of prayer and the grace of supplication, so that in loud acclamations I was enabled to praise and glorify his most holy name. When I got out of the cabin, and told some of the people what the Lord had done for me, alas! who could understand me or believe my report! None but to whom the arm of the Lord was revealed. I became a barbarian to them in talking of the love of Christ: his name was to me as ointment poured forth; indeed it was sweet to my soul, but to them a rock of offence. I thought my case singular, and every hour a day until I came to London, for I much longed to be with some to whom I could tell of the wonders of God's love towards me, and join in prayer to him whom my soul loved and thirsted after. I had uncommon commotions within, such as few can tell aught[536] about. Now the Bible was my only companion and comfort; I prized it much, with many thanks to God that I could read it for myself, and was not left to be tossed about or led by man's devices and notions. The worth of a soul cannot be told.—May the Lord give the reader an understanding in this. Whenever I looked in the Bible I saw things new, and many texts were immediately applied to me with great comfort; for I knew that to me was the word of salvation sent. Sure I was that the Spirit which indited the word opened my heart to receive the truth of it as it is in Jesus—that the same Spirit enabled me to act with faith upon the promises which were precious to me, and enabled me to believe to the salvation of my soul. By free grace I was persuaded that I had a part and lot in the first resurrection,[537] and was en-

lightened with the "light of the living," Job xxxiii. 30. I wished
for a man of God, with whom I might converse; my soul was
like the chariots of Aminadab, Canticles vi. 12. These, among
others, were the precious promises that were so powerfully applied
to me: "All things whatsoever ye shall ask in prayer, believing, ye
shall receive," Matt[hew]. xxi. 22. "Peace I leave with you, my
peace I give unto you," John xiv. 27. I saw the blessed Redeemer
to be the fountain of life, and the well of salvation. I experienced
him to be all in all; he had brought me by a way that I knew
not, and he had made crooked paths straight. Then in his name
I set up his Ebenezer,[538] saying, Hitherto He hath helped me: and
could say to the sinners about me, Behold what a Saviour I have!
Thus I was, by the teaching of that all glorious Deity, the great
One in Three, and Three in One, confirmed in the truths of the
Bible; those oracles of everlasting truth, on which every soul living
must stand or fall eternally, agreeably to Acts iv. 12. "Neither is
there salvation in any other, for there is no other name under
heaven given among men whereby we must be saved, but only
Jesus Christ." May God give the reader a right understanding in
these facts! "To him that believeth, all things are possible, but to
them that are unbelieving, nothing is pure," Titus i. 15.

[539]During this period we remained at Cadiz until our ship got
laden. We sailed about the 4th[540] of November; and, having a
good passage, we arrived in London the month following, to my
comfort, with heart-felt gratitude to God, for his rich and unspeakable mercies.

[541]On my return, I had but one text which puzzled me, or that
the devil endeavoured to buffet me with, viz. Rom[ans]. xi. 6.[542]
and as I had heard of the Rev. Mr. Romaine, and his great knowledge in the Scriptures, I wished much to hear him preach. One
day I went to Blackfriars church, and, to my great satisfaction and
surprise, he preached from that very text. He very clearly shewed
the difference between human works and free election, which is
according to God's sovereign will and pleasure.[543] These glad tid-
ings set me entirely at liberty, and I went out of the church rejoicing, seeing my spots[544] were those of God's children. I went

to Westminster chapel,[545] and saw some of my old friends, who were glad when they perceived the wonderful change that the Lord had wrought in me, particularly Mr. G. Smith,[546] my worthy acquaintance, who was a man of a choice spirit, and had great zeal for the Lord's service. I enjoyed his correspondence till he died in the year 1784. I was again examined in that same chapel, and was received into church-fellowship amongst them: I rejoiced in spirit, making melody in my heart to the God of all my mercies. Now my whole wish was to be dissolved, and to be with Christ— but, alas! I must wait my appointed time.

Miscellaneous Verses;
Or,
Reflections on the State of my Mind during my first Convictions of the Necessity of believing the Truth, and of
experiencing the inestimable Benefits of Christianity.

WELL may I say my life has been
One scene of sorrow and of pain;
From early days I griefs have known,
And as I grew my griefs have grown.

Dangers were always in my path,
And fear of wrath and sometimes death;
While pale dejection in me reign'd,
I often wept, by grief constrain'd.

When taken from my native land,
By an unjust and cruel band,
How did uncommon dread prevail!
My sighs no more I could conceal.

To ease my mind I often strove,
And tried my trouble to remove:
I sung and utter'd sighs between—
Assay'd to stifle guilt with sin.

But, O! not all that I could do
Would stop the current of my woe;
Conviction still my vileness shew'd;
How great my guilt—how lost to good.[547]

"Prevented, that I could not die,
Nor could to one sure refuge fly;
An orphan state I had to mourn,—
Forsook by all, and left forlorn."

Those who beheld my downcast mien,
Could not guess at my woes unseen:

They by appearance could not know
The troubles that I waded through.

Lust, anger, blasphemy, and pride,
With legions of such ills beside,
"Troubled my thoughts," while doubts and fears
Clouded and darken'd most my years.

"Sighs now no more would be confin'd—
They breath'd the trouble of my mind:"
I wish'd for death, but check'd the word,
And often pray'd unto the Lord.

Unhappy, more than some on earth,
I thought the place that gave me birth—
Strange thoughts oppress'd—while I replied,
"Why not in Ethiopia died?"

And why thus spar'd, when nigh to hell!—[548]
God only knew—I could not tell!—
"A tott'ring fence, a bowing wall,
I thought myself e'er since the fall."

Oft times I mus'd, and nigh despair,[549]
While birds melodious fill'd the air.
"Thrice happy songsters, ever free,"
How blest were they compar'd to me!

Thus all things added to my pain;
While grief compell'd me to complain;
When sable clouds began to rise,
My mind grew darker than the skies.

The English nation forc'd to leave,
How did my breast with sorrow heave!
I long'd for rest—cried "Help me, Lord!
Some mitigation, Lord, afford!"

Yet on, dejected, still I went—
Heart-throbbing woes within me pent;
Nor land, nor sea, could comfort give,
Nor aught my anxious mind relieve.

Weary with troubles, yet unknown
To all but God and self alone,
Numerous months for peace I strove,
Numerous foes I had to prove.

Inur'd to dangers, grief, and woes,
Train'd up 'midst perils, death, and foes,
I said, "Must it thus ever be?
No quiet is permitted me."

Hard hap, and more than heavy lot!
I pray'd to God, "Forget me not—
What thou ordain'st help me to bear;
But, O! deliver from despair!"

Strivings and wrestling seem'd in vain;
Nothing I did could ease my pain:
Then gave I up my work and will,
Confess'd and own'd my doom was hell!

Like some poor pris'ner at the bar,
Conscious of guilt, of sin, and fear,
Arraign'd, and self-condemn'd, I stood,[550]
"Lost in the world and in my blood!"

Yet here, 'midst blackest clouds confin'd,
A beam from Christ, the day-star, shin'd;
Surely, thought I, if Jesus please,
He can at once sign my release.

I, ignorant of his righteousness,
Set up my labours in its place;
"Forgot for why his blood was shed,
And pray'd and fasted in his stead."

He dy'd for sinners—I am one;
Might not his blood for me atone?
Tho' I am nothing else but sin,
Yet surely he can make me clean!

Thus light came in, and I believ'd;
Myself forgot, and help receiv'd!
My Saviour then I know I found,
For, eas'd from guilt, no more I groan'd.

O, happy hour, in which I ceas'd
To mourn, for then I found a rest!
My soul and Christ were now as one—
Thy light, O Jesus, in me shone!

Bless'd be thy name; for now I know
I and my works can nothing do;
"The Lord alone can ransom man—
For this the spotless Lamb was slain!"

When sacrifices, works, and pray'r,
Prov'd vain, and ineffectual were,
"Lo then I come!" the Saviour cry'd
And, bleeding, bow'd his head and dy'd.

He dy'd for all who ever saw
No help in them, nor by the law:
I this have seen and gladly own
"Salvation is by Christ alone!"[551]

CHAP. XI.

The Author embarks on board a ship bound for Cadiz—Is near being shipwrecked—Goes to Malaga—Remarkable for cathedral there—The Author disputes with a Popish priest—Picks up eleven miserable men at sea in returning to England—Engages again with Doctor Irving to accompany him to Jamaica and the Musquito shore—Meets with an Indian Prince on board—The Author attempts to instruct him in the truths of the Gospel—Frustrated by the bad example of some in the ship—They arrive on the Musquito shore with some slaves they purchased at Jamaica, and begin to cultivate a Plantation—Some account of the manners and customs of the Musquito Indians—Successful device of the Author's to quell a riot among them—Curious entertainment given by them to Doctor Irving and the author; he leaves[552] the shore and goes for Jamaica—Is barbarously treated by a man with whom he engaged for his passage—Escapes, and goes to the Musquito admiral, who treats him kindly—He gets another vessel, and goes on board—Instances of bad treatment—Meets Dr. Irving—Gets to Jamaica—Is cheated by his captain—Leaves the Doctor, and sails for England.

WHEN our ship was got ready for sea again, I was entreated by the captain to go in her once more; but, as I felt myself as happy as I could wish to be in this life, I for some time refused; however, the advice of my friends at last prevailed, and in full resignation to the will of God, I again embarked for Cadiz in March, 1775. We had a very good passage, without any material accident, until we arrived off the Bay of Cadiz; when one Sunday, just as we were going into the harbour, the ship struck against a rock, and knocked off a garboard plank, which is the next to the keel. In an instant all hands were in the greatest confusion, and began with loud cries to call on God to have mercy on them. Although I could not swim, and saw no way of escaping death, I felt no dread in my then situation, having no desire to live. I even rejoiced in spirit, thinking this death would be sudden glory. But the fulness of time was not yet come. The people near to me were very much astonished in seeing me thus calm and resigned; but I told them of the peace of God, which, through sovereign grace, I enjoyed, and these words were that instant in my mind:

> Christ is my pilot wise, my compass is his word;
> My soul each storm defies, while I have such a Lord.
> I trust his faithfulness and power,
> To save me in the trying hour.

> Though rocks and quicksands deep through all my passage lie,
> Yet Christ shall safely keep and guide me with his eye.
> How can I sink with such a prop,
> That bears the world and all things up?[553]

At this time there were many large Spanish flukers or passage vessels full of people crossing the channel, who, seeing our condition, a number of them came alongside of us. As many hands as could be employed began to work; some at our three pumps, and the rest unloading the ship as fast as possible. There being only a single rock, called the Porpus, on which we struck, we soon got off it, and providentially it was then high water; we therefore run the ship ashore at the nearest place to keep her from sinking. After many tides, with a great deal of care and industry, we got her repaired again. When we had dispatched our business at Cadiz, we went to Gibraltar, and from thence to Malaga, a very pleasant and rich city, where there is one of the finest cathedrals I had ever seen. It had been above fifty years in building, as I had heard, though it was not then quite finished; great part of the inside, however, was completed, and highly decorated with the richest marble columns, and many superb paintings; it was lighted occasionally by an amazing number of wax tapers of different sizes, some of which were as thick as a man's thigh; these, however, were only used on some of their grand festivals.

I was very much shocked at the custom of bull-baiting, and other diversions which prevailed here on Sunday evenings, to the great scandal of Christianity and morals. I used to express my abhorrence of it to a priest whom I met with. I had frequent contests about religion with the reverend father, in which he took great pains to make a proselyte of me to his church; and I no less to convert him to mine. On these occasions I used to produce my bible, and shewed him in what points his church erred. He then said he had been in England, and that every person there read the bible, which was very wrong; but I answered him, that Christ desired us to search the scriptures. In his zeal for my conversion, he solicited me to go to one of the universities in Spain, and declared that I should have my education free; and told me, if I got myself made a priest, I might in time become even Pope; and he said that Pope Benedict was a black man.[554] As I was ever desirous of learning, I paused some time upon this temptation, and thought by being crafty (by going to the university),[555] I might catch some with guile; but again[556] I began to think it would only be hypocrisy in me to embrace his offer, as I could not in conscience conform to the opinions of his church. I was therefore enabled to regard the word of God, which says, "Come out from amongst them"; and I[557] refused Father Vincent's offer. So we parted without conviction on either side.

Having taken at this place some fine wines, fruits, and money, we proceeded to Cadiz, where we took about two tons more of money, &c. and then sailed for England in the month of June. When we were about the north latitude 42, we had contrary winds for several days, and the ship did not make in that time above six or seven miles straight course. This made the captain exceedingly fretful and peevish; and I was very sorry to hear God's most holy name often blasphemed by him. One day, as he was in that impious mood, a young gentleman on board, who was a passenger, reproved him, and said, he acted wrong, for we ought to be thankful to God for all things, as we were not in want of any thing on board; and though the wind was contrary for us, yet it was fair for some others, who perhaps stood in more need of it than we. I immediately seconded this young gentleman with some boldness, and said we had not the least cause to murmur, for that the Lord was better to us than we deserved, and that he had done all things well. I expected that the captain would be very angry with me for speaking, but he replied not a word. However, before that time, or hour,[558] on the following day, being the 21st of June, much to our great joy and astonishment, we saw the providential hand of our benign Creator, whose ways with his blind creatures are past finding out. The preceding night I dreamed that I saw a boat immediately off the starboard main shrouds; and exactly at half past one o'clock the following day at noon, while I was below, just as we had dined in the cabin, the man at the helm cried out, A boat! which brought my dream that instant into my mind. I was the first man that jumped on the deck; and looking from the shrouds onward, according to my dream, I descried a little boat at some distance; but, as the waves were high, it was as much as we could do sometimes to discern her; we, however, stopped the ship's way, and the boat which was extremely small, came alongside with eleven miserable men, whom we took on board immediately. To all human appearance, these people must have perished in the course of an hour, or less; the boat being small, it barely contained them. When we took them up they were half drowned, and had no victuals, compass, water, or any other necessary whatsoever, and had only one bit of an oar to stir with, and that right before the wind; so that they were obliged to trust entirely to the mercy of the waves. As soon as we got them all on board, they bowed themselves on their knees, and, with hands and voices lifted up to heaven, thanked God for their deliverance; and I trust that my prayers were not wanting amongst them at the same time. This mercy of the Lord quite melted me, and I recollected his words, which I saw thus verified, in the 107th Psalm, "O give thanks unto the Lord, for he is good, for his mercy endureth for ever. Hungry and thirsty, their souls fainted in them. They cried unto the Lord in their trouble, and he delivered them out of their distresses. And he led them forth by the right way, that they might go to a city of habitation. O that men would praise the Lord for his goodness,

and for his wonderful works to the children of men. For he sat-
isfieth the longing soul, and filleth the hungry soul with
goodness."

"Such as sit in darkness and in the shadow of death:"

"Then they cried unto the Lord in their trouble, and he saved
them out of their distresses. They that go down to the sea in ships;
that do business in great waters; these see the works of the Lord,
and his wonders in the deep. Whoso is wise and will observe
these things, even they shall understand the loving kindness of the
Lord."[559]

The poor distressed captain said, "that the Lord is good; for,
seeing that I am not fit to die, he therefore gave me a space of
time to repent." I was very glad to hear this expression, and took
an opportunity, when convenient, of talking to him on the providence of God. They told us they were Portuguese, and were in
a brig loaded with corn,[560] which shifted that morning at five o
clock, owing to which the vessel sunk that instant with two of
the crew; and how these eleven got into the boat (which was
lashed to the deck) not one of them could tell. We provided them
with every necessary, and brought them all safe to London: and I
hope the Lord gave them repentance unto eternal life.[561]

At our arrival,[562] I was happy once more amongst my friends
and brethren till November, when my old friend, the celebrated
Dr. Irving, bought a remarkable fine sloop, about 150 tons. He
had a mind for a new adventure, in cultivating a plantation at
Jamaica and the Musquito Shore; he asked me to go with him,
and said that he would trust me with his estate in preference to
any one. By the advice, therefore, of my friends, I accepted of
the offer, knowing that the harvest was fully ripe in those parts,
and I hoped to be an instrument, under God, of bringing some
poor sinner to my well-beloved master, Jesus Christ. Before I
embarked, I found with the Doctor four Musquito Indians, who
were chiefs in their own country, and were brought here by some
English traders for some selfish ends.[563] One of them was the Musquito king's son, a youth of about eighteen years of age; and whilst
he was here he was baptized by the name of George. They were

going back at the government's expence, after having been in England about twelve months, during which they learned to speak pretty good English. When I came to talk to them, about eight days before we sailed, I was very much mortified in finding that they had not frequented any churches since they were here, and were baptized,[564] nor was any attention paid to their morals. I was very sorry for this mock Christianity, and had just an opportunity to take some of them once to church before we sailed. We embarked in the month of November 1775, on board of the sloop Morning Star, Captain David Miller, and sailed for Jamaica. In our passage I took all the pains that I could to instruct the Indian prince in the doctrines of Christianity, of which he was entirely ignorant; and, to my great joy, he was quite attentive, and received with gladness the truths that the Lord enabled me to set forth to him. I taught him in the compass of eleven days all the letters, and he could put even two or three of them together, and spell them. I had Fox's Martyrology with cuts,[565] and he used to be very fond of looking into it, and would ask many questions about the papal cruelties he saw depicted there, which I explained to him. I made such progress with this youth, especially in religion, that when I used to go to bed at different hours of the night, if he was in his bed, he would get up on purpose to go to prayer with me, without any other clothes than his shirt; and before he would eat any of his meals amongst the gentlemen in the cabin, he would first come to me to pray, as he called it. I was well pleased at this, and took great delight in him, and used much supplication to God for his conversion. I was in full hope of seeing daily every appearance of that change which I could wish; not knowing the devices of Satan, who had many of his emissaries to sow his tares[566] as fast as I sowed the good seed, and pull down as fast as I built up. Thus we went on nearly four-fifths of our passage, when Satan at last got the upper hand. Some of his messengers, seeing this poor heathen much advanced in piety, began to ask him whether I had converted him to Christianity, laughed and made their jest at him, for which I rebuked them as much as I could; but this treatment caused the prince to halt between two

opinions. Some of the true sons of Belial,[567] who did not believe
that there was any hereafter, told him never to fear the devil, for
there was none existing; and if ever he came to the prince, they
desired he might be sent to them. Thus they teazed the poor
innocent youth, so that he would not learn his book any more!
He would not drink nor carouse with these ungodly actors, nor
would he be with me even at prayers. This grieved me very much.
I endeavoured to persuade him as well as I could, but he would
not come; and entreated him very much to tell me his reasons for
acting thus. At last he asked me, "How comes it that all the white
men on board, who can read and write, observe the sun, and
know all things, yet swear, lie, and get drunk, only excepting
yourself?" I answered him, the reason was, that they did not fear
God; and that if any one of them died so, they could not go to,
or be happy with God. He replied, that if a certain person[568] went
to hell, he would go to hell too! I was sorry to hear this; and, as
he sometimes had the tooth-ach, and also some other persons in
the ship at the same time, I asked him if their tooth-ach made
him easy? he said, No. Then I told him, if he and these people
went to hell together, their pains would not make his any lighter.
This had great weight with him, it depressed his spirits much; and
he became ever after, during the passage, fond of being alone.
When we came into the latitude of Martinico, and near making
the land, one morning we had a brisk gale of wind, and, carrying
too much sail, the mainmast went over the side. Many people
were then all about the deck, and the yards, masts, and rigging,
came tumbling all about us, yet there was not one of us in the
least hurt, although some were within a hair's breadth of being
killed; and, particularly, I saw two men, who, by the providential
hand of God, were most miraculously preserved from being
smashed to pieces. On the fifth of January we made Antigua and
Montserrat, and ran along the rest of the islands: and on the four-
teenth we arrived at Jamaica. One Sunday, while we were there,
I took the Musquito, prince George, to church, where he saw the
sacrament administered. When we came out we saw all kinds of
people, almost from the church door for the space of half a mile

down to the water-side, buying and selling all kinds of commodities: and these acts afforded me great matter of exhortation to this youth, who was much astonished. Our vessel being ready to sail for the Musquito shore, I went with the Doctor on board a Guinea-man,[569] to purchase some slaves to carry with us, and cultivate a plantation; and I chose them all of my own countrymen, some of whom came from Lybia.[570] On the 12th[571] of February we sailed from Jamaica, and on the eighteenth arrived at the Musquito shore, at a place called Dupeupy. All our Indian guests now, after I had admonished them, and a few cases of liquor given them by the Doctor, took an affectionate leave of us, and went ashore, where they were met by the Musquito king, and we never saw one of them afterwards. We then sailed to the southward of the shore, to a place called Cape Gracias a Dios, where there was a large lagoon or lake, which received the emptying of two or three very fine large rivers, and abounded much in fish and land tortoise. Some of the native Indians came on board of us here; and we used them well, and told them we were come to dwell amongst them, which they seemed pleased at. So the Doctor and I, with some others, went with them ashore; and they took us to different places to view the land, in order to choose a place to make a plantation of. We fixed on a spot near a river's bank, in a rich soil; and, having got our necessaries out of the sloop, we began to clear away the woods, and plant different kinds of vegetables, which had a quick growth. While we were employed in this manner, our vessel went northward to Black River to trade.[572] While she was there, a Spanish guarda costa[573] met with and took her. This proved very hurtful, and a great embarrassment to us. However, we went on with the culture of the land. We used to make fires every night all around us, to keep off wild beasts, which, as soon as it was dark, set up a most hideous roaring. Our habitation being far up in the woods, we frequently saw different kinds of animals; but none of them ever hurt us, except poisonous snakes, the bite of which the Doctor used to cure by giving to the patient, as soon as possible, about half a tumbler of strong rum, with a good deal of Cayenne pepper in it. In this manner he cured two natives, and one of his own slaves. The Indians were exceedingly fond of the Doctor, and they had good reason for it; for I believe they never had such an useful man amongst them. They came from all quarters to our dwelling; and some *woolwow,* or flat-headed Indians,[574] who lived fifty or sixty miles above our river, and this side of the South Sea,[575] brought us a good deal of silver in exchange for our goods. The principal articles we could get from our neighbouring Indians were turtle oil, and shells, little silk grass, and some provisions; but they would not work at any thing for us, except fishing; and a few times they assisted to cut some trees down, in order to build us houses; which they did exactly like the Africans, by the joint labour of men, women, and children. I do not recollect any of them to have had more than two wives. These always accompanied their husbands when they came to our dwelling, and then they generally carried whatever they brought to us, and always squatted down behind their husbands. Whenever we gave them any thing to eat, the men and their wives ate separate.[576] I never saw the least sign of incontinence amongst them. The women are ornamented with beads, and fond of painting themselves; the men also paint, even to excess, both their faces and shirts; their favourite colour is red. The women generally cultivate the ground, and the men are all fishermen and canoe-makers. Upon the whole, I never met any nation that were so simple in their manners as these people, or had so little ornament in their houses. Neither had they, as I ever could learn, one word expressive of an oath. The worst word I ever heard amongst them when they were quarreling, was one that they had got from the English, which was, "you rascal." I never saw any mode of worship among them; but in this they were not worse than their European brethren or neighbours, for I am sorry to say that there was not one white person in our dwelling, nor any where else, that I saw in different places I was at on the shore, that was better or more pious than those unenlightened Indians; but they either worked or slept on Sundays; and, to my sorrow, working was too much Sunday's employment with ourselves; so much so, that in some length of time we really did not know one day from another. This mode of living laid the foundation of my decamping at last. The natives are well made and warlike; and they particularly boast of having never been conquered by the Spaniards. They are great drinkers of strong liquors when they can get them. We used to distill rum from pine-apples, which were very plentiful here; and then we could not get them away from our place. Yet they seemed to be singular, in point of honesty, above any other nation I was ever amongst. The country being hot, we lived under an open shed, where we had all kinds of goods, without a door or a lock to any one article; yet we slept in safety, and never lost any thing, or were disturbed. This surprised us a good deal; and the Doctor, myself, and others, used to say, if we were to lie in that manner in Europe we should have our throats cut the first night. The Indian governor goes once in a certain time all about the province or district, and has a number of men with him as attendants and assistants. He settles all the differences among the people, like the judges here, and is treated with very great respect. He took care to give us timely notice before he came to our habitation, by sending his stick as a token, for rum, sugar, and gunpowder, which we did not refuse sending; and at the same time we made the utmost preparation to receive his honour and his train. When he came with his tribe, and all our neighbouring chieftains, we expected to find him a grave reverend judge, solid and sagacious; but, instead of that, before he and his gang came in sight, we heard them very clamorous; and they even had plundered some of our good neighbouring Indians, having intoxicated themselves with our liquor. When they arrived we did not know what to make of our new guests, and would gladly have dispensed with the honour of their company. However, having no alternative, we feasted them plentifully all the day till the evening; when the Governor, getting quite drunk, grew very unruly, and struck one of our most friendly chiefs, who was our nearest neighbour, and also took his gold-laced hat from him. At this a great commotion took place;[577] and the Doctor interfered to make peace, as we could all understand one another, but to no purpose; and at last they became so outrageous, that the Doctor,

fearing he might get into trouble, left the house, and made the
best of his way to the nearest wood, leaving me to do as well as
I could among them. I was so enraged with the governor, that I
could have wished to have seen him tied fast to a tree, and flogged
for his behaviour; but I had not people enough to cope with his
party. I therefore thought of a stratagem to appease the riot. Rec-
ollecting a passage I had read in the life of Columbus, when he
was amongst the Indians in Jamaica,[578] where, on some occasion,
he frightened them, by telling them of certain events in the heavens, I had recourse to the same expedient, and it succeeded beyond my most sanguine expectations. When I had formed my
determination, I went in the midst of them, and taking hold of
the governor, I pointed up to the heavens. I menaced him and
the rest: I told them God lived there, and that he was angry with
them, and they must not quarrel so; that they were all brothers,
and if they did not leave off, and go away quietly, I would take
the book (pointing to the bible), read, and *tell* God to make them
dead. This was something like magic. The clamour immediately
ceased, and I gave them some rum and a few other things; after
which they went away peaceably; and the Governor afterwards
gave our neighbour, who was called Captain Plasmyah, his hat
again. When the Doctor returned, he was exceedingly glad at my
success in thus getting rid of our troublesome guests. The Musquito people within our vicinity, out of respect to the Doctor,
myself, and his people, made entertainments of the grand kind,
called in their tongue *tourrie* or *drykbot*. The English of this expression is, a feast of drinking about, of which it seems a corruption of language. The drink consisted of pine-apples roasted, and
casades[579] chewed or beaten in mortars; which, after lying some
time, ferments, and becomes so strong as to intoxicate, when
drank in any quantity. We had timely notice given to us of the
entertainment. A white family, within five miles of us, told us
how the drink was made; I and two others went before the time
to the village,[580] where the mirth was appointed to be held, and
there we saw the whole art of making the drink and also the kind
of animals that were to be eaten there. I cannot say the sight of

either the drink or the meat were enticing to me. They had some thousands of pine-apples roasting, which they squeezed, dirt and all, into a canoe they had there for the purpose. The casade drink was in beef barrels and other vessels, and looked exactly like hog-wash. Men, women, and children were thus employed in roasting the pine-apples, and squeezing them with their hands. For food they had many land torpins or tortoises, some dried turtle, and three large alligators alive, and tied fast to the trees. I asked the people what they were going to do with these alligators? and I was told they were to be eaten. I was much surprised at this, and went home not a little disgusted at the preparations. When the day of the feast was come, we took some rum with us, and went to the appointed place, where we found a great assemblage of these people, who received us very kindly. The mirth had begun before we came; and they were dancing with music: and the musical instruments were nearly the same as those of any other sable people; but, as I thought, much less melodious than any other nation I ever knew. They had many curious gestures in dancing, and a variety of motions and postures of their bodies, which to me were in no wise attracting. The males danced by themselves, and the females also by themselves, as with us. The Doctor shewed his people the example, by immediately joining the women's party, though not by their choice. On perceiving the women disgusted, he joined the males. At night there were great illuminations, by setting fire to many pine-trees, while the drykbot went round merrily by calabashes or gourds: but the liquor might more justly be called eating than drinking. One Owden, the oldest father in the vicinity, was drest in a strange and terrifying form. Around his body were skins adorned with different kinds of feathers, and he had on his head a very large and high head-piece, in the form of a grenadier's cap, with prickles like a porcupine; and he made a certain noise which resembled the cry of an alligator. Our people skipped amongst them out of complaisance, though some could not drink of their tourrie; but our rum met with customers enough, and was soon gone. The alligators were killed, and some of them roasted. Their manner of roasting is by digging a hole in the earth, and filling it with wood, which they burn to coal, and then they lay sticks across, on which they set the meat. I had a raw piece of the alligator in my hand: it was very rich: I thought it looked like fresh salmon, and it had a most fragrant smell, but I could not eat any of it. This merry-making at last ended without the least discord in any person in the company, although it was made up of different nations and complexions.

[581]The rainy season came on here about the latter end of May, which continued till August very heavily; so that the rivers were overflowed, and our provisions then in the ground were washed away. I thought this was in some measure a judgment upon us for working on Sundays, and it hurt my mind very much. I often wished to leave this place and sail for Europe; for our mode of procedure, and living in this heathenish form was very irksome to me. The word of God saith, "What does it avail a man if he gain the whole world, and lose his own soul?"[582] This was much and heavily impressed on my mind; and, though I did not know how to speak to the Doctor for my discharge, it was disagreeable for me to stay any longer. But about the middle of June I took courage enough to ask him for it. He was very unwilling at first to grant me my request;[583] but I gave him so many reasons for it, that at last he consented to my going, and gave me the following certificate of my behaviour:

> The bearer, Gustavus Vassa, has served me several years with strict honesty, sobriety, and fidelity. I can, therefore, with justice recommend him for these qualifications; and indeed in every respect I consider him as an excellent servant. I do hereby certify that he always behaved well, and that he is perfectly trust-worthy.
>   CHARLES IRVING.

Musquito shore, June 15, 1776

Though I was much attached to the Doctor, I was happy when he consented to my going.[584] I got every thing ready for my departure, and hired some Indians, with a large canoe, to carry me off. All my poor countrymen, the slaves, when they heard of my leaving them, were very sorry, as I had always treated them with care and affection, and did every thing I could to comfort the poor creatures, and render their condition easy. Having taken leave of my old friends and companions, on the 18th of June, accompanied by the Doctor, I left that spot of the world, and went southward above twenty miles along the river. There I found a sloop, the captain of which told me he was going to Jamaica. Having agreed for my passage with him and one of the owners, who was also on board, named Hughes, the Doctor and I parted, not without shedding tears on both sides. The vessel then sailed along the river till night, when she stopped in a lagoon within the same river. During the night a schooner, belonging to the same owners came in, and, as she was in want of hands, Hughes, the owner of the sloop, asked me to go in the schooner as a sailor, and said he would give me wages. I thanked him; but I said I wanted to go to Jamaica. He then immediately changed his tone, and swore, and abused me very much, and asked how I came to be freed! I told him, and said that I came into that vicinity with Dr. Irving, whom he had seen that day. This account was of no use; he still swore exceedingly at me, and cursed the master for a fool that sold me my freedom, and the Doctor for another in letting me go from him. Then he desired me to go in the schooner, or else I should not go out of the sloop as a free man. I said this was very hard, and begged to be put on shore again; but he swore that I should not. I said I had been twice amongst the Turks, yet had never seen any such usage with them, and much less could I have expected any thing of this kind among the Christians.[585] This incensed him exceedingly; and, with a volley of oaths and imprecations, he replied, "Christians! Damn you, you are one of St. Paul's men;[586] but by G——, except you have St. Paul's or St. Peter's faith, and walk upon the water to the shore, you shall not go out of the vessel!" which I now found was going amongst the Spaniards towards Carthagena, where he swore he would sell me.[587] I simply asked him what right he had

to sell me? But, without another word, he made some of his
people tie ropes round each of my ancles, and also to each wrist,
and another rope round my body, and hoisted me up without
letting my feet touch or rest upon any thing. Thus I hung, without
any crime committed, and without judge or jury, merely because
I was a freeman, and could not by the law get any redress from
a white person in those parts of the world. I was in great pain
from my situation, and cried and begged very hard for some
mercy, but all in vain. My tyrant in a rage brought a musquet out
of the cabin, and loaded it before me and the crew, and swore
that he would shoot me if I cried any more. I had now no alternative; I therefore remained silent, seeing not one white man on
board who said a word on my behalf. I hung in that manner from
between ten and eleven o'clock at night till about one in the
morning; when, finding my cruel abuser fast asleep, I begged some
of his slaves to slacken[588] the rope that was round my body, that
my feet might rest on something. This they did at the risk of
being cruelly used by their master, who beat some of them severely at first for not tying me when he commanded them. Whilst
I remained in this condition, till between five and six o'clock next
morning, I trusted & prayed[589] to God to forgive this blasphemer,
who cared not what he did, but when he got up out of his sleep
in the morning was of the very same temper and disposition as
when he left me at night. When they got up the anchor, and the
vessel was getting under way, I once more cried and begged to
be released; and now being fortunately in the way of their hoisting
the sails, they loosed me.[590] When I was let down, I spoke to one
Mr. Cox, a carpenter, whom I knew on board, on the impropriety
of this conduct. He also knew the Doctor, and the good opinion
he ever had of me. This man then went to the captain, and told
him not to carry me away in that manner; that I was the Doctor's
steward, who regarded me very highly, and would resent this
usage when he should come to know it. On which he desired a
young man to put me ashore in a small canoe I brought with me.
This sound gladdened my heart and I got hastily into the canoe,
and set off whilst my tyrant was down in the cabin; but he soon

spied me out, when I was not above thirty or forty yards from the vessel, and, running upon the deck with a loaded musquet in his hand, he presented it at me, and swore heavily and dreadfully, that he would shoot me that instant, if I did not come back on board. As I knew the wretch would have done as he said, without hesitation, I put back to the vessel again; but, as the good Lord would have it, just as I was alongside he was abusing the captain for letting me go from the vessel; which the captain returned, and both of them soon got into a very great heat. The young man that was with me, now got out of the canoe; the vessel was sailing on fast with a smooth sea; and I then thought it was neck or nothing,[591] so at that instant I set off again for my life, in the canoe, towards the shore; and fortunately the confusion was so great amongst them on board, that I got out of the reach of the musquet shot, unnoticed, while the vessel sailed on with a fair wind a different way; so that they could not overtake me without tacking:[592] but, even before that could be done, I should have been on shore, which I soon reached, with many thanks to God for this unexpected deliverance. I then went and told the other owner, who lived near that shore (with whom I had agreed for my passage) of the usage I had met with. He was very much astonished, and appeared very sorry for it. After treating me with kindness, he gave me some refreshment, and three heads of roasted Indian corn, for a voyage of about eighteen miles south, to look for another vessel. He then directed me to an Indian chief of a district, who was also the Musquito admiral, and had once been at our dwelling; after which I set off with the canoe across a large lagoon alone (for I could not get any one to assist me) though I was much jaded,[593] and had pains in my bowels, by means of the rope I had hung by the night before. I was therefore at different times unable to manage the canoe, for the paddling was very laborious. However, a little before dark, I got to my destined place, where some of the Indians knew me, and received me kindly. I asked for the admiral; and they conducted me to his dwelling. He was glad to see me, and refreshed me with such things as the place afforded; and I had a hammock to sleep in. They acted towards

me more like Christians than those whites I was amongst the last
night, though they had been baptized. I told the admiral I wanted
to go to the next port to get a vessel to carry me to Jamaica; and
requested him to send the canoe back which I then had, for which
I was to pay him. He agreed with me, and sent five able Indians
with a large canoe to carry me and[594] my things to my intended
place, about fifty miles; and we set off the next morning. When
we got out of the lagoon and went along shore, the sea was so
high that the canoe was oftentimes very near being filled with
water. We were obliged to go ashore, and drag her[595] across different necks of land; we were also two nights in the swamps,
which swarmed with musquito flies, and they proved troublesome
to us. This tiresome journey of land and water ended, however,
on the third day, to my great joy; and I got on board of a sloop
commanded by one captain Jenning. She was then partly loaded,
and he told me he was expecting daily to sail for Jamaica; and
having agreed with me to work my passage, I went to work accordingly. I was not many days on board before we sailed; but,
to my sorrow and disappointment, though used to such tricks, we
went to the southward along the Musquito shore, instead of steering for Jamaica. I was compelled to assist in cutting a great deal
of mahogany wood on the shore as we coasted along it, and load
the vessel with it, before she sailed. This fretted me much; but,
as I did not know how to help myself among these deceivers, I
thought patience was the only remedy I had left, and even that
was forced. There was much hard work and little victuals on
board, except by good luck we happened to catch turtles. On this
coast there was also a particular kind of fish called manatee, which
is most excellent eating, and the flesh is more like beef than fish;
the scales are as large as a shilling, and the skin thicker than I ever
saw that of any other fish.[596] Within the brackish waters along
shore there were likewise vast numbers of alligators, which made
the fish scarce. I was on board this sloop sixteen days, during
which, in our coasting, we came to another place, where there
was a smaller sloop called the Indian Queen, commanded by one
John Baker. He also was an Englishman, and had been a long time

along the shore trading for turtle shells and silver, and had got a good quantity of each on board. He wanted some hands very much; and, understanding I was a freeman, and wanted to go to Jamaica, he told me if he could get one or two men more,[597] that he would sail immediately for that Island; he also pretended to show[598] me some marks of attention and respect, and promised to give me forty five shillings sterling a month if I would go with him. I thought this much better than cutting wood for nothing. I therefore told the other captain that I wanted to go to Jamaica in the other vessel; but he would not listen to me: and, seeing me resolved to go in a day or two, he got the vessel under sail,[599] intending to carry me away against my will. This treatment mortified me extremely. I immediately, according to an agreement I had made with the captain of the Indian Queen, called for her boat, which was lying near us, and it came along-side; and by the means of a north pole shipmate which I met with in the sloop I was in, I got my things into the boat, and went on board of the Indian Queen, July the 10th. A few days after I was there, we got all things ready and sailed; but again, to my great mortification, this vessel still went to the south, nearly as far as Carthagena, trading along the coast, instead of going to Jamaica, as the captain had promised me: and, what was worst of all, he was a very cruel and bloody-minded man, and was a horrid blasphemer. Among others, he had a white pilot, one Stoker, whom he beat often as severely as he did some negroes he had on board. One night in particular, after he had beaten this man most cruelly, he put him into the boat, and made two negroes row him to a desolate key, or small island; and he loaded two pistols; and swore bitterly that he would shoot the negroes if they brought Stoker on board again. There was not the least doubt but that he would do as he said, and the two poor fellows were obliged to obey the cruel mandate; but, when the captain was asleep, the two negroes took a blanket, at the risque of their lives,[600] and carried it to the unfortunate Stoker, which I believe was the means of saving his life from the annoyance of insects. A great deal of entreaty was used with the captain the next day, before he would consent to let Stoker come

on board; and when the poor man was brought on board he was
very ill, from his situation during the night, and he remained so
till he was drowned a little time after. As we sailed southward we
came to many uninhabited islands, which were overgrown with
fine large cocoa-nut trees.[601] As I was very much in want of provisions, I brought a boat load of the nuts[602] on board, which lasted
me and others for several weeks, and afforded us many a delicious
repast in our scarcity. One day, before this, I could not help observing the providential hand of God, that ever supplies all our
wants, though in the ways and manner we know not. I had been
a whole day without food, and made signals for boats to come
off, but in vain. I therefore earnestly prayed to God for relief in
my need; and at the close of the evening I went off the deck. Just
as I laid down I heard a noise on the deck; and, not knowing
what it meant, I went directly on the deck again, when what
should I see but a fine large fish, about seven or eight pounds,
which had jumped aboard! I took it, and admired, with thanks,
the good hand of God; and what I considered as not less extraordinary, the captain, who was very avaricious, did not attempt to
take it from me, there being only him and I on board; for the
rest were all gone ashore trading. Sometimes the people did not
come off for some days: this used to fret the captain, and then he
would vent his fury on me by beating me, or making me feel in
other cruel ways. One day especially, in this wild, wicked, and
mad career, after striking me several times with different things,
and once across my mouth, even with a red burning stick out of
the fire, he got a barrel of gunpowder on the deck, and swore
that he would blow up the vessel. I was then at my wit's end,
and earnestly prayed to God to direct me. The head was out of
the barrel; and the captain took a lighted stick out of the fire to
blow himself and me up, because there was a vessel then in sight
coming in, which he supposed was a Spanish Guarda Costa,[603] and
he was afraid of falling into their hands. Seeing this, I got an axe,
unnoticed by him, and placed myself between him and the powder, having resolved in myself, as soon as he attempted to put the
fire in the barrel, to chop him down that instant. I was more than

an hour in this situation; during which he struck me often, still keeping the fire in his hand for this wicked purpose. I really should have thought myself justifiable in any other part of the world if I had killed him, and prayed to God, who gave me a mind which rested solely on himself. I prayed for resignation, that his will might be done: and the following two portions of his holy word, which occurred to my mind, buoyed up my hope, and kept me from taking the life of this wicked man. "He hath determined the times before appointed, and set bounds to our habitations," Acts xvii. 26. And, "Who is there among you that feareth the Lord, that obeyeth the voice of his servant, that walketh in darkness and hath no light? let him trust in the name of the Lord, and stay upon his God," Isaiah l. 10. And this, by the grace of God, I was enabled to do. I found him a present help in the time of need, and the captain's fury began to subside as the night approached: but I found,

> That he who cannot stem his anger's tide
> Doth a wild horse without a bridle ride.[604]

The next morning we discovered that the vessel which had caused such a fury in the captain was an English sloop. They soon came to an anchor where we were, and, to my no small surprise, I learned that Dr. Irving was on board of her on his way from the Musquito shore to Jamaica. I was for going immediately to see this old master and friend, but the captain would not suffer me to leave the vessel. I then informed the Doctor, by letter, how I was treated, and begged that he would take me out of the sloop: but he informed me that it was not in his power, as he was a passenger himself; but he sent me some rum and sugar for my own use. I now learned that after I had left the estate which I managed for this gentleman on the Musquito shore, during which the slaves were well fed and comfortable, a white overseer had supplied my place: this man, through inhumanity and ill-judged avarice, beat and cut the poor slaves most unmercifully; and the consequence was, that every one got into a large Puriogua canoe,

and endeavoured to escape; but, not knowing where to go, or
how to manage the canoe, they were all drowned; in consequence
of which the Doctor's plantation was left uncultivated, and he was
now returning to Jamaica to purchase more slaves and stock it
again.

[605]On the 14th of October, the Indian Queen arrived at Kingston in Jamaica. When we were unloaded I demanded my wages,
which amounted to eight pounds five shillings sterling;[606] but Captain Baker refused to give me one farthing, although it was the
hardest earned money I ever worked for in my life. I found out
Dr. Irving upon this, and acquainted him of the captain's knavery.
He did all he could to help me to get my money; and we went
to every magistrate in Kingston (and there were nine), but they
all refused to do any thing for me, and said my oath could not be
admitted against a white man. Nor was this all; for Baker threatened that he would beat me severely if he could catch me, for
attempting to demand my money; and this he would have done;
but that I got, by means of Dr. Irving, under the protection of
Capt. Douglas, of the Squirrel man of war.[607] I thought this exceedingly hard usage; though indeed I found it to be too much
the practice there to pay free negro men[608] for their labour in this
manner.

[609]One day I went with a free negro tailor, named Joe Dia-
mond, to one Mr. Cochran, who was indebted to him some trifling sum; and the man, not being able to get his money, began
to murmur. The other immediately took a horse-whip to pay him
with it; but by the help of a good pair of heels, the tailor got off.
Such oppressions as these made me seek for a vessel to get off the
island as fast as I could: and, by the mercy of God, I found a ship
in November bound for England, when I embarked with a convoy, after having taken a last farewell of Dr. Irving. When I left
Jamaica he was employed in refining sugars; and offered me a
place, but I refused. And some months[610] after my arrival in England I learned, with much sorrow, that this my amiable friend
was dead, owing to his having eaten some poisoned fish.

[611]We had many very heavy gales of wind in our passage; in

the course of which no material incident occurred, except that an American privateer,[612] falling in with the fleet, was captured and set fire to by his Majesty's ship the Squirrel.

[613]On January the seventh, 1777, we arrived at Plymouth. I was happy once more to tread upon English ground; and, after passing some little time at Plymouth and Exeter among some pious friends, whom I was happy to see, I went to London, with a heart replete with thanks to God for all past mercies.

Different transactions of the Author's life till the present time—His application to the late Bishop of London to be appointed a missionary to Africa—Some account of his share in the conduct of the late expedition to Sierra Leona—Petition to the Queen—His marriage—Conclusion.

SUCH were the various scenes to which I was a witness, and the fortune I experienced until the year 1777. Since that period, my life has been more uniform, and the incidents of it fewer than in any other equal number of years preceding; I therefore hasten to the conclusion of a narrative, which I fear the reader may think already sufficiently tedious.

I had suffered so many impositions in my commercial transactions in different parts of the world, that I became heartily disgusted with the seafaring life, and was determined not to return to it, at least for some time. I therefore once more engaged in service shortly after my return, and continued for the most part in this situation until 1784.[614]

Soon after my arrival in London, I saw a remarkable circumstance relative to African complexion, which I thought so extraordinary that I shall beg leave just to mention it: A white negro woman, that I had formerly seen in London and other parts, had married a white man, by whom she had three boys, and they were every one mulattoes, and yet they had fine light hair. In 1779, I served Governor Macnamara,[615] who had been a considerable time on the coast of Africa. In the time of my service I used to ask frequently other servants to join me in family prayer; but this only excited their mockery. However, the Governor, understanding that I was of a religious turn, wished to know what religion I was of; I told him I was a protestant of the church of England, agreeable to the thirty-nine articles of that church;[616] and that whomsoever I found to preach according to that doctrine, those I would hear. A few days after this, we had some more discourse on the same subject; when he said he would, if I chose, as he thought I might be of service in converting my countrymen to the Gospel-faith, get me sent out as a missionary to Africa. I at first refused going, and told him how I had been served on a like occasion by some white people the last voyage I went to Jamaica, when I attempted, (if it were the will of God) to be the means of converting the Indian prince; and said I supposed they would serve me worse than Alexander the coppersmith did St. Paul,[617] if I should attempt to go amongst them in Africa. He told me not to fear, for he would apply to the Bishop of London to get me ordained.[618] On these terms I consented to the Governor's proposal to go to Africa, in hope of doing good, if possible, amongst my countrymen; so, in order to have me sent out properly, we immediately wrote the following letters to the late Bishop of London:

To The Right Reverend Father in God, ROBERT, *Lord Bishop of London.*
THE MEMORIAL OF GUSTAVUS VASSA,[619]
    SHEWETH,
    THAT your memorialist is a native of Africa, and has a knowledge of the manners and customs of the inhabitants of that country.
    That your memorialist has resided in different parts of Europe for twenty-two years last past, and embraced the Christian faith in the year 1759.
    That your memorialist is desirous of returning to Africa as a missionary, if encouraged by your Lordship, in hopes of being able to prevail upon his countrymen to become Christians; and your memorialist is the more induced to undertake the same, from the success that has attended the like undertakings when encouraged by the Portuguese through their different settlements on the coast of Africa, and also by the Dutch; both governments encouraged the blacks, who by their education are qualified to undertake the

same, and are found more proper than European clergymen, unacquainted with the language and customs of the country.

Your memorialist's only motive for soliciting the office of a
missionary is, that he may be a means, under God, of reforming
his countrymen and persuading them to embrace the Christian
religion. Therefore your memorialist humbly prays your Lordship's
encouragement and support in the undertaking.

GUSTAVUS VASSA.

At Mr. Guthrie's, Tailor,
No. 17, Hedge-lane.

MY LORD, I have resided near seven years on the coast of
Africa, for most part of the time as commanding officer. From the
knowledge I have of the country and its inhabitants, I am inclined
to think that the within plan will be attended with great success,
if countenanced by your Lordship. I beg further to represent to
your Lordship, that the like attempts, when encouraged by other
governments, have met with uncommon success; and at this very
time I know a very respectable character, a black priest, at Cape
Coast Castle.[620] I know the within-named Gustavus Vassa, and
believe him a moral good man. I have the honour to be,

My Lord,
Your Lordship's
Humble and obedient Servant,
Grove, 11th March, 1779.
MATT. MACNAMARA.

This letter was also accompanied by the following from Dr.
Wallace, who had resided in Africa for many years, and whose
sentiments on the subject of the African mission were the same
with Governor Macnamara's:

MY LORD,   *March 13, 1779.*

I have resided near five years in Senegambia, on the coast of
Africa, and have had the honour of filling very considerable em-
ployments in that province. I do approve of the within plan, and
think the undertaking very laudable and proper, and that it de-

serves your Lordship's protection and encouragement, in which case it must be attended with the intended success. I am, my Lord,
Your Lordship's
humble and obedient Servant,
THOMAS WALLACE.

With these letters I waited on the Bishop, by the Governor's desire, and presented them to his Lordship. He received me with much condescension and politeness; but, from some certain scruples of delicacy, and saying the Bishops were not of opinion in sending a new missionary to Africa, he declined to ordain me.

My sole motive for thus dwelling on this transaction, or inserting these papers, is the opinion which gentlemen of sense and education, who are acquainted with Africa, entertain of the probability of converting the inhabitants of it to the faith of Jesus Christ, if the attempt were countenanced by the legislature.

Shortly after this I left the Governor, and served a nobleman in the Dorsetshire militia, with whom I was encamped at Coxheath for some time;[621] but the operations there were too minute and uninteresting to make a detail of.

In the year 1783, I visited eight counties in Wales, from motives of curiosity. While I was in that part of the country, I was led to go down into a coal-pit in Shropshire, but my curiosity nearly cost me my life; for while I was in the pit the coals fell in, and buried one poor man, who was not far from me: upon this I got out as fast as I could, thinking the surface of the earth the safest part of it.

In the spring of 1784, I thought of visiting old ocean again. In consequence of this I embarked as steward on board a fine new ship called the London, commanded by Martin Hopkins, and sailed for New York. I admired this city very much; it is large and well-built, and abounds with provisions of all kinds. [While we lay here, a circumstance happened which I thought extremely singular:—One day a malefactor was to be executed on a gallows; but with condition that if any woman, having nothing on but her shift, married the man under the gallows, his life was to be saved. This extraordinary privilege was claimed; a woman presented herself; and the marriage ceremony was performed.][622]

[623]Our ship having got laden, we returned to London in January 1785. When she was again ready for another voyage, the captain being an agreeable man, I sailed with him from hence in the spring, March 1785, for Philadelphia. On the 5th of April we took our departure from the land's end, with a pleasant gale; and, about nine o'clock that night the moon shone bright, and the sea was smooth, while our ship was going free by the wind at the rate of about four or five miles an hour.—At this time another ship was going nearly as fast as we on the opposite point, meeting us right in the teeth, yet none on board observed either ship until we struck each other forcibly head and head, to the astonishment and consternation of both crews. She did us much damage, but I believe we did her more; for when we passed by each other, which we did very quickly, they called to us to bring to, and hoist out our boats,[624] but we had enough to do to mind ourselves; and in about eight minutes we saw no more of her. We refitted as well as we could the next day, and proceeded on our voyage, and in May arrived at Philadelphia.

[625]I was very glad to see this favourite old town once more; and my pleasure was much increased in seeing the worthy Quakers, freeing and easing the burthens of many of my oppressed African brethren. It rejoiced my heart when one of these friendly people took me to see a free-school they had erected for every denomination of black people, whose minds are cultivated here, and forwarded to virtue; and thus they are made useful members of the community. Does not the success of this practice say loudly to the planters, in the language of scripture—"Go ye, and do likewise?"[626]

In October 1785, I was accompanied by some of the Africans, and presented this address of thanks to the gentlemen called Friends or Quakers, in Whitehart-court,[627] Lombard-street:

GENTLEMEN,

By reading your book, intitled, A Caution to Great Britain and her Colonies, concerning the Calamitous State of the enslaved Negroes,[628] We, part of the poor, oppressed, needy, and much degraded negroes, desire to approach you, with this address of thanks, with our inmost love and warmest acknowledgments; and with the deepest sense of your benevolence, unwearied labour, and kind interposition, towards breaking the yoke of slavery, and to administer a little comfort and ease to thousands and tens of thousands of very grievously afflicted and too heavy burthened negroes.

Gentlemen, could you, by perseverance, at last be enabled, under God, to lighten in any degree the heavy burthen of the afflicted, no doubt it would, in some measure, be the possible means under God of saving the souls of many of the oppressors; and if so, sure we are that the God, whose eyes are ever upon all his creatures, and always rewards every true act of virtue, and regards the prayers of the oppressed, will give to you and yours those blessings which it is not in our power to express or conceive, but which we, as a part of those captivated, oppressed, and afflicted people, most earnestly wish and pray for.[629]

These gentlemen received us very kindly, with a promise to exert themselves on behalf of the oppressed Africans; and we parted.

While in town,[630] I chanced once to be invited to a Quaker's wedding. The simple and yet expressive mode used at their solemnizations is worthy of note. The following is the true form of it:

Near the close of a meeting for worship, wherein there are frequently seasonable exhortations from some of their ministers, the bride[631] and bridegroom stand up, and, taking each other by the hand in a solemn manner, the man audibly declares to this purpose:

"Friends, in the fear of the Lord, and before this assembly, I take this my friend, M. N. to be my wife; promising, through divine assistance, to be unto her a loving and faithful husband until it shall please the Lord by death to separate us:"[632] And the woman makes the like declaration. Then the man and woman sign their names to the certificate; and as many witnesses as have a mind.[633] I had the honour to subscribe mine to a certificate in Whiteheart-Court, Lombard-Street.[634] This mode I highly recommend.[635]

We returned to London in August, and our ship not going immediately to sea, I shipped as a steward in an American ship called the Harmony, Captain John Willett, and left London in March 1786, bound to Philadelphia. Eleven days after sailing, we carried our foremast away.[636] We had a nine weeks passage, which caused our trip not to succeed well, the market for our goods proving bad; and, to make it worse, my commander began to play me the like tricks as others too often practise on free negroes in the West Indies. But, I thank God, I found many friends here who in some measure prevented him. On my return to London in August, I was very agreeably surprised to find, that the benevolence of government adopted the plan of some philanthropic individuals, to send the Africans from hence to their native quarter, and that some vessels were then engaged to carry them to Sierra Leona; an act which redounded to the honour of all concerned in its promotion, and filled me with prayers and much rejoicing.[637] There was then in the city a select committee of gentlemen for the black poor, to some of whom I had the honour of being known; and as soon as they heard of my arrival, they sent for me to the committee. When I came there, they informed me of the intention of government; and, as they seemed to think me qualified to superintend part of the undertaking, they asked me to go with the black poor to Africa.[638] I pointed out to them many objections to my going; and particularly I expressed some difficulties on the account of the slave-dealers, as I would certainly oppose their traffic in the human species by every means in my power. However, these objections were over-ruled by the gentlemen of the committee, who prevailed on me to consent to go; and recommended me to the honourable Commissioners of his Majesty's Navy, as a proper person to act as commissary for government in the intended expedition; and they accordingly appointed me, in November 1786, to that office, and gave me sufficient power to act for the government in the capacity of commissary; having received my warrant and the following order:

By the principal Officers and Commissioners of his Majesty's Navy.

WHEREAS you are directed, by our warrant of the 4th of last month, to receive into your charge, from Mr. Joseph Irwin,[639] the surplus provisions remaining of what was provided for the voyage, as well as the provisions for the support of the black poor, after the landing at Sierra Leona, with the clothing, tools, and all other articles provided at government's expence; and as the provisions were laid in at the rate of two months for the voyage, and for four months after the landing, but the number embarked being so much less than we expected, whereby there may be a considerable surplus of provisions, clothing, &c. these are, in addition to former orders, to direct and require you to appropriate or dispose of such surplus to the best advantage you can for the benefit of government, keeping and rendering to us a faithful account of what you do therein. And for your guidance in preventing any white persons going, who are not intended to have the indulgence of being carried thither, we send you herewith a list of those recommended by the committee for the black poor, as proper persons to be permitted to embark, and acquaint you that you are not to suffer any others to go who do not produce a certificate from the committee for the black poor, of their having their permission for it. For which this shall be your warrant. Dated at the Navy Office, January 16, 1787.

To Mr. Gustavus Vassa, Commissary of Provisions and Stores for the Black Poor to Sierra Leona.
J. HINSLOW.
GEO. MARSH.
W. PALMER.

I proceeded immediately to the executing of my duty on board the vessels destined for the voyage, where I continued till the March following.

During my continuance in the employment of government I was struck with the flagrant abuses committed by the agent, and endeavoured to remedy them, but without effect. One instance, among many which I could produce, may serve as a specimen. Government had ordered to be provided all necessaries (slops,[640] as they are called, included) for 750 persons; however, not being able to muster more than 426,[641] I was ordered to send the superfluous slops, &c. to the king's stores at Portsmouth;[642] but, when I demanded them for that purpose from the agent, it appeared they had never been bought, though paid for by government. But that was not all, government were not the only objects of peculation;[643] these poor people suffered infinitely more; their accommodations were most wretched; many of them wanted beds, and many more clothing and other necessaries. For the truth of this, and much more, I do not seek credit from my own assertion. I appeal to the testimony of Capt. Thompson, of the Nautilus,[644] who convoyed us, to whom I applied in February 1787 for a remedy, when I had remonstrated to the agent in vain, and even brought him to be a witness of the injustice and oppression I had complained of.[645] I appeal also to a letter written by these wretched people, so early as the beginning of the preceding January, and published in the Morning Herald, on the fourth of that month, signed by twenty of their chiefs.[646]

I could not silently suffer government to be thus cheated, and my countrymen plundered and oppressed, and even left destitute of the necessaries for almost their existence. I therefore informed the Commissioners of the Navy of the agent's proceeding; but my dismission was soon after procured by the unjust means of Samuel Hoare, banker[647] in the city; and he moreover,[648] empowered the same agent to receive on board, at the government expence, a number of persons as passengers, contrary to the orders I received. By this I suffered a considerable loss in my property: however, the Commissioners were satisfied with my conduct, and wrote to Capt. Thompson, expressing their approbation of it.

Thus provided, they proceeded on their voyage; and at last, worn out by treatment, perhaps, not the most mild, and wasted by sickness, brought on by want of medicine, clothes, bedding, &c. they reached Sierra Leona just at the commencement of the rains.[649] At that season of the year it is impossible to cultivate the lands; their provisions therefore were exhausted before they could derive any benefit from agriculture; and it is not surprising that many, especially the Lascars,[650] whose constitutions are very tender, and who had been cooped up in ships from October to June, and accommodated in the manner I have mentioned, should be so wasted by their confinement as not long to survive it.

Thus ended my part of the long-talked of expedition to Sierra Leona; an expedition, which, however unfortunate in the event, was humane and politic in its design, nor was its failure owing to government; every thing was done on their part; but there was evidently sufficient mismanagement attending the conduct and execution of it to defeat its success.[651]

I should not have been so ample in my account of this transaction, had not the share I bore in it been made the subject of partial animadversion, and even my dismission from my employment thought worthy of being made, by Hoare and others, matter[652] of public triumph. The motive which might influence any person to descend to a petty contest with an obscure African, and to seek gratification by his depression, perhaps it is not proper here to enquire into or relate, even if its detection were necessary to my vindication;[653] but I thank Heaven it is not. I wish to stand by my own integrity, and not to shelter myself under the impropriety of another; and I trust the behaviour of the Commissioners of the Navy to me entitles me to make this assertion; for after I had been dismissed, March 24,[654] I drew up a memorial thus:

To The Right Honourable the Lords Commissioners
of his Majesty's Treasury.
The Memorial and Petition of GUSTAVUS VASSA, a black man,
late Commissary to the Black Poor, going to AFRICA.
HUMBLY SHEWETH,
    THAT your Lordships' memorialist was, by the Honourable the Commissioners of his Majesty's Navy, on the 4th of December last, appointed to the above employment by warrant from that board;

That he accordingly proceeded to the execution of his duty on board of the Vernon, being one of the ships appointed to proceed to Africa with the above poor;

That your memorialist, to his great grief and astonishment, received a letter of dismission, from the Honourable Commissioners of the Navy, by your Lordships' orders:

That, conscious of having acted with the most perfect fidelity and the greatest assiduity in discharging the trust reposed in him, he is altogether at a loss to conceive the reasons of your Lordships' having altered the favourable opinion you were pleased to conceive of him, sensible that your Lordships would not proceed to so severe a measure without some apparent good cause; he therefore has every reason to believe that his conduct has been grossly misrepresented to your Lordships, and he is the more confirmed in his opinion, because, by opposing measures of others concerned in the same expedition, which tended to defeat your Lordships' humane intentions, and to put the government to a very considerable additional expence, he created a number of enemies, whose misrepresentations, he has too much reason to believe, laid the foundation of his dismission. Unsupported by friends, and unaided by the advantages of a liberal education, he can only hope for redress from the justice of his cause, in addition to the mortification of having been removed from his employment, and the advantage which he reasonably might have expected to have derived therefrom. He has had the misfortune to have sunk a considerable part of his little property in fitting himself out, and in other expences arising out of his situation, an account of which he here annexes. Your memorialist will not trouble your Lordships with a vindication of any part of his conduct, because he knows not of what crimes he is accused; he, however, earnestly entreats that you will be pleased to direct an enquiry into his behaviour during the time he acted in the public service; and, if it be found that his dismission arose from false representations, he is confident that in your Lordships' justice he shall find redress.

Your petitioner therefore humbly prays that your Lordships will take his case into consideration, and that you will be pleased to order payment of the above referred to account, amounting to 32£.4s. and also the wages intended, which is most humbly submitted. *London, May 12, 1787.*

The above petition was delivered into the hands of their Lordships, who were kind enough, in the space of some few months afterwards, without hearing, to order me 50£. sterling—that is 18£. wages for the time (upwards of four months) I acted a faithful part in their service.—Certainly the sum is more than a free negro would have had in the western colonies!!!

[655]From that period to the present time my life has passed in an even tenor, and great part of my study and attention has been to assist in the cause of my much injured countrymen.

March the 21st, 1788, I had the honour of presenting the Queen with a petition on behalf of my African brethren, which was received most graciously by her Majesty:[656]

To the QUEEN's *Most Excellent Majesty*.
MADAM,

YOUR Majesty's well known benevolence and humanity embolden[657] me to approach your royal presence, trusting that the obscurity of my situation will not prevent your Majesty from attending to the sufferings for which I plead.

Yet I do not solicit your royal pity for my own distress: my sufferings, although numerous, are in a measure forgotten. I supplicate your Majesty's compassion for millions of my African countrymen, who groan under the lash of tyranny in the West Indies.

The oppression and cruelty exercised to the unhappy negroes there, have at length reached the British legislature, and they are now deliberating on its redress; even several persons of property in slaves in the West Indies have petitioned parliament against its continuance, sensible that it is as impolitic as it is unjust and what is inhuman must ever be unwise.

Your majesty's reign has hitherto been distinguished by private acts of benevolence and bounty; surely the more extended the misery is, the greater claim it has to your Majesty's compassion, and the greater must be your Majesty's pleasure in administering to its relief.

I presume, therefore, gracious Queen, to implore your interposition with your royal consort, in favour of the wretched Africans; that, by your Majesty's benevolent influence, a period may now be put to their misery; and that they may be raised from the condition of brutes, to which they are at present degraded, to the rights and situation of men,[658] and be[659] admitted to partake of the blessings of your Majesty's happy government; so shall your Majesty enjoy the heart-felt pleasure of procuring happiness to millions, and be rewarded in the grateful prayers of themselves, and of their posterity.

And may the all-bountiful Creator shower on your Majesty, and the Royal Family, every blessing that this world can afford, and every fulness of joy which divine revelation has promised us in the next.

I am your Majesty's most dutiful and devoted servant to command,

GUSTAVUS VASSA,

The oppressed Ethiopian.

No. 53, Baldwin's-Gardens.

The negro consolidated act, made by the assembly of Jamaica last year, and the new act of amendment now in agitation there, contain a proof of the existence of those charges that have been made against the planters relative to the treatment of their slaves.[660] I hope to have the satisfaction of seeing the renovation of liberty and justice, resting on the British government, to vindicate the honour of our common nature. These are concerns which do not perhaps belong to any particular office: but, to speak more seriously to every man of sentiment, actions like these are the just and sure foundation of future fame; a reversion,[661] though remote, is coveted by some noble minds as a substantial good. It is upon these grounds that I hope and expect the attention of gentlemen in power. These are designs consonant to the elevation of their rank, and the dignity of their stations; they are ends suitable to the nature of a free and generous government; and, connected with views of empire and dominion, suited to the benevolence and solid merit of the legislature. It is a pursuit of substantial greatness.—May the time come—at least the speculation to me is pleasing—when the sable people shall gratefully commemorate the auspicious aera of extensive freedom: then shall those persons[662] particularly be named with praise and honour, who generously proposed and stood forth in the cause of humanity, liberty, and good policy; and brought to the ear of the legislature designs worthy of royal patronage and adoption.[663] May Heaven make the British senators the dispersers of light, liberty and science, to the uttermost parts of the earth: then will be glory to God on the highest, on earth peace, and good-will to men.—Glory, honour, peace, &c. to every soul of man that worketh good; to the Britons first, (because to them the Gospel is preached), and also to the nations. "Those that honour their Maker have mercy on the poor."[664] "It is righteousness exalteth a nation; but sin is a reproach to any people:[665] destruction shall be to the workers of iniquity,[666] and the wicked shall fall by their own wickedness."[667] May the blessings of the Lord be upon the heads of all those who commiserated the cases of the oppressed negroes, and the fear of God prolong their days; and may their expectations be filled with gladness! "The liberal devise liberal things, and by liberal things shall stand," Isaiah xxxii. 8. They can say with pious Job, "Did not I weep for him that was in trouble; Was not my soul grieved for the poor?" Job xxx. 25.

[668]As the inhuman traffic of slavery is now taken into[669] the consideration of the British legislature, I doubt not, if a system of commerce was established in Africa, the demand for manufactures would most rapidly augment, as the native inhabitants would[670] insensibly adopt the British fashions, manners, customs, &c. In proportion to the civilization, so will be the consumption of British manufactures.

The wear and tear of a continent, nearly twice as large as Europe, and rich in vegetable and mineral productions, is much easier conceived than calculated.

A case in point.—It cost the Aborigines of Britain little or nothing in clothing, &c. The difference between their forefathers and the present generation, in point of consumption, is literally infinite. The supposition is most obvious. It will be equally immense in Africa.—The same cause, viz. civilization, will ever have the same effect.

It is trading upon safe grounds. A commercial intercourse with Africa opens an inexhaustible source of wealth to the manufacturing interests of Great Britain,[671] and to all which the slave-trade is an objection.

If I am not misinformed, the manufacturing interest is equal, if not superior, to the landed interest, as to the value, for reasons which will soon appear. The abolition of slavery, so diabolical, will give a most rapid extension of manufactures, which is totally and diametrically opposite to what some interested people assert.

The manufacturers of this country must and will, in the nature and reason of things, have a full and constant employ, by supplying the African markets.

Population, the bowels and surface of Africa, abound in valuable and useful returns; the hidden treasures of centuries will be brought to light and into circulation. Industry, enterprize, and mining, will have their full scope, proportionably as they civilize. In a word, it lays open an endless field of commerce to the British manufacturers and merchant adventurers. The manufacturing interest and the general interests are synonimous. The abolition of slavery would be in reality an universal good.

Tortures, murder, and every other imaginable barbarity and iniquity are practised upon the poor slaves with impunity. I hope the slave-trade will be abolished. I pray it may be an event at hand. The great body of manufacturers, uniting in the cause, will considerably facilitate and expedite it; and, as I have already stated, it is most substantially their interest and advantage, and as such the nation's at large, (except those persons concerned in the manufacturing neck-yokes, collars, chains, hand-cuffs, leg-bolts, drags,[672] thumb-screws, iron-muzzles, and coffins; cats, scourges, and other instruments of torture used in the slave trade). In a short time one sentiment alone will prevail, from motives of interest as well as justice and humanity. Europe contains one hundred and twenty millions of inhabitants. Query.—How many millions doth Africa contain? Supposing the Africans, collectively and individually, to expend 5£ a head in raiment and furniture yearly when civilized, &c. an immensity beyond the reach of imagination!

This I conceive to be a theory founded upon facts, and therefore an infallible one. If the blacks were permitted to remain in their own country, they would double themselves every fifteen years. In proportion to such increase will be the demand for manufactures. Cotton and indigo grow spontaneously in most parts of Africa; a consideration this of no small consequence to the manufacturing towns of Great Britain. It opens a most immense, glorious, and happy prospect—the clothing, &c. of a continent ten thousand miles in circumference, and immensely rich in productions of every denomination in return for manufactures.

[673]Since the first publication of my Narrative, I have been in a great variety of scenes in many parts of Great Britain, Ireland, and Scotland, an account of which might well be added here;[674] but as this would swell the volume too much,[675] I shall only observe in general, that in May 1791, I sailed from Liverpool to Dublin where I was very kindly received, and from thence to Cork, and then travelled over many counties in Ireland. I was every where exceedingly well treated, by persons of all ranks. I found the people extremely hospitable, particularly in Belfast, where I took my passage on board of a vessel for Clyde, on the 29th of January, and arrived at Greenock on the 30th. Soon after I returned to London, where I found persons of note from Holland and Germany, who requested me to go there; and I was glad to hear that an edition of my Narrative had been printed in both places, also in New York. I remained in London till I heard the debate in the house of Commons on the Slave Trade, April the 2d and 3d. I then went to Soham in Cambridgeshire, and was married on the 7th of April to Miss Cullen, daughter of James and Ann Cullen, late of Ely.[676]

I have only therefore to request the reader's indulgence, and conclude. I am far from the vanity of thinking there is any merit in this Narrative; I hope censure will be suspended, when it is considered that it was written by one who was as unwilling as unable to adorn the plainness of truth by the colouring of imagination. My life and fortune have been extremely chequered, and my adventures various. Even those I have related are considerably abridged. If any incident in this little work should appear uninteresting and trifling to most readers, I can only say, as my excuse for mentioning it, that almost every event of my life made an impression on my mind, and influenced my conduct. I early accustomed myself to look at the hand of God in the minutest occurrence, and to learn from it a lesson of morality and religion; and in this light every circumstance I have related was to me of importance. After all, what makes any event important, unless by it's observation we become better and wiser, and learn "to do justly, to love mercy, and to walk humbly before God!"[677] To those who are possessed of this spirit, there is scarcely any book or incident so trifling that does not afford some profit, while to others the experience of ages seems of no use; and even to pour out to them the treasures of wisdom is throwing the jewels of instruction away.[678]

THE END.

EXPLANATORY AND TEXTUAL NOTES

1 The letter "To the Reader" appears in eds. 5–9.

In ed. 4 only, immediately following the title page, is "TO THE MOST REVEREND FATHER IN GOD, ROBERT, Lord Archbishop of Dublin, &c. This edition of my Narrative is humbly Inscribed (as a small Token of my Gratitude for his unequalled Beneficence) BY HIS GRACE'S MOST OBLIGED, AND MOST OBEDIENT, HUMBLE SERVANT, GUSTAVUS VASSA. *Dublin, 30th May,* 1791."

2 The attack in *The Oracle* reads:

It was well observed by Chubb, that there is no absurdity, however gross, but popular credulity has a throat wide enough to swallow it. It is a fact that the Public may depend on, that *Gustavus Vasa,* who has publicly asserted that he was kidnapped in Africa, never was upon that Continent, but was born and bred up in the Danish Island of Santa Cruz, in the West Indies. *Ex hoc uno disce omnes* [this one fact tells all]. What, we will ask any man of plain understanding, must that cause be, which can lean for support on falsehoods as audaciously propagated as they are easily detected?

Modern Patriotism, which wantons so much in sentiment, is *really* founded rather in private interested views, than in a regard for the Public Weal. The conduct of the friends to the Abolition is a proof of the justice of this remark. It is a fact, of which, perhaps, the People are not apprized, but which it well becomes them to know, that WILBERFORCE and the THORNTONS are concerned in settling the Island of Bulam in Sugar Plantations; of course their interests clash with those of the present Planters and hence their clamour against the Slave Trade.

"Old Cato is as great a Rogue as You."

["Chubb" probably refers to Thomas Chubb (1679–1747), whose assessment of human credulity can be found in *A Discourse on Miracles, Considered as Evidence to Prove the Divine Original of a Revelation* (London, 1741): "Man is a creature not only *capable* of being imposed upon by *others,* but likewise of imposing upon *himself.* . . . As men are thus *capable* of misleading themselves, so *sometimes,* and under *some circumstances,* the delusion is *catching*" (72–73).

The writer in *The Oracle* refers to William Wilberforce (1759–1833), leader in the House of Commons of the movement to abolish the slave trade, along with Henry Thornton (1760–1815), chairman of the Sierra Leone Company Court of Directors, and William Thornton (1761–1828), a slave-owning West Indian Quaker who moved to the United States and who supported his friend Henry Smeathman's proposal for resettling Afro-Britons in Sierra Leone. None of them participated in the short-lived scheme of the Bulama Island Association to set up an agricultural colony off the coast of Western Africa, which the West Indian planters rightly saw as a potential commercial threat to their own interests.

The quotation is from Alexander Pope, *The Epistle to Bathurst* (London, 1733), 68.]

3 The attack in *The Star* reads:
The Negroe, called GUSTAVUS VASA, who has published an history of his life, and gives so admirable an account of the laws, religion, and natural productions of the interior parts of Africa; and in which he relates his having been kidnapped in his infancy, is neither more nor less, than a native of the Danish island of Santa Cruz.
Both newspaper attacks appeared while Equiano was in Scotland, preparing and promoting the 5th edition of his book.

4 [Equiano's note]
      —"Speak of me as I am,
Nothing extenuate, nor set down aught
In malice."—. [William Shakespeare, *Othello* 5:2:342.]

5 [Equiano's note]
      I may now justly say,
"There is a lust in man no charm can tame,
Of loudly publishing his [our] neighbour's shame;
On eagles wings immortal scandals fly,
But [While] virtuous actions are but born and die."*

London. The Country Chronicle and Weekly Advertiser for Essex, Herts, Kent, Surry, Middlesex, &c. Tuesday, February 19th, 1788.—Postscript.
"We are sorry the want of room prevents us from giving place to the favors of GUSTAVUS VASSA on the Slave Trade. The zeal of this worthy African, in favour of his brethren, would do honour to any colour or to any cause."
[Equiano's verse quotation is taken, with minor changes indicated in brackets, from Stephen Harvey's translation of Juvenal, *Satire* 9, first published in 1697.]

6 [Equiano's note] My friend Mrs. Baynes, formerly Miss Guerin, at Southhampton, and many others of her friends.
John Hill, Esq. Custom-house, Dublin.

Admiral Affleck.
Admiral George Balfour, Portsmouth.
Captain Gallia, Greenock.
Mrs. Shaw, James-street, Covent-Garden, London.

7 Candid: fair-minded.

8 *"Edinburgh, June* 1792" in eds. 8 and 9; ed. 6 reads, *"London, Dec.* 30, 1792"; ed. 7 reads, *"London, August* 1793."

9 In eds. 5–9.

10 Ult.: contraction for *ultimo*, meaning *last*.

11 In eds. 5–9.

12 In eds. 1 and 2, this address, followed by the "List of Subscribers," is placed immediately after the title page.

13 Equiano's description of himself as humble and unpretentious is quite conventional for writers of autobiographies during the period. A writer of a spiritual autobiography, such as Equiano's, would be especially aware of the danger of sounding too proud. By "unlettered" he means lacking formal education, particularly in the classical languages of Greek and Latin. Two kinds of *countrymen* appear in this letter: those he addresses are his political countrymen, whose culture and values he has embraced and to whom he appeals as a British subject with the right to petition the members of Parliament; those he refers to in the letter itself are his fellow native Africans, his countrymen by birth.

14 *March* 1789: ed. 1 reads, "Union-Street, Mary-le-bone, March 24, 1789"; ed. 2 reads, "No. 10, Union-Street, Mary-le-bone, Dec. 24, 1789"; eds. 3 and 4 read, "No. 4, Taylor's Buildings, St. Martin's-Lane, October 30, 1790"; ed. 5 reads, "June 1792"; ed. 6 reads, "December 1792"; eds. 7 and 8 read, "March 1789."

15 In eds. 3–9.

16 In eds. 3–9.

17 In eds. 3–9.

18 In eds. 5–9.

19 In eds. 5–9.

20 In eds. 6–9.

21 In eds. 6–9.

22 In eds. 8 and 9.

23 In eds. 5–9.

24 In eds. 3–9.

25 See Othello's speech in Shakespeare, *Othello* 1.3.89: "Yet, by your gracious patience, I will a round unvarnished tale deliver of my whole course of love."

26 N.B.: nota bene, note well. This paragraph appears only in eds. 8 and 9.

27 "The kind reception . . . African": in eds. 3–9.

28 In eds. 1–9, although varying in content.

29 In eds. 6–9.

30 In eds. 7–9.

31 In eds. 8 and 9.

32 In ed. 9 only.

33 In ed. 9 only.

34 In eds. 4–9. Robert Fowler (1726?–1801) was the Anglican Archbishop of Dublin (1779–1801).

35 In eds. 5–9.

36 The "history of neither a saint, a hero, nor a tyrant" was increasingly seen in the seventeenth and eighteenth centuries as the proper subject for autobiography, biography, and the novel. In his *Rambler* 60 (13 October 1750), Samuel Johnson (1709–1784) tells us why:

> Our passions are therefore more strongly moved, in proportion as we can more readily adopt the pains or pleasures proposed to our minds, by recognising them as once our own, or considering them as naturally incident to our state of life. It is not easy for the most artful writer to give us an interest in happiness or misery, which we think ourselves never likely to feel, and with which we have never yet been made acquainted. Histories of the downfall of kingdoms, and revolutions of empires, are read with great tranquillity; the imperial tragedy pleases common auditors only by its pomp of ornament, and grandeur of ideas; and the man whose faculties have been engrossed by business, and whose heart never fluttered but at the rise or fall of stocks, wonders how the attention can be seized, or the affections agitated by a tale of love.

37 Countrymen: used here to mean those born in the same geographical area, in the widest sense, Africa.

38 Providence is God as the designer, caretaker, and superintendent of the world and its inhabitants, especially humankind. As the derivation of the term from the Latin *pro-video* (to look forward) implies, events in God's creation happen by plan, not chance. And because God is benevolent, all events, no matter how apparently evil, are part of the grand design whose outline has been revealed to humans in the Bible. Equiano's references here to being "a particular favourite," and elsewhere to particular providences convey his belief that God has invested the events of his individual life with significance not as easily recognized in the lives of most humans.

39 That is, nearly on the equator.

40 Abyssinia: the ancient name for modern Ethiopia.

41 The passage in brackets appears only in the 1st ed. of 1789.

42 [Equiano's note, eds. 8 and 9] See the Observations on a Guinea Voyage, in a series of letters, addressed to the Rev. T. Clarkson, by Jas. Field, Stanfield, in 1788, page 21—"I never saw a happier race of people than those of the kingdom of Benin, seated in ease and plenty, the Slave Trade, and its unavoidable bad effects excepted; every thing bore the appearance of friendship, tranquillity, and primitive independence."

[Equiano quotes from Letter 4 of Stanfield (d. 1824), *Observations on a Voyage to the Coast of Africa, in a Series of Letters to Thomas Clarkson, by James Field Stanfield, Formerly a Mariner in the African Trade*. The immediate context of Stanfield's observation is probably also relevant here: he is responding to the assertions made by proponents of the slave trade that West Indian slavery was a material improvement in the living conditions of Africans. The manuscript of Stanfield's *Observations* was approved for publication by the Society for Effecting the Abolition of the Slave Trade, which ordered the printing of three thousand copies of it for distribution.

Equiano's homeland was that of the present Igbo people of modern Nigeria; scholars' attempts to locate Essaka have been so far unsuccessful.]

43 [Equiano's note, eds. 1–9] See Benezet's Account of Guinea throughout.

[Anthony Benezet (1713–1784), *Some Historical Account of Guinea, Its Situation, Produce, and the General Disposition of Its Inhabitants. With an Inquiry into the Rise and Progress of the Slave Trade, Its Nature, and Lamentable Effects* (London, 1788). Much of Equiano's description of Africa, as he indicates, parallels that found in Benezet, which in turn is largely an acknowledged digest of previous accounts by European travelers. Benezet's writings against the slave trade were republished and distributed throughout Britain after his death by the Society for Effecting the Abolition of the Slave Trade.

Equiano's emphasis on the sanctity of marriage and the consequent severe punishment for adultery contrasts sharply with the common proslavery assertions of African sexual promiscuity, which, the apologists for slavery claimed, accounted for the low birthrate among slaves that required the constant resupply provided by the slave trade. For example, James Grainger (1721?–1766), *An Essay on the More Common West-India Diseases* (London, 1764): "Black women are not so prolific as the white inhabitants, because they are less chaste. . . ." (14).]

44 [Equiano's note, eds. 1–9] When I was in Smyrna [under the dominion of Turkey] I have frequently seen the Greeks dance after this manner.

45 The ancestor of the modern banjo.

46 Stickado: xylophone.

47 Calico, or muslin: types of cotton cloth.

48 Highland: Scottish.

49 [Equiano's note, eds. 1–9] The bowl is earthen, curiously figured, to which a long reed is fixed as a tube. This tube is sometimes so long as to be borne by one, and frequently, out of grandeur, by two boys.

50 Such "refinements" were usually associated with the French during the period.

51 Plantain: a type of banana that must be cooked before being eaten.

52 Eadas: from a West African word for an edible tuberous plant.

53 Indian corn: what is commonly known in North America as corn and in Europe as maize; distinguished from Guinea corn, or millet.

54 In only the 1st ed. the passage "by pouring . . . certain place" reads "by pouring out a small portion of the food, in a certain place."

55 Only the 1st ed. reads "is gotten."

56 [Equiano's note, eds. 1–9] When I was in Smyrna I saw the same kind of earth, and brought some of it with me to England; it resembles musk in strength, but is more delicious in scent, and is not unlike the smell of a rose.

57 Equiano's description would probably have reminded his readers of a well-known passage from Michel Adanson (1727–1806), *A Voyage to Senegal, the Isle of Goree, and the River Gambia* (London, 1759):

> Which way soever I turned my eyes on this pleasant spot, I beheld a perfect image of pure nature: an agreeable solitude, bounded on every side by a charming landskip; the rural situation of cottages in the midst of trees; the ease and indolence of the Negroes, reclined under the

shade of their spreading foliage; the simplicity of their dress and manners; the whole revived in my mind, the idea of our first parents, and
I seemed to contemplate the world in its primeval state (54).

Adanson's passage reappears frequently in the anti–slave trade works of
the period, including Benezet's *Account* and Thomas Day (1748–1789) and
John Bicknell, *The Dying Negro* (London, 1773), a poem Equiano quotes
later in his *Narrative*. Adanson's comment was so popular because it could
be used as eyewitness evidence to refute the proslavers' argument that they
were saving Africans from the hardships of their homeland by removing
them to the West Indies.

58 Stout: strong, powerful.

59 Trepan: to ensnare, to trick.

60 Contemporaneous accounts disagree. For example, James Grainger
(1721?–1766), in *The Sugar-Cane. A Poem* (London, 1764), 2:75, notes,
"teeth-fil'd Ibbos or *Ebboes*, as they are more commonly called, are a numerous nation. Many of them have their teeth filed, and blackened in an
extraordinary manner. They make good slaves when bought young; but are,
in general, foul feeders, many of them greedily devouring the raw guts of
fowls: They also feed on dead mules and horses; whose carcases, therefore,
should be buried deep, that the Negroes may not come at them. But the
surest way is to burn them; otherwise they will be apt, privily, to kill those
useful animals, in order to feast on them." In *An Essay on the More Common West-India Diseases. . . . To which Are Added, Some Hints on the Management . . . of Negroes* (London, 1764), he remarks, "In the Ibbo country,
the women chiefly work; they, therefore, are to be preferred to the men of
the same country at a negroe sale. . . ." (7).

Bryan Edwards (1743–1800) says:

. . . All the Negroes imported from these vast and unexplored regions
[the Bight of Benin] . . . are called in the West Indies *Eboes*; and in
general they appear to be the lowest and most wretched of all the
nations of Africa. In complexion they are much yellower than the
Gold Coast and Whidah Negroes; but it is a sickly hue, and their eyes
appear as if suffused with bile, even when they are in perfect health.
I cannot help observing too, that the conformation of the face, in a
great majority of them, very much resembles that of the baboon. . . .

The great objection to the Eboe as slaves, is their constitutional
timidity, and despondency of mind; which are so great as to occasion
them very frequently to seek, in a voluntary death, a refuge from their
own melancholy reflections. They require therefore the gentlest and
mildest treatment to reconcile them to their situation; but if their
confidence be once obtained, they manifest as great fidelity, affection,

and gratitude, as can reasonably be expected from men in a state of slavery. The females of this nation are better labourers than the men, probably from having been more hardly treated in Africa.

The depression of spirits which these people seem to be under, on their first arrival in the West Indies, gives them an air of softness and submission, which forms a striking contrast to the frank and fearless temper of the Koromantyn Negroes. Nevertheless, the Eboes are in fact more truly savage than any nation of the Gold Coast; inasmuch as many tribes among them . . . have been, without doubt, accustomed to the shocking practice of feeding on human flesh. . . .

Of the religious opinions and modes of worship of the Eboes, we know but little; except that . . . they pay adoration to certain reptiles, of which the guana (a species of lizard) is in the highest estimation. They universally practice circumcision. . . . (*The History, Civil and Commercial, of the British Colonies in the West Indies. In Two Volumes* [London, 1793], 2: 69–71).

61 The relativity of the significance of skin color was often remarked by Equiano's contemporaries; for example, Adanson notes in *A Voyage* that "It came into my head, that my colour, so opposite to the blackness of the Africans, was the first thing that struck the children: those poor little creatures were then in the same case as our own infants, the first time they see a Negroe" (74).

62 [Equiano's note, eds. 1–9] See Benezet's account of Africa throughout.

[Equiano seems to be referring to what is essentially an earlier version of *Some Historical Account of Guinea: A Short Account of that Part of Africa, Inhabited by the Negroes. With Respect to the Fertility of the Country; the Good Disposition of Many of the Natives, and the Manner by which the SLAVE TRADE Is Carried on. Extracted from Divers Authors, in Order to Shew the Iniquity of that Trade, and the Falsity of the ARGUMENTS usually Advanced in its Vindication. With Quotations from Several Persons of Note, viz. GEORGE WALLIS, FRANCIS HUTCHESON, and JAMES FOSTER. . . . The Second Edition, with Large Additions and Amendments* (Philadelphia, 1762).]

63 Compare Willem Bosman's observation, quoted in Benezet's *Account* (155):

If the person who occasioned the beginning of the war be taken, they will not easily admit him to ransom, though his weight in gold be offered, for fear he should in future form some new design against their repose.

64 Oblation: an offering.

65 Of the name Olaudah, Edwards remarks, in his Introduction to the facsimile reprint of the first edition of the *Narrative*, "The second element of the name may be either *ude*, 'fame' . . . or *uda*, 'resonant, resounding. . . .' The latter seems more likely, though I have been told that a name composed of *ola*, 'ornament,' and *ude*, having the sense of 'ornament of fame,' might signify 'fortunate.' But I know of no occurrence of any such name in modern times" (lxxiv).

66 Certain times: during menstruation.

67 Only the 1st ed. reads "A virgin."

68 [Equiano's note, eds. 1–9] See also Lieut. Matthew's Voyage, p. 123. [The reference is to *A Voyage to the River Sierra-Leone, on the Coast of Africa; Containing an Account of the Trade and Productions of the Country, and of the Civil and Religious Customs and Manners of the People; in a Series of Letters to a Friend in England. By John Matthews, Lieutenant in the Royal Navy; During his Residence in that Country in the Years 1785, 1786, and 1787* (London, 1788). Matthews describes a very similar custom in Africa. Matthews was one of the principal witnesses for the slavery interest at the hearings held in Parliament on the slave trade.]

69 [Equiano's note, eds. 1–9] An instance of this kind happened at Montserrat, in the West Indies, in the year 1763. I then belonged to the ship Charming Sally, Capt. Doran.—The chief mate, Mr. Mansfield, and some of the crew being one day on shore, were present at the burying of a poisoned negro girl. Though they had often heard of the circumstance of the running in such cases, and had even seen it, they imagined it to be a trick of the corpse bearers. The mate therefore desired two of the sailors to take up the coffin, and carry it to the grave. The sailors, who were all of the same opinion, readily obeyed; but they had scarcely raised it to their shoulders before they began to run furiously about, quite unable to direct themselves, till at last, without intention, they came to the hut of him who had poisoned the girl. The coffin then immediately fell from their shoulders against the hut, and damaged part of the wall. The owner of the hut was taken into custody on this, and confessed the poisoning.—I give this story as it was related by the mate and crew on their return to the ship. The credit which is due to it I leave with the reader.
[Slave owners in general were quite anxious about their vulnerability to being poisoned by their domestic slaves. For example, in 1740, slaves in New York City were accused of conspiring to poison their masters; and *The London Chronicle* (8 April 1789) carried stories of slaves in Jamaica and London accused of "the horrid practice of administering poison."]

70 [Equiano's note, eds. 6–9] See 1 Chron. 1. 33. Also John Brown's [A] Dictionary of the [Holy] Bible [Edinburgh, 1788] on the same verse.

[Equiano's linking of Africans with Jews reflects the widespread belief among both supporters and opponents of the slave trade that, in the words of John Gill (1697–1771), cited below in the *Narrative*, ". . . all *Africa* and a considerable part of *Asia* were possessed by the four sons of *Ham* and their posterity. . . ." (73). The point of contention between the two sides was over the issue of whether these descendants of Ham were, like him, cursed for his having mocked Noah. If so, they were doomed to be "most wicked and miserable, and few of them have hitherto enjoyed the light of the gospel" (Brown [1722–1787], *Dictionary*, 2:573). Since Brown's *Dictionary* is arranged topically and does not annotate particular verses, Equiano is probably thinking here (and again in Chapter XI, when he cites Brown) of Matthew Henry (1662–1714), *An Exposition of the Old Testament, in Four Volumes* (London, 1710), the eighth edition of which (Edinburgh, 1772) he bought in London on 2 May 1777.

Equiano certainly knew the discussions of the subject found in Granville Sharp (1735–1813), *The Just Limitation of Slavery* (London, 1776); Thomas Clarkson (1760–1846), *Essay on the Slavery and Commerce of the Human Species* (London, 1786); and Ottobah Cugoano (1757?–1791+), *Thoughts and Sentiments on the Evil and Wicked Traffic of the Slavery and Commerce of the Human Species* (London, 1787).]

71 John Gill, *An Exposition of the Old Testament, in which Are Recorded the Original of Mankind, of the Several Nations of the World, and of the Jewish Nation in Particular. . . .* (London, 1788), 158.

72 *The Truth of the Christian Religion. In Six Books. By Hugo Grotius. Corrected and Illustrated with Notes by Mr. Le Clerc. To which Is Added, a Seventh Book, Concerning this Question, What Christian Church We Ought to Join Ourselves to? By the Said Mr. Le Clerc. Ninth Edition. Done into English by John Clarke* (London, 1786).

73 Confirmed . . . Bedford: eds. 1 and 2 read: "confirmed by the scripture chronology." See Arthur Bedford (1668–1745), *The Scripture Chronology Demonstrated by Astronomical Calculations, and also by the Year of Jubilee, and the Sabbatical Year among the Jews; or, An Account of Time from the Creation of the World. . . .* (London, 1730), 229.

74 Law of retaliation: *lex talionis*, the law of an eye for an eye and a tooth for a tooth.

75 [Equiano's note, eds. 1–9] Page 178 to 216.

76 [Equiano's note, eds. 1–9] Philos. Trans. No. 476. Sect. 4. cited by the Rev. Mr. Clarkson, p. 205.

[Clarkson quotes the concluding sentence of John Mitchel, "Causes of the Different Colours of Persons in Different Climates," a paper read at meetings of the Royal Society from 3 May to 14 June 1744. Mitchel's paper is found in *The Philosophical Transactions (From the Year 1743 to the Year 1750) Abridged and Disposed under General Heads. . . . By John Martyn* [1699–1768] (London, 1756), 10:926–49.

Mitchel's larger conclusions may be relevant to Equiano's position on color:

> From what has been said about the cause of the colour of black and white people, we may justly conclude, that they might very naturally be both descended from one and the same parents, as we are otherwise better assured from Scripture, that they are . . . for the different colours of people have been demonstrated to be only the necessary effects and natural consequences of their respective climes, and ways of life . . . that they are the most suitable for the preservation of health, and the ease and convenience of mankind in these climes, and ways of living: so that the black colour of the negroes of *Africa*, instead of being a curse denounced on them, on account of their forefather *Ham*, as some have idly imagined, is rather a blessing, rendering their lives, in that intemperate region, more tolerable, and less painful: whereas, on the other hand, the white people, who look on themselves as the primitive race of man, from a certain superiority of worth, either supposed or assumed, seem to have the least pretention to it of any, either from history or philosophy; for they seem to have degenerated more from the primitive and original complexion, in *Noah* and his sons, than even the *Indians* and negroes; and that to the worst extreme, the most delicate, tender, and sickly (10:947).
>
> . . . we do not affirm, that either Blacks or Whites were originally descended from one another, but that both were descended from people of an intermediate tawny colour; whose posterity became more and more tawny, i.e. black, in the southern regions, and less so, or white, in the northern climes: whilst those who remained in the middle regions, where the first men resided, continued of their primitive tawny complexions; which we see confirmed by matter of fact, in all the different people in the world (10:948).]

77 [Equiano's note, eds. 1–9] Same page.

[Clarkson quotes from a *Treatise upon the Trade from Great Britain to Africa, by an African Merchant* (London, 1772), which is a proslavery tract.]

78 Equiano quotes from the description of "The good Sea-Captain" in Thomas Fuller (1608–1661) *The Holy State* (Cambridge, 1642):

> *In taking a prize* [capturing an enemy ship and all that it contains] *he most prizeth the mens lives whom he takes*; though some of them may chance to be Negroes or Savages. 'Tis the custome of some to cast them overbord, and there's an end of them: for the dumbe fishes will

tell no tales. But the murder is not so soon drown'd as the men. What, is a brother by the half bloud no kinne? A Savage hath God to his father by creation, though not the Church to his mother, and God will revenge his innocent bloud. But our Captain counts the image of God nevertheless his image cut in ebony as if done in ivory, and in the blackest Moores he sees the representation of the King of heaven. (129)

79 [Equiano's note, eds. 1–9] Acts xvii. 26.

80 Arts . . . exercise: eds. 1–4 read "art of war; my daily exercise."

81 Mouths . . . continued: eds. 1–7 read "mouths, and ran off with us into the nearest wood. Here they tied our hands, and continued."

82 Equiano's use of *deliverance* here to mean only physical salvation, as opposed to its later meaning in the *Narrative* of spiritual salvation, parallels the dual use of the term in spiritual biographies, including fictional ones, like *Robinson Crusoe* (1719), by Daniel Defoe (1660–1731). During the stage of his life before being exposed to Christianity, Equiano fails to yet recognize that, from a theological perspective, release from the slavery of sin is far more important than release from bodily bondage.

83 Them: eds. 1–4 read "it."

84 Reads "small comfort" in eds. 1–5.

85 Smith: blacksmith.

86 Reads "flogging" in eds. 1–8.

87 Only ed. 1 reads "(as in ours)."

88 I lay. . . . I expected: only ed. 1 reads "I lay hid. I then gave myself up for lost entirely, and expected."

89 Adapted or misremembered from Sir John Denham (1615–1669), *Cooper's Hill* (1642):
> Now ev'ry leaf, and ev'ry moving breath
> Presents a foe, and ev'ry foe a death. (lines 287–288)

90 Only ed. 1 reads "and not to be ill-treated."

91 Only ed. 1 reads "through many different countries, and a number of large woods."

92 The use of language was considered a uniquely human achievement, separating humans from animals; hence, the more civilized the people, the more developed, or copious, the language was thought to be.

93 Only ed. 1 reads "they indulged us together."

94 Equiano refers to the four stages of the African slave trade: the original capture by other Africans and transportation to the coast, during which many died from hunger, thirst, and exhaustion; the middle passage across the Atlantic, when disease and despair posed the most lethal threats; the seasoning, or period between arrival in the West Indies and full-time employment on the plantations, when the Africans were somewhat gradually introduced to the life of forced labor and when they were suddenly introduced to a new and therefore deadly disease environment; and the final stage of enslavement.

95 Equiano may be subtly reminding his readers of the common abolitionist argument that sugar could be profitably cultivated in Africa by free native labor.

96 The phrase "they are known . . . *core*" added in 5th and subsequent eds.
Core: cowry, a shell used as currency in West Africa.

97 Equiano must mean 172 pounds of cowry shells, because the price of slaves during the century ranged between 100 and 300 pounds apiece.

98 Suffer me: allow me.

99 Bound: enslaved.

100 Uncircumcised: like the Jews, Equiano uses this contemptuous label to distinguish other races from his own; at the same time, it reminds his readers of the Jewish-African relationship he sees.

101 Equiano refers to fortune here because, as a pagan, he still saw life as a matter of chance, rather than as a working out of Providential design and order.

102 Discovered: revealed.

103 Eat: a variant spelling of *ate*.

104 Equiano may be making the point that these Africans, the ones who have direct contact with the Europeans, are consequently the most morally corrupted. In *Thoughts upon Slavery* (London, 1774), John Wesley (1703–1791) says, "the Negroes who inhabit the coast of *Africa* . . . are represented by them who have no motive to flatter them, as remarkably sensible. . . . as industrious, . . . As fair, just, and honest in all their dealings, unless where Whitemen have taught them otherwise, . . . And as far more mild, friendly and kind to Strangers, than any of our Forefathers were" (16).

105 Pomkins: pumpkins.

106 Mechanics: skilled craftsmen or artisans.

107 Sound: healthy.

108 These two sentences were revised twice: the 1st ed. reads ". . . into terror when I was carried on board. I was immediately . . ."; the 3rd ed. reads ". . . into terror, which I am yet at a loss to describe; and the then feelings of my mind when carried on board. I was immediately . . ."; the final revision first appears in the 5th ed.

109 Long hair: only ed. 1 reads "loose hair."

110 Windlass: a winch, or crank, used to wind a heavy rope or chain to lift a weight.

111 Nettings: "a sort of fence, formed of an assemblage of ropes, fastened across each other" (William Falconer (1732–1769), *An Universal Dictionary of the Marine* [London, 1784; first published in 1769], hereafter cited in the notes as Falconer). These nettings were placed along the sides of the ship to form a caged enclosure to prevent the slaves from jumping overboard to try to escape or commit suicide.

112 The abolitionists frequently argued that the slave trade brutalized the enslavers as well as the enslaved. The tyrannical captain became almost a stock figure in the literature. The apologists for slavery argued that the trade served as a nursery for seamen. Evidence supports the abolitionists' claims that the trade was even more lethal, on an average percentage basis, for the crews than for the slaves. The Privy Council in 1789 estimated that the average mortality rate for slaves during the middle passage was 12.5 percent. Modern estimates of the mortality rate of 15 percent for slaves mean that of the approximately 10 million Africans taken to the Americas between 1600 and 1900, about 1.5 million died at sea. More than twice that number of African slaves died during the same period either while still in Africa or on their way to the Orient. The mortality rate of the much smaller number of marine slavers is estimated at about 20 percent. For both slaves and enslavers, the death rate varied with length of voyage, time, and age.

113 Foremast: the term *ship* was "particularly applied to a vessel furnished with three masts, each of which is composed of a lower mast, top mast, and top-gallant mast, with the usual machinery thereto belonging. The mast . . . placed at the middle of the ship's length, is called the main-mast, . . . that which is placed in the fore-part, the fore-mast, . . . and that which is towards the stern [the rear] is termed the mizen-mast" (Falconer).

114 Spell or magic: the anchor.

115 Boat: "a small open vessel, conducted on the water by rowing or sailing" (Falconer).

116 Necessary tubs: latrines.

117 Quadrant: "an instrument used to take the altitude of the sun or stars at sea, in order to determine the latitude of the place; or the sun's azimuth, so as to ascertain the magnetical variation" (Falconer).

118 Parcels: groups.

119 Made us jump: as a sign of health and strength.

120 The 1st ed. reads ". . . the houses were built with stories . . ."; the 2nd ed. reads ". . . the houses were built with bricks and stories . . ."; the final revision first appears in the 5th ed.

121 From . . . Africa: only ed. 1 reads "from those in Africa."

122 Equiano refers to what was known as the *scramble*, described from the perspective of an observer by Alexander Falconbridge (d. 1792) in *An Account of the Slave Trade on the Coast of Africa* (London, 1788):

> On a day appointed, the negroes were landed, and placed altogether in a large yard, belonging to the merchants to whom the ship was consigned. As soon as the hour agreed on arrived, the doors of the yard were suddenly thrown open, and in rushed a considerable number of purchasers, with all the ferocity of brutes. Some instantly seized such of the negroes as they could conveniently lay hold of with their hands. Others, being prepared with several handkerchiefs tied together, encircled with these as many as they were able. While others, by means of a rope, effected the same purpose. It is scarcely possible to describe the confusion of which this mode of selling is productive. It likewise causes much animosity among the purchasers, who, not unfrequently upon these occasions, fall out and quarrel with each other. The poor astonished negroes were so much terrified by these proceedings, that several of them, through fear, climbed over the walls of the court yard, and ran wild about the town; but were soon hunted down and retaken (34).

Falconbridge's *Account* was written at the behest of the Society for Effecting the Abolition of the Slave Trade, which printed and distributed six thousand copies of it.

123 Devoted: doomed.

124 Sloop: "a small vessel furnished with one mast" (Falconer).

125 Snow: "generally the largest of all two-masted vessels employed by Europeans, and the most convenient for navigation" (Falconer).

126 Pascal (d. 1787): appointed lieutenant, 9 December 1745; commander, 21 August 1759; post-captain, 20 June 1765. Pascal commanded the *Industrious Bee* as early as 5 June 1752, when he announced in *The Virginia Gazette* a reward for four men who had jumped ship.

127 This would have been a rather high price for a young, untrained boy, though in times of war, as at this point in Equiano's life, the price was somewhat inflated because of the disruption of the supply of slaves from Africa. Compare Granville Sharp's comment in *A Representation of the Injustice and Dangerous Tendency of Tolerating Slavery; or of Admitting the Least Claim of Private Property in the Persons of Men, in England* . . . (London, 1769):

> . . . a stout young Negro, who can read and write, and is approved of in domestic service, is sold for no more than thirty pounds in England; whereas it is certain, that such a one might be sold, at least, for the same sum in the West Indies; and sometimes, perhaps, for near double the money. . . . (43–44).

128 At this point in his life, Equiano is of course being deceived by those who tell him he is returning to his country, but they are also being ironically prophetic because once he experiences life in England he always sees it, rather than North America or the West Indies, as his home.

129 Idea: reads "sound" only in the 1st ed.

130 Pascal probably renamed Equiano to hide his status as a slave: Some British officers went so far as to carry their own slaves to sea in the King's ships, but this was best done under disguise, for naval opinion in general and the Admiralty's in particular inclined to regard a man-of-war as a little piece of British territory in which slavery was improper (N.A.M. Rodger, *The Wooden World: An Anatomy of the Georgian Navy* [London: Fontana Press, 1990], 160).
By being renamed *Gustavus Vassa*, Equiano becomes the namesake of Gustavus I, or Gustavus Vassa (1496–1560), the noble Swede who led his people to freedom from Danish rule in 1521–23 and went on to become a very successful king of liberated Sweden. But a British audience also associated the name with eighteenth-century arguments over political freedom in Britain because the government of Sir Robert Walpole had used the Licensing Act of 1737 to block the planned performance in 1738 of Henry Brooke's transparently anti-Walpole play, *Gustavus Vasa, The Deliverer of his Country.* Although published in 1739, the play was not staged in England until 1805, when it was performed at Covent Garden. (Retitled *The Patriot*, the play was performed in 1742 in Dublin.) Republication of *Gustavus Vasa* in 1761, 1778, 1796, and 1797 kept the play and its discourse of political slavery before the British public, and in the nineteenth century William Wordsworth considered using Vasa as the subject of an epic poem. *The Poetical Works of John Scott* (London, 1782) includes the suggestion that scenes from the play be subjects for paintings.
Slaves were often given ironically inappropriate names of powerful his-

torical figures like Caesar and Pompey to emphasize their subjugation to their masters' wills. Equiano probably expected his readers to recognize the parallel between the Swedish freedom fighter and the modern leader of his people's struggle against the slave trade, as well as the irony of his initial resistance to his new name.

131 And by which name I have been known ever since: only ed. 1 reads "and was obliged to bear the present name, by which I have been known ever since."

Except for its appearance on the title page, the name Olaudah Equiano was never used by the author of *The Interesting Narrative* in either public or private written communication. Whether in print, unpublished correspondence, or in his will, he always identified himself as Gustavus Vassa.

132 The English generally tended to consider sharks to be inedible. Sharks frequently followed slave ships, drawn to them by the bodies of dead slaves thrown overboard in the course of the middle passage. Considered one of the greatest terrors of the sea, the shark was often brutally treated when caught, and what Equiano witnesses is probably a case of gratuitous cruelty. Returning the finless shark to the ocean dooms it to a lingering and painful death.

133 People; I; eds. 1–5 read "people, though I."

134 Baker had been with Pascal at least since 20 June 1755, when his name appeared with Pascal's on the muster book of the *Roebuck* (PRO ADM 36/6472). Documents in the London Public Records Office (PRO) are identified by their class codes and piece numbers. In this and subsequent notes the following class codes are cited: ADM (Admiralty); PROB (Prerogative Court of Canterbury); PRIS (King's Bench Prison); PC (Privy Council Office); RG (General Register Office); T (Treasury); and TS (Treasury Solicitor).

135 America: though a native of North America, he was a British subject since the United States of America did not officially exist until 1783.

136 Archipelago: the islands of Greece. Baker died at sea on 21 February 1759 (PRO ADM 36/6367).

137 Discovered: revealed.

138 Kill and eat me: reads "kill me to eat" only in the 1st ed.

139 Grampus: a kind of whale, often used to refer to the killer whale.

140 Quarter-deck: "the Quarter of a ship [is] . . . that part of a ship's side which lies towards the stern [rear]. . . . Although the lines by which the quarter and bow [front] of a ship, with respect to her length, are only

imaginary, . . . if we were to divide the ship's sides into five equal portions, the names of each space would be readily enough expressed. Thus the first, from the stern, would be the quarter; the second, abaft [behind] the mid-ships; the third, the midships; the fourth before the midships; and the fifth, the bow" (Falconer).

141 Compare "seamen have a custom when they meet a *whale,* to fling him out an empty *tub* by way of amusement, to divert him from laying violent hands upon the ship" (Jonathan Swift [1667–1745], "The Preface" to *A Tale of a Tub* [London, 1704]).

142 As Equiano says earlier, this was an exceptionally long voyage, almost twice the normal time of about seven weeks.

143 Equiano actually reached Falmouth, England, via Newfoundland, Canada, on 14 February 1754. He joined the crew of the *Roebuck* 6 August 1755 (PRO ADM 36/6472). Equiano must either have been born before 1745 or been younger than he says he was when he was kidnapped: if he had been eleven years old when he was kidnapped, more than a year seems to have passed, though he now tells us he "was near twelve years of age." He has told us that six or seven months passed between his being kidnapped and his arrival on the coast of Africa; his trip to Barbados must have taken about two months; he was in Barbados for almost two weeks; his voyage to Virginia should have taken about a week; he was in Virginia for perhaps a month; and the passage to England took thirteen weeks. At least thirteen months have passed. He may have exaggerated his own age because the younger he was when he left Africa, the less credible his memory of his homeland would be.

Equiano's memory fails him at other times: he misremembers the dates of his first seeing George Whitefield and the celebration in Charleston of the repeal of the Stamp Act later in his *Narrative;* several of the revisions he makes after the first edition readjust the time scheme of his story.

144 Edwards points out in his Introduction that other Black writers had used the motif of the talking book. Equiano appears to be paraphrasing a similar account by a fellow Afro-Briton of a talking book found in James Albert Ukawsaw Gronniosaw, *A Narrative of the Most Remarkable Particulars in the Life of James Albert Ukawsaw Gronniosaw, an African Prince, As Related by Himself* (Bath, 1772):

. . . and when first I saw [my master] read, I was never so surprized in my life, as when I saw the book talk to my master, for I thought it did, as I observed him to look upon it, and move his lips.—I wished it would do so to me. As soon as my master had done reading, I followed him to the place where he took the book, being mightily delighted with it, and when nobody saw me, I opened it and put my ears down close upon it, in great hopes that it would say something to me; but was very sorry, and greatly disappointed when I found it would not speak, this thought immediately presented itself to me, that every body and every thing despised me because I was black (10).

In John Marrant (1755–1791), *Narrative of the Lord's Wonderful Dealings with John Marrant* (London: 2nd ed. 1785), the daughter of the king of the Indians is mystified by Marrant's Bible:

> His daughter took the book out of my hand a second time; she opened it, and kissed it again; her father bid her give it to me, which she did; but said, with much sorrow, the book would not speak to her (27).

In his *Thoughts and Sentiments on the Evil and Wicked Traffic of the Slavery and Commerce of the Human Species, Humbly Submitted to the Inhabitants of Great Britain, By Ottobah Cugoano, a Native of Africa,* Cugoano includes a similar episode of an illiterate person misunderstanding how reading works:

> The Inca opened it eagerly, and turning over the leaves, lifted it to his ear: This, says he, is silent; it tells me nothing; and threw it with disdain to the ground (80).

Cugoano's unacknowledged source for the anecdote is William Robertson (1721–1793), *The History of America* (London: 2nd ed., 1778), 2:175.

Yet another version of the story appears in *The Life, History, and Unparalleled Sufferings of John Jea, The African Preacher. Compiled and Written by Himself* (Portsea, 1812?):

> My master's sons also endeavoured to convince me, by their reading in the behalf of their father; but I could not comprehend their dark sayings, for it surprised me much, how they could take that blessed book into their hands, and to be so superstitious as to want to make me believe that the book did talk with them; so that every opportunity when they were out of the way, I took the book, and held it up to my ears, to try whether the book would talk with me or not, but it proved to be all in vain, for I could not hear it speak one word. . . .(33).

145 Him: reads "her" only in the 1st ed.

146 Nicholas Dobree II, born around 1727, in St. Peter Port, Guernsey.

147 Pascal, a lieutenant since 9 December 1745, became the first lieutenant on the *Roebuck* on 13 July 1756; the muster book identifies Baker as his servant, and "Gust. Vasa" as the captain's servant (PRO ADM 36/6472).

148 The Nore: an area near the mouth of the Thames where naval military fleets assembled during this period.

149 Man of war: "ships of war are properly equipped with artillery, ammunition, and all the necessary martial weapons and instruments for attack

or defence. They are distinguished from each other by their several ranks or classes" (Falconer). Because the next few pages of Equiano's *Narrative* are full of naval terminology, a general note from Falconer on the different classes, or rates, of men of war, and the significance of the *Royal George* may be helpful:

Rates [are] the orders or classes into which the ships of war are divided, according to their force and magnitude. . . .

The British fleet is accordingly distributed into six rates, exclusive of the inferior vessels that usually attend on naval armaments; as sloops of war, armed ships, bomb-ketches, fire-ships and . . . schooners commanded by lieutenants.

Ships of the first rate mount 100 cannon. . . . They are manned by 850 men. . . . Ships of the second rate carry 90 guns upon three decks. . . . Ships of the third rate carry from 64 to 80 cannon. . . . Ships of the fourth rate mount from 60 to 50 guns, upon two decks, and the quarter deck. . . . All vessels of war, under the fourth rate, are usually comprehended under the general names of frigates, and never appear in the line of battle[,]. . . . a general name given to the arrangement or order in which a fleet of ships of war are disposed to engage an enemy. . . .

Nothing more evidently manifests the great improvement of the marine art, and the degree of perfection to which it has arrived in England, than the facility of managing our first rates; which were formerly esteemed incapable of government, unless in the most favourable weather of the summer. In testimony of this observation we may, with great propriety, produce the example of the Royal George, which, during the whole course of the late war [the Seven Years War], was known to be as easily navigated, and as capable of service, as any of the inferior ships of the *line*, and that frequently in the most tempestuous seasons of the year.

The *Royal George* was still newsworthy because it had sunk while being repaired in 1782, drowning 800 people, and plans and attempts were made through the 1780s to salvage parts of the ship.

The *Roebuck* was a fifth rate 40 (that is, with 40 guns).

150 The Royal Navy had the authority to forcibly draft experienced seamen into service by boarding incoming merchant vessels or sending press-gangs ashore to impress, or press, those they wanted. Since Britain was fighting France in the Seven Years' War of 1756–1763 (called in North America the French and Indian War), the first truly worldwide war, the Navy's press-gangs were very active.

At the end of this chapter, Equiano becomes a member of a press-gang led by Pascal. In 1760, Pascal faced the prospect of legal prosecution for pressing men he wrongly thought were deserters from the Navy. In a letter to the Admiralty Board dated 5 May 1760, Francis Holburne (1704–1771), the King's Harbourmaster at Plymouth (1757–1765), supported Pascal, and the Board followed his recommendation that His Majesty's Solicitor be ordered to defend Pascal, should he be prosecuted (PRO/ADM/1/932).

151 Eds. 1–2 read "Immediately afterwards the press-gang."

152 An engagement: reads "a battle" only in the 1st ed.
Falconer defines *engagement* as "in a naval sense, implies a particular or general battle at sea; or an action of hostility between single ships, or *detachments*, or *squadrons* of ships of war."

153 Prize: "a vessel taken from the enemy by a ship of war, privateer, or armed merchantman" (Falconer). The captain and crew divided the value of the prizes among themselves.

154 Frigate: "a light nimble ship, built for the purposes of sailing swiftly. These vessels mount from twenty to thirty-eight guns, and are esteemed excellent cruizers" (Falconer). The ship he sees was indeed "French-built": the *Ambuscade*, a 5th rate 40, was the converted French *Embuscade*, captured by the British navy on 21 April 1746.

155 Jib: "the foremost sail of a ship" (Falconer).

156 Colours: "the flags or banners which distinguish the ships of different nations" (Falconer).

157 Portsmouth: "In England, the royal dockyards are at Chatham, Portsmouth, Plymouth, Deptford, Woolwich, and Sheerness. His Majesty's ships and vessels of war are generally moored at these ports, during the time of peace; and such as want repairing are taken into the docks, examined, and refitted for service" (Falconer).

158 Admiral John Byng (1704–1757) had been sent with thirteen ships and one army battalion to relieve the British garrison on Minorca besieged by numerically superior French troops. Outmaneuvered by a fleet of twelve French ships on 20 May 1756, Byng retreated, with the troops, to Gibraltar, and Minorca fell to the French on 28 May. Brought home under arrest for cowardice, disaffection, and neglect of duty, he was found guilty only of the latter. When King George II refused to pardon him, Byng was executed at Portsmouth on 14 March 1757. The public was furious with both Byng and the government, which was widely thought to have prosecuted Byng as a scapegoat for the ministry's failure to wage war vigorously.

159 An 8-gun vessel. Seamen were often lent for brief periods of time from one ship to another.

160 A 2nd rate 90.

161 They were the children of Maynard and Elizabeth Guerin: Eliza-beth Martha (b. 1721); Maynard Peter (1726–1760); and Mary (b. 1728), who became, on 1 May 1774, the second wife of Arthur Baynes, surgeon general to the garrison at Gibraltar, who died at the age of 65 in Southamp-ton on 25 March 1789 (PRO PROB 11/1182). While he served on the *Roebuck*, Pascal's wages were paid on 24 March 1757 to "Maynard Guerin Atty," who obviously acted as Pascal's authorized agent, the same role he was playing for the members of several army regiments at the time of his death on 6 May 1760. His two sisters were his only heirs (PRO PROB 11/856). In his will (PROB 11/1142), Pascal calls Mrs. Baynes, the former Mary Guerin, "my Cousin," to whom he leaves his "Shirt Pin as it origi-nally belonged to her ffamily [sic]."

162 Chilblain: skin inflammation of the hand or foot caused by the cold.

163 Mortification: gangrene.

164 Pascal served on the *Preston* as first lieutenant from 7 January 1757 to 10 November 1757 (PRO ADM 36/6367), when he was discharged to serve on the *Jason* from 10 November 1757 to 27 December 1757 (PRO ADM 36/6365). With him went his servant Baker and the captain's servant "Gustavus Vavasa" [sic].
    Duke of Cumberland: Duke of C—— in eds. 1–7. William Augustus, late duke of Cumberland (1721–1765), was the uncle of the reigning king of Britain, George III (1738–1820). Cumberland defeated the Jacobite rebels at Culloden in 1746 so thoroughly that he was given the nickname of "The Butcher." But in October 1757 he felt obligated to resign from the army, having been defeated at Hastenbeck in July and compelled to evacuate Hanover. Hence, Equiano helped to bring him back to Britain in disgrace.

165 Top: "a sort of platform, surrounding the lower mast-head, from which it projects on all sides like a scaffold" (Falconer). The fore-top was the top on the fore-mast.

166 D——d: damned.

167 Equiano has forgotten that between service on the *Preston* and the *Royal George*, Pascal and his servant "Gustavus Vassor" [sic] were on the *Ja-son* from 11 November to 27 December 1757 (PRO ADM 36/5888; PRO ADM 36/5743). Pascal entered the muster list of the *Royal George* as a 6th lieutenant on 27 December 1757; his servant "Gustavus Vasser" [sic] en-tered on 12 January 1758. Pascal was not demoted from 1st to 6th lieu-tenant; he went from being the senior lieutenant on a smaller ship to being the lieutenant with the least seniority on the largest ship in the Royal Navy (PRO ADM 36/5743). Each 1st and 2nd rate ship had six lieutenants.

168 With an authorized complement of 880 men, a 1st rate 100 like the *Royal George* often had on board well over 1,100 people, including dependents and purveyors of goods, when in a home port. In addition, ships usually carried livestock to supply fresh food while in port and at sea. When the *Royal George* sank while under repair at Spithead in August 1782, over 800 of the 1,100 onboard drowned, half of the victims thought to be women and children. In the eighteenth century, very few people, including seamen, knew how to swim.

169 A 2nd rate 90. The names of Pascal and his servant "Gustavus Vasser" [sic] appear on the muster book of the *Namur* as of 27 January 1758. On 2 August 1758 he became 3rd lieutenant on the *Namur* (PRO ADM 36/6253).

170 Edward Boscawen (1711–1761), called "Old Dreadnought," was already one of the most distinguished commanders in the navy because of his behavior at the taking of Porto Bello (1739) and at the siege of Cartagena (1741).

171 The British, under Lord Loudon, had failed to take Louisburg in June-September 1757. Louisburg guarded the mouth of the St. Lawrence river and thus the approach by water to Quebec and Montreal in the French colony of Canada.

172 Maintop gallant-mast head: "A mast, with regard to it's [sic] length, is either formed of one single piece, which is called a *pole mast*, or composed of several pieces joined together, each of which retains the name of mast separately. The lowest of these is accordingly named the lower-mast . . . the next in heighth [sic] is the top-mast, . . . which is erected at the head of the former; and the highest is the top-gallant mast, . . . which is prolonged from the upper end of the top mast. Thus the two last are no other than a continuation of the first upwards" (Falconer). The maintop gallant-mast head is thus the top of the ship's middle, or main mast. "Admiral of the fleet, the highest officer under the admiralty of Great-Britain: when he embarks on any expedition, he is distinguished by the union flag at the main-top-mast head. Vice-Admiral . . . the officer next in rank and command to the admiral; his flag is displayed at the fore top mast-head. Rear-Admiral . . . the officer next in rank and command to the vice-admiral, and who carries his flag at the mizen-top mast-head" (Falconer). Until 1864 these three ranks were further subdivided, in descending order, into Red, White, and Blue squadrons.

173 Admiral Sir Samuel Cornish (d. 1770), whose greatest victory would be the capture of Manila in the Spanish Philippines on 5 October 1762. The *Lenox* was a 3rd rate 74.

174 Teneriffe: largest of the Canary Islands. They reached Teneriffe on 13 March 1758 and left it on 20 April (PRO ADM 52/950).

175 Sugar loaf: a conical pile of refined sugar.

176 They reached Halifax Harbor on 10 May and Louisburg on 2 June (PRO ADM 52/950).

177 Colonel James Wolfe (1727–1759), after playing a major role in the taking of Louisburg, was appointed major general of the successful attack on Quebec, where he was killed during the battle of the Heights of Abraham on 13 September 1759, the final assault on the city. He was immortalized in Benjamin West's painting of his heroic end.

178 A 3rd rate 80.

179 Highlander: a Scotsman. Recently, during the Jacobite Rebellion of 1745–46, the most able enemies of the English, the Highlanders performed in the Seven Years' War with great distinction and ferocity on the British side. Equiano's account of the capture of an "Indian King" is corroborated by contemporaneous records: General James Wolfe to Lord George Germain, Louisbourg, 1 July 1758 (Germain Papers, part of Brigadier General Jeffrey Amherst Papers, William L. Clements Library, Ann Arbor, Michigan); Journals of James Thompson, Sr., 1758–1883, Reel M–2312, vol. 1, Archives Nationales du Quebéc.

180 Batteries: a battery was "A Place to plant guns on" (*A Military and Sea Dictionary* [London, 1711]).
Playing upon: firing upon.

181 Fireship: "an old vessel filled with combustible materials, and fitted with grappling-irons to hook, and set fire to, the enemies [sic] ships in battle, &" (Falconer).
George Balfour died in 1794.

182 Laforey, another junior captain: reads "another junior captain, Laforey" only in the 1st ed.
Sir John Laforey (1729?–1796) was commander of the *Hunter* sloop of war.

183 Eds. 1–5 read "a sixty-four, called the Bienfaisant, they brought off." This 3rd rate 64 was captured on 25 July 1758.

184 Would: eds. 1–4 read "could."

185 The city, defended by the French and Canadians under the command of Governor Drucour, fell to the British and Colonial forces led by Vice-Admiral Boscawen, Colonel Wolfe, and General Lord Jeffrey Amherst (1717–1797) on 26 July 1758. The assault had begun on 30 May.

186 Sir Charles Hardy (1716?–1780) and Philip Durell (d. 1766). Hardy's flagship was the 1st rate 100 *Royal William;* Durell's was the *Princess Amelia.*

187 Sounding: "the operation of trying the depth of the water, and the quality of the ground, by means of a plummet, . . . sunk from a ship to the bottom: (Falconer).

188 Ensign: "a large standard, or banner, hoisted on a long pole over the poop [,] . . . the highest and aftmost deck of a ship . . . [,] and called the ensign-staff" (Falconer).

189 Broadside: "in a naval engagement, the whole discharge of the artillery on one side of a ship of war . . ." (Falconer).

190 *Somerset*: a 3rd rate 64.

191 Admiral Hubert de Conflans, soon to be defeated by Admiral Sir Edward Hawke (flagship the *Royal George*) at the battle of Quiberon Bay at the mouth of the Loire River in northwestern France, 20–22 November 1759.

192 Bending a sail: "fastening it to it's [sic] yard [,] . . . a long piece of timber suspended upon the masts of a ship, to extend the sails to the wind" (Falconer).

193 Wore: the past tense of a variant of *veer*, to change course. Stood after: chased.

194 East-Indiaman: a vessel trading with India and owned by the East India Company.

195 Strike: "used to express the lowering of the colours, in token of surrender, to a victorious enemy" (Falconer).

196 Starting our water: pumping water from the ship. The *Namur* ran aground in the beginning of November 1758 (PRO ADM 52/950).

197 Eds. 1–4 read "between two and three years."

198 The entry in the parish register for 9 February reads "Gustavus Vassa a Black born in Carolina 12 years old."

199 Thomas Wilson (1663–1755), *An Essay towards an Instruction for the Indians; Explaining the Most Essential Doctrines of Christianity. Which May Be of Use to Such Christians, as Have not well Considered the Meaning of the Religion they Profess; or, Who Profess to Know GOD, but in Works Do Deny Him. in Several Short and Plain Dialogues. . . .* (London, 1740). Equiano probably refers to one of the later editions, such as *The Knowledge and Practice of Christianity Made Easy to the Meanest Capacities: or, an Essay towards an Instruction for the Indians* (London, 1781).

200 Eds. 1–7 read "Miss Guerin did me the honour to stand as godmother."

201 Rendezvous-house: a place, usually an inn near the Thames, where the commanding officer of a press-gang lodged his gang, received volunteers, gathered information, and which he used as the base of operations for impressing seamen from local taverns.

202 Wherry: "a light sharp boat, used in a river or harbour for carrying passengers from place to place" (Falconer).

203 Waterman: one who manages a boat or ferry.

204 Land's End: the westernmost point of southern England.

205 Levant: the eastern shore of the Mediterranean.

206 [Equiano's note] He had drowned himself in endeavouring to desert.
Mole: "a name given in the Mediterranean to a long pier, or artificial bulwark of masonry, extending obliquely across the entrance of a harbour, in order to break the force of the sea from the vessels which are anchored within" (Falconer).

207 Watered: took on fresh water for drinking.

208 *Culloden*: 3rd rate 74; *Conqueror*: 3rd rate 70.

209 Slipping their cables: releasing the ropes that held them.

210 Gunwales, or gunnels: "the upper edge of a ship's side" (Falconer).

211 Misquoted from Alexander Pope's translation of Homer's *Iliad*, which reads:

> O King! oh Father! hear my humble Pray'r. . . .
> If *Greece* must perish, we thy Will obey,
> But let us perish in the Face of Day. (17:728–32)

212 Admiral de la Clue Sabran.

213 Crowd sail: "to carry an extraordinary force of sail upon a ship, in order to accelerate her course on some important occasion" (Falconer).

214 *Newark*: a 2nd rate 80.

215 *Redoutable*: a 74-gun ship.

216 Equiano's consistent misspelling of Cape Lagos, on the southwestern corner of Portugal. The French defeat at Lagos Bay, 17–19 August 1759, by Boscawen destroyed France's hopes of combining its Atlantic fleet based at Brest with its Mediterranean fleet at Toulon in preparation for the planned invasion of Scotland by Marshal Comte Maurice de Saxe.

217 About . . . turned: eds. 1–2 read "In less than a minute the midnight for a certain space seemed turned."

218 Middle deck: of a three-deck ship.

219 Match-tub: containing the smoldering combustible material used to light the fuses and thus fire the ship's guns.

220 Reads "to the dear Miss Guerin" in only the 1st ed.

221 Vice-Admiral of the blue Thomas Broderick (d. 1769).

222 Pascal and his servant "Gustavus Vasser" [sic] were discharged on 20 August 1759 from the *Namur* because Pascal advanced to the command of the "*Etna*" (PRO ADM 36/6256). Equiano is using the term *captain* loosely, referring not to rank but to responsibility. The official rank of captain was that of post-captain, which Pascal did not attain until 20 June 1765. Informally, the commanding officer of any royal naval vessel, whatever his rank, was called captain, as were the commanders of merchant vessels. Hence, Pascal, though still a lieutenant, was now a "captain." Under him was a lieutenant of the fireship, Isaac Lewis (PRO ADM 32/5).

223 Schools were commonly established on the larger ships to educate the many boys aboard who were destined to become professional seamen and officers, positions which required a relatively high degree of literacy and mathematical knowledge.

224 The Havannah: the capital of Cuba, then a colony of Spain.

225 George II died on 25 October 1760 and was succeeded by his grandson George III.

226 The fleet left Spithead on 29 March but because of contrary winds did not reach Belle Isle until 7 April 1761.
Keppel: Commodore Augustus Keppel (1725–1786), later (1782) First Viscount Keppel. During the eighteenth century, *Commodore* was a temporary title given to a post-captain who had the responsibilities of a rear admiral (that is, command of a division of the squadron) but, because of lack of seniority, not the rank.
Belle-Isle: the siege and conquest of this island in Quiberon Bay by the combined sea and land forces under Keppel and General Studholme Hodgson, respectively, against the French garrison commanded by General Chevalier de Saint Croix took place 7 April–8 June 1761.

227 All official records identify him as John Mundall, Gunner (PRO ADM 32/5; PRO ADM 1/5301). His "very indifferent morals" probably contributed to his conviction by a court martial on 7 April 1762 on charges of "Breach of Discipline and other Misbehaviour" while serving under "Captain Paschal" [sic] on "the Aetna Fireship" (PRO ADM 1/5301).

228 Reads "the 20th of April" only in the 1st ed.

229 Who told him his time was short: ed. 1 reads "who told him time was short."

230 Half-deck: "the inferior ships of the line are equipped with two decks and a half, and frigates, sloops, &c. with one gun-deck and a half" (Falconer).

231 Waist: "that part of a ship which is contained between the quarterdeck and fore-castle, being usually a shallow space, with an ascent of several steps to either of those places." The forecastle was "a short deck placed in the fore-part of the ship, above the upper deck" (Falconer).

232 Sir John Clarke (d. 1775) was the acting captain of the *Lynne*, a 5th rate 44, 15 January–30 May 1761 (PRO ADM 36/5981).

233 Cutwater: "the foremost part of a ship's prow" (Falconer).

234 Hatchway or hatch: "a square or oblong opening in the deck of a ship, of which there are several, forming the passages from one deck to another, and into the *hold* or lower apartments. . . . Hatches is also, although improperly, a name applied by sailors to the covers or lids of the hatchways" (Falconer).
Combings: the raised sides of the hatch.

235 The Lieutenant of the *Aetna*, Isaac Lewis, was killed 8 April 1761, "Landing Men on Belle Isle" (PRO ADM 32/5).

236 Frapping: "the act of passing three, four, or five turns of a cable round the hull, or frame of a ship, in the middle, to support her in a great storm, when it is apprehended that she is not strong enough to resist the violent efforts of the sea" (Falconer).
Hawser: "a large rope" (Falconer).

237 Crazy: broken down.

238 Again Equiano is mistaken in his dates: Pascal and his servant, "Gustavus Vassor" [sic] served on the *Jason* 11 November–27 December 1757, when they transferred to the *Royal George*.

239 Hold: "the whole interior cavity or belly of a ship, or all that part of her inside which is comprehended between the floor and the lower-deck, throughout her whole length" (Falconer).
Keel: "the principal piece of timber in a ship, which is usually first laid on the blocks in building. If we compare the carcase of a ship to the skeleton of the human body, the keel may be considered as the back-bone, and the timbers as the ribs" (Falconer).

240 After-hold: "a general name given to all that part of the hold which lies abaft [behind] the main-mast" (Falconer).
Ballast: "a certain portion of stone, iron, gravel, or such like materials, deposited in a ship's hold, when she has either no cargo, or too little to bring her sufficiently low in the water. It is used to counter balance the effort of the wind upon the masts, and give the ship a proper stability, that she may be enabled to carry sail without danger of oversetting" (Falconer).

241 Only the 1st ed. reads "the 8th of April," the correct date.

242 Major General John Craufurd (ca. 1725–1764) was taken prisoner on 3 May.

243 Breastwork: "a Work rais'd to cover Men against the Enemies [sic] Cannon and small Shot . . . and must be made of Earth, and not of Stones, lest they, being beaten to Pieces, do Mischief" (*A Military and Sea Dictionary*).

244 Citadel: "a Fort with Four, Five, or Six Bastions [great walls], raised on the most advantageous Ground about a City, the better to command it, and divided from it by an *Esplanade*, or open Space, the better to hinder the Approach of an Enemy" (*A Military and Sea Dictionary*). "In regard to the situation of a citadel . . . if the town lies near a navigable river or lake, it should be placed near the entrance, to prevent the approach of an enemy with ships; and if the place is a sea-port, the citadel should be placed near the harbour, so as to command it from one end to the other; that it may protect the ships lying in it, and secure the place against any bombardment" (John Muller [1699–1784], *A Treatise Containing the Elementary Part of Fortification* [London, 2nd ed. 1756]), 198.

245 Butt: a large cask.

246 John Milton (1608–1674), *Paradise Lost* (London, 1674), 1:175.

247 Suffered me: permitted me.

248 Shells or carcases: "The shell is a great hollow ball, filled with powder, which, falling into the works of a fortification, &c. destroys the most substantial buildings by it's [sic] weight; and, bursting asunder, creates the greatest disorder and mischief by it's [sic] splinters" (Falconer).

249 Bomb-proofs: bomb shelters.

250 Stanhope: Sir Thomas Stanhope (d. 1770).
Swiftsure: a 3rd rate 70.
Basse-road: should read *Basque Road*. A road is "a bay or place of anchorage, at some distance from the shore, on the sea-coast, whither ships or vessels occasionally repair, to receive intelligence, orders, or necessary supplies" (Falconer). Lying between the Ile de Ré (or Rhe) and the Ile d'Oleron, the Basque Road leads to the French naval base of Rochefort.

251 Bomb-vessel: "a small ship particularly calculated to throw [mortar] shells into a fortress" (Falconer).

252 Spring: "a rope passed out of one extremity of a ship and attached to a cable proceeding from the other, when she lies at anchor. It is usually performed to bring the ship's broadside, or battery of cannon, to bear upon some distant object; as another ship, or a fortress on the coast" (Falconer).

253 *Nassau*: a 3rd rate 70.

254 Grapplings: iron hooks used to pull vessels together.

255 Dennis: Sir Peter Denis (d. 1778).
Howe: Richard Howe, Earl (1726–1799).
On 4 January 1762, Great Britain declared war on Spain, France's ally.
Wasp: an 8-gun sloop.

256 [Equiano's note, eds. 1–9.] Among others whom we brought from Bayonne, were two gentlemen who had been in the West Indies, where they sold slaves; and they confessed they had made at one time a false bill of sale, and sold two Portuguese white men among a lot of slaves.
[Cartel: "a ship commissioned in time of war to exchange the prisoners of two hostile powers; also to carry any particular request or proposal from one to another: for this reason the officer who commands her is particularly ordered to carry no cargo, ammunition, or implements of war, except a single gun for the purpose of firing signals" (Falconer). Portugal was Britain's ally during the Seven Years' War.]

257 [Equiano's note, eds. 1–9.] Some people have it, that sometimes before persons die, their ward is seen; that is, some spirit, exactly in their likeness, though they are themselves at other places at the same time. One day while we were at Bayonne, Mr. Mondle saw one of our men, as he thought in the gun room; and a little after, coming on the quarter-deck, he spoke of the circumstance of this man to some of the officers. They told him that this man was then out of the ship, in one of the boats with the lieutenant; but Mr. Mondle would not believe it, and we searched the ship, when we found the man was actually out of her; and when the boat returned sometime afterwards, we found the man had been drowned the very time Mr. Mondle thought he saw him.

258 Then: "when" in eds. 1 and 2.

259 Although the war was effectively over, the Treaty of Paris, which recognized most of Britain's great territorial gains at the expense of the French, was not signed until 10 February 1763.

260 Captain's clerk: Patrick Hill (PRO ADM 32/5).
Rule of three: the rule for calculating the fourth proportional number from three given numbers: the fourth is to the third as the second is to the first.

261 Daniel Queen: listed in the *Aetna*'s pay book as Daniel Quin, able seaman.
Mess: "a particular company of officers or crew of a ship, who eat, drink, and associate together" (Falconer).

262 Had: eds. 1–5 read "have."

263 Could: eds. 1–8 read "did."

264 Hanger: a short, curved broadsword that hangs from the belt.

265 West-Indiamen: ships that carried trade to the West Indies.

266 Faint at different times: reads "faint different times" in eds. 1 and 2.

267 And encouraged my hopes: "and I still entertained hopes" in eds. 1–8.

268 Would not: "could not" only in 1st ed.

269 Prize-money: in wartime, crews shared the value of the prizes—the captured ships and their cargoes.

270 This incident in Equiano's life predates by almost a decade the Mansfield Decision discussed in the Introduction.

271 "Said, 'If your . . . I . . . it.' ": reads "said if my . . . he . . . it." only in the 1st ed.

272 With . . . burst: ed. 1 reads "while my heart was ready to burst." Pascal's apparently unaccountable behavior toward Equiano may be explained by some information not found in the *Narrative*. "Gustavus Vassan" [sic] had been promoted from the status of servant to the naval rating, or status, of able seaman on 29 September 1762 (PRO ADM 32/5), thus making it much harder for Pascal to hide his condition as a slave when Pascal, along with other British officers, was permitted to enter the service of Britain's ally Portugal in an attempt to upgrade the latter's navy.

273 Guinea: 21 shillings; a pound was worth 20 shillings.

274 "And they did at last": reads "and, indeed, at last," in eds. 1–5.

275 [Equiano's note in eds. 1–9.] Thus was I sacrificed to the envy and resentment of this woman, for knowing that the lady whom she had succeeded in my master's good graces designed to take me into her service; which, had I once got on shore, she would not have been able to prevent. She felt her pride alarmed at the superiority of her rival in being attended by a black servant; it was not the less to prevent this than to be revenged on me, that she caused the captain to treat me thus cruelly.

[As Equiano implies, having a black servant was a common eighteenth-century mark of conspicuous consumption.]

276 *Aeolus* frigate: a 5th rate 32.

277 [Equiano's note in eds. 1–9.] "The dying Negro," a poem originally published in 1773. Perhaps it may not be deemed impertinent here to add, that this elegant and pathetic [emotionally moving] little poem was oc-

casioned, as appears by the advertisement prefixed to it, by the following incident: "A black who a few days before, had run away from his master, and got himself christened, with intent to marry a white woman, his fellow servant, being taken, and sent on board a ship in the Thames, took an opportunity of shooting himself through the head."

[Equiano conflates and misquotes lines from the first three editions of Thomas Day and John Bicknell, *The Dying Negro, a Poetical Epistle, from a Black, Who Shot Himself on Board a Vessel in the River Thames, to his Intended Wife.* (London, 1773).]

278 "Illumined" in eds. 1–4.

279 Milton, *Paradise Lost*, 1:65–68. The second line of Milton's text reads "And rest can never dwell . . ."

280 Quaker: during the eighteenth century, the Society of Friends, or Quakers, put increasing pressure on its members to renounce slavery, eventually threatening slave dealers or owners with expulsion. The need to repeat the threat suggests that King was not the only Quaker to ignore the strictures of the society. He was probably the same Robert King involved in a legal action on 13 April 1769 against Walter Tullideph "for Slaves and other live Stock and Plantation" in Montserrat (PRO PC 2/113).

281 What Captain Doran fears is well expressed by Sir John Fielding (d. 1780) in *Extracts from Such of the Laws, as Particularly Relate to the Peace and Good Order of this Metropolis . . . A New Edition. . . .* (London, 1768):

The immense Confusion that has arose in the Families of Merchants and other Gentlemen who have Estates in the *West-Indies*, from the great Number of Negro Slaves they have brought into this Kingdom, also deserves the most serious Attention; many of these Gentlemen have either at a vast Expence caused some of these Blacks to be instructed in the necessary Qualifications of a domestic Servant, or else have purchased them after they have been instructed; they then bring them to *England* as cheap Servants, having no Right to Wages; they no sooner arrive here, than they put themselves on a Footing with other Servants, become intoxicated with Liberty, grow refractory, and either by Persuasion of others, or from their own Inclinations, begin to expect Wages according to their own Opinion of their Merits; and as there are already a great Number of black Men and Women who have made themselves so troublesome and dangerous to the Families who brought them over as to get themselves discharged; they enter into Societies, and make it their Business to corrupt and dissatisfy the Mind of every fresh black Servant that comes to *England*; first, by getting them christened or married, which they inform them makes them free (tho' it has been adjudged by our most able Lawyers, that neither of these Circumstances alter the Master's Property in a Slave).

However it so far answers their Purpose, that it gets the Mob on their Side, and makes it not only difficult but dangerous to the Proprietor of these Slaves to recover the Possession of them, when once they are spirited away; and indeed it is the less Evil of the two, to let them go about their Business, for there is great Reason to fear that those Blacks who have been sent back to the Plantations, after they have lived some time in a Country of Liberty, where they have learnt to write and read, been acquainted with the Use, and entrusted with the Care of Arms, have been the occasion of those Insurrections that have lately caused and threatened such Mischief and Dangers to the Inhabitants of, and Planters in the Islands of the *West-Indies*; it is therefore to be hoped that these Gentlemen will be extremely cautious for the future, how they bring Blacks to *England*, for besides that they are defeated in the Ends that they propose by it, it is a Species of Inhumanity to the Blacks themselves, who while they continue Abroad in a Degree of Ignorance so necessary to render a State of Slavery supportable, are in some Measure contented with their Condition, and chearfully submit to those severe Laws which the Government of such Persons makes necessary; but they no sooner come over, but the Sweets of Liberty and the Conversation with free Men and Christians, enlarge their Minds, and enable them too soon to form such Comparisons of different Situations, as only serve when they are sent back again to imbitter their State of Slavery, to make them restless, prompt to conceive, and alert to execute the blackest Conspiracies against their Governors and Masters (143–45).

282 Very thankful: reads "very grateful" only in the 1st ed.

283 "My" lacking in eds. 1–8.

284 Followed . . . until: ed. 1 reads "followed her with my eyes and tears until."

285 To refine wine: to purify or clarify it.

286 Gauging: determining the capacity of vessels.

287 Droggers: coasting vessels used in the West Indies.

288 And other places: reads "and others" in eds. 1–7.

289 These; reads "those" in eds. 1–4.

290 "A day" appears in eds. 3–9.

291 [Equiano's note in eds. 1–9.] These pisterines are of the value of a shilling. [The following phrase, "a day," was added in the 8th and 9th eds.]

292 Man of feeling: someone who could empathize with others.

293 Farthing: a fourth of a penny, the smallest English coin.

294 King's Bench: King's Bench Prison for debtors. Checking the Prison Commitment Books and the Inquest Reports on deaths in the King's Bench has not led to a certain identification of the Montserrat official to whom Equiano refers, but the fact that he relies on hearsay information, combined with some coincidences, suggests that he may be mistakenly thinking of Michael White, confirmed in 1764 as deputy lieutenant governor of Montserrat. Although White's will shows that he died a wealthy man (PR PROB 11/1128), *The Gentleman's Magazine* for February 1785 (and consequently published some time after February) says simply that on 15 February died "Hon[orable] Michael White, Lieut. Gov. of Montserrat." Another Michael White was committed to the King's Bench Prison on 18 April and not discharged until 29 November 1785 (PRO PRIS 5/1). Writing several years after the facts and perhaps under the influence of wishful thinking, Equiano may have confused the two Michael Whites.

295 The last war: the American Revolution. He may have taken advantage of the disruption caused by the capture of Montserrat in 1782 by the French.

296 Christian master: one of many times in his *Narrative* Equiano uses *Christian* ironically, or even sarcastically, to stress the frequent incongruity between the profession of Christianity and the practice, particularly among slave owners.

297 The first cost: the price the master paid for him.

298 Coopers: barrel makers.

299 Thousand pounds current: a thousand pounds in local, or soft currency; equal to about 571 pounds sterling, or hard currency, at the contemporaneous rate of exchange.

300 Eds. 1–4 read "So much are men blinded."

301 Stripes: floggings.

302 Cut most shockingly: castrated.

303 One Mr. Drummond . . . running away.: this paragraph is lacking in the 1st ed., and in eds. 2–7, begins "One Mr. D——."

304 A separate paragraph in eds. 2–9.

305 [Equiano's note in eds. 1–9.] Mr. Dubury, and many others in Montserrat.

306 [Equiano's note in eds. 1–9.] Sir Philip Gibbes, Bart. [Baronet] Barbadoes. [The following was added to the note in the 9th ed.] See his *Instructions for the Treatment of Negroes, inscribed to the Society for propagating the*

Gospel in foreign Parts, 1786. (Sold by Shepperson and Reynolds, London) p. 32, 33.

"If negroes decrease in number, the decrease must be ever imputed to a want of care, or a want of judgment in the treatment of them.—All animals, rational and irrational, are known to increase in all countries where ease and plenty prevail, and where want and oppression are not felt. This is universally acknowledged: so that where the decrease happens, the design of Providence to increase and multiply is unwisely, as well as impiously, frustrated by the want of care and humanity, or the want of judgment and attention. The people of Barbadoes need not extend their inquiries to distant countries. At St. Vincents they may learn, that a vessel from Africa bound to Barbadoes, I believe, since the commencement of the present century, was stranded on that island. Such of the people as saved themselves from shipwreck settled at St. Vincents. Under all these difficulties which men must suffer from such a misfortune, in an almost uninhabited island (for St. Vincents at that time had very few native Indians) these Africans made a settlement, and have increased to a very considerable number.—Here is a proof, that the negroes will increase even in this climate, when they do not live and labour under circumstances that obstruct population."

[Equiano is not quoting from the 1786 edition, which has only thirty pages, but from the *Second Edition, with Additions* of 1788. Gibbes (1731–1815) was one of Equiano's original subscribers.]

307 Lying: being given time for rest and recovery while, and immediately after, giving birth.

308 [Equiano's note.] Benezet's Account of Guinea, p. 16. [Equiano's information comes from pp. 72–80, which, in turn, Benezet acknowledges, is derived from William Burke (1729–1798) and Edmund Burke (1729–1797), *An Account of the European Settlements in America* (London: 2nd ed., 1758).]

309 Compare Burke, *An Account*: ". . . notwithstanding that the climate is in every respect, except that of being more wholesome, exactly resembling the climate from whence they come . . ." (2:124).

310 The reference to sealing wax echoes an oft-repeated account first found in Sir Hans Sloane (1660–1753), *A Voyage to the Islands Madera, Barbados, Nieves, St. Christophers and Jamaica. . . .* (London, 1707).

311 During pleasure: as long as the master pleased.

312 "Other" added in eds. 6–9.

313 "I have often asked . . . bear to do' ": added in eds. 3–9; "It is not uncommon . . . God bless them": added in eds. 5–9.

314 Milton, *Paradise Lost* 2: 616–18. Milton's second line reads, "View'd first their lamentable lot, and found."

315 Charles Town: Charleston, South Carolina.

316 Either a bit's worth (six-pence): reads, in 1st ed. only, "either a bit, worth six pence."

317 This act, passed 8 August 1688, is frequently mentioned by the opponents of the slave trade. For example, Benezet refers to it in his *Account of Guinea* (1788), 70. In contrast to the treatment of Black slaves, an act passed 3 October 1688 in Barbados declared that poor White apprentices, upon proven mistreatment, would be set free from their master or mistress. As the first major British settlement in the West Indies (1627), Barbados established precedents followed by the other colonies regarding the status and treatment of slaves.

318 Equiano is probably trying to sound unbiased by using examples from the geographical and racial extremes of humankind, commonly thought to be neither Negroes nor Caucasians. On the "Samiade," compare Oliver Goldsmith (1728–1774), *An History of the Earth, and Animated Nature* (London, 1774):

> The first distinct race of men is found round the polar regions. The Laplanders, the Esquimaux Indians, the Samoeid Tartars, the inhabitants of Nova Zembla, the Borandians, the Greenlanders, and the natives of Kamskatka, may be considered as one peculiar race of people, all greatly resembling each other in their stature, their complexion, their customs, and their ignorance. . . . These nations not only resemble each other in their deformity, their dwarfishness, the colour of their hair and eyes, but they have all, in a great measure, the same inclinations, and the same manners, being all equally rude, superstitious, and stupid. (2:214)

For the Hottentots, compare "An Account of the Cape of Good Hope; by Mr. John Maxwell. Philosophical Transaction No. 310, p. 2423," in *Memoirs of the Royal Society; or, a New Abridgment of the Philosophical Transactions. . . . By Mr. [Benjamin] Baddam* (London: 3rd ed., 1745):

> The *Hottentots* . . . are a race of men distinct both from *Negroes* and *European Whites*; for their hair is woolly, short and frizzled; their noses flat, and lips thick; but their skin is naturally as white as ours. . . . Mr. *Maxwel* takes them to be the most lazy, and ignorant part of mankind. . . . (60, 61).

Equiano might better have followed the advice Benezet offers in his *Account of Guinea* (1788):

> But nothing shews more clearly how unsafe it is to form a judgment of distant people from the accounts given of them by travellers, who have taken but a transient view of things, than the case of the Hot-

tentots, . . . those several nations of Negroes who inhabit the most
southern part of Africa: *these people* are represented by several authors,
who appear to have very much copied their relations one from the
other, as so savage and barbarous as to have little of human, but the
shape: but these accounts are strongly contradicted by others, particularly Peter Kolben [1675–1726], who has given a circumstantial relation of the disposition and manners of those people. He was a man
of learning, sent from the court of Prussia solely to make astronomical observations there; and having no interest in the slavery of the
Negroes, had not the same inducement as most other relators had, to
misrepresent the natives of Africa (85).

319 [Equiano's note in eds. 3–9.] In his "Cursory Remarks."
[The passage to which Equiano refers is a footnote on page 38 of James
Tobin, *Cursory Remarks upon the Reverend Mr. Ramsay's Essay* (London, 1785).
James Ramsay (1733–1789) had published *An Essay on the Treatment and
Conversion of African Slaves in the Sugar Colonies* in 1784. Equiano had ear-
lier defended his friend Ramsay, a subscriber to the *Narrative*, and attacked
Tobin's writings, in *The Public Advertiser*, 28 January 1788.
In a manuscript volume in the Rhodes House Library, Oxford, Ramsay mentions Equiano twice:
Gustavus Vasa, is a well known instance of what improvement a Negroe is capable. He was kidnapped when about 11 years old perhaps
above 1000 miles in land. He continued a slave for many years till he
by his industry bought out his own freedom. He has learned to read
and write: and in vindication of the rights of his colour has not been
afraid to contend in Argument with men of high rank [Thomas
Townshend, Lord Sidney (1733–1800), for example], and acuteness
of parts. But the extent of his abilities appeared very clearly, when
Government resolved to return the Negroes lately to Africa. Those
to whom the mangement of the expedition was committed, dreaded
so much his influence over his countrymen, that they contrived to
procure an order for his being sent ashore. In particular, his knowledge of the Scriptures is truly surprising, and shows that he could
study and really understand them.

A letter addressed "To Civis," who had published a newspaper article defending slavery, begins, "Sir, After taking a competent time
to frame your answer concerning the inferiority of the Negroe race
you have in your letter of Aug. 19th [in *The Morning Chronicle and
London Advertiser*] thought proper to group all your adversaries together, that you might level them at a single volley. But Benezet Junior, Humanitas, Christian and Goodenough [all pseudonyms of
writers against the slave trade who published responses to "Civis" in

The Morning Chronicle], not being sufficiently numerous to entitle you to a triumph, Mr. Ramsay and Mr. [John] Newton [(1725–1807), author of the anti-slave-trade *Thoughts upon the African Slave Trade*, 1788] are added and poor Gustavus Vasa is made in shape of a pig to bring up the rear. . . . [In his letter of 19 August "Civis" says, "If I were even to allow some share of merit to Gustavus Vasa, Ignatius Sancho, &c. it would not prove equality more, than a pig having been taught to fetch a card, letters, &c. would show it not to be a pig, but some other animal."] I think it is not quite fair to attack persons who give their names to the public, in a mask; while you yourself wish to fight in Masquerade, I have no desire to make the discovery. . . . You are hurt at being proposed to be pitted against Gustavus Vasa. [In his letter to "Civis," printed 11 July 1788, "Christian" writes, "Now I am far from thinking Civis one of the lowest of the white race; I dare say he is a very respectable person. Yet, from any thing that has appeared under his name, I should not fear to have a black correspondent of yours, Gustavus Vasa, pitted against him, and the publick left to determine which of the two has the best claim to humanity."] As a Christian you must allow that the knowledge of Revelation is the most sublime science, that can adorn human nature. Now with out wishing to imitate your sneering manner or to express the least contempt for your abilities, of which I sincerely entertain an high opinion I propose that the point of inferiority may be determined, by your favorite Mr. Gibbons [Edward Gibbon, (1737–1794), author of *The Decline and Fall of the Roman Empire,* Vol. 1, 1776, widely considered a mocker of Christianity] from your or Vasa's most sensible account of your religion." (MSS BRIT EMP. S.2)

[Ramsay's manuscript letter is a preliminary draft of the letter printed in the 11 September 1788 issue of *The Morning Chronicle* under the pseudonym "George Fox," the name of the founder (1624–1691) of the Society of Friends or Quakers.]

320 Reads "begotten on a black woman" only in the 1st ed.

321 Exodus 7:1–25.

322 Need: "read" only in the 1st ed.

323 [Equiano's footnote in eds. 8 and 9.] See the Observations on a Guinea Voyage, in a series of letters to the Rev. T. Clarkson, by James Field, Stanfield, in 1788, p. 21, 22.—"The subjects of the king of Benin, at Gatoe, where I was, had their markets regular and well stocked; they teemed with luxuries unknown to the Europeans."

324 Adapted from Beelzebub's speech in Milton, *Paradise Lost*, 2: 332–40. According to Matthew 12:24, Beelzebub is "the prince of the devils."

325 Reads "transactions with Europeans" in eds. 1 and 2.

326 Equiano seems to confuse Brimstone Hill, the location of the defending fortress on St. Christopher's (St. Kitts) island, with one of the volcanoes near Plymouth, on Montserrat.

327 The following two paragraphs are lacking in eds. 1 and 2.

328 Viz.: *videlicet*, namely.

329 In eds. 1–5, reads "Some time in the year 1763."

330 "Burthen" added in eds. 2–9.

331 "Him" lacking only in 1st ed.

332 Stove: past participle of *stave*: to put a hole in.

333 Only the 1st ed. reads "my master told me."

334 Oftentimes felt much hunger: only the 1st ed. reads "felt much hunger oftentimes."

335 Geneva: gin.

336 Whites: "Europeans" only in the 1st ed.

337 Presently: soon.

338 Presumably to keep the knowledge of Christianity from the slaves. There was much dispute during the period over whether Christianity, with its doctrine of the equality of souls, posed a revolutionary threat to the institution of slavery, or whether its promise of an afterlife that could compensate for the sufferings endured in the present served to support the institution.

339 Predestinarian: one who believes that external forces, not one's own choices, determine the events and direction of one's life. If Equiano refers to his African childhood beliefs, they were quite compatible with the side of Methodism associated with George Whitefield, who emphasized a Calvinistic faith in election, or predestination, whereby God has chosen some few people to be saved and the rest to be eternally damned. John Wesley, Whitefield's cofounder of Methodism, was relatively Arminian in his faith, stressing the role of free will in the attainment of salvation through Christ available to all true believers.

340 Puncheons: large casks for holding liquids.

341 Punt: an open boat with squared ends and a flat bottom, propelled in shallow water by a pole.

342 Sounding: where he could touch bottom.

343 A separate paragraph in eds. 2–9.

344 Phrase "then with us" lacking in eds. 1 and 2.

345 Served his time: been apprenticed for a specified period.

346 Liberty, which is but nominal: reads "liberty; and even this is but nominal" only in the 1st ed.

347 I have not been able to identify the source of these lines, although the concluding phrase—"makes a slave of man"—is taken from William Cowper (1731–1800), *The Task, A Poem in Six Books* (London, 1785), 5: 643. Equiano may be the author of the lines. He includes an original poem at the end of chapter 10, and was recognized as a poet during his lifetime. In *The Baviad, A Paraphrastic Imitation of the First Satire of Persius* (London, 1791), William Gifford (1756–1826) invokes Equiano in his satire on the Della Cruscan poetry of Robert Merry (1755–1798):

What the ladies may say to such a swain [Merry], I know not; but certainly he is prone to run wild, die, &c. &c. Such indeed is the combustible nature of this gentleman, that he takes fire at every female signature in the papers: and I remember that when Olaudo [sic] Equiano (who, for a black, is not ill-featured) tried his hand at a soft sonnet, and by mistake subscribed it Olauda, Mr. Merry fell so desperately in love with him, and "yelled out such syllables of dolour" [cf. William Shakespeare, *Macbeth*, Act 4, scene 3] in consequence of it, that "the pitiful-hearted" [cf. Thomas Betterton, *King Henry IV, with the Humours of Sir John Falstaff. A Tragi-Comedy* (1700), Act 2, scene 4] negro was frightened at the mischief he had done, and transmitted in all haste the following correction to the editor—"For Olauda, please to read Olaudo, the black MAN" (pp. 38–39).

I have found neither the sonnet nor the correction Gifford mentions.

348 Still remembering: reads "and, remembering" only in the 1st ed.

349 Freedom . . . should: eds. 1–7 read "freedom in time, if it should."

350 To prove: to test.

351 "he ever saw" in eds. 1–4.

352 Tierce: 42 gallons.

353 "Metal" in eds. 1–5.

354 *Wise*: "skilled in hidden arts," Samuel Johnson (1709–1784), *A Dictionary of the English Language* (London, 1755).

355 Phrase "sold my things well" lacking in eds. 1–7.

356 Ague: a recurrent chill.

357 Repeal of the Stamp Act: Although Equiano sets this event in 1765, the Stamp Act was repealed by Parliament in London on 18 March 1766, and news of the repeal reached America in May.

358 "Me" lacking in eds. 1–5.

359 Bastinadoes: beating with a cudgel or stick.

360 Eds. 1–4 read "1764." The reference to the Repeal of the Stamp Act earlier means that the year was 1766, unless Equiano is conflating that event with those of 1765.

361 Not a separate paragraph in the 1st ed.

362 Unlike members of the Church of England or Roman Catholics, Quakers believed that the Bible's teachings were supplemented by individual divine inspiration, the "inner light" available to both men and women, that could be shared in public meetings. These particular messages from God were not always comprehensible by others. Equiano's anecdote anticipates the more famous episode recorded by James Boswell (1740–1795) in 1763 in his *Life of Johnson* (London, 1791):

Next day, Sunday, July 31, I told him I had been that morning at a meeting of the people called Quakers, where I had heard a woman preach. JOHNSON. "Sir, a woman's preaching is like a dog's walking on his hinder legs. It is not done well; but you are surprized to find it done at all."

The egalitarian Quakers did not recognize an authority standing between the believer and God, and thus did not have a class of clergy (minister, preacher, or priest) separate from a congregation. As Equiano later discovered, when no member of a meeting was prompted to speak, public worship was conducted silently, a frequent occurrence.

363 Since George Whitefield (1714–1770) did not leave Great Britain between 7 July 1765 and 16 September 1768, Equiano could not have heard the famous Methodist preacher in Philadelphia during 1766 or 1767. He probably heard him in Savannah, Georgia, in February 1765. The weekly newspaper *The Georgia Gazette* (14 and 21 February) reported that Whitefield was in the city on the 9th, while the sloop *Prudence*, on which Equiano served under Thomas Farmer, was in port between the 7th and the 16th.

364 Whitefield was both praised and condemned for the fervor with which he preached, especially to the poor, who were often ignored by his more conservative and less evangelical fellow Anglican ministers. William Hogarth (1697–1764) satirizes his style of preaching in the print *Credulity, Superstition, and Fanaticism. A Medley* (London, 1762).

365 Not a separate paragraph in the 1st ed.

366 No use to murmur at: eds. 1–4 read "no use to encounter with."

367 Not a separate paragraph in the 1st ed.

368 Dance in at: ed. 1 reads "dance with at."

369 With him: "to him" in the 1st ed. only.

370 Notes: banknotes, or paper money.

371 Compare the moral of Aesop's fable "The Dog and the Shadow": "Beware lest you lose the substance by grasping at the shadow."

372 Manumission: emancipation from slavery or bondage.

373 And a heart replete with thanks to God: added in eds. 2–9.

374 And I had expressed: reads "and that I had expressed" in eds. 1–5.

375 [Equiano's note in eds. 1–9.] Acts xii. 9.

376 Elijah is carried to heaven in 2 Kings 2:1–18.

377 Now became: "was become" in eds. 1–5.

378 Local currency was normally inflated in relation to pounds sterling.

379 Vasa . . . have: eds. 1–4 read "Vasa, I had, or now I have"; ed. 5 reads "Vasa, I had, or now have, or by any."

380 Liber D: book, or register D. The use of authenticating documentation, including correspondence, became a hallmark of eighteenth-century autobiographical and biographical writings, both fictional and nonfictional. The technique is epitomized in Boswell's *Life of Johnson*.

381 Pleasant: "calm" in eds. 1–8.

382 And river: lacking in eds. 1–4.

383 Not a separate paragraph in the 1st ed.

384 Came . . . free man: only the 1st ed. reads "came, he told him I was a free man; and when Mr. Read applied to him to deliver me up, he said he knew nothing of the matter."

385 Gaol: jail.

386 For a while: eds. 1–8 read "for a little."

387 *Yea-ma-chra*: an Indian name for the area near Savannah.

388 Must have retarded: "must retard" in eds. 1 and 2.

389 During the several years: "for the many years" only in the 1st ed.

390 Not a separate paragraph in the 1st ed.

391 Not a separate paragraph in the 1st ed.

392 When: "that" in eds. 1–4.

393 This: "his" in eds. 1–6.

394 The very worst: eds. 1–8 read "the worst."

395 Not a separate paragraph in the 1st ed.

396 By mere dint of reason: "by my former experience" in the 1st ed. only.

397 Traverse: "in navigation, implies a compound course, or an assembly of various courses, lying at different angles with the meridian. . . . The true course and distance resulting from this diversity of courses is discovered by collecting the difference of latitude and departure of each course, and reducing the whole into one departure and one difference of latitude, according to the known rules of trigonometry" (Falconer). Equiano may be saying that he does not know how to use a traverse board, "a thin piece of board, marked with all the points of the compass, and having eight holes bored in each, and eight small pegs hanging from the center of the board. It is used to determine the different courses run by a ship during the period of the watch; and to ascertain the distance of each course" (Falconer).

398 Not a separate paragraph in the 1st. ed.

399 Observation: "the art of measuring the altitude of the sun or a star, in order to determine the latitude, or the sun's azimuth" (Falconer).

400 Hit the islands: eds. 1–4 read "hit upon the islands."

401 Not a separate paragraph in the 1st ed.

402 Sable: lacking in eds. 1–4.

403 In eds. 1–4 the paragraph ends with "no small measure." The addition appears in eds. 5–9.

404 In the two-volume eds. 1 and 2, the engraving of *Bahama Banks*, with its accompanying biblical quotations, serves as frontispiece to vol. 2. In ed. 3, it precedes ch. 7. In eds. 4–9, it precedes ch. 8.

405 By: "with" in eds. 1–4. The King James Version reads "with."

406 Equiano has transposed verses 25 and 26.

407 Quotation lacking in eds. 1–4. The King James Version reads "all safe to land."

408 Reads "fourth of February" in eds. 1–5.

409 Made . . . water: leaked.

410 Helm: "a long and flat piece of timber, or an assemblage of several pieces, suspended along the hind part of a ship's stern-post, where it turns upon hinges to the right or left, serving to direct the course of the vessel, as the tail of a fish guides the body. The helm is usually composed of three parts . . . the rudder, the tiller, and the wheel, except in small vessels, where the wheel is unnecessary" (Falconer).

Lee-beam: *lee* is "an epithet used by seamen to distinguish that part of the hemisphere to which the wind is directed, from the other part whence it arises: which latter is accordingly called *to windward*" (Falconer).

411 Breakers: "a name given by sailors to those billows [large rolling waves] that break violently over rocks lying under the surface of the sea. They are distinguished both by their appearance and sound, as they cover that part of the sea with a perpetual foam, and produce a hoarse and terrible roaring, very different from what the waves usually have in a deeper bottom. When a ship is unhappily driven amongst breakers, it is hardly possible to save her, as every billow that heaves her upwards serves to dash her down with additional force, when it breaks over the rocks or sand beneath it" (Falconer).

412 Eds 1–7 lack the phrase "and besides being broken."

413 Small . . . island: ed. 1 reads "small key or island."

414 Things: added in eds. 3–9.

415 Dutch Creole: a person of Dutch descent born in the Western Hemisphere.

416 Want: lack.

417 Partly: "entirely" in the 1st ed. only.

418 Not a separate paragraph in the 1st ed.

419 Before refrigeration became possible, the only way to preserve meat was by heavily salting it.

420 New Providence: the capital of the Bahamas.

421 "Obbico" in eds. 1 and 2: modern-day Abaco. Andros is actually the largest Bahamian island.

422 Keys: only ed. 9 reads "quays."

423 Hoy: "a small vessel, usually rigged as a sloop, and employed for carrying passengers and luggage from one place to another" (Falconer).

424 Schooner: "a small vessel with two masts" (Falconer).

425 To look after wrecks: not in the sense of *to care for*, but rather to look for wrecked ships to pillage.

426 The wreck: ed. 1 reads "our wreck."

427 Foundering: sinking.

428 Buoy of the anchor: "a sort of closed cask, or block of wood, fastened by a rope to the anchor, to determine the place where the anchor is situated, that the ship may not come too near it, to entangle her cable about the stock, or the flukes of it" (Falconer). The crew hope to pull the vessel toward the anchor, which is in deeper water than they are.

429 "At" lacking in 1st ed. only.

430 Our eyes: only the 1st ed. reads "The eyes of us all."

431 Boat-hook: "an iron hook with a sharp point on the hinder end thereof, to stick into a piece of wood, a ship's side, &c. It is stuck upon a long pole or shaft, . . . by the help of which a person in the boat may either hook anything to confine the boat in a particular place, or push her off by the sharp point attached to the back of the hook" (Falconer).

432 Catguts: used to make the strings of musical instruments.

433 Not a separate paragraph in the 1st ed.

434 Not a separate paragraph in the 1st ed.

435 Martinico: modern-day Martinique.

436 There was much contemporaneous debate about whether slaves were relatively worse off in the British West Indies than in the French, where their treatment was regulated, at least in theory but not always in practice, since 1685 by the Code Noir. Underlying the debate was the dispute over whether slavery was best regulated by the metropolitan European government in Paris or London, or by the local Caribbean governments.

437 That is, before the hurricane season suspended maritime travel.

438 Shuffling: shifty or deceitful behavior.

439 Grenades: the Grenadines.

440 Advertise myself: in case anyone had a claim on him as a fugitive slave.

441 Freedom: eds. 1–7 read "freeman."

442 In this . . . all night: lacking only in the 1st ed.

443 Cherry Garden Stairs: a landing place on the south bank of the Thames, about four miles below Westminster Palace.

444 "Was" added in eds. 8 and 9.

445 Master: not an owner, but an employer who will teach him the skill of hairdressing.

446 Three parts of the French horn: "The tones of the *French Horn* are soft, rich, and mellow" *The Musical Dictionary* (London, 1835).

447 According to the ledgers for Poor Rates and Cleansing Rates, Francis Grigory and John Grigory lived in different houses in Coventry-court, Haymarket, in 1767. The former may be the Francis Gregory who received his B.A. from Christ Church, Oxford, in 1742; the latter may be the John Gregory who received his B.A. from St. Mary Hall, Oxford, in 1727. Francis had lived in Coventry-court since at least 1764 and is probably the man Equiano refers to; John does not appear in the ledgers until 1767.

Barter: in arithmetic, "The computation of the quantity or value of one commodity, to be given for a known quantity and value of another; the 'rule' or method of computing this" (*Oxford English Dictionary*).

Alligation: "The arithmetical rule that teaches to adjust the price of compounds, formed of several ingredients of different values" (Johnson, *Dictionary*).

448 Thank: "thanked" in eds. 1–8.

449 Master: of a ship, that is.

450 Equiano's comments on the Turks may be seen as unintentionally ironic. Although he does not say much about slavery in the Middle East, Islamic slave traders had taken as many as 4 million slaves from Africa before the European transatlantic slave trade began and perhaps an additional 3 million in the nineteenth century, after most of the European trade ended.

451 Franks, or Christians: since the time of the Crusades, when many of the European invaders originated from what is now France, the Turks used the terms *Frank* and *Christian* interchangeably. The infidel Christians were segregated from the Muslim population to avoid religious corruption of the latter by the former.

452 Not a separate paragraph in the first edition.

453 Inquisition: the institution within the Roman Catholic Church established to identify and prosecute heretics.

Among the major disagreements between the Roman Catholic Church and Protestantism are those over the relationship between the Bible and divine truth and the way to salvation. For most Protestants, including Anglicans, the Bible is sufficient for salvation, containing all that a believer needs to know, and accessible to the individual believer; Roman Catholic doctrine maintains that the Bible is necessary but not sufficient, needing to be supplemented by the teachings of the Church Fathers who wrote after the composition of the Bible, which is best mediated to laypeople through the

EXPLANATORY AND TEXTUAL NOTES

Church, that is, by those properly trained to read it. Some Protestant sects, notably the Quakers, while rejecting the doctrine of mediation by a Church, held that the Bible must be supplemented by postbiblical personal revelations and visitations by the Holy Spirit. Roman Catholics and Protestants also disagree about which books of the Bible are canonical. Hence, the importation of Bibles, particularly Protestant ones, was perceived in Roman Catholic countries as spreading heresy and undermining the authority of the Church.

454 Garden of Eden: I have found no reference to a garden with this name in Oporto in contemporaneous travelers' accounts.

455 The host: the consecrated bread or wafer of Holy Communion.
Te Deum: Te Deum laudamus (We praise Thee, O God), the first words of a Latin hymn used on special occasions of celebration.

456 Not a separate paragraph in the 1st ed.

457 Galley: "a kind of low flat-built vessel, furnished with one deck, and navigated with sails and oars, particularly in the Mediterranean" (Falconer). The galley slaves, who included convicts and non-Christian prisoners of war, were often noted by contemporaneous travelers to southern France and Italy. See, for example, Letter XIV in Tobias Smollett (1721–1771), *Travels through France and Italy* (London, 1766).

458 Ferdinand IV (1751–1825) and Maria Carolina (1752–1814).

459 Mammon: the demonic god of worldliness and materialism.

460 Thinking one was . . . venture on: lacking only in the 1st ed.

461 Locusts: locust-tree beans.
Pulse: edible seeds of pod-bearing plants.

462 Standgate-creek: Stangate Stairs is a landing place on the south bank of the Thames, opposite Westminster Palace.

463 Not a separate paragraph in the 1st ed.

464 Discovered: revealed.

465 We: "I" in eds. 1–5.

466 Were: "was" in eds. 1–5.
Throughout the British West Indies, of which Jamaica was by far the most populous (with about 300,000 people; Barbados had 100,000), more than 90 percent of the total population of 500,000 were of African descent on the eve of the American Revolution. By comparison, at midcentury, of the approximately 2 million people in the North American colonies that would become the United States, overall about 20 percent were of African descent, but within those colonies the rate ranged from 2 percent in Massachusetts

to 60 percent in South Carolina. Blacks composed 44 percent of the population of Virginia, 20 percent of Georgia, and 2.4 percent of Pennsylvania. In England, with 6.5 million people in 1771, the 14,000–20,000 Blacks made up less than 0.2 percent of the total population and were concentrated in the slave-trading ports of Bristol, Liverpool, and especially London.

467 Situation of a gentleman: Equiano plays upon the difference between birth and behavior in definitions of a *gentleman*. By Johnson's first definition, a *gentleman* is "A man of birth; a man of extraction, though not noble"; by his second, "A man raised above the vulgar by his character or post" (*Dictionary*). Here, as elsewhere in his *Narrative*, Equiano implies that though a man may have the status of a gentleman (Johnson's first definition), he can fail to behave like one (Johnson's second definition).

468 Neptune: Roman god of the sea.

469 Late: "since" in eds. 1–5 because Phipps (1744–1792) succeeded his father, Constantine Phipps, as 2nd Baron Mulgrave of Ireland in 1775, two years "since" the voyage (he received an English peerage as Lord Mulgrave 16 June 1790). By the time of the publication of the 6th ed. of the *Narrative*, in 1793, he had become "late," having died 10 October 1792. Mulgrave was one of Equiano's original subscribers.
  Horatio Nelson (1758–1805), later Viscount Nelson, the hero of the naval Battle of Trafalgar, in which he died, was a member of this Arctic expedition.

470 The expedition is most fully described in *A Voyage towards the North Pole Undertaken by His Majesty's Command 1773. By Constantine John Phipps* (London, 1774), an account on which Equiano relies for some of his own details and phrasing, though Equiano includes information not found in Phipps. The *Race Horse* and the *Carcass* were structurally reinforced bomb vessels.

471 Skiffington Lutwidge, or Lutwych.

472 Tow: broken hemp fiber. Aqua fortis: nitric acid.

473 It happened: "Unfortunately it happened" in eds. 1–5.

474 Unfortunately: lacking in eds. 1–5.

475 Equiano's data on the apparatus agree with those found in Phipps's account, which includes an illustration and explanation of Doctor Irving's invention.

476 Sea horse: "Arctick Walrus. . . . This animal, which is called by the Russians Morse, from thence by our seamen corrupted Sea Horse" (Phipps, 184). This name for the walrus appears in Samuel Johnson's *Dictionary* (London, 1755) and was still in use in the twentieth century.

477 We were stopt . . . body of ice: compare Phipps's "the ice was one compact impenetrable body . . . (42).

478 We had generally . . . uncommon scene: compare Phipps's "had not the mildness of the weather, the smooth water, bright sunshine, and constant day-light, given a cheerfulness and novelty to the whole of this striking and romantick scene" (31).

479 Some of our people. . . . they dispersed: compare Phipps's "At six in the morning the officers returned from the island; in their way back they had fired at, and wounded a sea-horse, which dived immediately, and brought up with it a number of others. They all joined in an attack upon the boat, wrested an oar from one of the men, and were with difficulty prevented from staving or oversetting her; but a boat from the *Carcass* joining ours, they dispersed" (57–58).

480 *Natural* state: in the theological condition of Adam and Eve after the Fall into sin in the Garden of Eden. Equiano is referring to a stage in the process described by William Romaine (1714–1795) in *A Treatise upon the Life of Faith* (London, 1764), a process more fully experienced in chapter X of the *Narrative*:

Faith is the gift of God (7). . . . They [sinners like Adam and Eve] found themselves fallen creatures, and they felt the sad consequences of the fall, namely, total ignorance in the understanding of God and his ways, an open rebellion against him in the will, and an entire enmity in the heart, a life spent in the service of the world, the flesh, and the devil; and on all these accounts guilty before God, and by nature children of wrath. When they were convinced of those truths in their judgments, and the awakened conscience sought for ease and deliverance, then they found they were helpless and without strength. They could take no step or do any thing, which could in the least save them from their sins. Whatever method they thought of, it failed them upon trial, and left conscience more uneasy than before. Did they purpose to repent? They found such a repentance, as God would be pleased with, was the gift of Christ. . . . Suppose they thought of reforming their lives, yet what is to become of their old sins? (12–13).

What method then shall [a sinner] take? The more he strives to make himself better, the worse he finds himself. He sees the pollution of sin greater. He finds in himself a want of all good, and an inclination to all evil (15). . . . The gospel finds him in this condition, as the good samaritan did the wounded traveller, and brings him good news. It discovers to him the way of salvation contrived in the covenant of grace, and manifests to him what the ever blessed Trinity had therein purposed, and what in the fulness of time was accomplished (16–17).

The corruption of our nature by the fall, and our recovery through

Jesus Christ, are the two leading truths in the christian religion. . . . for a sinner will never seek after nor desire Christ, farther than he feels his guilt and his misery; nor will he receive Christ by faith, till all other methods of saving himself fail; nor will he live upon Christ's fulness farther than he has an abiding sense of his own want of him (22–23). Every man in his natural state before the grace of Christ, and the inspiration of his Spirit, has no faith (29–30).

481 E. N. E.: east northeast.

482 S. W.: southwest.

483 Now . . . prospect: eds. 1–5 read "and now, having a prospect."

484 Booms: "certain long poles run out from different places in the ship to extend the bottoms of particular sails" (Falconer).

Chuck, or chock: "a sort of wedge used to confine a cask or other weighty body, in a certain place, and to prevent it from fetching way when the ship is in motion" (Falconer).

485 Phipps says that they "made Orfordness" on 24 September (74).

486 Phipps ends on a less pessimistic note: "There was also most probability, if ever navigation should be practicable to the Pole, of finding the sea open to the Northward after the solstice; the sun having then exerted the full influence of his rays, though there was enough of the summer still remaining for the purpose of exploring the seas to the Northward and Westward of Spitsbergen" (76).

Equiano's conclusion is closer in spirit to that of *The Journal of a Voyage Undertaken by Order of His Present Majesty, for Making Discoveries towards the North Pole. . . .* (London, 1774): "Thus ended a voyage, which seems to have determined the question so much agitated concerning the navigation to the north pole, and proved . . . that no passage would ever be found practicable in that direction" (101). This work was reprinted in 1788.

In the surviving musters for this voyage of the *Racehorse* (PRO/ADM/36/7490), which cover the period 24 May–31 October 1773, Charles Irving, surgeon, is listed as having come aboard on 26 April. The name Vassa does not appear; however, there is a Gustavus Weston on the musters. He joined the expedition on 17 May and is identified as being an able seaman, aged 28, born in South Carolina. Given that the spelling of foreign-sounding names was often at best approximate on the muster lists, given that the personal and professional data match those found on earlier musters, in Equiano's own estimate of his birth date, and the place of birth recorded at his baptism, and given that Mulgrave was a subscriber of *The Interesting Narrative*, Gustavus Weston was almost certainly Gustavus Vassa. Because the muster and pay books of the *Racehorse* are lacking for the period between October 1773 and January 1775, I have been unable to determine precisely when Gustavus Weston was discharged from the ship, but he was definitely gone by the latter date.

487 Ere it be to late: "ere it was too late" in eds. 1–5.

488 Given the Methodist belief (consistent with the Thirty-Nine Articles that constitute the doctrine of the Church of England) in the necessity of divine grace for salvation, Equiano's attempt to achieve salvation on his own is doomed to failure, and his dissatisfaction with his present condition is inevitable.

489 Person . . . with me: reads "person amongst my acquaintance that agreed with me" only in the 1st ed.

490 Only 1st ed. reads "other methods still."

491 "Quakers . . . remained" in eds. 6–9. Eds. 1–3 read "quakers, where the word of God was neither read or preached, so that I remained"; eds. 4 and 5 read "Quakers, which was at times held in silence, and I remained."

492 Edified: "satisfied" only in the 1st ed.

493 "At length I" only in the 1st ed.

494 Presumably, what Equiano means is that Judaism availed him nothing because it has a much less fully developed concept of an afterlife than is found in the Christian faiths.

495 The first four books of the New Testament: Matthew, Mark, Luke, and John.

496 Turks: since the Turks were conventionally seen as brutal infidels, comparing hypocritical or false Christians unfavorably to them was a common rhetorical ploy used by satirists. For an example, see Hogarth's *Credulity*, where the smiling Turk is clearly a more sane and positive figure than the lunatic Methodists he (and we) observe.

497 Union-stairs: a landing place on the north bank of the Thames, about 3½ miles downriver from Westminster Palace.

498 "April the fourth" in eds. 1–5.

499 Information: "notice" only in the 1st ed.

500 Combined piece of business: the mate, captain, and Kirkpatrick conspired against Annis.

501 *Habeas corpus*: "you shall have the body," a legal writ used to release someone from illegal restraint.

502 Tipstaff: constable or bailiff, so-called because, as a sign of his office, he carried a staff with a metal tip.

503 Granville Sharp (1735–1813), who subscribed for two copies of the *Narrative*: this may have been Equiano's first of several encounters with the great abolitionist, who had brought the Somerset case before Mansfield in 1772. Sharp later told his niece, Jemima Sharp, that Equiano had been recommended to him by General James Edward Oglethorpe (1696–1785), the philanthropic founder of Georgia, originally a slave-free colony (Sharp papers at Hardwicke Court, Gloustershire). Equiano's personal opinion of Sharp is expressed in what he wrote on the flyleaf of one of his books:

Gustavus V.

His Book.

Given to him
By that Truly Pious,
And Benevolent man
Mr. Granville Sharp.
April the 13th 1779.
London.

On 19 March 1783, Sharp recorded in his journal that "Gustavus Vassa, a negro, called on me, with an account of 130 negroes being thrown alive into the sea" (Prince Hoare [1755–1834], *Memoirs of Granville Sharp* [London, 1820], 236). Equiano brought Sharp the report in the *Morning Chronicle and London Advertiser* (18 March 1783) of the case of the slave ship *Zong*, whose captain, falsely asserting a lack of water, threw 132 sick Africans into the sea so that the owner of the cargo could make a claim for the insurance money on them.

504 Situation . . . was told: reads "situation; and also was told" only in the 1st ed.

505 The *London Chronicle* (27 April 1774) gives a different account of the Annis affair, which was newsworthy in part because Kirkpatrick's behavior was clearly illegal in light of the well-known Mansfield decision in the Somerset case of 1772:

A few days ago a Merchant, who had kept a Black Servant some years, having some words with him they parted by consent; and the Black had his Master's leave to go; he accordingly went, and entered himself as a Cook on board a West India ship; the Master hearing where he was, went with two Gentlemen and two Watermen and took the poor Fellow by violence, tying his hands and legs, and carried him on board a ship bound to St. Kitt's, on which he was put in chains to be carried into slavery; but several Gentlemen seeing the transaction, employed an Attorney to serve the Merchant with a habeas corpus to produce the body: the habeas was returned that the body was not to be found, though it is said the ship did not sail through the Downs for St. Kitt's till some days after the habeas was served; therefore the

Gentlemen have ordered the Attorney to proceed against the Master; and also on the Captain's return to proceed against him for violently and by force taking a man out of the kingdom.

506 Ed. 9 reads "which I felt was grievous."

507 Isaiah 65:24.

508 Dissenting minister: either a Protestant who was not a member of the Church of England, or one of the Methodist lay preachers who, beginning in 1760, took out licenses as dissenting preachers.

509 Because Equiano names Anglican churches in Westminster, the dissenting minister identifies him as a Church of England man.

510 Love feast: religious gatherings intended to commemorate Christ's Last Supper and Christian fellowship. As Equiano soon discovers, the soul, not the body, was fed.

511 Calling and election of God: the Calvinistic belief that divine grace, or salvation, was freely given by God, not earned by humans through their actions, or good works. Those who are to be saved have been predestined by God; thus faith is sufficient, and good works may be a sign of salvation but not a cause.

512 Primitive Christians: those living in the early days of the faith, before the establishment of churches and the rise of doctrinal disputes.

513 Quoted from Robert Robinson (1735–1790), "Come Thou fount of every blessing," No. 417 in *The Methodist Hymn Book* (1933 ed.).

514 Quick: alive.

515 This sounds like a conflated reference to both the catechetic form of Thomas Wilson, *An Essay towards an Instruction for the Indians*, a copy of which Equiano had been given when he was baptized, and which he subsequently lost, and to the content of Laurence Harlow, *The Conversion of an Indian, in a Letter to a Friend* (London, 1774).

516 Reverend . . . speak; Reads "reverend gentleman speak" in 1st ed.; "reverend gentleman Mr. G. speak" in eds. 2–7: "reverend gentleman (Mr. Green) speak" in ed. 8.

517 "Agreeable" in eds. 1 and 2.

518 [Equiano's note, lacking in eds. 1–5.] Romans, chapter viii, verses 1, 2, 3.

519 Eds. 1–7 read "Rev. Mr. P——."
Henry Peckwell (1747–1787), Calvinistic divine and writer, who frequently preached at the Chapel, in the New Way, Westminster.

Lamentations 3:39: "Wherefore doth a living man complain, a man for the punishment of his sins?"

520 Me: lacking only in ed. 9.

521 James 2: 10.

522 Not a separate paragraph in the 1st ed.

523 Communicant: a person entitled to receive the sacrament of Communion.

524 "Mr. G.S." in eds. 1–7.

George Smith (d. 1784) was praised by prison reformers, including John Howard (1726?–1790), for his management of the Tothill-fields, or Westminster, Bridewell (a bridewell was a house of correction in which prisoners were forced to work). In his *State of the Gaols in London, Westminster, and Borough of Southwark. . . .* (London, 1776), William Smith says of George Smith, "The present keeper is a sober, careful, pious man; reads prayers and exhorts the prisoners every day, and sometimes oftener; by such a conduct he tames the fierce and abandoned savage, and makes those hardened wretches preserve a decent deportment, which is a very rare thing in most of the other gaols, where they appear like so many disorderly fiends, cloathed with wickedness, and steeled with daring effrontery" (26).

525 Joseph Alleine (1634–1668), *An Alarme to Unconverted Sinners* (1673), frequently republished in the eighteenth century.

526 On the morning: begins a new paragraph in eds. 1–8.

527 Reads "or all that day" only in 1st ed.

528 [Equiano's note, lacking in eds. 1–5.] See page 101 [86 in this Penguin ed.].

529 "Neither is there salvation in any other: for there is none other name under heaven given among men, whereby we must be saved."

530 "Isa. xxv. 7." added in eds. 8 and 9.

531 Romans 7:9.

532 "Jesus answered, 'Verily, verily, I say unto thee, Except a man be born of water and *of* the Spirit, he cannot enter into the kingdom of God.' "

533 [Equiano's note in eds. 1–9.] John xvi. 13, 14, &.

534 Free grace: the phrase is somewhat redundant because *grace* means God's love and protection freely given to the sinner.

535 Equiano alludes to Acts of the Apostles 8:26–39, where the Ethiopian eunuch accepts Christ as his Savior and is baptized by Philip. *Ethiopian* was a term used to describe any Black African.

536 [Equiano's note in eds. 1–9.] Acts xxii. 17.

537 A part and lot in: eds. 1–5 read "a part in." The first resurrection was that of Jesus.

538 Set up his Ebenezer: Ebenezer was the name of the stone Samuel set up to commemorate God's role in his victory at Mizpeh over the unbelievers (1 Samuel 7:12). Equiano is of course using the term figuratively.

539 Not a separate paragraph in the 1st ed.

540 Reads "fourth" in eds. 1–5.

541 Not a separate paragraph in the 1st ed.

542 "And if by grace, then *is it* no more of works: otherwise grace is no more grace. But if *it be* of works, then is it no more grace: otherwise work is no more work."

543 Romaine's *A Seasonable Antidote against Popery. In a Dialogue upon Justification* (London, 1757) gives us the gist of what Equiano heard him preach:
And hereby the Believer is entitled to immortal Happiness, on Account of what Christ hath done for him, the Comfort of which he enjoys by what the Holy Spirit hath wrought in him, viz. a believing Apprehension and Conviction that he has an Interest in the Righteousness of the God-Man. This is I think the true Gospel of Jesus Christ, which is evidently no Covenant of Faith and Repentance, but a Revelation of Grace and Mercy, and in which we have the free Promises of eternal Life, but not annexed to the Performance of Faith and Repentance, as Works of Man, or the terms or Conditions of the Covenant, but to Jesus Christ, and to the perfect Obedience, and full Satisfaction he hath made for Sin: For the Gift of God is eternal Life through Jesus Christ our Lord (6–7).
This justifying Faith is the Gift of the Holy Spirit. He gives us Evidence of our being justified, by bearing his Testimony with our Spirits, that we are the Children of God, and these Fruits do not justify us, but prove us to be justified, as the Fruits upon a Tree don't make it alive, but prove it to be alive (33–34).

544 Spots: sins.

545 Not the Anglican St. Margaret's of Westminster, in which he had been baptized, but the New Way Chapel, where he had earlier heard Peckwell preach.

546 Eds. 1–7 read "Mr. G——S——."

547 The 1st ed. only reads "how lost from God!"

548 Only the 1st ed. reads "spared nigh to hell?—."

549 Only the 1st ed. reads "mused, nigh despair." In the preceding stanza, compare Equiano's " 'A tott'ring fence, a bowing wall' " to John and Charles Wesley's translation of Psalm 62, II. 15–16: "Lo! As a bowing wall ye stand, / And as a tottering fence."

550 Only the 1st ed. reads "self-condemned."

551 [Equiano's note in eds. 1–9.] Acts iv. 12. [Equiano is not directly quoting the Bible here, but rather paraphrasing and condensing the message of Acts 4:10–12, is the biblical passage displayed in the *Narrative*'s frontispiece. In the preceding stanza, compare Equiano's " 'Lo then I come!' the Saviour cry'd / And, bleeding, bow'd his head and dy'd" to l. 8 of John and Charles Wesley's short hymn based on Mark 14:32: "Then I come to die with Thee."

552 Eds. 1–8 read "author, who leaves."

553 Adapted from "The Spiritual Victory," No. 312 in Augustus Montague Toplady (1740–1778), *Psalms and Hymns for Public and Private Worship. Collected (for the Most Part), and Published, by Augustus Toplady* (London, 1776).

554 Benedict XIV was pope from 1740 to 1758. Father Vincent may be making something of a joke here: the general of the Jesuits was called "The Black Pope," and Benedict XIV was generally considered to be anti-Jesuit.

555 Parenthetical phrase lacking in eds. 1–5.

556 Eds. 1–5 lack "again."

557 Eds. 1–5 lack "I." Equiano quotes from 2 Corinthians 6:17: "Wherefore come out from among them, and be ye separate, saith the Lord, and touch not the unclean *thing*; and I will receive you."

558 Eds. 1–5 lack "or hour."

559 Equiano is selectively quoting from the psalm.

560 Corn: a general word for cereal grains, but not maize.

561 Eds. 1 and 2 read "unto life eternal."

562 Eds. 1–5 lack "At our arrival,".

563 Musquito Indians: a corruption of "Miskito," a people living on the Caribbean coast of Central America who, although their king was nominally under the authority of the governor of Jamaica, were in effect mili-

tary allies of Britain against Spain and rebellious slaves. According to Thomas Jefferys (d. 1771), in *The West India Atlas* (London, 1794), "The Mosquitoes were divided into four principal tribes, under the protection of the English: their chiefs have the commissions of Captain, General, Admiral, &c. which were given them with some presents by the Governor of Jamaica, whom they did regard as the King of the World. The implacable hatred they bear to the Spaniards, by whom their ancestors were driven from the fertile plains they enjoyed near Lake Nicaragua, goes almost as far back as the discovery of America, and their friendship for the English is as old as the expeditions of the Buccaniers against their common enemy" (11).

564 And were baptized: eds. 1–4 read "to be baptized." The revision, though grammatically clumsy, is more consistent with the sense of the rest of the sentence: to baptize the Indians without teaching them Christian theology and morality was indeed to practice mock religion.

565 John Fox (1517–1587), *The Acts and Monuments of the Church, or Book of Martyrs*, an anti–Roman Catholic work often reprinted in the eighteenth century in abridged editions with "cuts," or woodcut illustrations.

566 Tares: weed seeds.

567 Belial: a demonic personification mentioned in 2 Corinthians 6:15.

568 A certain person: eds. 1 and 2 read "if these persons."

569 Guinea-man: a ship coming from the coast of Guinea, Africa, with a cargo of slaves.

570 [Equiano's note.] See John Brown's Scripture Dictionary, 1 Chron. i. 33. Also Purver's Bible, with Notes on Gen. xxv. 4. [Neither the phrase "some of whom came from Lybia" nor the note appear in eds. 1–4. Anthony Purver (1702–1777), *A New and Literal Translation of All the Books of the Old and New Testament; with Notes Explanatory. . . .* (London, 1764): "Alexander Polyhistor & Cleodemus Malchus, who both wrote the History of the Barbarians in Greek, say that Apher, one Abraham's Offspring, led an Army against Libya, and getting the Victory, settled there; from whom his Posterity were called Africans" (1:47)].

571 Eds. 1–7 read "the twelfth."

572 Black River: called Rio Tinto by the Spaniards.

573 Guarda costa: a ship of the Spanish Colonial coast guard.

574 *Woolwow* or flat-headed Indians, Ulua Indians, who flattened the heads of their infants by binding them. In Jefferys's *West-India Atlas*, the "Woolvas" are located to the south of the "Moskito King's Party," in present-day Nicaragua.

575 South Sea: the Pacific Ocean.

576 Only ed. 1 reads "ate it separate."

577 Eds. 1 and 2 read "commotion taken place."

578 Eds. 1–8 read "Columbus, when he was amongst the Indians in Mexico or Peru." On his fourth voyage, to frighten the Indians of Jamaica into supplying his men with provisions, Columbus used his knowledge of an impending lunar eclipse to convince them that his God could punish them with a famine if they continued to refuse his requests.

579 Casades: cassava.

580 How the drink was made; I and: eds. 1–2 read "how the drink was made, and I and."

581 Not a separate paragraph in the 1st ed.

582 Matthew 16:26.

583 Eds. 1 and 2 read "grant my request."

584 To my going: lacking in eds. 1–5.

585 Only the 1st ed. reads "amongst Christians."

586 Perhaps a reference to Paul's Epistle to the Galatians 3:28: "There is neither Jew nor Greek, there is neither bond nor free, there is neither male nor female: for ye are all one in Christ Jesus." Or perhaps to Paul's epistle to Philemon, in which he returns a slave, Onesimus, to his master, telling the latter to receive him "Not now as a servant, but above a servant, a brother beloved, specially to me, but how much more unto thee, both in the flesh, and in the Lord?" (Philemon 16).

On a less spiritual level, the con artists found around St. Paul's in London were called "St. Paul's men."

587 Carthagena: in Spanish New Granada, now Colombia.

588 Slacken: eds. 1–2 read "slack."

589 Eds. 1–7 read "I trust I prayed."

590 Loosed me: eds. 1–5 read "released me."

591 Neck or nothing: all or nothing, a desperate attempt.

592 Tacking: changing course.

593 Jaded: wearied.

594 Me and: lacking in eds. 1–7.

595 Eds. 1 and 2 lack "her."

596 Manatee: the sea cow, an aquatic mammal.

597 Eds. 1–5 lack "men more."

598 Only ed. 1 lacks "show."

599 Under sail: eds. 1–2 read "to sail."

600 At the risque of their lives: lacking in eds. 1–5.

601 Cocoa-nut trees: eds. 1 and 2 read "cocoa nuts."

602 Of the nuts: eds. 1 and 2 read "of them."

603 Spanish Guarda Costa: eds. 1–5 read "a Spaniard."

604 Adapted from *Love's Last Shift* 2:7, a play by Colley Cibber (1671–1757).

605 Not a separate paragraph in the 1st ed.

606 Ed. 1 reads "eight pounds and five shillings sterling."

607 Captain Stair Douglass of the *Squirrel*, a 6th rate 20.

608 Free negro men: only ed. 1 reads "free men."

609 Not a separate paragraph in the 1st ed.

610 Sugars . . . months: Eds. 1–8 read "sugars; and some months."

611 Not a separate paragraph in the 1st ed.

612 Privateer: "a vessel, armed and equipped by particular merchants, and furnished with a military commission by the admiralty, or the officers who superintend the marine department of a country, to cruise against the enemy, and take, sink, or burn their shipping, or otherwise annoy them as opportunity offers. These vessels are generally governed on the same plan with his majesty's ships, although they are guilty of many scandalous depredations, which are very rarely practised by the latter" (Falconer).

613 Not a separate paragraph in the 1st ed.

614 Engaged in service: worked as a servant.

615 Matthias Macnamara was appointed lieutenant governor at James Island in 1774 and governor of Senegambia in November 1775. In August 1777, after he had lost two civil suits brought against him by a subordinate, the Council of Trade removed him as governor.

616 Thirty-nine Articles: the articles of faith, published in 1563, that constitute the Creed of the Church of England.

617 Alexander the coppersmith did St. Paul: a reference to Paul's Second Epistle to Timothy 4:14–15:

14. Alexander the coppersmith did me much evil: the Lord reward him according to his works:

15. Of whom be thou ware also; for he hath greatly withstood our words.

618 Bishop of London: Robert Lowth (1710–1787).

619 Memorial: a written petition and/or statement of facts.

620 Philip Quaque (1741–1816), the Black Anglican minister at Cape Coast Castle.

621 A nobleman in the Dorsetshire militia: probably George Pitt (1721–1803), Baron Rivers, colonel of the Dorset militia from 1757, and an original subscriber for two copies of Equiano's *Narrative*. The camp at Coxheath, near Maidstone in Kent, was the largest of the military camps established in early 1778 throughout southern England in anticipation of a French invasion.

622 The bracketed passage appears only in eds. 1–4 and was probably inadvertently dropped by the printer in later editions.

623 Not a separate paragraph in the 1st ed.

624 Eds. 1 and 2 read "boat."

625 Not a separate paragraph in the 1st ed.

626 Luke 10:37.

627 Here and below "Whitehart-court" reads "Gracechurch-Court" in eds. 1 and 2. Whitehart-court, a doglegged street connecting Lombard and Gracechurch Streets, was often called White heart (or hart) yard, Gracechurch street during the eighteenth century.

628 First published by Benezet in Philadelphia in 1766 with the title *A Caution and Warning to Great Britain and her Colonies. . . .* , and retitled for the 1767 London ed., this antislavery tract was printed in 1784 and 1785 eds. by the Quakers' printer, James Phillips, and distributed by the Society of Friends to all the principal members of government and the Parliament, as well as to clergymen throughout the country. The Quakers had earlier distributed in the same way Benezet's *The Case of Our Fellow-Creatures, the Oppressed Africans*. (Minutes of Meeting for Sufferings, 25 February 1785; Minutes of the Committee on the Slave Trade, 14 and 20 March 1784: the Library of the Society of Friends House, London).

629 According to the copy in John Kemp's commonplace book, 1786, MS Box X3/2, in the Library of the Society of Friends House, London, this letter was "Presented by Gustavus Vassa and Seven others the 21st Octr. 1785."

630 In town: London.

631 Near the close . . . the bride: eds. 1–5 read "After the company have met they have seasonable exhortations by several of the members; the bride. . . ."

632 . . . until it . . . separate us: eds. 1–5 read ". . . till death separate us. . . ."

633 Then . . . a mind: Eds. 1–5 read "Then the two first sign their names to the record, and as many more witnesses as have a mind."

634 Whiteheart-Court: eds. 1–2 read "Gracechurch-Court."

Because the monthly records of this meeting house were destroyed by fire in 1821 I have not been able to identify the married couple with certainty. "Gustavus Vassa" does not appear on any of the "Registers of the Marriages of the People called Quakers, belonging to the Quarterly Meeting of London & Middlesex" (PRO RG 6/495; PRO RG 6/965). Until 1775, the quarterly records include the names of witnesses at the various monthly meetings, and between 1775 and 1790 none of the brides married at Gracechurch Street has the initials "M.N." If we assume that the printer mistook Equiano's "H" for an "N," and that the wedding took place while Equiano was in London between August 1785 and March 1786, the wedding was that of Richard Berry and Marsha Hulme on 7 December 1785 (PRO RG 6/965).

The initials "M.N.," however, may not be intended to refer to the actual name of the bride in the particular wedding Equiano witnessed. Since he tells us that he is giving "the true form" of the ceremony, he may be appropriating for use in the "form," or model, of a Quaker wedding the same initials used to represent the names of those to be married in "The Form of Solemnization of Matrimony" found in the Anglican *Book of Common Prayer*: "I PUBLISH the Banns of Marriage between M. of— and N. of —."

635 The conclusion of this paragraph was much revised, in part to reflect Equiano's changed marital status, which of course rendered his flippant reference to his availability inappropriate. The 1st ed. lacks the phrase "Lombard-Street. This mode I highly recommend." Eds. 2–4 close the paragraph with "Lombard-Street.—My hand is ever free—if any female Debonair [eligible young woman] wishes to obtain it, this mode I recommend."

Note that by inserting the letter of thanks to the Quakers and his description of the Quaker wedding, both set in London, Equiano has digressed from the chronology of his narrative.

636 Carried our foremast away: the foremast broke off and went overboard.

637 For the plan, see *Plan of a Settlement to Be Made near Sierra Leona, on the Grain Coast of Africa. Intended more particularly for the Service and Happy Establishment of Blacks and People of Colour, to Be Shipped as Freemen under the*

Direction of the Committee for Relieving the Black Poor, and under the Protection of the British Government. By Henry Smeathman, Esq. Who Resided in that Country near Four Years (London, 1786).

Smeathman (d. 1786) had spent time in Africa conducting research for a treatise on termites and while there had married into the families of the local African rulers, King Tom and Cleveland, whose father was English. His concern for the presence and plight of Blacks under British rule was prompted by Britain's defeat in the American Revolution: "And whereas many black persons, and people of Colour, Refugees from America, disbanded from his Majesty's Service by sea or land, or otherwise distinguished objects of British humanity, are at this time in the greatest distress, they are invited to avail themselves of the advantages of the plan proposed" (16–17). The charitable impulse was complemented by the desire to abolish the slave trade and to demonstrate that Africa could generate wealth without being forced to export its human resources. In February 1786, Smeathman brought his proposal for a multiracial settlement in Africa to the Committee for the Relief of the Black Poor, headed by Jonas Hanway (1712–1786), a group of London businessmen who raised more than £1,000 to provide relief, health care, clothing, and jobs to needy Blacks. The committee approved a version of the plan in May and quickly received a promise from the Treasury of up to £14 per person to support transporting the settlers of the projected self-governing village of Granville Town (named in honor of Sharp, the philanthropist and abolitionist), in The Province of Freedom to be established on land bought from local African authorities. The political constitution of the projected community was outlined in Sharp's *A Short Sketch of Temporary Regulations (until Better Shall Be Proposed), for the Intended Settlement on the Grain Coast of Africa, near Sierra Leone* (London, 1786).

A letter from the government to the Committee for the Black Poor reveals a sense of urgency:

> I am commanded by the Lords Commissioners of His Majesty's Treasury to acquaint you that they have taken Measures for the Civil Officers apprehending such Blacks as they may meet with committing any Act of Vagrancy who have received the Bounty of the public on Condition of their going to Serra [sic] Leona, with an Intention to have them sent from Time to Time on Board the Ships prepared to convey them to the place of their Destination and the better to enable My Lords to carry their Intentions into Execution, I am directed to desire You will send them a List of the Names of such as have received the said Bounty, and who are not now on board the Ships, and to request that You will favour them with any Observations that may occur to You or any other Plan that You are of Opinion may more effectually carry the Intentions of this Board respecting the sending the Blacks to Serra Leona into Execution with as little delay as possible. (PRO T 27/38, dated 4 December 1786)

The Morning Herald (2 January 1787) reported that the authorities acted promptly:

> The Mayor has given orders to the City Marshals, the Marshalmen, and Constables, to take up all the blacks they find begging about the streets, and to bring them before him, or some other Magistrate, that they may be sent home, or to the new colony that is going to be established in Africa; near twenty are already taken up, and lodged in the two Compters [the Poultry and Wood Street city prisons for debtors].

638 Equiano was the only person of African descent to be involved in the organization of the project. His full title of "Commissary on the part of the Government" expresses the importance of his position: in addition to overseeing supplies, he was to act as the official representative of the British government in dealings with the local African authorities in Sierra Leone.

639 Only the 1st ed. reads "Mr. Irving."

Upon Smeathman's sudden death on 1 July 1786, his clerk and friend, Joseph Irwin, who had never been to Africa, was the freed slaves' own choice to succeed Smeathman as agent conductor of the resettlement project. Irwin was dead by the time *The Interesting Narrative* was first published.

640 Slops: ready-made clothes.

641 Copies of Equiano's muster lists for the *Atlantic*, *Belisarius*, and *Vernon* transport ships are in PRO T 1/643 (no. 487). The settlers were not exclusively Black and included mixed-race couples. His lists total 459 people: 344 Blacks (290 men, 43 women, 11 children) and 115 Whites (31 men, 75 women, 9 children). The muster numbers continued to rise and fall because people who left, were expelled, or died before and during the passage were often replaced by others.

642 The king's stores: the royal naval storehouses.

643 Peculation: embezzlement.

644 Thompson: Thomas Boulden Thompson (1766?–1828), whose command of the *Nautilus* was officially confirmed on 27 March 1786, two months after he had been given the commission. He did not receive the rank of post-captain until 22 November 1790.

One of the reasons for Equiano's dismissal was Thompson's letter of 21 March 1787 complaining to the Navy Board "of the conduct of Mr Gustavus Vasa, which has been, since he held the situation of Commissary, turbulent and discontented, taking every means to actuate the minds of the Blacks to discord: and I am convinced that unless some means are taken to quell his spirit of sedition, it will be fatal to the peace of the settlement and dangerous to those intrusted with the guiding it." Thompson also complains of Irwin's conduct (PRO T 1/643). Sharp, too, expresses disapproval of

Equiano's behavior in a letter of July 1787 to Sharp's brother (Prince Hoare, *Memoirs of Granville Sharp* [London, 1820], 313). The comments by Thompson and Sharp are similar in content to those printed in the 29 December 1786 issue of *The Morning Herald*. Thompson was an abolitionist who testified before a House of Commons committee in 1790.

Nautilus: a 16-gun sloop.

645 [Equiano's note, lacking in eds. 1–8.] He then told the agent before me, he was informed by Mr. Steele, M.P. [Thomas Steele (1753–1823), joint secretary to the Treasury Board, 1783–91, member of Parliament, and one of Equiano's original subscribers] that the said expedition had cost 33,000£ and he desired that the things might be had.

[The government expended 15,679£ 13 s. 4 d. on the Black Poor (PRO T 29/60, 29 July 1789).]

646 Equiano may refer to the following item in the 2–5 January issue of *The Morning Herald* (I have not found a 4 January issue):

Six of the leaders of these poor deceived people, Captains of hundreds and Captains of fifties [the divisions of the intended settlers], came up last week from the Belisarius and Atlantic, at Gravesend, and waited upon Lord George Gordon [(1751–1793). Gordon gained notoriety in 1780 for his role in the anti–Roman Catholic Gordon riots, but because of his opposition to the transportation of convicts was seen in the last years of his life as a champion of social underdogs], to pray the continuance of his protection, and to stop their sailing, till the meeting of parliament, that the public might know their unhappy situation. Their poverty is made the pretence for their transportation, and the inferior orders of them decoyed on board the ships, are already subjected to a treatment and controul, little short of the discipline of Guinea-men [ships of the slave trade].

Irwin's response was published in the 13 January issue of the same newspaper.

647 [Equiano's note, lacking in eds. 1–8.] Witness Thomas Steele, Esq. M.P. of the Treasury, and Sir Charles Middleton, Bart. &. I should publicly have exposed him, (even in writing falsely of me last March) were it not out of respect to the worthy Quakers and others.

[Sir Charles Middleton (1726–1813), Baronet, later Lord Barham, and from 1778 to 1790 comptroller of the navy; rear admiral of the white (24 September 1787), rear admiral of the red (21 October 1790), vice-admiral of the white (1 February 1793), vice-admiral of the red (12 April 1794), admiral of the blue (1 June 1795). An active opponent of the African slave trade, Middleton had appointed Equiano commissary, and he was one of the original subscribers to *The Interesting Narrative*. Middleton had been Ramsay's commanding officer in 1755, when Ramsay served in the Royal Navy as assistant surgeon, and acted as the clergyman Ramsay's patron, presenting him in 1781 to the livings of Teston and Nettlestead, Kent. Ramsay died in Middleton's London home 20 July 1789.

Samuel Hoare (1751–1825): one of the Quaker members of the Committee for the Black Poor, succeeding Jonas Hanway on the latter's death on 5 September 1786 as chairman; treasurer of the Society for Effecting the Abolition of the Slave Trade; and a partner in the banking house of Barnet, Hill, Barnet, and Hoare in Lombard Street: a very powerful enemy. Equiano had already named Hoare as an opponent in a letter to *The Public Advertiser*, 14 July 1787.

Equiano was dismissed while the vessels were at Plymouth, awaiting their final embarkation for Africa.]

648 . . . by the unjust means . . . and he moreover. . . . : eds. 1–8 read "by means of a gentleman in the city, whom the agent, conscious of his [that is, Joseph Irwin's own] peculation, had deceived by letter, and whom, moreover. . . ."

649 The 411 passengers still aboard when the vessels left Plymouth on 9 April 1787 arrived on the African coast on 9 May.

650 Lascars: East Indian sailors, usually classified in the period as Blacks. Approximately 50 such sailors, stranded in Britain by ships of the East India Company, sought resettlement in Africa.

651 The government's role ended with the payment of transportation costs. The Province of Freedom was conceived as a self-governing, free settlement, not as a British colony. It was "unfortunate in the event" in that the settlers who had not died of disease had been dispersed in December 1789, when a local African chieftain, King Jimmy, destroyed the town in misdirected retaliation for the abduction of some of his people by a United States slave ship.

652 . . . made, by Hoare and others, matter: eds. 1–8 read "Made by some a matter."

653 [Equiano's note, keyed in eds. 1–4 to "triumph" in the sentence above.] See the Public Advertiser, July 14, 1787.
[Equiano's letter to *The Public Advertiser* reads:
An extract of a letter from on board one of the ships with the Blacks, bound to Africa, having appeared on the 2nd and 3rd inst. in the public papers, wherein injurious reflexions, prejudicial to the character of Vasa, the Black Commissary, were contained, he thinks it necessary to vindicate his character from these misrepresentations, informing the public, that the principal crime which caused his dismission, was an information he laid before the Navy Board, accusing the Agent of unfaithfulness in his office, in not providing such nec-

essaries as were contracted for the people, and were absolutely necessary for their existence, which necessaries could not be obtained
from the Agents. The same representation was made by Mr. Vasa to
Mr. Hoare, which induced the latter, who had before appeared to be
Vasa's friend, to go to the Secretary of the Treasury, and procure his
dismission. The above Gentleman impowered the Agent to take many
passengers in, contrary to the orders given to the Commissary.]

654 After his dismissal, Equiano was soon attacked by "X" in *The Public Advertiser* (11 April 1787):
The Public will naturally suspend their belief as to the improbable
tales propagated concerning the Blacks, especially as the cloven hoof
of the author of those reports is perfectly manifest. That one of the
persons employed in conducting those poor people is discharged, is
certainly true, his own misconduct having given too good reason for
his dismission. The Blacks have never refused to proceed on the voyage, but the ships have been delayed at Plymouth by an accidental
damage which one of them received in a gale of wind. To sum up
all, should the expedition prove unsuccessful, it can only be owing
to the over-care of the committee, who, to avoid the most distant
idea of compulsion, did not even subject the Blacks to *any* government, except such as they might chuse for themselves. And among
such ill-informed people, this delicacy may have fatal consequences.
Three days later, the same newspaper carried another anonymous attack:
The expedition of the Blacks to Sierra leone is not in the least retarded by the dismission of V——the Black who was appointed to
superintend the Blacks.
    The assertions made by that man that the Blacks were to be treated
as badly as West-India negroes, and that he was discharged to make
room for the appointment of a man who would exercise tyranny to
those unfortunate men, shew him to be capable of advancing falsehoods as deeply black as his jetty face. The true reason for his being
discharged, was gross misbehaviour, which had not only rendered him
disagreeable to the officers and crew, but had likewise drawn on him
the dislike of those over whom he had been appointed. . . .
    . . . Let us hear no more of those *black* reports which have been
so industriously propagated; for if they are continued, it is rather more
than probable that most of the *dark* transactions of a *Black* will be
brought to *light*.

655 This paragraph is lacking only in the 1st ed.

656 [Equiano's note.] At the request of some of my most particular
friends I take the liberty of inserting it here.
[Her Majesty was Queen Charlotte (1744–1818), Royal Consort of King

George III. Benezet, through the American-born painter Benjamin West (1738–1820), had petitioned her on the same subject in 1783.]

657 Eds. 1 and 2 read "emboldens."

658 Eds. 1–5 read "freemen." Perhaps in response to the emphasis during the French Revolution on the universal rights of man, Equiano's revision is intended to suggest that no distinction between free and unfree men should exist: all should be free if they are men.

659 Be: lacking in eds. 1–5.

660 *The Consolidated Slave Act of Jamaica*, passed 2 March 1792, replacing the act of 1788, actually diminished some of the penalties against the brutality of slave owners prescribed by the earlier law. In a letter of 9 April 1792, Edmund Burke accurately characterized the act to Henry Dundas (1742–1811) as "arrant trifling."

661 Reversion: a legal term meaning the return to the grantor, or to his or her estate if the grantor has died, of a granted estate after the grant has expired.

662 [Equiano's note in eds. 1–9.] Granville Sharp, Esq; The Rev. Thomas Clarkson; the Rev. James Ramsey [sic]; our approved friends, men of virtue, are an honour to their country, ornamental to human nature, happy in themselves, and benefactors to mankind!

[Equiano's relationships with Ramsay and Sharp have been discussed earlier. Clarkson (1760–1846), author of *An Essay on the Slavery and Commerce of the Human Species, Particularly the African* (London, 1786) and the two-volume *History of the Abolition of the African Slave-Trade* (London, 1808), like Ramsay and Sharp, was a subscriber to the *Narrative*, and also a friend of Equiano. To help Equiano promote the sale of his book, on 9 July 1789 he wrote to the Reverend Mr. Jones of Trinity College, Cambridge:

Dear Sir

I take the Liberty of introducing to your Notice Gustavus Vassa, the Bearer, a very honest, ingenious, and industrious African, who wishes to visit Cambridge. He takes with him a few Histories containing his own Life written by himself, of which he means to dispose to defray his Journey. Would you be so good as to recommend the Sale of a few and you will confer a favour on your already obliged and obedient Servant

Thomas Clarkson. (Cambridgeshire County Record Office: Vassa 132/B 1–17).]

663 It is upon these grounds . . . worthy of royal patronage and adoption: compare Maurice Morgann (1726–1802), *Plan for the Abolition of Slavery in the West Indies* (London, 1772), 33:

It is upon these grounds that I hope and expect the attention of men of power. These are designs consonant to the elevation of their rank, and the dignity of their station. These are ends suitable to the nature of a free and generous government, and connected with the views of empire and dominion, worthy of ambition. These are ends suited to the benevolence and solid merit of our Sovereign, and to the views of a regulated and moral pursuit of a well-earned and substantial greatness.

The time may come, at least the speculation is pleasing, when an united people of various habit and complexion, shall with one tongue gratefully commemorate the auspicious aera of universal freedom—and then shall those Persons be named with praise and honour, who, quitting the narrow and hackneyed track of business, had generously embraced proposals of moral, as well as political tendency, and brought to the ear of the Sovereign, designs worthy of his royal adoption and patronage.

664 Proverbs 14:31.

665 Proverbs 14:34.

666 Proverbs 10:29.

667 Proverbs 11:5.

668 The following nine paragraphs had earlier been published, in substantially the same form and language, in *The Public Advertiser* (31 March 1788), and on 13 March 1788 Equiano had addressed them privately to Lord Hawkesbury (Charles Jenkinson [1729–1808], created Baron Hawkesbury in 1786, president of the Board of Trade, 1786–1804).

669 Is now taken into: eds. 1–5 read "is to be taken into."
Although it would take nineteen years to complete, the parliamentary struggle to end the slave trade began in May 1788, when the issue of abolition was brought forward in the House of Commons. In a letter from Ramsay to [Mr. Baker?], dated 6 September 1788 (Society of Friends House Library, London: Thompson-Clarkson collection, 3/156), Ramsay suggests that Equiano greet every returning member of Parliament with a written address protesting against the slave trade. We do not know if his suggestion was acted upon.

670 Would: eds. 1–8 read "will."
Equiano's call for the replacement of the slave trade had been anticipated by earlier writers, including Benezet and Malachy Postlethwayt (1707–1767), the latter in *Britain's Commercial Interest Explained and Improved* (London, 1757). The philanthropically inspired Province of Freedom had been intended as well to reap economic benefits for Britain, and in 1790, before he learned that Granville Town had been destroyed, Sharp published anony-

mously *Free English Territory in Africa*, proposing the creation of the St. George's Bay Company for trade. Commercial interests played an even greater part in the design of the settlement established by the Sierra Leone Company, incorporated by Parliament in 1791 to build Freetown on the physical and economic remains of the Province of Freedom. Along with the survivors of Granville Town, more than a thousand Afro-Britons, resettled from Nova Scotia, established Freetown in February 1792. Henry Thornton (1760–1815), future chairman of the Sierra Leone Company Court of Directors, and John Clarkson (1764–1828), brother of Thomas and future recruiting agent for the company as well as governor of the colony, were both among Equiano's original subscribers.

671 [Equiano's note, lacking in eds. 1–8.] In the ship Trusty, lately for the new settlement of Sierra Leona, in Africa, were 1300 pairs of shoes (an article hitherto scarcely known to be exported to that country) with several others equally new, as articles of export.—Thus will it not become the interest as well as the duty of every artificer, mechanic, and tradesman, publicly to enter their protest against this traffic of the human species? What a striking— what a beautiful contrast is here presented to view, when compared with the cargo of a slave-ship! Every feeling heart indeed sensibly participates of the joy, and with a degree of rapture reads barrels of *flour* instead of *gunpowder—biscuits and bread* instead of *horsebeans—implements of husbandry* instead of *guns* for destruction, rapine, and murder—and various articles of *usefulness* are the pleasing substitutes for the *torturing thumb-screw* and the *galling chain*, &.

672 Drags: weights attached to the leg to impede movement.

673 This paragraph is lacking in eds. 1–4.

674 [Equiano's note, lacking in eds. 1–5.] Viz. Some curious adventures beneath the earth,˙ in a river in Manchester,—and a most astonishing one under the Peak of Derbyshire—and in Sept. 1792, I went 90 fathoms down St. Anthony's Colliery, at Newcastle, under the river Tyne, some hundreds of yards on Durham side.

675 But as this: reads "but this" in eds. 6–9.

676 [Equiano's note, lacking in eds. 1–4.] See Gentleman's Magazine for April 1792, Literary and Biographical Magazine and British Review for May 1792, and the Edinburgh Historical Register or Monthly Intelligencer for April 1792.
[*The Gentleman's Magazine*, 62:384, reads, "At Soham, co. Cambridge, Gustavus Vassa, the African, well known in England as the champion and advocate for procuring a suppression of the slave-trade, to Miss Cullen, daughter of Mr. C. of Ely, in same county."
The Soham Register for Marriages, No. 220, reads, "Gustavus Vassa (an African) of the Parish of St. Martin in the Fields in the Co. of Middlesex

Bachelor, and Susanah [sic] Cullen of this Parish Spnr [spinster] were Married in this Church by License from Drs [Doctors] Commons this seventh Day of April in the Year One Thousand seven Hundred and ninety two By me Charles Hill Curate." The marriage was witnessed by Francis Bland and Thomas Cullen. "Susan Cullen" is listed as a subscriber in the 3rd (1790) and 4th (1791) eds. of the *Narrative*.

Gustavus and Susanna Vassa had two daughters: Ann Mary (or Maria), born 16 October 1793 and baptized 30 January 1794; and Joanna, born 11 April and baptized 29 April 1795. Ann Mary (or Maria) died 21 July 1797, and Susanna was buried 21 February 1796, aged 34. Joanna inherited on her twenty-first birthday in 1816 Vassa's estate, worth £950, equivalent to about £80,000 or $120,000 in 1994.]

677 Micah 6:8.

678 Equiano died 31 March 1797. His death is recorded in *The Gentleman's Magazine* (for April 1797), 67:356, in the "Obituary of remarkable Persons": "In London, Mr. Gustavus Vasa, the African, well known to the publick by the interesting narrative of his life, supposed to be written by himself."

Granville Sharp wrote to his niece Jemima on 27 February 1811 that he had seen Equiano, "a sober honest man," in his last moments: "I went to see him when he lay upon his death bed, and had lost his voice so that he could only whisper" (Granville Sharp Papers, Gloustershire Record Office).

APPENDICES

APPENDIX A

The Frontispieces and Title Pages of the First London (1789) and New York (1791) Editions

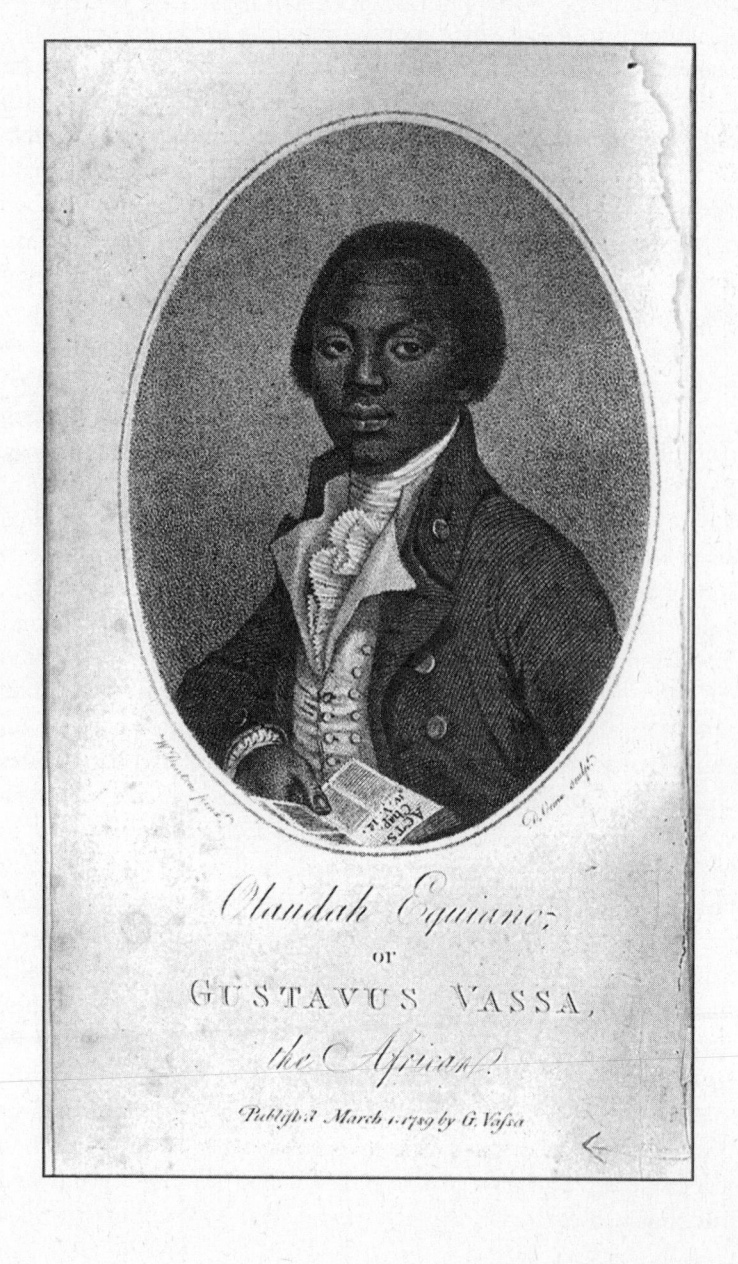

Olaudah Equiano,

OR

GUSTAVUS VASSA,

the African.

Publish'd March 1. 1789 by G. Vassa.

Henry Sole

THE

INTERESTING NARRATIVE

OF

THE LIFE

OF

OLAUDAH EQUIANO,

OR

GUSTAVUS VASSA,

THE AFRICAN.

WRITTEN BY HIMSELF.

VOL I.

Behold, God is my salvation; I will trust and not be afraid, for the Lord Jehovah is my strength and my song; he also is become my salvation.
And in that day shall ye say, Praise the Lord, call upon his name, declare his doings among the people. Isaiah xii. 2, 4.

LONDON:

Printed for and sold by the AUTHOR, No. 10, Union-Street, Middlesex Hospital;

Sold also by Mr. Johnson, St. Paul's Church-Yard; Mr. Murray, Fleet-Street; Messrs. Robson and Clark, Bond-Street; Mr. Davis, opposite Gray's Inn, Holborn; Messrs. Shepperson and Reynolds, and Mr. Jackson, Oxford-Street; Mr. Lackington, Chiswell-Street; Mr. Mathews, Strand; Mr. Murray, Prince's-Street, Soho; Mess. Taylor and Co. South Arch, Royal Exchange; Mr. Button, Newington-Causeway; Mr. Parsons, Paternoster-Row; and may be had of all the Booksellers in Town and Country.

[Entered at Stationer's Hall.]

Tiedone Sculp.

Olaudah Equiano

or

GUSTAVUS VASSA

the African.

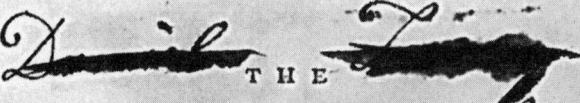

THE
INTERESTING NARRATIVE

OF

THE LIFE

OF

OLAUDAH EQUIANO,

OR

GUSTAVUS VASSA,

THE AFRICAN.

WRITTEN BY HIMSELF.

VOL I.

*Behold, God is my salvation : I will trust and not
be afraid, for the Lord Jehovah is my strength
and my song ; he also is become my salvation.
And in that day shall ye say, Praise the Lord, call
upon his name, declare his doings among the people,
Isaiah xii. 2, 4.*

FIRST AMERICAN EDITION.

N E W - Y O R K :

PRINTED and Sold BY W. DURELL, *at his*
Book-Store and Printing-Office, No. 19, Q. Street.
M,DCC,XCI.

APPENDIX B

A Note on the Illustrations

The frontispiece was painted ("pinx[i]t") by the miniaturist William Denton, about whom very little is known beyond the fact that he exhibited portraits at the Royal Academy from 1792 to 1795. Denton's painting was reproduced ("sculp[si]t") in stipple and line engraving by Daniel Orme (1766–1832?), at the beginning of what was to become a distinguished career as a miniaturist portrait painter. Orme exhibited at the Royal Academy between 1797 and 1801 and was appointed engraver to King George III. All the evidence we have, such as Vassa's registering his book in his own name at Stationers' Hall and marketing it himself, suggests that he would have chosen the artists to create his likeness.

Not surprisingly, when the frontispiece to the ninth edition is compared to that of the first, the inscribed names show considerable wear, and the portrait itself is a later state of the original print, with some interestingly subtle changes. In the ninth edition, the eyes of Equiano appear to be more open and more directly looking at the viewer. Given his increasingly strong control of the production and distribution of his *Interesting Narrative* (by the seventh edition he is no longer selling it through others), Equiano may well have had an influence on the new emphasis of his portrait, which seems to reflect the growing assertiveness manifested in his verbal additions and revisions. It, too, is addressed "To the Reader."

The print of *Bahama Banks*, which was the frontispiece to volume 2 of the two-volume first and second editions, is after a painting by Samuel Atkins (1760–1810), who in 1789 had already begun to establish his reputation as a marine painter. His work was exhibited at the Royal Academy in 1787–88, 1791–96, and 1804–8. Both Atkins and Denton were subscribers to the original edition of *The Interesting Narrative*, and the choice of them, along with Orme, as illustrators reflects Equiano's artistic taste and business acumen in selecting such talented men at or near the beginnings of their careers. The presence of the painters' names on the subscription list suggests that they may even have donated their talents to what they considered a worthy cause, whose success would enhance their own reputations as well as the author's.

The illustrations were reengraved by Cornelius Tiebout (1777–1832) for the unauthorized New York City edition of 1791. A painter as well as an engraver, Tiebout was a subscriber to the New York City edition. In 1793 he went to London to study under the engraver James Heath (1757–1834), returning to New York City by 1796. The engraving business Tiebout began with his brother Andrew and others failed around 1822, after which he settled in Kentucky, where he died.

The painting on the cover of the Penguin Edition of Equiano's works, beautiful though it is, is almost certainly not that of Equiano, who was first suggested as the sitter in 1961. The resemblance between the sitter and Equiano's frontispiece is merely superficial, and the sitter's dress indicates that the portrait was very probably painted before 1765, a period when Equiano was usually outside of England.

APPENDIX C

List of Subscribers to the First Edition

His Royal Highness the Prince of
Wales
His Royal Highness the Duke of
York

A

The Right Hon. the Earl of
Ailesbury
Admiral Affleck
Mr. William Abington, 2 copies
Mr. John Abraham
James Adair, Esq.
Reverend Mr. Aldridge
Mr. John Almon
Mrs. Arnot
Mr. Joseph Armitage
Mr. Joseph Ashpinshaw
Mr. Samuel Atkins
Mr. John Atwood
Mr. Thomas Atwood
Mr. Ashwell
J.C. Ashworth, Esq.

B

His Grace the Duke of Bedford
Her Grace the Duchess of
Buccleugh
The Right Rev. the Lord Bishop
of Bangor
The Right Hon. Lord Belgrave

The Rev. Doctor Baker
Mrs. Baker
Matthew Baillie, M.D.
Mrs. Baillie
Miss Baillie
Miss J. Baillie
David Barclay, Esq.
Mr. Robert Barrett
Mr. William Barrett
Mr. John Barnes
Mr. John Basnett
Mr. Bateman
Mrs. Baynes, 2 copies
Mr. Thomas Bellamy
Mr. J. Benjafield
Mr. William Bennett
Mr. Bensley
Mr. Samuel Benson
Mrs. Benton
Reverend Mr. Bentley
Mr. Thomas Bently
Sir John Berney, Bart.
Alexander Blair, Esq.
James Bocock, Esq.
Mrs. Bond
Miss Bond
Mrs. Borckhardt
Mrs. E. Bouverie
————Brand, Esq.
Mr. Martin Brander
F.J. Brown, Esq. M.P. 2 copies
W. Buttall, Esq.
Mr. Buxton
Mr. R.L.B.

Mr. Thomas Burton, 6 copies
Mr. W. Button

C

The Right Hon. Lord Cathcart
The Right Hon. H.S. Conway
Lady Almiria Carpenter
James Carr, Esq.
Charles Carter, Esq.
Mr. James Chalmers
Captain John Clarkson, of the
    Royal Navy
The Rev. Mr. Thomas Clarkson,
    2 copies
Mr. R. Clay
Mr. William Clout
Mr. George Club
Mr. John Cobb
Miss Calwell
Mr. Thomas Cooper
Richard Cosway, Esq.
Mr. James Coxe
Mr. J.C.
Mr. Croucher
Mr. Cruickshanks
Ottobah Cugoano, or John
    Stewart

D

The Right Hon. the Earl of
    Dartmouth
The Right Hon. the Earl of
    Derby
Sir William Dolben, Bart.
The Reverend C.E. De Coetlogon
John Delamain, Esq.
Mrs. Delamain
Mr. Davis
Mr. William Denton
Mr. T. Dickie

Mr. William Dickson
Mr. Charles Dilly, 2 copies
Andrew Drummond, Esq.
Mr. George Durant

E

The Right Hon. the Earl of Essex
The Right Hon. the Countess of
    Essex
Sir Gilbert Elliot, Bart. 2 copies
Lady Anne Erskine
G. Noel Edwards, Esq. M.P.
    2 copies
Mr. Durs Egg
Mr. Ebenezer Evans
The Reverend Mr. John Eyre
Mr. William Eyre

F

Mr. George Fallowdown
Mr. John Fell
F.W. Foster, Esq.
The Reverend Mr. Foster
Mr. J. Frith
W. Fuller, Esq.

G

The Right Hon. the Earl of
    Gainsborough
The Right Hon. the Earl of
    Grosvenor
The Right Hon. Viscount Gallway
The Right Hon. Viscountess
    Gallway
————Gardner, Esq.
Mrs. Garrick
Mr. John Gates
Mr. Samuel Gear

Sir Philip Gibbes, Bart. 6 copies
Miss Gibbes
Mr. Edward Gilbert
Mr. Jonathan Gillett
W.P. Gilliess, Esq.
Mrs. Gordon
Mr. Grange
Mr. Wiliam Grant
Mr. John Grant
Mr. R. Greening
S. Griffiths
John Grove, Esq.
Mrs. Guerin
Reverend Mr. Gwinep

H

The Right Hon. the Earl of
  Hopetoun
The Right Hon. Lord Hawke
Right Hon. Dowager Countess of
  Huntingdon
Thomas Hall, Esq.
Mr. Haley
Hugh Josiah Hansard, Esq.
Mr. Moses Hart
Mrs. Hawkins
Mr. Haysom
Mr. Hearne
Mr. William Hepburn
Mr. J. Hibbert
Mr. Jacob Higman
Sir Richard Hill, Bart.
Reverend Rowland Hill
Miss Hill
Captain John Hills, Royal Navy
Edmund Hill, Esq.
The Reverend Mr. Edward Hoare
William Hodges, Esq.
Reverend Mr. John Holmes,
  3 copies
Mr. Martin Hopkins
Mr. Thomas Howell

Mr. R. Huntley
Mr. J. Hunt
Mr. Philip Hurlock, jun.
Mr. Hutson

J

Mr. T.W.J. Esq.
Mr. James Jackson
Mr. John Jackson
Reverend Mr. James
Mrs. Anne Jennings
Mr. Johnson
Mrs. Johnson
Mr. William Jones
Thomas Irving, Esq. 2 copies
Mr. William Justins

K

The Right Hon. Lord Kinnaird
William Kendall, Esq.
Mr. William Ketland
Mr. Edward King
Mr. Thomas Kingston
Reverend Dr. Kippis
Mr. William Kitchener
Mr. John Knight

L

The Right Reverend the Lord
  Bishop of London
Mr. John Laisne
Mr. Lackington, 6 copies
Mr. John Lamb
Bennet Langton, Esq.
Mr. S. Lee
Mr. Walter Lewis
Mr. J. Lewis
Mr. J. Lindsey

Mr. T. Litchfield
Edward Loveden Loveden,
    Esq. M.P.
Charles Lloyd, Esq.
Mr. William Lloyd
Mr. J.B. Lucas
Mr. James Luken
Henry Lyte, Esq.
Mrs. Lyon

M

His Grace the Duke of
    Marlborough
His Grace the Duke of
    Montague
The Right Hon. Lord Mulgrave
Sir Herbert Mackworth, Bart.
Sir Charles Middleton, Bart.
Lady Middleton
Mr. Thomas Macklane
Mr. George Markett
James Martin, Esq. M.P.
Master Martin, Hayes-Grove, Kent
Mr. William Massey
Mr. Joseph Massingham
John M'Intosh, Esq.
Paul Le Mesurier, Esq. M.P.
Mr. James Mewburn
Mr. N. Middleton
T. Mitchell, Esq.
Mrs. Montague, 2 copies
Miss Hannah More
Mr. George Morrison
Thomas Morris, Esq.
Miss Morris
Morris Morgann, Esq.

N

His Grace the Duke of
    Northumberland
Captain Nurse

O

Edward Ogle, Esq.
James Ogle, Esq.
Robert Oliver, Esq.

P

Mr. D. Parker
Mr. W. Parker
Mr. Richard Packer, jun.
Mr. Parsons, 6 copies
Mr. James Pearse
Mr. J. Pearson
J. Penn, Esq.
George Peters, Esq.
Mr. W. Phillips
J. Philips, Esq.
Mrs. Pickard
Mr. Charles Pilgrim
The Hon. George Pitt, M.P.
Mr. Thomas Pooley
Patrick Power, Esq.
Mr. Michael Power
Joseph Pratt, Esq.

Q

Robert Quarme, Esq.

R

The Right Hon. Lord Rawdon
The Right Hon. Lord Rivers,
    2 copies
Lieutenant General Rainsford
Reverend James Ramsay,
    3 copies
Mr. S. Remnant, jun.
Mr. William Richards,
    2 copies

Mr. J.C. Robarts
Mr. James Roberts
Dr. Robinson
Mr. Robinson
Mr. C. Robinson
George Rose, Esq. M.P.
Mr. W. Ross
Mr. William Rouse
Mr. Walter Row

S

His Grace the Duke of St.
    Albans
Her Grace the Duchess of St.
    Albans
The Right Reverend the Lord
    Bishop of St. David's
The Right Hon. Earl Stanhope,
    3 copies
The Right Hon. the Earl of
    Scarbrough
William, the Son of Ignatius
    Sancho
Mrs. Mary Ann Sandiford
Mr. William Sawyer
Mr. Thomas Seddon
W. Seward, Esq.
Reverend Mr. Thomas Scott
Granville Sharp, Esq. 2 copies
Captain Sidney Smith, of the
    Royal Navy
Colonel Simcoe
Mr. John Simco
General Smith
John Smith, Esq.
Mr. George Smith
Mr. William Smith
Reverend Mr. Southgate
Mr. William Starkey
Thomas Steel, Esq. M.P.
Mr. Staples Steare
Mr. Joseph Stewardson

Mr. Henry Stone, jun.
    2 copies
John Symmons, Esq.

T

Henry Thornton, Esq. M.P.
Mr. Alexander Thomson, M.D.
Reverend John Till
Mr. Samuel Townly
Mr. Daniel Trinder
Reverend Mr. C. La Trobe
Clement Tudway, Esq.
Mrs. Twisden

U

Mr. M. Underwood

V

Mr. John Vaughan
Mrs. Vendt

W

The Right Hon. Earl of Warwick
The Right Reverend the Lord
    Bishop of Worcester
The Hon. William Windham,
    Esq. M.P.
Mr. C.B. Wadstrom
Mr. George Walne
Reverend Mr. Ward
Mr. S. Warren
Mr. J. Waugh
Josiah Wedgwood, Esq.
Reverend Mr. John Wesley
Mr. J. Wheble
Samuel Whitbread, Esq. M.P.

Reverend Thomas Wigzell
Mr. W. Wilson
Reverend Mr. Wills
Mr. Thomas Wimsett
Mr. William Winchester
John Wollaston, Esq.
Mr. Charles Wood
Mr. Joseph Woods

Mr. John Wood
J. Wright, Esq.

Y

Mr. Thomas Young
Mr. Samuel Yockney

APPENDIX D

List of Subscribers to the New York Edition

A

Rev. Burgiss Allison, Principal of
the Academy at Bordentown
John Applegate, Queen-Street,
N.Y.
John Alsop, jun. 12 copies
John Ashfield, No. 44, William
Street
Mary Alsop, Middletown, Con-
necticut
Joseph Wright Alsop, do. [ditto]
Joel Allyn, do.

B

William Brown, Esq., Middletown,
Connecticut
John Belding, Weathersfield, do.
Col. William M. Bloggett, do.
James Bulkley, do.
Abraham Boudoine, N.Y.
John Beers, Suffolk county, S.N.Y.
12 copies
John Bedient, N.Y.
Samuel Borrowe, do.
Joseph Ball, Boston
John O. Bogart, N.Y.
Cornelius Brinkerhoof, do.
John Bowne, jun. do.
Samuel Bowne, do.
Thomas Burling, C.M.
George Bowne, jun.

C

Jacob Conkline, N.Y.
Elijah Cock, do.
Job Cook, do.
Hugh Chard, New Castle, S.N.Y.
Francis Courtney, Ulster county,
do.
Jesse Cole, Middletown,
Connecticut
Joseph Churchell, do.
Jonathan Collins, do.
William Crosby, do.
Timothy Canfield, do.

D

Thomas Dobson, Book-Seller,
Phila. 100 copies
Cornelius Davis, N.Y.
John Durell, do.
Samuel Dodge, do.
Samuel M. Dickenson,
Middletown, Connecticut
Stephen Dehart, Eliz. Town, N.J.
George Duryee, jun. Bushwick,
Long-Island
Carson Dickenson

E

Isaac Eccleston, Antigua

F

Rev. Benjamin Foster, N.Y.
Bezaleel Fisk, Middletown,
   Connecticut
David S. Franks, N.Y.
Bela F. Frost
John Ferris, Wilmington
George Fox, N.Y.

G

Nathan Gellem, Middletown,
   Connecticut
William Green, Newcastle

H

Ichabod B. Hasley, Eliz. Town,
   N.J. 12 copies
Rev Adam Hamilton, Westfield,
   Connecticut
John Harrison, printer, N.Y.
John Hamilton, do.
John Hendrick, Eliz. Town, N.J.
John Hinckman
Doctor Lee Hall, Middletown,
   Connecticut
Samuel Hutchinson, do.
Jacob Hamerson, Weathersfield,
   do.
Calvin Hall, Middletown, do.
Hezekiah Hulbert, do.
Samuel Harris, do.
T. Hosmer, do.
John Haydock, N.Y.
Jeremiah Hallett, do.

J

David Richard Floyd Jones,
   Q. county, S.N.Y.

K

Abigail Kenyon, do.
John Kent, Broad-Way, N.Y.

L

Samuel Le Count, N.Y.
Philip K. Lawrence, do.
Loins and Wright, do. 6 copies
Richard R. Lawrence, do.

M

William Martin, N.Y.
James Main, do.
John Murray, jun. do.
John Miller, Water-street, do.
Robert Mott, 2 copies
William Manning, jun. N.J.
John Meriam
Thomas Mason, Philadelphia
Hugh Montgomery, N.Y.
Alexander M'Rea, Middletown
Asahel M'Rea, do.

P

Nathaniel Pearsall, No. 36, Queen
   street, N.Y.
Peter Palmer, do.
Benjamin Pomroy, Middletown,
   Connecticut
Doctor Jared Potter, Wallingford,
   do.

R

Ezekel Robins, Queen street,
   N.Y.
Thomas Ross, do.

Isaac Riley, Middletown,
  Connecticut, 60 copies
John I. Richey, N.Y.
John Remmy, jun. do.
Rev. William Rogers. D.D.
  Professor of English and
  Oratory, in the College of
  Philadelphia
Noah Reest
Jesse Riley, Weathersfield,
  Connecticut
Matthew I. Russel, Esq.
  Middletown
Roger Riley, Esq. Berlin,
  Connecticut
Theophilus M. Robinson,
  Wellingford, Connect.

S

Daniel Stansburg, N.Y.
Solomon Smith, N.J. Sussex C.
  Minisink, 6 copies
Isaac Spinning, do.
Aaron Sharpless, N.Y., 12 copies
Peter Slote, do.
Abraham H. Schenck, do.
Nathaniel Smith, do.
Melancthon Smith, Esq. do.
Allyn Southmayd, Middletown,
  Connecticut

Peter A. Schenck, N.Y.
Peter T. Schenck, Long-Island
Joshua Stors, Middletown
Lemuel Stoors, do.
Jehosuphat Starr, do.

T

Cornelius Tiebout, copper-plate
  engraver, N.Y.
Alexander Tiebout, do.
Walter Towndsend, North Castle
Andrew Thompson, N.Y.
Jacob Fee, do.
Doctor Ebenezer Tray,
  Middletown, Connecticut

U

Andrew Underhill

W

T.P. Wills, N. Jersey
William V. Wagener, N.Y.
Joseph Webb, Weathersfield,
  Connecticut
Seth Wetmore, Middletown, do.

APPENDIX E

Correspondence and Other Writings of Gustavus Vassa, or Olaudah Equiano, Not Published in The Interesting Narrative.

1. For *The Public Advertiser*, 4 April 1787.[1]

We are sorry to find that his Majesty's Commissary for the African Settlement has sent the following letter to Mr. John Stewart [Ottobah Cugoano], Pall Mall:

At Plymouth, March 24, 1787.

Sir,
    These with my respects to you. I am sorry you and some more are not here with us. I am sure [Joseph] Irwin, and [Patrick] Fraser the Parson, are great villains, and Dr. Currie. I am exceeding much aggrieved at the conduct of those who call themselves gentlemen. They now mean to serve (or use) the blacks the same as they do in the West Indies. For the good of the settlement I have borne every affront that could be given, believe me, without giving the least occasion, or ever yet resenting any.
    By Sir Charles Middleton's letter to me, I now find Irwin and Fraser have wrote to the Committee and the Treasury, that I use the white people with arrogance, and the blacks with civility, and stir them up to mutiny: which is not true, for I am the greatest peace-maker that goes out. The reason for this lie is, that in the presence of these two I acquainted Captain [Thomas Boulden] Thompson of the Nautilus sloop, our convoy, that I would go to London and tell of their roguery; and further insisted on Captain Thompson to come on board of the ships, and see the wrongs done to me and the people; so Captain Thompson came and saw it, and ordered the things to be given according to contract—which is not yet done in many things—and many of the black people have died for want of their due. I am grieved in every respect. Irwin never meant well to the people, but self-interest has ever been his end: twice this week [the Black Poor] have taken him, bodily, to the Captain, to complain of him, and I have done it four times.
    I do not know how this undertaking will end; I wish I had never been

327

involved in it; but at times I think the Lord will make me very useful at last.

I am, dear Friend,
With respect, yours,
"G. VASA."
The Commissary for the Black Poor.

2. For *The Public Advertiser*, 14 July 1787.

An extract of a letter from on board one of the ships with the Blacks, bound to Africa, having appeared on the 2nd and 3rd inst. in the public papers,[2] wherein injurious reflexions, prejudicial to the character of Vasa, the Black Commissary, were contained, he thinks it necessary to vindicate his character from these misrepresentations, informing the public, that the principal crime which caused his dismission, was an information he laid before the Navy Board, accusing the Agent [Irwin] of unfaithfulness in his office, in not providing such necessaries as were contracted for the people, and were absolutely necessary for their existence, which necessaries could not be obtained from the Agents. The same representation was made by Mr. Vasa to Mr. Hoare, which induced the latter, who had before appeared to be Vasa's friend, to go to the Secretary of the Treasury, and procure his dismission. The above Gentleman impowered the Agent to take many passengers in, contrary to the orders given to the Commissary.

(Mr. Vasa).

3. The Address of Thanks of the Sons of Africa to the Honourable Granville Sharp, Esq.[3]

Honourable and Worthy Sir,   December 15, 1787.
    Give us leave to say, that every virtuous man is a truly honourable man; and he that doth good hath honour to himself: and many blessings are upon the head of the just, and their memory shall be blessed, and their works praise them in the gate.

    And we must say, that we, who are a part, or descendants, of the much-wronged people of Africa, are peculiarly and greatly indebted to you, for the many good and friendly services that you have done towards us, and which are now even out of our power to enumerate.

    Nevertheless, we are truly sensible of your great kindness and humanity; and we cannot do otherwise but endeavour, with the utmost sincerity and thankfulness, to acknowledge our great obligations to you, and, with the most feeling sense of our hearts, on all occasions to express and manifest our gratitude and love for your long, valuable, and indefatigable labours and benevolence towards using every means to rescue our suffering brethren in slavery.

Your writings, Sir, are not of trivial matters, but of great and essential things of moral and religious importance, worthy the regard of all men; and abound with many great and precious things, of sacred writ, particularly respecting the laws of God, and the duties of men.

Therefore, we wish, for ourselves and others, that these valuable treatises may be collected and preserved, for the benefit and good of all men, and for an enduring memorial of the great learning, piety, and vigilance of our good friend the worthy Author. And we wish that the laws of God, and his ways of righteousness set forth therein, may be as a path for the virtuous and prudent to walk in, and as a clear shining light to the wise in all ages; and that these and other writings of that nature, may be preserved and established as a monument or beacon to guide or to warn men, lest they should depart from the paths of justice and humanity; and that they may more and more become means of curbing the vicious violators of God's holy law, and to restrain the avaricious invaders of the rights and liberties of men, whilever the human race inhabits this earth below.

And, ever honourable and worthy Sir, may the blessing and peace of Almighty God be with you, and long preserve your valuable life, and make you abundantly useful in every good word and work! And when God's appointed time shall come, may your exit be blessed, and may you arise and for ever shine in the glorious world above, when that Sovereign Voice, speaking with joy, as the sound of many waters, shall be heard, saying, "Well done, thou good and faithful servant: enter thou into the joy of thy Lord!" It will then be the sweetest of all delights for ever, and more melodious than all music! And such honour and felicity will the blessed God and Saviour of his people bestow upon all the saints and faithful servants who are redeemed from among men, and saved from sin, slavery, misery, pain, and death, and from eternal dishonour and wrath depending upon the heads of all the wicked and rebellious.

And now, honourable Sir, with the greatest submission, we must beg you to accept this memorial of our thanks for your good and faithful services towards us, and for your humane commiseration of our brethren and countrymen unlawfully held in slavery.

And we have hereunto subscribed a few of our names, as a mark of our gratitude and love. And we are, with the greatest esteem and veneration, honourable and worthy, Sir, your most obliged and most devoted humble servants.

OTTOBAH CUGOANO.	JASPER GOREE.
JOHN STUART.	GUSTAVUS VASA.
GEORGE ROBERT MANDEVILLE.	JAMES BAILEY.

WILLIAM STEVENS.   THOMAS OXFORD.
JOSEPH ALMAZE.   JOHN ADAMS.
BOUGHWA GEGANSMEL.   GEORGE WALLACE.

4. For *The Public Advertiser*, 28 January 1788.

To J. T. [James Tobin] Esq; Author of the BOOKS called CURSORY
REMARKS & REJOINDER.

Sir,

That to love mercy and judge rightly of things is an honour to man, no
body I think will deny; but "if he understandeth not, nor sheweth compassion to the sufferings of his fellow-creatures, he is like the beasts that
perish." Psalm lix verse 20.

Excuse me, Sir, if I think you in no better predicament than that exhibited in the latter part of the above clause; for can any man less ferocious
than a tiger or a wolf attempt to justify the cruelties inflicted on the negroes in the West Indies? You certainly cannot be susceptible of human pity
to be so callous to their complicated woes! Who could but the Author of
the Cursory Remarks so debase his nature, as not to feel his keenest pangs
of heart on reading their deplorable story? I confess my cheek changes colour
with resentment against your unrelenting barbarity, and wish you from my
soul to run the gauntlet of Lex Talionis[4] at this time; for as you are so fond
of flogging others, it is no bad proof of your deserving a flagellation yourself. Is it not written in the 15th chapter of Numbers, the 15th and 16th
verses, that there is the same law for the stranger as for you?

Then, Sir, why do you rob him of the common privilege given to all
by the Universal and Almighty Legislator? Why exclude him from the en-
joyment of benefits which he has equal right to with yourself? Why treat
him as if he was not of like feeling? Does civilization warrant these incur-
sions upon natural justice? No. —Does religion? No. —Benevolence to all
is its essence, and do unto others as we would others should do unto us,
its grand precept—to Blacks as well as Whites, all being the children of the
same parent. Those, therefore, who transgress those sacred obligations, and
here, Mr. Remarker, I think you are caught, are not superior to brutes
which understandeth not, nor to beasts which perish.

From your having been in the West Indies, you must know that the facts
stated by the Rev. Mr. [James] Ramsay are true; and yet regardless of the
truth, you controvert them. This surely is supporting a bad cause at all
events, and brandishing falsehood to strengthen the hand of the oppressor.
Recollect, Sir, that you are told in the 17th verse of the 19th chapter of
Leviticus, "You shall not suffer sin upon your neighbour"; and you will not
I am sure, escape the upbraidings of your conscience, unless you are fortu-

nate enough to have none; and remember also, that the oppressor and the oppressed are in the hands of the just and awful God, who says, Vengeance is mine and I will repay—repay the oppressor and the justifier of the oppression. How dreadful then will your fate be? The studied and torturing punishments, inhuman, as they are, of a barbarous planter, or a more barbarous overseer, will be tenderness compared to the provoked wrath of an angry but righteous God! who will raise, I have the fullest confidence, many of the sable race to the joys of Heaven, and cast the oppressive white to that doleful place, where he will cry, but will cry in vain, for a drop of water!

Your delight seems to be in misrepresentation, else how could you in page 11 of your Remarks, and in your Rejoinder, page 35, communicate to the public such a glaring untruth as that the oath of a free African is equally admissable in several courts with that of a white person? The contrary of this I know is the fact at every one of the islands I have been, and I have been at no less than fifteen. But who will dispute with such an invective fibber? Why nobody to be sure; for you'll tell, I wish I could say truths, but you oblige me to use ill manners, you lie faster than Old Nick can hear them. A few shall stare you in the face:

What is your speaking of the laws in favour of the Negroes?

Your description of the iron muzzle?

That you never saw the infliction of a severe punishment, implying thereby that there is none?

That a Negro has every inducement to wish for a numerous family?

That in England there are no black labourers?

That those who are not servants, are in rags or thieves?

In a word, the public can bear testimony with me that you are a malicious slanderer of an honest, industrious, injured people!

From the same source of malevolence the freedom of their inclinations is to be shackled—it is not sufficient for their bodies to be oppressed, but their minds must also? Iniquity in the extreme! If the mind of a black man conceives the passion of love for a fair female, he is to pine, languish, and even die, sooner than an intermarriage be allowed, merely because the complexion of the offspring should be tawney—A more foolish prejudice than this never warped a cultivated mind—for as no contamination of the virtues of the heart would result from the union, the mixture of colour could be of no consequence. God looks with equal good-will on all his creatures, whether black or white—let neither, therefore, arrogantly condemn the other.

The mutual commerce of the sexes of both Blacks and Whites, under the restrictions of moderation and law, would yield more benefit than a prohibition—the mind free—would not have such a strong propensity toward the black females as when under restraint: Nature abhors restraint, and for ease either evades or breaks it. Hence arise secret amours, adultery, fornication and all other evils of lasciviousness! hence that most abandoned boasting of the French Planter, who, under the dominion of lust, had the shameless impudence to exult at the violations he had committed against Virtue, Religion, and the Almighty—hence also spring actual murders on infants, the procuring of abortions, enfeebled constitution, disgrace, shame, and a thousand other horrid enormities.

Now, Sir, would it not be more honour to us to have a few darker visages than perhaps yours among us, than inundation of such evils? and to provide effectual remedies, by a liberal policy against evils which may be traced to some of our most wealthy Planters as their fountain, and which may have smeared the purity of even your own chastity?

As the ground-work, why not establish intermarriages at home, and in our Colonies? and encourage open, free, and generous love upon Nature's own wide and extensive plan, subservient only to moral rectitude, without distinction of the colour of a skin?

That ancient, most wise, and inspired politician, Moses, encouraged strangers to unite with the Israelites, upon this maxim, that every addition to their number was an addition to their strength, and as an inducement, admitted them to most of the immunities of his own people. He established marriage with strangers by his own example—The Lord confirmed them— and punished Aaron and Miriam for vexing their brother for marrying the Ethiopian—Away then with your narrow impolitic notion of preventing by law what will be a national honour, national strength, and productive of national virtue—Intermarriages!

Wherefore, to conclude in the words of one of your selected texts, "If I come, I will remember the deeds which he doeth, prating against us with malicious words."

I am Sir,
Your fervent Servant,
GUSTAVUS VASSA, the Ethiopian and the King's late Commissary for the
    African Settlement.
Baldwin's Garden, Jan. 1788.

5. FOR *THE PUBLIC ADVERTISER*, 5 FEBRUARY 1788.

To MR. GORDON TURNBULL, Author of an "Apology for NEGRO SLAVERY."

Sir,

I am sorry to find in your Apology for oppression, you deviate far from the Christian precepts, which enjoin us to do unto others as we would others should do unto us. In this enlightened age, it is scarcely credible that a

man should be born and educated, in the British dominions especially, possessed of minds so warped as the author of the Cursory Remarks and yourself. Strange that in a land which boasts of the purest light of the Gospel,
and the most perfect freedom, there should be found advocates of oppression—for the most abject and iniquitous kind of slavery. To kidnap our fellow creatures, however they may differ in complexion, to degrade them into
beasts of burthen, to deny them every right but those, and scarcely those we
allow to a horse, to keep them in perpetual servitude, is a crime as unjusti-
fiable as cruel; but to avow and defend this infamous traffic required the
ability and the modesty of you and Mr. Tobin. Certainly, Sir, you were perfectly consistent with yourself attacking as you did that friend to the rights
of mankind, the Rev. James Ramsay. Malignity and benevolence do not well
associate, and humanity is a root that seldom flourishes in the soil of a
planter. I am not therefore surprised that you have endeavoured to depre-
ciate his noble Essay on the Treatment and Conversion of African Slaves &c.
That learned and elegant performance written in favour of a much injured
race of men, we are happy to think has had a good effect in opening the
eyes of many of his countrymen to the sufferings of their African brethren;
for the Apostle calls us brethren; but if I may form a conjecture from your
writings; the Apostles have very small credit either with you or your worthy partner in cruelty, Mr. Tobin; for can any man be a Christian who asserts that one part of the human race were ordained to be in perpetual
bondage to another? Is such an assertion, consistent with that spirit of
meekness, of justice, of charity, and above all, that brotherly love which it
enjoins? But we trust that in spite of your *hissing* zeal and impotent malevolence against Mr. Ramsay, his noble purpose of philanthropy will be productive of much good to many, and in the end through the blessing of God,
be a means of bringing about the abolition of Slavery. To the Reverend
Gentleman we return our most unfeigned thanks and heartfelt gratitude,
and we also feel ourselves much indebted to all those gentlemen who have
stepped forward in our defence, and vindicated us from the aspersions of
our tyrannical calumniators.

You and your friend, J. Tobin, the cursory remarker, resemble Demetrius,
the silversmith, seeing your craft in danger, a craft, however, not so innocent or justifiable as the making of shrines for Diana, for that though wicked
enough, left the persons of men at liberty, but yours enslaves both body
and soul—and sacrifices your fellow-creatures on the altar of avarice. You,
I say, apprehensive that the promulgation of truth will be subversive of your
infamous craft, and destructive of your iniquitous gain, rush out with the
desperation of assassins, and attempt to wound the reputation of the reverend Essayist by false calumnies, gross contradictions of several well-known
facts, and insidious suppression of others. The character of that reverend
Gentleman to my knowledge (and I have known him well both here and
in the West Indies for many years) is irreproachable. Many of the facts he

relates I know to be true, and many others still more shocking, if possible, have fallen within my own observation, within my own feeling; for were I to enumerate even my own sufferings in the West Indies, which perhaps I may one day offer to the public, the disgusting catalogue would be almost too great for belief. It would be endless to refute all your false assertions respecting the treatment of African slaves in the West Indies; some of them, however, are gross; in particular, you say in your apology page 30, "That a Negro has every inducement to wish a numerous family, and enjoys every pleasure he can desire." A glaring falsehood! But to my great grief, and much anguish in different islands in the West Indies, I have been a witness to children torn from their agonized parents, and sent off wherever their merciless owners please, never more to see their friends again. In page 34 of the same elaborate and pious work, you offer an hypothesis, that the Negro race is an inferior species of mankind: Oh fool! See the 17th chapter of the Acts, verse 26, "God hath made of one blood all nations of men, for to dwell on all the face of the earth, &c." Therefore, beware of that Scripture, which says, Fools perish for lack of knowledge.

GUSTAVUS VASSA, the Ethiopian,
and late Commissary for the African Settlement

Baldwin's Gardens.

6. FOR THE PUBLIC ADVERTISER, 13 FEBRUARY 1788.

To the Senate of GREAT BRITAIN.

Gentlemen,
    May Heaven make you what you should be, the dispensers of light, liberty and science to the uttermost parts of the earth; then will be glory to God on the highest—on earth peace and goodwill to man:—Glory, honour, peace, &c. to every soul of man that worketh good; to the Britons first (because to them the Gospel is preached) and also to the nations: To that truly immortal and illustrious advocate of our liberty, Granville Sharp, Esq., the philanthropist and justly Reverend James Ramsay, and the much to be honoured body of gentlemen called Friends, who have exerted every endeavour to break the accursed yoke of Slavery, and ease the heavy burthens of the oppressed Negroes. "Those that honour their Maker have mercy on the Poor";—and many blessing are upon the heads of the just. —May the fear of the Lord prolong their days, and cause their memory to be blessed, and may their numbers be increased, and their expectations filled with gladness, for commiserating the poor Africans, who are counted as beasts of burthen by base-minded men. May God ever open the mouths of these

worthies to judge righteously, and plead the cause of the poor and needy—
for the liberal devise liberal things, and by liberal things shall stand; and they
can say with the pious Job, "Did I not weep for him that was in trouble?
Was not my soul grieved for the Poor?"

It is righteousness exalteth a nation, but sin is a reproach to any people.
—Destruction shall be to the workers of iniquity—and the wicked shall perish by their own wickedness. —May the worthy Lord Bishop of London
be blessed for his pathetic[5] and humane sermon on behalf of the Africans,
and all the benevolent gentlemen who are engaged in the laudable attempt
to abolish Slavery, and thereby prevent many savage barbarities from being
daily committed by the enslavers of men, to whom the Lord has pronounced
wrath, anguish, and tribulation, &. to the sons of Britain first (as having the
Gospel preached amongst them) and also to the nations—.

AETHIOPIANUS.

7. Letter from Gustavus Vassa, late Commissary for the African Settlement, to the Right Honourable Lord Hawkesbury.[6]

My Lord,   London, 13th March 1788.

As the illicit Traffic of Slavery is to be taken into consideration of the
British Legislature, I have taken the Liberty of sending you the following
Sentiments, which have met the Approbation of many intelligent and com-
mercial Gentlemen.

Sir,
A SYSTEM of commerce once established in Africa, the Demand for
Manufactories will most rapidly augment, as the native Inhabitants will sen-
sibly adopt our Fashions, Manner, Customs, &c. &c.

In proportion to the Civilization, so will be the Consumption of British
Manufactures.

The Wear and Tear of a Continent, nearly twice as large as Europe, and
rich in Vegetable and Mineral Productions, is much easier conceived than
calculated. A Case in point. It cost the Aborigines of Britain little or nothing in Cloathing, &c. The Difference between our Forefathers and us, in
point of Consumption, is literally infinite. The Reason is most obvious. It
will be equally immense in Africa. The same Cause, viz. Civilization, will
ever produce the same Effect. There are no Book or outstanding Debts, if
I may be allowed the Expression. The Word Credit is not to be found in
the African Dictionary; it is standing upon safe Ground.

A commercial Intercourse with Africa opens an inexhaustible Source of

Wealth to the manufacturing Interest of Great Britain; and to all which the Slave Trade is a physical Obstruction.

If I am not misinformed, the manufacturing Interest is equal, if not superior to the landed Interest as to Value, for Reasons which will soon appear. The Abolition of the diabolical Slavery will give a most rapid and permanent Extension to Manufactures, which is totally and diametrically opposite to what some interested People assert.

The Manufactories of this Country must and will in the nature and Reason of Things have a full and constant Employ by supplying the African Markets. The Population, Bowels, and Surface of Africa abound in valuable and useful Returns; the hidden treasuries of Countries will be brought to Light and into Circulation.

Industry, Enterprise, and Mining will have their full Scope, proportionably as they civilize. In a Word, it lays open an endless Field of Commerce to the British Manufacturer and Merchant Adventurer.

The manufacturing Interest and the general Interest of the Enterprise are synonimous; the Abolition of Slavery would be in reality an universal Good, and for which a partial Ill must be supported.

Tortures, Murder, and every other imaginable Barbarity are practised by the West India Planters upon the Slaves with Impunity. I hope the Slave Trade will be abolished: I pray it may be an Event at hand. The great Body of Manufacturers, uniting in the Cause, will considerably facilitate and expedite it; and, as I have already stated, it is most substantially their Interest and Advantage, and as such the Nation at large. In a short Space of Time One Sentiment alone will prevail, from Motives of Interest as well as Justice and Humanity.

Europe contains One hundred and Twenty Millions of Inhabitants; Query, How many Millions doth Africa contain? Supposing the Africans, collectively and individually, to expend Five Pounds a Head in Raiment and Furniture yearly, when civilized, &c. —an Immensity beyond the Reach of Imagination: This I conceive to be a Theory founded upon Facts; and therefore an infallible one. If the Blacks were permitted to remain in their own Country they would double themselves every Fifteen Years: In Proportion to such Increase would be the Demand for Manufactures. Cotton and Indigo grow spontaneously in some Parts of Africa: A Consideration this of no small Consequence to the manufacturing Towns of Great Britain.

The Chamber of Manufactories of Great Britain, held in London will be strenuous in the Cause. It opens a most immense, glorious, and happy Prospect.

The Cloathing, &c. of a Continent Ten thousand Miles in Circumference, and immensely rich in Productions of every Denomination, would make an interesting Return indeed for our Manufactures, a free Trade being established.

I have, my Lord, the Honour to subscribe myself,

Your Lordships very humble and devoted Servant,
GUSTAVUS VASSA,
the late Commissary for the African Settlement.
No. 53, Baldwin's Gardens, Holborn.

8. FOR *THE PUBLIC ADVERTISER*, 28 APRIL 1788.

To the Rev. Mr. RAYMUND HARRIS, *the* Author *of the* Book *called—*
"Scripture Researches on the *Licitness* of the *Slave Trade.*"[7]

SIR,

THE Subject of Slavery is now grown to be a serious one, when we
consider the buying and selling of Negroes not as a clandestine or piratical
business, but as an open public trade, encouraged and promoted by Acts
of Parliament. Being contrary to religion, it must be deemed a national
sin, and as such may have a consequence that ought always to be dreaded.
—May God give us grace to repent of this abominable crime' before it be
too late! I could not have believed any man in your office would have dared
to come forth in public in these our days to vindicate the accursed Slave
Trade on any ground; but least of all by the law of Moses, and by that of
Christ in the Gospel. As you are so strenuous in bringing in the blessed and
benevolent Apostle, Paul, to support your insinuations, with respect to Slavery, I will here attack you on the Apostle's ground. The glorious system of
the Gospel destroys all narrow partiality, and makes us citizens of the world,
by obliging us to profess universal benevolence; but more especially are we
bound, as Christians, to commiserate and assist, to the utmost of our power,
all persons in distress, or captivity. Whatever the Worshipful Committee of
the Company of Merchants trading to Africa, and their hirelings, may think
of it, or their advocate, the Rev. Mr. Harris, we are not to do evil that
good may come, though some of our Statesmen and their political deceivers
may think otherwise. We must not for the sake of Old England, and its
African trade, or for the supposed advantage or imaginary necessities of the
American colonies, lay aside our Christian charity, which we owe to all the
rest of mankind; because whenever we do so we certainly deserve to be
considered in no better light than as an overgrown society of robbers—a
mere banditti, who perhaps may love one another, but at the same time are
at enmity with all the rest of the world. Is this according to the law of Nature? For shame! Mr. Harris. In your aforesaid book I am sorry to find you
wrest the words of St. Paul's Epistle to Philemon. St. Paul did not entreat
Philemon to take back his servant Onesimus in his former capacity, as you
have asserted, in order to render bondage consistent with the principles of
revealed religion; but St. Paul said expressly, not now as a servant, but above
a servant, a brother beloved, &c. —So, Mr. Harris, you have notoriously

wrested St. Paul's words; in the other texts, where St. Paul recommends submission to servants for conscience sake, he at the same time enjoins the master to entertain such a measure of brotherly love towards his servant, as must be entirely subversive of the African trade, and West India slavery. —And though St. Paul recommends Christian Patience under servitude; yet at the same time he plainly insinuates, that it is inconsistent with Christianity. —The apostle's right to have detained Onesimus, even without the master's consent, is sufficiently implied in the 8th verse. —The dignity of Christ's kingdom doth not admit of Christians to be slaves to their brothers. —Canst thou be made free, says the apostle to the Christian Servant, choose it rather; for he that is called of the Lord being a servant, is the free man of the Lord; ye are bought with a price, be not therefore the servants of men. —Sir, to me it is astonishing, you should in the open face of day, so strangely pervert the apostle's meaning in the 16th verse. —Of this epistle, which you cite strongly in favour of slavery, when the whole tenor of it is in behalf of the slave, I think if you were not hired, you must necessarily observe and acknowledge this matter beyond dispute: and if you were well acquainted with the Bible, you would have seen the very time St. Paul sent Onesimus back to his former master. He then was a Minister or a Preacher of the Gospel. This is corroborated by a variety of circumstances; pray see the epistle to the Colossians. —Surely every reasonable Christian must suppose St. Paul mad, according to the doctrine presumed in your book, to send Onesimus to be a slave and private property the very time when the Christians had all one heart, one mind, and one spirit; and all those who had property sold it, and they had all things common amongst them. You, Sir, as a Clergyman ought to have considered this subject well; I think you have done no credit to the doctrine of Christ, in asserting, that Onesimus was to be received by Philemon for ever as a slave. —St. Paul in his epistles enjoins servants to submission, and not to grieve on the account of their temporal estate. For if, instead of this, he had absolutely declared the iniquity of slavery, tho' established and authorised by the laws of a temporal government, he would have occasioned more tumult than reformation: among the multitude of slaves there would have been more striving for temporal than spiritual happiness; yet it plainly appears by the insinuations which immediately follow, that he thought it derogatory to the honour of Christianity, that men who are bought with the inestimable price of Christ's blood, shall be esteemed slaves, and the private property of their fellow-men. And had Christianity been established by temporal authority in those countries where Paul preached, as it is at present, in this kingdom, we need not doubt but that he would have urged, nay, compelled the masters, as he did Philemon, by the most pressing arguments, to treat their quondam slaves, not now as servants, but above servants—a brother beloved —May God open your eyes while it is called to-day, to see aright, before you go hence and be no more seen. —Remember the God who has said, Vengeance is mine, and I will repay not only the oppressor, but also the justifier of the oppression.

SIR,
I am fervently thine,
GUSTAVUS VASSA,
The African.
Baldwin's Gardens.

9. FOR *THE PUBLIC ADVERTISER,* 19 JUNE 1788.[8]

To the Honourable and Worthy Members of the BRITISH SENATE.

Gentlemen,

Permit me, one of the oppressed natives of Africa, thus to offer you the warmest thanks of a heart glowing with gratitude for your late humane interference on the behalf of my injured countrymen. May this and the next year bear record of deeds worthy of yourselves! May you then complete the glorious work you have so humanely begun in this, and join with the public voice in putting an end to an oppression that now so loudly calls for redress! The wise man saith, *Prov.* xiv. 34, "Righteousness exalteth a nation, but sin is a reproach to any people." May all the noble youths I heard speak in our favour in the Senate, be renowned for illustrious deeds, and their aspiring years crowned with glory! May the all bountiful Creator, the God whose eyes are ever upon all his creatures, who ever rewards all virtuous acts, and regards the prayers of the oppressed, make you that return, which I and my unfortunate countrymen are not able to express, and shower on you every happiness this world can afford, and every fulness of which Divine Revelation has promised us in the next! Believe me, Gentlemen, while I attended your debate on the Bill for the relief of my countrymen, now depending before you, my heart burned within me, and glowed with gratitude to those who supported the cause of humanity. I could have wished for an opportunity of recounting to you not only my own sufferings, which, though numerous, have been nearly forgotten, but those of which I have been a witness for many years, that they might have influenced your decision; but I thank God, your humanity anticipated my wishes, and rendered such recital unnecessary. Our cries have at length reached your ears, and I trust you are already in some measure convinced that the Slave Trade is as impolitic as inhuman, and as such must ever be unwise. The more extended our misery is, the greater claim it has to your compassion, and the greater the pleasure you must feel in administering to its relief. The satisfaction, which, for the honour of human nature, this distinguished act of compassion gave you, was as visible as felt, and affected me much. From the particular favours shewed me by many of your worthy Members, espe-cially your Honourable Chairman Mr. Whitbread, Sir P. Burrell, Sir William Dolben, the Hon. G. Pitt,[9] &. &. I beg thus to express my most grateful acknowledgments, and I pray the good and gracious God ever to distinguish them by his choicest blessings! —And if it should please Providence to enable me to return to my estate in Elese, in Africa, and to be happy enough to see any of these worthy senators there, as the Lord liveth, we will have such a libation of pure virgin palm-wine, as shall make their hearts glad!!!—And we will erect two altar[s]—one to Pity*—the other to Freedom—to perpetuate their benevolence to my countrymen.

I am, with the most devoted respect, Honourable and Most Worthy Senators, Your grateful and lowly Servant, GUSTAVUS VASSA, the African.

Baldwin's Gardens, June 18, 1788.

*J.R. and T.C.[10]

10. FOR *THE MORNING CHRONICLE AND LONDON ADVERTISER*, 27 JUNE 1788.

To the Author of the POEM ON HUMANITY.[11]
Worthy Sir,

In the name of the poor injured Africans, I return you my innate thanks; with prayers to my God ever to fill you with the spirit of philanthropy here, and hereafter receive you into glory. During time may you exert every endeavour in aiding to break the accursed yoke of slavery, and ease the heavy burthens of the oppressed Africans. Sir, permit me to say, "Those that honour their Maker have mercy on the poor"; and many blessings are upon the heads of the Just. May the fear of the Lord prolong your days, and cause your memory to be blessed, and your expectations filled with gladness, for commiserating the poor Africans, who are counted as beasts of burthen by base-minded men. May God ever enable you to support the cause of the poor and the needy. The liberal devise liberal things, and by liberal things shall stand; and may you ever say with the pious Job, "Did not I weep for him that was in trouble? Was not my soul grieved for the poor?" May the all-seeing God hear my prayers for you and crown your works with abounding success! pray you excuse what you here see amiss. I remain with thanks and humble respect.

Yours to Command,
GUSTAVUS VASSA.
The Oppressed African.
Now at No. 13, Tottenham-Street,
Wednesday June 25, 1788.

Editorial Note:

We cannot but think the letter a strong argument in favour of the *natural abilities*, as well as *good feelings*, of the Negro Race, and a solid answer in their favour, though manifestly written in haste, and we print it exactly from the original. As to the question of their *stupidity*, we are sincere friends to *commerce*, but we would have it flourish without *cruelty*.

11. For *The Public Advertiser*, 28 June 1788.

To the Right Hon. LORD SYDNEY.[12]
My Lord,

Having been present last Wednesday [25 June] at the debate on the Slave Bill, now depending in the House of Lords, I with much surprize heard your Lordship combat the very principle of the Bill, and assert that it was founded in mistaken humanity. At the first, such assertion would appear rather paradoxical. If imposing a restraint on the cruelities practised towards wretches who never injured us, be mistaken humanity, what are the proper channels through which it ought to be directed? However, as your Lordship gave reasons for your opinion, I do not wish either to tax your humanity or candour, but on the contrary believe you were misled by your information. Your Lordship mentioned you had been told by Captain Thompson, under whose convoy the natives of Africa were lately sent out to Sierra Leona, that shortly after their arrival there, some of them embraced the first opportunity of embarking for the West Indies, some of the Lascars, rather than work, lay down among the bushes and died, and that the humane intentions of the Government were frustrated, and the expectations of all concerned in the enterprize disappointed. Now, my Lord, without impeaching the veracity of that gentleman, or controverting the facts he related, permit me to explain the cause of the ill success of that expedition, which I hope will sufficiently obviate the inferences your Lordship drew from them.

When the intention of sending those people to Sierra Leona was first conceived, it was thought necessary by Government to send a Commissary on their part to Superintend the conduct of the Agent who had contracted for carrying them over, and I being judged a proper person for that purpose was appointed Commissary by the Commissioners of the Navy, the latter end of 1786. In consequence I proceeded immediately to the execution of my duty on board one of the vessels destined for the voyage, where I continued till the March following.

During my continuance in the employment of Government, I was struck with the flagrant abuses committed by the Agent, and endeavoured to remedy them, but without effect. One instance, among many which I could produce, may serve as a specimen: Government had ordered to be provided all necessaries (slops as they are called included) for 750 persons; however not being able to muster more than 426, I was ordered to send the superfluous slops, &. to the King's stores at Portsmouth, but when I demanded them for that purpose from the Agent, it appeared they had never been bought, tho' paid for by Government. —But that was not all, Government were not the only objects of peculation; these poor people suffered infinitely more—their accommodations were most wretched, many of them wanted beds, and many more cloathing and other necessaries. —For the truth of this, and much more, I do not seek credit on my assertion. I appeal to the testimony of Captain Thompson himself, to whom I applied in February 1787, for a remedy, when I had remonstrated to the Agent in vain, and even brought him to a witness of the injustice and oppression I complained of. —I appeal also to a letter written by these wretched people, so early as the beginning of the preceeding January, and published in *The Morning Herald* of the 4th of that month, signed by twenty of their Chiefs.

My Lord, I could not silently suffer Government to be thus cheated, and my countrymen plundered and oppressed, and even left destitute of the necessaries for almost their existence—I therefore informed the Commissioners of the Navy of the Agent's proceedings—but my dismission was soon after procured by means of his friend, a Banker in the City, possibly his partner in the contract. By this I suffered a considerable loss in my property, and he, it is said, made his fortune; however, the Commissioners were satisfied with my conduct, and wrote to Captain Thompson, expressing their approbation of it.

Thus provided, they proceeded on their voyage, and at last worn out by treatment, perhaps not the most mild, and wasted by sickness, brought on by want of medicine, cloathes, bedding, &. &. they reached Sierra Leona, just at the commencement of the rains—At that season of the year, it is impossible to cultivate the lands; their provisions therefore were exhausted before they could derive benefit from agriculture. —And it is not surprising that many, especially the Lascars, whose constitutions are very tender, and who had been cooped up in a ship from October to June, and accommodated in the manner I have mentioned, should be so wasted by their confinement as not long to survive it. —As for the native Africans who remained, there was no object for their industry; and surely, my Lord, they shewed a much less indulgent spirit in going to the West-Indies than staying at Sierra Leona to starve.

The above facts and many more instances of oppression and injustices, not only relative to the expedition to Sierra Leona, but to the Slave Trade in general, I could incontrovertibly establish, if at any time it should be judged necessary to call upon me for that purpose.

I am, my Lord,
Your Lordship's most respectful and
obedient Servant,
GUSTAVUS VASSA, the African.

Tottenham Street No. 13, June 26.

12. FOR *THE MORNING CHRONICLE AND LONDON ADVERTISER*, 15 JULY 1788.

To the Honourable Sir WILLIAM DOLBEN, Bart.[13]
Sir,

We beg your permission to lay in this manner our humble thankfulness before you, for a benevolent law obtained at your motion, by which the miseries of our unhappy brethren, on the coast of Africa, may be alleviated, and by which the lives of many, though destined for the present to a cruel slavery, may be preserved, as we hope, for future and for greater mercies.

Our simple testimony is not much, yet you will not be displeased to learn, that a few persons of colour, existing here, providentially released from the common calamity, and feeling for their kind, are daily pouring forth their prayers for you, Sir, and other noble and generous persons who will not (as we understand) longer suffer the rights of humanity to be confounded with ordinary commodities, and passed from hand to hand, as an article of trade.

We are not ignorant, however, Sir, that the best return we can make is, to behave with sobriety, fidelity, and diligence in our different stations, whether remaining here under the protection of the laws, or colonizing our native soil, as most of us wish to do, under the dominion of this country; or as free labourers and artizans in the West India islands, which, under equal laws, might become to men of colour places of voluntary and very general resort.

But in whatever station, Sir, having lived here, as we hope, without reproach, so we trust that we and our whole race shall endeavour to merit, by dutiful behaviour, those mercies, which, humane and benevolent minds seem to be preparing for us.

THOMAS COOPER.
GUSTAVUS VASSA.
OTTOBAH CUGOANA STEWARD.
GEORGE ROBERT MANDEVIL.

JOHN CHRISTOPHER.
THOMAS JONES.

For ourselves and Brethren

Sir W. DOLBEN is highly gratified with the kind acceptance his endeavours to promote the liberal designs of the Legislature have met from the worthy natives of Africa; whose warm sense of benefits, and honourable resolution of showing their gratitude by their future conduct in steadiness and sobriety, fidelity, and diligence, will undoubtedly recommend them to the British Government, and he trusts, to other Christian powers, as most worthy of their further care and attention; yet as he is but one among many who are equally zealous for the accomplishment of this good work, he must earnestly desire to decline any particular address upon the occasion. Duke-Street, Westminster, 1788.

13. FOR *THE MORNING CHRONICLE AND LONDON ADVERTISER*, 15 JULY 1788.

To the Right Honourable WILLIAM PITT.

Sir,
   We will not presume to trouble you with many words. We are persons of colour, happily released from the common calamity, and desirous of leaving at your door, in behalf of our Brethren, on the Coast of Africa, this simple, but grateful acknowledgment of your goodness and benevolence towards our unhappy race.

THOMAS COOPER.
GUSTAVUS VASSA.
OTTOBAH CUGOANA STEWARD.
GEORGE ROBERT MANDEVIL.
JOHN CHRISTOPHER.
THOMAS JONES.

For ourselves and Brethren.

14. FOR *THE MORNING CHRONICLE AND LONDON ADVERTISER*, 15 JULY 1788.

To the Right Honourable CHARLES JAMES FOX.

Sir,
   We are men of colour, happily, ourselves, emancipated from a general calamity by the laws of this place, but yet feeling very sensibly for our kind,

and hearing, Sir, that, in their favour, you have cooperated with the minister [Pitt], and have nobly considered the rights of humanity as a common
cause, we have thereupon assumed the liberty (we hope, without offence)
of leaving this simple, but honest token of our joy and thankfulness at your
door.

THOMAS COOPER.
GUSTAVUS VASSA.
OTTOBAH CUGOANA STEWARD.
GEORGE ROBERT MANDEVIL.
JOHN CHRISTOPHER.
THOMAS JONES.

For ourselves and Brethren.

15. GUSTAVUS VASSA THE AFRICAN'S PRINTED SOLICITATION, DATED NOVEMBER 1788, FOR SUBSCRIPTIONS TO THE FIRST EDITION OF *THE INTERESTING NARRATIVE* (KEELE UNIVERSITY LIBRARY SPECIAL COLLECTIONS, REFERENCE 74/12632)[14]

London, November, 1788.

TO THE NOBILITY, GENTRY, AND OTHERS.

PROPOSALS

For publishing by Subscription

THE INTERESTING

NARRATIVE

OF THE

LIFE

OF

Mr. *Olaudah Equiano,*

OR

Gustavus Vasa,

THE AFRICAN.

WRITTEN BY HIMSELF:

Who most respectfully solicits the Favour of the Public.

The Narrative contains the following Articles:

The Author's Observations on his Country, and the different Nations in Africa; with an Account of their Manners and Customs, Religion, Marriages, Agriculture, Buildings, &c. —His Birth—The Manner how he and his Sister were kidnapped, and of their accidentally meeting again in Africa—His Astonishment at sight of the Sea, the Vessel, White Men, Men on Horseback, and the various Objects he beheld on his first Arrival in England; particularly a Fall of Snow—An Account of Five Years Transactions in the Wars, under Admiral Boscawen, &c. from 1757 to the Peace in December 1762—Of his being immediately after sent into Slavery, in the West Indies—Of the Treatment, and cruel Scenes of punishing the Negroes—The manner of obtaining his Freedom—The verification of Five remarkable Dreams, or Visions; particularly in being shipwrecked in 1767, and picking up Eleven miserable Men at Sea in 1774, &c.—The wonderful Manner of his Conversion to the Faith of CHRIST JESUS, and his Attempt to convert an Indian Prince—Various Actions at Sea and Land, from 1777 to the present Time, &c. &c.

CONDITIONS.

I.   This Work shall be neatly printed on a good Paper, in a Duodecimo, or Pocket Size, and comprized in two handsome Volumes.

II.   Price to Subscribers Seven Shillings bound, or Six Shillings unbound; one half to be paid at subscribing, and the other on the delivery of the Books, which will be very early in Spring.

III. A few Copies will be printed on Fine Paper, at a moderate advance of Price. It is therefore requested, that those Ladies and Gentlemen who may choose to have paper of that quality, will please to signify the same at subscribing.

IV.   In Volume I, will be given an elegant Frontispiece of the Author's Portrait.

SUBSCRIPTIONS *are taken in by the following Booksellers:*

Mr. [John] Murray, Fleet-Street; Mess. [James] Robson and [William] Clark[e], Bond-Street; Mr. [Lockyer] Davis, opposite Gray's Inn, Holborn; Messrs. [John] Shepperson and [Thomas] Reynolds, Oxford-Street; Mr. [James] Lackington, Chiswell-Street; Mr. [David] Mathews, Strand; Mr. [David or John] Murray, Prince's Street, Soho; Mr. Taylor and Co. South Arch, Royal Exchange; Mr. Thomson, Little Pultney-Street, Golden Square; Mr. [William] Harrison, No. 154, Borough; Mr. Hallowell, Cockhill, Ratcliff; Mr. [William?] Button, Newington Causeway; Mr. Burton, over the Brook, Chatham; and by the Booksellers in Dover, Sandwich, Exeter, Portsmouth, and Plymouth.

16. HOLOGRAPH LETTER FROM GUSTAVUS VASSA TO JOSIAH WEDGWOOD WRITTEN ON THE PRINTED SOLICITATION FOR SUBSCRIPTIONS TO *The Interesting Narrative*, DATED NOVEMBER 1788 (KEELE UNIVERSITY LIBRARY SPECIAL COLLECTIONS, REFERENCE 74/12632)

Worthy Sir &c. this my Dutiful Respect to you I Pray you to Pardon this freedom I have taken in beging [*sic*] your favour, or the apperence [*sic*] of your Name amongst others of my Worthy friends.—& you will much oblige your Huml. Servt. to Command. Gustavus Vassa
The African

17. FOR *THE PUBLIC ADVERTISER*, 14 FEBRUARY 1789

To the Committee for the Abolition of the Slave Trade at Plymouth.

Gentlemen,

Having seen a plate representing the form in which Negroes are stowed on board the Guinea ships, which you are pleased to send to the Rev. Mr. [Thomas] Clarkson, a worthy friend of mine,[15] I was filled with love and gratitude towards you for your humane interference on behalf of my oppressed countrymen. Surely this case calls aloud for redress! May this year bear record of acts worthy of a British Senate, and you have the satisfaction of seeing the completion of the work you have so humanely assisted us in. With you I think it the indispensable duty of every friend of humanity, not to suffer themselves to be led away with the specious but false pretext drawn from the supposed political benefits this kingdom derives from the continuance of this iniquitous branch of commerce. It is the duty of every man,

every friend to religion and humanity, to assist the different Committees
engaged in this pious work; reflecting that it does not often fall to the lot
of individuals to contribute to so important a moral and religious duty as
that of putting an end to a practise which may, without exaggeration, be
stiled one of the greatest evils now existing on earth. —The wise man saith,
"Righteousness exalteth a nation, but sin is a reproach to any people." Prov.
xiv. 34.

Permit me, Gentlemen, on behalf of myself and my brethren, to offer
you the warmest effusions of hearts over flowing with gratitude for your
pious eforts, which it is my constant prayer may prove successful.

With the best wishes for health and happiness,

I am, Gentlemen,

Your obedient, humble Servant,

GUSTAVUS VASSA, the African.

Feb. 7, 1789, No. 10, Union Street,
Middlesex Hospital.

18. FOR *THE DIARY; OR WOODFALL'S REGISTER*, 25 APRIL 1789.

To Mr. WILLIAM DICKSON, formerly Private Secretary to the Hon. Edward Hay, Governor of the Island of Barbadoes.[16]

Sir,

We who have perused your well authenticated Book, entitled LETTERS
ON SLAVERY, think it a duty incumbent on us to confess, that in our
opinion such a work cannot be too much esteemed; you have given but
too just a picture of the Slave Trade, and the horrid cruelties practised on
the poor sable people in the West Indies, to the disgrace of Christianity.
Their injury calls aloud for redress, and the day we hope is not far distant,
which may record one of the most glorious acts that ever passed the British
Senate—we mean an Act for the total Abolition of the Slave Trade.

It is the duty of every man who is a friend to religion and humanity
(and such you have shewn yourself to be) to shew his detestation of such
inhuman traffick. Thank to God, the nation at last is awakened to a sense
of our sufferings, except the Oran Otang philosophers, who we think will
find it a hard task to dissect your letters. Those who can feel for the distresses of their own countrymen, will also commiserate the case of the poor
Africans.

Permit us, Sir, on behalf of ourselves and the rest of our brethren, to
offer you our sincere thanks for the testimony of regard you have shewn
for the poor and much oppressed sable people.

With our best wishes that your praise-worthy publication may meet with the wished-for success, and may the all-bountiful Creator bless you with health and happiness, and bestow on you every blessing of time and eternity.

We are,
Sir,
Your most obedient humble servants,
OLAUDAH EQUIANO, or GUSTAVUS VASA.
OTTOBAH CUGOANO, or JOHN S[T]UAR[T].
YAHNE AELANE, or JOSEPH SANDERS.
BROUGHWAR JOGENSMEL, or JASPER GOREE.
COJOH AMMERE, or GEORGE WILLIAMS.
THOMAS COOPER.
WILLIAM GREEK.
GEORGE MANDEVILLE.
BERNARD ELLIOT GRIFFITHS.

19. ADVERTISEMENT IN THE *MORNING STAR*, 29 APRIL, 1 MAY 1789.[17]

This Day is published,

The Interesting Narrative of the Life of
OLAUDAH EQUIANO;
OR,
GUSTAVUS VASSA, THE AFRICAN,
Written by himself.

THIS Work is neatly printed on a good paper, in a duodecimo, or pocket size, and comprised in two handsome volumes. Price 7s. unbound.

In Vol. I. is given an elegant Frontispiece of the Author's Portrait. Vol. II. a Plate shewing the manner the Author was shipwrecked in 1767.

The Narrative contains the following Articles:

The Author's observations on his country, and the different nations in Africa; with an account of their manners and customs, religion, marriages, agriculture, buildings, &c. his birth, the manner how he and his sister were kidnapped, and of their accidentally meeting again in Africa. His astonishment at the sight of the sea, the vessel, white men, men on horseback, and the various objects he beheld on his first arrival in England; particularly a fall of snow. An account of five years transactions in the wars, under Admiral Boscawen, &c. from 1757 to the peace in December, 1762. Of his being immediately after sent into slavery in the West Indies. Of the treatment, and the cruel scenes of punishing the negroes; the manner of obtaining his freedom; the verification of five remarkable dreams or visions; particularly in being shipwrecked in 1767, and picking up eleven miserable men at sea, in 1775, &c. The wonderful manner of his conversion to the Faith of Christ Jesus, and his attempt to convert an Indian Prince. Various actions at sea and land, from 1777, to the present time.

The books are sold by the Author, No. 10, Union-street, Middlesex Hospital; and by the following Booksellers: Mr. [Joseph] Johnson, St. Paul's Church Yard; Mr. [John] Murray, Fleet-Street; Mess. [James] Robson and [William] Clark[e], Bond-Street; Mr. [Lockyer] Davis, opposite Gray's Inn, Holborn; Messrs. [John] Shepperson and [Thomas] Reynolds, Oxford-Street; Mr. [James] Lackington, Chiswell-Street; Mr. [David] Mathews, Strand; Mr. [David or John] Murray, Prince's Street, Soho; Mr. Taylor and Co. South Arch, Royal Exchange; Mr. Hallowell, Cockhill, Ratcliff; Mr. [William?] Button, Newington Causeway; Mr. Burton, over the Brook, Chatham; Mr. S[hirley]. Woolmir [Woolmer], Exeter; Mr. [John] Parsons, Paternoster-row; and Mr. H[enry]. Trapp, No. 1, Paternoster-row.

20. FROM *ARIS'S BIRMINGHAM GAZETTE*, MONDAY, 14 JUNE 1790.

December 24, 1789.

This Day is published,
The Second, and corrected Edition of
The interesting NARRATIVE of the LIFE of OLAUDAH EQUIANO, or GUSTAVUS VASSA, the African. Written by himself.

From the Reception this Work has met with, from above Seven Hundred Persons of all Denominations—the Author humbly Thanks his numerous Friends for past Favours; and as a new Edition is now out, he most respectfully solicits the Favour and Encouragement of the candid and unprejudiced Friends of the Africans.

This Work is neatly printed on a good Paper, in a Duodecimo, or Pocket Size, and comprised in two handsome Volumes. Price 6s. unbound—and 4s. 6d. if six Copies are taken.

In Volume I. is given an elegant Frontispiece of the Author's Portrait. Volume II a Plate shewing the Manner the Author was shipwrecked in 1767.

The Narrative contains the following Articles—The Author's Observations on his Country, and the different Nations in Africa; with an Account of their Manners and Customs, Religion, Marriages, Agriculture, Buildings, &c.—His Birth—The Manner how he & his Sister were kidnapped, and of their accidentally meeting again in Africa—His Astonishment at the Sight of the Sea, the Vessel, White Men, Men on Horseback, and the various

Objects he beheld on his first Arrival in England, particularly a Fall of Snow—An Account of five Years Transactions in the Wars, under Admiral Boscawen, &c. from 1757 to the Peace in December, 1762—Of his being immediately after sent into Slavery in the West Indies—Of the Treatment, and the cruel Scenes of punishing the Negroes—The Manner of obtaining his Freedom.—The Verification of five remarkable Dreams or Visions; particularly in being shipwrecked in 1767, and picking up eleven miserable Men at Sea in 1775, &c.—The wonderful Manner of his Conversion to the Faith of Christ Jesus, and his Attempt to convert an Indian Prince—Various Actions at Sea and Land, from 1777 to the present Time.

Sold by the Author, at Mr. [William] Bliss's, Grocer, Aston-street; T[homas]. Pearson, and M[yles]. Swinney, Printers, in High-street; and Mr. [Edward] Piercy, Bull-street, Birmingham; likewise by Mr. [J.W.] Piercy, Printer, in Coventry.[18]

21. FROM *ARIS'S BIRMINGHAM GAZETTE*, MONDAY, 28 JUNE 1790.

To the Printer of the Birmingham Gazette.

SIR,   June 19, 1790.

HAVING received great Marks of Kindness from the under-mentioned Gentlemen of this Town, who have subscribed to my Narrative: particularly from Mess. Charles and Sampson Lloyd, and Families, and Dr. [William] Gilby.

Dr. [Edward] Johnstone
John Taylor, Esq.
Sam[uel] Garbet, Esq.
Sam[uel] Galton, Esq.
W[illia]m Russell, Esq.
Rev. Dr. [Joseph] Priestley
Rev. Mr. [J.] Riland
Rev. Mr. Pearce
Rev. Mr. Bass
William Smith
Samuel Ford
Peter Capper
Joseph Randell
Joseph Gibbons
Thomas Robinson
Thomas Laurence
John Ward
Thomas Price

Mess. John Hammonds
James Osborn
William Sprigg
John Freer, jun.
S. Ryland
John Harwood
Thomas King
Wm. Humphreys
G. Humphreys
Thomas Colemore
Samuel Colemore
Richard Gibbs
James Bedford
William Medley
William Hicks
John Cope
John Robbins
Mess. Cockle

James Bingham

John Jukes

Matt[hew] Boulton, Esq.

Edward Palmer, Esq.

Mess. Henry Perkins

George Simcox

Thomas Green

Thomas Parkes

Sam[uel] Pemberton

John Lee

John Dickenson

Thomas Ketland

Joseph Rabone

Edward Webb

Samuel Baker

William Hunt

Mrs. Wiggin

William Cope

John Biddle

Thomas Francis

William Reynolds

Joseph Cotterell

James Gottington

Benjamin Freeth

John Lowe, jun.

I beg you to suffer me, thus publicly to express my grateful Acknowledgments to them for their Favours, and for the Fellow-feeling they have discovered for my very poor and much oppressed Countrymen; these Acts of Kindness and Hospitality, have filled me with a longing Desire to see these worthy Friends on my own Estate in Africa, when the richest Produce of it should be devoted to their Entertainment; they should there partake of the luxuriant Pine-apples, and the well flavoured virgin Palm-wine; and to heighten the Bliss I would burn a certain Kind of Tree, that would afford us a Light as clear and brilliant as the Virtues of my Guests.

I am Sir, your humble Servant,
GUSTAVUS VASA, the African.

The Narratives are Sold by the Author, at Mr. Bliss', Grocer, Aston-street, and by T. Pearson, and T. Wood, Booksellers, in High-street, Birmingham, at 6s. a Copy, and 4s. 6d. to those who take six Copies.

22. FROM THE MANCHESTER MERCURY, & HARROP'S GENERAL ADVERTISER, TUESDAY, 20 JULY 1790

This Day is Published
The second and corrected EDITION of the interesting
Narrative of the
LIFE of OLAUDAH EQUIANO;
Or GUSTAVUS VASSA, the AFRICAN.
Written by himself.
From the reception this work has met with, from above seven hundred persons of all denominations, the Author humbly thanks his numerous friends,

for past favours; and as a New Edition is now out, he most respectfully solicits the favour and encouragement of the candid and unprejudiced friends
of the Africans.

This work is neatly printed on a good paper, in a duodecimo, or pocket
size, and comprised in two handsome volumes. Price 6s. unbound—and 4s.
6d. to those who take six copies.

In volume I. is given an elegant frontispiece of the Author's Portrait.
Volume II a plate shewing the manner the Author was shipwrecked in 1767.
The narrative contains the following articles

The Author's observation on his country, and the different nations in
Africa; with an account of their manners and customs, religion, marriages,
agriculture, buildings, &c. —His birth—The manner how he & his Sister
were kidnapped, and of their accidentally meeting again in Africa—His astonishment at the sight of the sea, the vessel, white men, men on horseback, and the various objects he beheld on his first arrival in England;
particularly a fall of snow—An account of five years transactions in the wars,
under Admiral Boscawen, &c. from 1757, to the peace in December, 1762—
Of his being immediately after sent into slavery in the West-Indies—Of the
treatment, and the cruel scenes of punishing the Negroes—The manner of
obtaining his freedom.—The verification of five remarkable dreams or visions; particularly in being shipwrecked in 1767, and picking up eleven miserable men at sea, in 1775, &c.—The wonderful manner of his conversion
to the faith of Christ Jesus, and his attempt to convert an Indian Prince.—
Various actions at sea and land, from 1777 to the present time.

The above narrative is to be had of Mr. Harrop, printer, & J. Thompson, bookseller, Market-street-lane, Manchester; and of the Author, at Mrs.
Lord's, No. 12, Spring gardens.[19]

23. FROM THE SHEFFIELD REGISTER, YORKSHIRE, DERBYSHIRE, & NOTTINGHAMSHIRE UNIVERSAL ADVERTISER, FRIDAY, 20 AUGUST 1790.

This Day was published
A SECOND AND CORRECTED EDITION,
Of the interesting Narrative of
THE LIFE OF OLAUDAH EQUIANO,
OR
GUSTAVUS VASSA, THE AFRICAN,
Written by himself.
The Author humbly thanks his numerous friends for the reception this Work
has met with from above Seven Hundred Persons of all denominations; and
as a New Edition is now out, he most respectfully solicits the Favour and
Encouragement of the candid and unprejudiced Friends of the AFRICANS.

This Work is neatly printed on a good Paper, in a Duodecimo, or Pocket Size, and comprised in two handsome Volumes. Price 6s. unbound.

In Vol. I. is given an elegant Portrait of the Author; in Vol. II a Plate shewing the Manner in which the Author was shipwrecked in 1767.

The Narrative contains the following Articles. The Author's Observations on his Country, and the different Nations in Africa; with an Account of their Manners and Customs, Religion, Marriages, Agriculture, Buildings, &c.—His Birth—The Manner how he & his Sister were kidnapped, and of their accidental Meeting again in Africa—His Astonishment at the Sight of the Sea, the Vessel, white Men, Men on Horseback, and the various Objects he beheld on his first Arrival in England; particularly a Fall of Snow— An Account of five Years Transactions in the Wars, under Admiral Boscawen, from 1757 to the Peace in December, 1762—Of his being immediately after sent into Slavery in the West Indies—Of the Treatment, and the cruel Scenes of punishing the Negroes—The Manner of obtaining his Freedom.— The Verification of five remarkable Dreams or Visions; particularly in being shipwrecked in 1767, and picking up eleven miserable Men at Sea in 1775, &c.—The wonderful Manner of his Conversion to the Faith of Christ Jesus, and his Attempt to convert an Indian Prince.—Various Actions at Sea and Land, from 1777, to the present Time.

Sold by the Printer [Joseph Gales] hereof, and by the Author, at the Rev. Mr. [Thomas] Bryant's, in Sheffield—who makes Allowance to Booksellers.[20]

24. SUSANNAH ATKINSON [WIFE OF LAW ATKINSON] OF MOULD GREEN [NEAR HUDDERSFIELD] TO GUSTAVUS VASSA, 29 MARCH 1791 [CAMBRIDGESHIRE RECORD OFFICE].

Mould Green March 29th 1791

Since my much valued Friend did not receive the few lines directed to Halifax—and since my Husband has come Home and informed me you wish'd to have a few lines from me—I could not think of going to Manchester without leaving you a few lines—hoping you are *here* to receive it— for tho' your Friend Susannah Atkinson will not be here to see you—yet she leaves her *Law* who will always meet *you*, my Friend[,] with pleasure— nor will *he* be the only one who will see you here with pleasure—Miss Frith who is so kind as to become my housekeeper—will be also glad to see you—I am sorry to hear you are low—suffer yourself not to be hurt with triffles [*sic*] since you must in this transitory and deceitful World [you must CROSSED OUT] meet with many unpleasing changes—I was sorry we should be so unfortunate as to recommend you to any who should in the least slight you—which seem'd to be the case at Elland—but I sincerely hope you have since experienced that friendship and civility from those you have been with—which has amply made up for the treatment you there received—but you have a friend above who can afford you more *real* comfort than Mortals here can give—not but friends are a Blessing—and afford that comfort—which I hope you will *never* want—but it is I believe absolutely necessary that we should meet with rebuffs—otherwise our Affections would be wholly placed *here*—which would in the end prove our destruction—but I ought to check my pen, as you have seen more of the World than me—and must of course know how to place a proper dependence on both God and Man—may he ever direct and watch over you—fear not—those who depend on *him* he will defend—and also in *the end befriend*—should I ever be so happy to see you again—(and I hope and trust I shall) I hope I need not say how happy I shall always be to see you—this I flatter myself you are assured of—I thank you for your picture—believe me we shall value it much—we will have it Framed—and hung with our own Family who are doing now—I hope you *may* see it—it wont be done the next time you come—but hope you will see it the time *after* next—till then may God preserve and Guide you—and believe me to be *ever* sincerely your well wisher—and Friend—Susannah Atkinson N.B. Miss Haigh and Cousin Tinkler [?] leave their Respects.[21]

25. FROM *THE LEEDS MERCURY*, 19 APRIL 1791, FOLLOWING NOTICE OF A SUBSCRIPTION DRIVE TO SUPPORT THE LONDON ABOLITION SOCIETY

To the PRINTER of the LEEDS MERCURY.

Leeds, April 16th.

Having received particular marks of kindness from Mr. Law Atkinson and Family, of Huddersfield, and many Gentlemen and Ladies, &c., of and near this town, who have purchased my genuine and interesting Narrative; I beg to offer them my warmest thanks; and also to the friends of humanity here, on behalf of my much oppressed countrymen, whose case calls aloud for redress—May this year bear record of acts worthy of a British Senate, and you have a satisfaction of seeing the completion of the work you have so humanely assisted in:—'Tis now the duty of everyone, who is a friend to religion and humanity, to assist the different Committees engaged in this pious work. Those who can feel for the distresses of their own countrymen, will also comiserate the case of the poor Africans. Since that it does not often fall to the lot of individuals to contribute to so important a moral and religious duty, as that of putting an end to a practice, which may, without exaggeration, be stiled one of the greatest evils now existing on the earth, it may be hoped, that each one will now use his utmost endeavours for that purpose. The Wise Man saith—"Righteousness exalteth a nation, but sin is a reproach to any people."

Permit me, dear friends, on behalf of myself and countrymen, to offer you the warmest effusions of a heart replete with gratitude.

I am, with constant prayers for your health and happiness,
Worthy friends,
Your respectful humble Servant,
GUSTAVUS VASSA,
The African.

26. FROM *THE YORK CHRONICLE*, FRIDAY, 22 APRIL 1791 [YORK REFERENCE LIBRARY]

This day is published,
In one handsome volume, twelves, on good paper,
Price Four Shillings sewed.
The THIRD EDITION, CORRECTED and ENLARGED,
of the Interesting
NARRATIVE of the LIFE of
OLAUDAH EQUIANO,
or
GUSTAVUS VASSA,
THE AFRICAN.
WRITTEN by HIMSELF.—With an elegant PRINT of the AUTHOR; and a plate shewing the manner in which he was ship-wrecked.

The kind reception which this Work has met with from many hundred persons of all denominations, demands the Author's most sincere thanks to his numerous friends; and he most respectfully solicits the favour and encouragement of the candid and unprejudiced friends of the Africans.

The General Magazine and Impartial Review, for July 1789, characterizes this Work in the following terms:—"This is 'a round unvarnish'd Tale' of the chequered adventures of an African, who early in life was torn from his native country by those savage dealers in a trade disgraceful to humanity, and which has fixed a stain on the legislature of Britain. The narrative appears to be written with much truth and simplicity.—The Author's account of the manners of the natives of his own province (Eboe) is interesting and pleasing."

The Book may be had of the Author at Mr. [William] Tuke's in Castlegate, and of Mr. [Robert] Spence in Ousegate, York.[22]

27. FROM *THE FREEMAN'S JOURNAL* (DUBLIN), 31 MAY–2 JUNE 1791.

This day is published,
In one handsome volume, Twelves, on good Paper,
Price Four Shillings, sewed:
The FOURTH EDITION, corrected and enlarged, of the
Interesting Narrative of the Life of
OLAUDAH EQUIANO,
Or GUSTAVUS VASSA—the AFRICAN.
Written by himself—With an elegant Print of the
AUTHOR; and a Plate shewing the manner in which he was shipwrecked.

The kind reception which this Work has met with in England, from many hundred persons of all denominations, demands the Author's most sincere thanks to his numerous Friends; and he most respectfully solicits the favour and encouragement of the candid and unprejudiced friends of the Africans.

The General Magazine and Impartial Review, for July 1789, characterizes this Work in the following terms:—"This is 'a round unvarnished tale' of the chequered adventures of an African who early in his life was torn from his native country by those savage dealers in a traffic disgraceful to humanity and which has fixed a stain on the Legislature of Britain. The narrative appears to be written with much truth and simplicity.—The Author's account of the manners of the natives of his own province (the Eboes) is interesting and pleasing."

The book will be had of the Author at 151 Capel-street; Mr. William Sleater [11] 28 Dame-street; and by Mr. P[atrick]. Byrne.[23]

28. FROM *THE BELFAST NEWS-LETTER*, 20 DECEMBER 1791.

This Day is published, (in one handsome Volume, Twelves, on good Paper, Price 4s. sewed) the 4th Edition, corrected and enlarged, of the interesting Narrative of the Life of OLAUDAH EQUIANO: or, GUSTAVUS VASSA, the AFRICAN; Written by himself.—With an elegant Print of the Author; and a Plate shewing the Manner in which he was shipwrecked.—The Narrative contains

The Author's Observations on his Country, and the different Nations in Africa; with an Account of their Manners and Customs, Religion, Marriages, Agriculture, Buildings—The Manner how he and his Sister were kidnapped, and of their accidentally meeting again in Africa—His Astonishment at the Sight of the Sea, the Vessel, white Men, and the various Objects he beheld on his first Arrival in England, particularly a Fall of Snow—An Account of five Years Transactions in the Wars.

The General Magazine and Impartial Review, for June 1789, characterizes this Work in the following Terms:—"This is 'a Round unvarnish'd Tale' of the chequered Adventures of an African, who, early in Life, was torn from his native Country by those savage Dealers in a Traffic disgraceful to Humanity, and which has fixed a Stain on the Legislature of Britain.—The Narrative appears to be written with much Truth and Simplicity.—The Author's Account of the manners of the Natives of his own Province (Eboe) is interesting and pleasing."

To be had of the Author, at Mr. Mullan's on the Quay; at Mr. Samuel Neilson's, Waring-street; and the Booksellers in Town.[24]

29. HOLOGRAPH LETTER TO THE REV. G. WALKER AND FAMILY IN NOTTINGHAM.[25]

London Feby the 27.th—1792
Dr. Revd. & Worthy friends &c.

This with my Best of Respects to you & wife with many Prayers that you both may ever be Well in Souls & Bodys—& also your Little Lovely Daughter—I thank you for all kindnesses which you was please[d] to show me, may God ever Reward you for it—Sir, I went to Ireland & was there 8 1/2 months—& sold 1900 copies of my narrative. I came here on the 10th inst.—& I now mean as it seem Pleasing to my Good God!—to leave London in about 8—or, 10 Days more, & take me a Wife—(one Miss Cullen—) of Soham in Cambridge shire—& when I have given her about 8 or 10 Days Comfort, I mean Directly to go Scotland—and sell my 5th. Editions—I Trust that my going about has been of much use to the Cause of the abolition of the accu[r]sed Slave Trade—a Gentleman of the Committee the Revd. Dr. Baker has said that I am more use to the Cause than half the People in the Country—I wish to God, I could be so. A noble Earl of Stanhope has Lately Consulted me twice about a Bill which his Ld.ship now mean[s] to bring in to the House to allow the sable People in the wt Indias the Rights of taking an oath against any White Person—I hope it may Pass, tis high time—& will be of much use. —may the Lord Bless all the friends of Humanity. Pray Pardon what ever you here see amiss—I will be Glad to see you at my Wedg. —Pray give my best Love To the Worthy & Revd. Mr. Robinson, & his—also to my friends Coltman—and Mr. & Mrs. Buxton—I Pray that the Good Lord may make all of that family Rich in faith as in the things of this World—I have [a] Great Deal to say if I ever have the Pleasure to see you again—I have been in the uttermust hurry ever since I have being in this wickd. Town. —& I only came now to save if I can, £232, I Lent to a man, who [is] now Dying.

Pray Excuse ha[ste]—will be Glad to hear from you—& do very much beg
your Prayers as you ever have mine—& if I see you no more here Below
may I see you all at Last at Gods Right Hand—where parting will be no
more—Glory to God that J. Christ is yet all, & in all, to my Poor Soul—
    I am with all Due Respects
    yours to Command—
    Gustavus Vassa
    The African
—at Mr. Hardys No. 4 Taylors Building
    Chandos street, Covent Garden

[Reverse side]
London twenty seventh February 1792
The Revd. G. Walker
P.S. you see how I am confused—Pray excuse this mistake of the frank—
for Mr. Houseman
Pray mind the Africans from the Pulpits

30. From *The Glasgow Advertiser and Evening Intelligencer*, from Friday, 27 April to Monday, 30 April 1792

This day is published.
(In one handsome Volume Twelves, on good paper,
price 4s. sewed)
The FOURTH Edition of the interesting NARRATIVE
of the LIFE of
OLAUDAH EQUIANO;
Or,
GUSTAVUS VASSA, THE AFRICAN:
Written by himself.
With an elegant Print of the Author, and a Plate shewing
the Manner in which he was ship-wrecked.

The Narrative contains the following Articles:
    The Author's observations on his country, and the different nations in
Africa; with an account of their Manners and Customs, Religion, Marriages,
Agriculture, Buildings—The manner how he and his Sister were kidnapped,
and of their accidentally meeting again in Africa—His astonishment at the
sight of the Sea, the Vessels, White Men, and the various objects he beheld
on his first arrival in England, particularly a Fall of Snow—An account of
five years Transactions in the Wars.

The General Magazine and Impartial Review, for July 1787 [*sic*], characterizes this work in the following terms:—"This is 'a round unvarnished tale' of the chequered adventures of an African, who, early in life, was torn from his native country by those savage dealers in a traffic disgraceful to humanity, and which has fixed a stain on the Legislature of Britain. The narrative appears to be written with much truth and simplicity. The author's account of the manners of the natives of his own province (Eboe) is interesting and pleasing."

To be had of the Author, at the King's Arms Inn, Trongate, and of the Booksellers in this city.[26]

31. FROM *THE CALEDONIAN MERCURY* [EDINBURGH], SATURDAY, 21 MAY 1792.

This day is published,
In one handsome volume 12mo, on good paper,
Price 4s. sewed
The Fourth Edition of the Interesting Narrative of the Life of
OLAUDAH EQUIANO;
Or GUSTAVUS VASSA, THE AFRICAN:
Written by Himself.
With an elegant Print of the Author, and a Plate shewing
the Manner in which he was ship-wrecked.
The Narrative contains the following Articles:

The Author's Observations on his Country, and the different Nations in Africa; with an Account of their Manners and Customs, Religion, Marriages, Agriculture, Buildings; the manner how he and his sister were kidnapped, and of their accidentally meeting again in Africa. His astonishment at the sight of the sea, the vessels, white men, and the various objects he beheld on his first arrival in England, particularly a fall of snow. An account of five years transactions in the Wars.

The General Magazine and Impartial Review, for July 1787 [*sic*], characterizes this work in the following Terms:—"This is a round unvarnish'd Tale of the Chequered Adventures of an African, who early in Life, was torn from his native country, by those savage dealers in a traffic disgraceful to humanity, and which has fixed a stain on the Legislature of Britain. The Narrative appears to be written with much truth and simplicity. The Author's Account of the manners of the natives of his own province (Eboe) is interesting and pleasing."

To be had of the Author, at Mr. Wilson's Hair-dresser, Anchor Close, and the Booksellers in town.

32. For *The Edinburgh Evening Courant,* Saturday, 26 May 1792.

To the GENERAL ASSEMBLY of the CHURCH OF SCOTLAND now convened.

———

GENTLEMEN,

PERMIT me, one of the oppressed natives of Africa, to offer you the warmest thanks of a heart glowing with gratitude on the unanimous decision of your debate of this day—It filled me with love towards you. It is no doubt the indispensable duty of every man, who is a friend to religion and humanity, to give his testimony against that iniquitous branch of commerce the slave trade. It does not often fall to the lot of individuals to contribute to so important a moral and religious duty, as that of putting an end to a practice which may, without exaggeration, be stiled one of the greatest evils now existing on the earth. —The Wise Man saith, "Righteousness exalteth a nation, but sin is a reproach to any people." Prov. xiv. 34.

Gentlemen, permit me, on behalf of myself and my much oppressed countrymen, to offer you the warmest effusions of a heart overflowing with hope from your pious efforts. It is my constant prayer that these endeavours may prove successful—And with best wishes for your health, happiness temporal and spiritual, I am, Gentlemen,

Your most respectful humble servant, &c. &c.

GUSTAVUS VASSA the African.

At Mr. M'Laren's, turner, second stair above Chalmers's Close, High Street—where my Narrative is to be had.

Edinburgh, May 24, 1792.[27]

33. Holograph letter to Thomas Hardy in PRO TS 24/12/2.[28]

Edinburg May 28th.—1792

Dr. Sir, &c. &c.

With Respect I take this oppertunity to acquaint you (by Mr. Ford—an acquaintance of mine who is to go to Day for London) that I am in health—hope that you & Wife is well—have sold books at Glasgow & Paisley, & came here on the 10th. ult. I hope next month to go to Dunde, Perth, & Aberdeen. —Sir, I am sorry to tell you that some Rascal or Rascals have asserted in the news parpers viz. Oracle of the 25th. of april, & the Star. 27th.—that I am a native of a Danish Island, Santa Cruz, in the Wt. Indias. The assertion has hurted the sale of my Books—I have now the aforesaid Oracle & will be much obliged to you to get me the Star, & take care of it till you see or hear from

me—Pray ask Mr. & Mrs. Peters who Lodged in the next Room to me, if they
have found a Little Round Gold Breast Buckel, or broach, sett in, or with fine
stones—if they have, I will pay them well for it. —& if they have found it pray
write to me on that account Directly. & if tis not found you need not write
on that account* (& the Direction is to me, to be left at the Post Office here.)
My best Respect to my fellow members of your society.[29] I hope they do yet
increase. I do not hear in this place that there is any such societys—I think Mr.
Alexr. Mathews in Glasgow told me that there was (or is) some there—Sir. on
Thursday the 24th. Inst. —I was in the General assembly of the Church of
Scotland, now Convened, & they agreed unanimously on a petition, or an ad-
dress to the House of Lords to abolish the Slave Trade—& on which account
I gave them an address of thanks in two news papers which is well Recd.[30] I
find the Scotchmen is not Like the Irish—or English—nor yet in their
Houses—which is to High—Especially here. But thanks to God the Gospel is
Plantifully preached here—& the Churches, or Karks[31] is well filled—I hope
the good Lord will enable me to hear & to profit, & to hold out to the end—
& keep me from all such Rascals as I have met with in London—Mr. Lewis
wrote me a Letter within 12 Days after I Left you & acquaintd. me of that vil-
lain who owed me above 200£—Dying on the 17th. of April—& that is all
the Comfort I got from him since—& now I am again obliged to slave on
more than before if possible—as I have a Wife.

   May God ever keep you & me from atachment to this evil World, & the
things of it—I think I shall be happy when time is no more with me, as I am
Resolved ever to Look to Jesus Christ—& submit to his Preordainations.

   Dr. Sir,—I am with Christian Love to you & Wife—&c.

Gustavus Vassa
The African

P.S.—pray get me the Gentlemens. Magazine for April 1792 & take Care of
it for me.[32]

   *it was wreped up in a bit of paper.

34. FROM THE *ABERDEEN JOURNAL*, MONDAY, 20 AUGUST 1792.

This Day is published,
(In one handsome Volume Twelves, on good Paper,
price 4s. sewed)
The FIFTH Edition of the interesting NARRATIVE
of the LIFE of
OLAUDAH EQUIANO;

OR,
GUSTAVUS VASSA, THE AFRICAN:
Written by himself.
With an elegant Print of the Author, and a plate shewing
the manner in which he was shipwrecked.
The narrative contains the following articles:

The Author's observations on his country, and the different nations in
Africa; with an account of their Manners and Customs, Religion, Marriages,
Agriculture, Buildings—The manner how he and his Sister were kidnapped,
and of their accidentally meeting again in Africa—His astonishment at the
sight of the Sea, the vessels, White Men, and the various objects he beheld
on his first arrival in England, particularly a Fall of Snow—An account of
five years Transactions in the Wars.

————————

The General Magazine and Impartial Review, for July 1789, characterizes this
work in the following terms:—"This is 'a round unvarnish'd tale' of the chequered adventures of an African, who, early in life, was torn from his native
country by those savage dealers in traffic disgraceful to humanity, and which
has fixed a stain on the Legislature of Britain. The narrative appears to be
written with much truth and simplicity. The author's account of the manners of the natives of his own province (Eboe) is interesting and pleasing."

To be had, on Thursday next, of the Author, at Mr. Spalding's, Marishal
Street; of Messrs Angus and Son, Mr. Brown, and the other booksellers.

35. FROM *THE NEWCASTLE CHRONICLE, OR,*
WEEKLY ADVERTISER, AND REGISTER OF NEWS,
COMMERCE, AND ENTERTAINMENT (NEWCASTLE)
15 SEPTEMBER 1792.

This Day is published,
(In one handsome Volume Twelves, on good Paper, Price
4s. Sewed)
THE FIFTH EDITION of the interesting
NARRATIVE of the LIFE of
OLAUDAH EQUIANO;
or,
GUSTAVUS VASSA, THE AFRICAN:
WRITTEN BY HIMSELF.
With an elegant PRINT of the AUTHOR.
And a PLATE shewing the Manner in which he was ship-wrecked.
The Narrative contains the following Articles:

The Author's Observations on his Country, and the different Nations in Africa; with an Account of their Manners and Customs, Religion, Marriages, Agriculture, Buildings—The Manner how he and his Sister were kidnapped, and of their accidentally meeting again in Africa—His Astonishment at the Sight of the Sea, the Vessels, white Men, and the various Objects he beheld on his first Arrival in England, particularly a Fall of Snow—An Account of five Years Transactions in the Wars.

The General Magazine and Impartial Review, for June 1789, characterizes this Work in the following Terms:—"This is 'a round unvarnish'd Tale' of the chequered Adventures of an African, who, early in Life, was torn from his native Country by those savage Dealers in a Traffic disgraceful to Humanity, and which has fixed a Stain on the Legislature of Britain.—The Narrative appears to be written with much Truth and Simplicity. The Author's Account of the Manners of the Natives of his own Province (Eboe) is interesting and pleasing."

To be had of the Author, Gustavus Vassa, at Mr. Robert Denton's, opposite the Turk's Head, Bigg-Market, Newcastle, and of the Booksellers in this Town.

36. Gustavus Vassa to Josiah Wedgwood
[Quotation by Courtesy of the Trustees of the Wedgwood Museum, Barlaston, Staffordshire, England]

London, August 21st. 1793

Dr. & Worthy Sir, &c.

I am with great respects—hope you are Well.

Dr. Sir I hope you do remember that you did once tell me, if that I was to be molested by the press gang to Write to Mr. Phillip Steven—at the Admiralty—I will now take it a great favour to inform me, if I may act so in Case I am molested—I mean next Week to be in Bristol where I have some of my narrative engaged—& I am very apt to think I must have enemys there—on the account of my Publick spirit to put an end to Slavery—or reather [sic] in being active to have the Slave Trade Abolished. Dr. Sir, I leave London on friday the 23d. inst. therefore will take it a particular favour if you will be kind enough as to Direct to me few Lines at the post office—till Calld. for—Bristol.

Worthy sir, &c. &c.

I am with all Due respt.

ever yrs. To Command &c.

Gustavus Vassa

The African

37. JOSIAH WEDGWOOD TO GUSTAVUS VASSA (DRAFT)
[QUOTATION BY COURTESY OF THE TRUSTEES OF THE WEDGWOOD MUSEUM, BARLASTON, STAFFORDSHIRE, ENGLAND]

[Endorsed Sept. 19. 1793]

Dear Sir

Your letter of the 21st of Augt came here in due course & would have been answd sooner but I have been from home for five weeks.

When I was in London if you had been molested by any press gang I would have applied personally to Mr Stevens in your behalf, & might have procured you relief before they had time to carry you away, but your writing from Bristol in case of an accident of that kind would not I fear have the same effect.

I hope you will not be in any danger, but if it should be otherwise you may direct a letter to Mr. Byerley No. 5 Greek St. Soho acquainting him with your situation & he will take the necessary steps with Mr Stevens in your favor.

With best wishes for your health & safety

I am Sr. your frd & servt

JW[35]

38. FROM THE NORFOLK CHRONICLE, 22 FEBRUARY 1794. [THIS AND THE FOLLOWING ADVERTISEMENT APPEARED ON THE SAME TWO DAYS IN YARRINGTON & BACON'S NORWICH MERCURY]

IN THE PRESS
And will be published, ready to be delivered on the 12th of
March next,
The EIGHTH EDITION, enlarged,
OF
THE
LIFE
Of OLAUDAH EQUIANO;
OR,
Gustavus Vassa,
THE AFRICAN
WRITTEN BY HIMSELF.

Containing the Author's observations on his country, the manner in which he and his Sister were kidnapped, of the treatment he received during the term of his slavery, and the manner of obtaining his freedom, &c. &c. With a Portrait of the Author, and a View of his being shipwrecked.

The work will be printed in one handsome volume twelves, price 4s. (Formerly sold for 7s.) on a good paper.

Subscriptions taken in by the Author, at Mr. [Jacob] Johnson's, Bridge-street, St. George's [Colegate parish]; and by Mr. [William] Stevenson, at the Norfolk Arms, in the Market-place, Norwich. As it is intended to pub-lish a List of Subscribers, the Author would be happy to have the names of such friends as mean to subscribe by the 6th of March at farthest.

For the Character of this Narrative see the Monthly Review for June; and also General Magazine, or Impartial Review for July 1789.

39. FROM *THE NORFOLK CHRONICLE*, 15 MARCH 1794.

GUSTAVUS VASSA, the AFRICAN.
To the Inhabitants of this City and its Environs,
And also of Bury St. Edmund.
GENTLEMEN,
PERMIT me, one of the oppressed Natives of Africa, to offer you the warmest thanks of a heart glowing with gratitude to you for your fellow feeling for the Africans and their cause:—Having received marks of kind-ness from you who have subscribed to my interesting Narrative, I heartily wish all of you every blessing that this world can afford, and all fullness of joy in the next world.

Gentlemen,

I am, with profound respect and gratitude, &c.
                    GUSTAVUS VASSA.
Norwich, March 14th, 1794.
N.B. Subscribers and others may now have the Narrative of the Author, at Mr. [Jacob] Johnson's, Bridge-street, St. George's [Colegate], and of Mr. [William] Stevenson, at the Norfolk Arms, in the Market-place, price 4s.

40. GUSTAVUS VASSA TO REVEREND PETER PECKARD, UNDATED (FERRAR PAPERS, MAGDALENE COLLEGE, CAMBRIDGE)

The Revd Dr. Peckard

Very kind & worthy Sir.—
This with my Dutiful Respect—pray pardon this Liberty of mine in Dis-turbing of you. I will take it a Particular favour if you will be kind enough to see me a minute or two—
Very kind & Worthy Sir—

I am with all Due Respects
Gustavus Vassa

Explanatory Notes: Appendix E

1 *The Public Advertiser, The Morning Chronicle,* and *The Diary* were pro-Pitt London newspapers subsidized at the time by the Treasury, under the direction of George Rose (1744–1818), one of the original subscribers to *The Interesting Narrative.*

2 The *"Extract of a letter from a gentleman [the Reverend Patrick Fraser] on board the Ship Atlantic, off Santa Cruz, Teneriffe"* appeared in *The London Chronicle* and *The Morning Chronicle, and London Advertiser*:

> I take this opportunity of informing you, that we arrived here on Saturday last, after a most pleasant passage of 13 days from Plymouth. I have the pleasure to inform you, that we are all well, and that the poor blacks are in a much more healthy state than when we left England. Vasa's discharge and the dismission of [William] Green and [Lewis] Rose, are attended with the happiest effects. Instead of that general misunderstanding under which we groaned through their means, we now enjoy all the sweets of peace, lenity, and almost uninterrupted harmony. The odious distinction of colours is no longer remembered, and all seem to conspire to promote the general good. The people are now regular in their attendance upon divine service on the Sundays, and on public prayers during the week; they do not, as formerly, absent themselves purposely on such occasions, for no other reasons whatever than that I am white. We have upwards of 20 blacks who receive instruction every day from the school-master; and I am happy to acquaint you, that some of them promise to make excellent scholars. I am this day to appoint another school on board of the Vernon, under the direction of Mr. Smith. In short, Sir, our affairs upon the whole are so much changed for the better, that I flatter myself with the pleasing hope that we may still do well, and enjoy the blessing of Providence in the intended settlement.

3 Quoted from Prince Hoare, *Memoirs of Granville Sharp* (London, 1820), 374–375. Sharp was one of the founders of the Society for Effecting the Abolition of the Slave Trade [hereafter SEAST], formally organized on May 22, 1787.

4 The law of retribution, of an eye for an eye.

5 Pathetic: emotionally moving.
Bishop of London: Dr. Beilby Porteus (1731–1808), bishop of London 1787–1808, had delivered the first abolitionist speech by a prominent An-

glican divine while he was still bishop of Chester, *A Sermon Preached before the Incorporated Society for the Propagation of the Gospel in Foreign Parts: at Their Anniversary Meeting in the Parish Church of St. Mary-Le-Bow, on February 21, 1783....* (London, 1784). Calling the disruption of the slave trade, "that opprobrious traffic, in which this country has for too long taken the lead" (18), one of the unintended beneficial consequences of the civil war with the American colonies, Porteus notes that "It is believed (on very just grounds, and after the maturest consideration of the subject) by men of great judgment and long experience in the management of West-India estates, that if the Negroes on any of our plantations were emancipated *gradually* (for every improvement of their situation must be *very gradual* [emphasis in original]) ... and retained afterwards by their owners as day labourers at a certain fair stipulated price, it would be an alteration no less advantageous to the planter, than kind and compassionate to the Negroe" (24). Porteus concludes by addressing the slave traders:

> Let then our countrymen make haste to relieve, as far as they are able, the calamities they have brought on so large a part of the human race; let them endeavour to wipe away the reproach of having delivered over so many fellow-creatures to a most heavy temporal bondage, both by contributing to soothe and alleviate that as much as possible, and by endeavouring to rescue them from the still more cruel bondage of ignorance and sin. (33– 34)

6 PRO BT 6/10, 325–330. Charles Jenkinson (1729–1808), created Baron Hawkesbury in 1786, President of the Board of Trade, 1786–1804. Equiano published a slightly revised version of this letter in *The Public Advertiser,* 31 March 1788.

7 Raymund Harris, *Scripture Researches on the Licitness of the Slave-Trade, Shewing its Conformity with the Principles of Natural and Revealed Religion, Delineated in the Sacred Writings of the Word of God* (London, 1788). Harris, whose real name was Hormasa, was a Spanish-born Jesuit. For his efforts on behalf of the slave trade and slavery, Harris received an award of £100 from the city of Liverpool. Among the responses to Harris were the Reverend William Hughes (d. 1798), *An Answer to the Rev. Mr. Harris's "Scriptural Researches on the Licitness of the Slave-Trade"* (London, 1788) and the Reverend James Ramsay, *An Examination of the Rev. Mr. Harris's Scriptural Researches on the Licitness of the Slave Trade* (London, 1788).

8 This letter was also published in the 20 June 1788 issue of *The Morning Chronicle, and London Advertiser.*

9 With the exception of Sir Peter Burrell (1754–1820), Samuel Whitbread (1726–1796), William Dolben (1727–1814), and George Pitt (1751–1828), all members of the House of Commons, were original subscribers to Equiano's *Narrative.*

10 Probably references to James Ramsay and Thomas Clarkson.

11 Samuel Jackson Pratt, *Humanity, or the Rights of Nature, a Poem: in Two Books. By the Author of Sympathy* (London, 1788).

12 Thomas Townsend (1733–1800), created Baron Sydney in 1783, Home Secretary of State, 1784–1789, and President of the Board of Control, 1784–1790.

13 Dolben (1727–1814) led the successful legislative fight in 1788 for a law regulating the overcrowding of slave ships.

14 I thank Mark Jones for bringing this and the following item to my attention.

15 The plate is reproduced in Clarkson, *History of the Rise, Progress, and Accomplishment of the Abolition of the Slave Trade by the British Parliament* (London, 1808), facing 2: 111.

16 William Dickson, *Letters on Slavery. . . . To Which Are Added, Addresses to the Whites, and to the Free Negroes of Barbadoes: and Accounts of Some Negroes Eminent for their Virtues and Abilities* (London, 1789). Dickson was a subscriber to Equiano's *Narrative*.

17 I thank Erin Sadlack for bringing this item to my attention.

18 William Bliss was one of Equiano's subscribers. In addition to being a stamp distributor, according to the *Universal British Directory 1793–1798*, Thomas Pearson was a "Printer, Bookseller, Stationer, and General Almanack Vender, Printer of *Aris's Birmingham Gazette*, & Proprietor of the Machine for ruling Accompt-books, 99 High-street"; Myles Swinney a "Letter-founder, Printer, Bookseller, Stationer, and Publisher of the *Birmingham and Stafford Chronicle*, Stamp and Medicine Vender, 75 High-street"; and Edward Piercy a "Printer, Bookseller, Stationer, & Medicine Vender, Bull-st." A "Mr. Pearson" was a member of the Society for Effecting the Abolition of the Slave Trade.

19 Edmond Holme's 1788 *A Directory for the Towns of Manchester and Salford, for the Year 1788* (Manchester: Printed for the Author) includes "Harrop Joseph, gent. Bury street, Salford," "Harrop James, printer and stationer, Marketplace," and "Thomson John, writing stationer, at Mrs. Lighthasle's milliner, Queen street, St. Ann's." Both James and Joseph Harrop were members of the Society for Effecting the Abolition of the Slave Trade.

20 Bryant was a member of the Society for Effecting the Abolition of the Slave Trade. During his book promotion tours in the provinces, Equiano apparently recruited, or at least identified, potential members for the Lon-

don Corresponding Society, a radical working-class organization begun on 25 January 1792 by Thomas Hardy (1752–1832), the Society's first Secretary, to promote the widening of the electorate. For example, Equiano brought Bryant to Hardy's attention: see the letter from Hardy to Bryant dated 8 March 1792 in British Library Add. Ms. 27, 811 ("Original Letter Book of the London Corresponding Society"), fols. 4v–5r, part of the Francis Place Collection. In his *Memoir of Thomas Hardy, Founder of, and Secretary to, the London Corresponding Society* (London, 1832), Hardy says that his letter to Bryant was "[t]he first correspondence of the Society" (14).

Equiano lived in Lydia and Thomas Hardy's house in Covent Garden while he revised the fifth edition (1792) of his *Interesting Narrative*: in his *Memoir*, Hardy refers to Equiano's "writing memoirs of his life" (15). Equiano's letter to the Reverend Walker (Letter 29) was mailed from Hardy's house.

21 Peter Barfoot and John Wilkes, compilers of *The Universal British Directory 1793–1798* (London, 1798), list John and Thomas Haighs as Huddersfield merchants and manufacturers; John and George Tinker as Huddersfield merchants and woolstaplers; and several people named Haigh and Tinker among the gentry and tradesmen in the nearby villages of Slaighwaite, Lockwood, Dalton, and Quarmby.

22 Tuke, a Quaker and member of the Society for Effecting the Abolition of the Slave Trade, was a tea-dealer; Spence (buried 9 August 1824, aged 75), was a bookseller. The same page prints the transcript of part of the slave-trade debate in the House of Commons, including William Wilberforce's statements.

23 Sleater, one of Equiano's Dublin subscribers, was printer for the Anglo-Irish parliament; Byrne, on the other hand, was a successful Roman Catholic bookseller and printer supporting the Irish nationalist opposition, Catholic emancipation, and parliamentary reform. He published the *Universal Magazine*, which sympathetically covered the progress of the French Revolution. He also later published the political pamphlets of Wolfe Tone, the Irish radical, and became printer to the Catholic Committee and to the United Irishmen.

24 In her article, "Equiano in Belfast," Nini Rogers says of Neilson, "In 1791 possibly the most radical member of Belfast's secret committee and then the United Irishmen was Samuel Neilson, son of a Presbyterian minister, thriving woolen draper and editor of the movement's newspaper, the *Northern Star*. Even among Belfast's radical families he was spoken of as a hot head and Wolfe Tone and Thomas Russell (that other influential outsider in Belfast politics) nicknamed him 'the Jacobin' " (75).

25 Reproduced from a photocopy in the Cambridgeshire County Record Office of the original autograph letter in the Hornby Library of the Liverpool City Library. Reproduced with the permission of the Liverpool

Libraries and Information Services. Walker was one of Equiano's original subscribers.

26 Andrew Dunbar was the inn-keeper at the sign of the King's Arms,
Trongate.

27 In London, *The Gazetteer and New Daily Advertiser* (30 May 1792) published a notice of Equiano's activities in Edinburgh:

> GUSTAVUS VASA, with his *white* wife, is at Edinburgh, where he has
> published a letter of thanks to the General Assembly of the Church of
> Scotland, for their just and humane interference upon the question of
> the SLAVE TRADE [emphasis in the original].

28 This letter was one of the documents seized when the authorities arrested its addressee, on 12 May 1794. Hardy was tried and acquitted on 5 November 1794 on a charge of high treason for his role in the London
Corresponding Society.

29 Equiano must have been one of the earliest members of the London
Corresponding Society, which had only about seventy members at the beginning of April 1792. Mary Thale estimates that by November 1794, the
number of members, the highest to date, was still less than eight hundred.

30 See Letter 32.

31 Karks: kirks, the Scottish word for churches.

32 Equiano refers to the issue that carried the announcement of his marriage to Miss Cullen.

33 *The Universal British Directory of Trade and Commerce . . .*, 5 vols. (London, 1791–98), 1:20, identifies "Ph. Stephens, Esq; F[ellow]. R[oyal]. S[oci-
ety]." As both the first secretary to the Lords Commissioners at the Admiralty
Office and first secretary in the Marine Department. Wedgwood (1730–1795)
was also a Fellow of the Royal Society. Thomas Byerley was Wedgwood's
nephew and personal secretary at Wedgwood's home, 5 Greek Street, Soho,
in London. Philip Stevens (1723–1809), M.P. for Sandwich, 1768–1806, was
first secretary of the Admiralty Board, 1759–1795.

The Will and Codicil of Gustavus Vassa [Olaudah Equiano]

In the Name of God Amen. I Gustavus Vassa of Addle Street Aldermanbury in the City of London Gentleman being sound in mind and Body and in perfect health and firm in my belief of a future State in the death and Corruption of the Body and hopeful in the rise of the Soul depending in the Mercy of God my Creator for forgiveness of my Sins Give Devise and Bequeath unto my Friends John Audley and Edward Ind both of Cambridge Esquires All my real and personal Estate of what Nature Kind or sort soever either in possession reversion remainder or expectancy and which Estate and property I have dearly earned by the Sweat of my Brow in some of the most remote and adverse Corners of the whole world to solace those I leave behind me. To Hold to them the said John Audley and Edward Ind their Executors Administrators and Assigns In Trust that they the said John Audley and Edward Ind shall and do receive and take the produce and profits arising from my Estate both real and personal and apply the same or a sufficient part thereof towards the Board Maintenance and Education of my two infant Daughters Ann Maria and Johanna Vassa until they shall respectively attain their respective Ages of Twenty one years. Then Upon this further Trust that from and after their Attaining their said Age of Twenty one years equally to be divided between them Share and Share alike but if either of them shall happen to die then I give and bequeath the Share of her so dying to the Survivor of them but in Case of the decease of both my Children before they arrive at their said Age of Twenty one years then and in that Case I give devise and bequeath the whole of my Estate and Effects hereinbefore given one Moiety thereof to the Treasurer and Directors of the Sierra Leona Company for the Use and Benefit of the School established by the said Company at Sierra Leona and the other Moiety thereof to the Treasurer and Directors of the Society instituted at the Spa Fields Chapel* on the twenty second day of September one thousand seven hundred and ninety five for

* The Methodist Spa Fields Chapel was a large hall, which had been licensed in 1777 as a dissenting meeting house in the parish of St. James, Clerkenwell. The license was cancelled when the Countess of Huntington (1707–1791) opened her Chapel on Palm Sunday, 28 March 1779. Unaffiliated with the Huntingdon Connexion, the Society mentioned in the will was later known as the London Missionary Society.

sending Missionaries to preach the Gospel in Foreign parts. I Do hereby Give and Bequeath unto the said John Audley and Edward Ind the Sum of Ten Pounds each. And I do hereby nominate constitute and appoint the said John Audley and Edward Ind Executors of this my last Will and Testament hereby revoking and making void all and every other Will and Wills at any time heretofore by me made and do declare this to be my last will and Testament. In Witness whereof I have hereunto set my hand and Seal this twenty eighth day of May in the year of our Lord one thousand seven hundred and ninety six.

[Signed] Gustavus Vassa

Signed Sealed Published and declared by the above named Gustavus Vassa as and for his last Will and Testament in the Presence of us who at his request and in his Presence have subscribed our Names as Witnesses thereto. Elizabeth Melliora Cooss No. 9 Adam Street. J. Gillham No. 9 Adam Street Adelphi. George Streetin, Clerk to Mr. Gillham.

THE SCHEDULE or Inventory of the principal part of my Estate and Effects which I am possessed of at the Time of making this my Will

Two Acres of Copyhold Pasture Ground with the Appurtenances thereunto belonging situate lying and being in Sutton and Mepal in the Isle of Ely and County of Cambridge which devolves to me [and] my heirs or assigns after the decease of Mrs. Ann Cullen of Fordham in Cambridgeshire by the last Will and Testament of my late Wife Susanna Vassa[.] And I have Mrs. Cullen's Bond for one Quarter of her Worth[:] One Annuity of James Parkinson Esquire of the Leverian Museum* Blackfriars road in the County of Surrey of the yearly value of Twenty six pounds thirteen Shillings and Eight pence;

One other Annuity of Francis Folkes and Frances his wife of Pleasant passage near Mother Red Caps† Hampstead Road in the County of Middlesex of the yearly value of Fifty Eight pounds two Shillings and Eight pence;

One other Annuity of Mrs Ann Leybourn of Westwell in the County of Oxford of the yearly value of One hundred pounds all payable quarterly[.]

* Through a lottery, Parkinson (ca. 1730–1813) had acquired in 1784 Sir Ashton Lever's Museum, a collection of curiosities and specimens of natural history. After failing to sell the collection to the queen of Portugal and the empress of Russia, he moved it to a building called the "Museum Leveriarum," at the corner of Blackfriars Road and Albion Street. When the British Museum declined to buy it in 1806, Parkinson dispersed the collection at a sixty-five-day auction.
† At a time when the numbering of houses was only beginning, residences were commonly identified by their proximity to local landmarks, like the Mother Red Caps inn.

Three hundred pounds secured to me by an Assignment of the Lease of Plaisterers Hall situate in Addle Street No. 25 in the City of London[.]*

Sundry Household Goods and Furniture wearing Apparel and printed Books at present on the Premises at Plaisterers Hall[;]

The Sum of Three hundred pounds at present undisposed of and such other Property as I may in future accumulate.

I do hereby desire my Executors to insure the Lives on which the several Annuities are granted at the Assurance Office in Bridge Street Blackfriars[.]

The Deeds of which Estate are lodged in the possession of James Gillham Attorney No. 9 Adam Street Adelphi or with Messrs. Down[,] Thornton and Compy Bankers Bartholomew Lane in the City of London.

[Signed] Gustavus Vassa.

Witnesses[:] Eliz[abe]th Melliora Cooss. Js. Gillham. George Streetin Cl[er]k to Mr. Gillham.†

---

* Equiano was living in Plaisterers' Hall when he composed his will. The Hall belonged to one of the City of London livery companies. The Plaisterers' Company, chartered in 1501, used the Hall as a source of rental income, leasing it to others, who in turn leased its rooms to various occupants. Equiano must have been a sub-tenant of William Rolfe, a goldsmith who signed a 21-year lease of the Hall on 24 December 1790 (Guildhall Ms. 6121/4). During the period of Equiano's occupancy, the Company usually held its meetings in the nearby Queens Head Tavern (Guildhall Ms. 6122/5). The original Hall was destroyed in the Great Fire of 1666; Equiano lived in the one rebuilt in 1669, designed by Sir Christopher Wren (1632–1723), and which burned down in 1882. A description of Wren's design ("Brewer's Book of Particulars. 1860," kept in Plaisterers' Hall) and the plan of the building in 1790 (Guildhall Ms. 6143) show that the Hall had ample room for more than one tenant at a time.

I am very grateful to Henry Mott, Clerk of the Plaisterers' Company, for allowing me to consult records held in Plaisterers' Hall.

† After Equiano's death on 31 March 1797, his will was proved in London in the Prerogative Court of Canterbury (because his estate involved more than one diocese) on 8 April 1797. A marginal note reads, "The Testator was formerly as within described but late of the Parish of Saint Mary leBon in the County of Middlesex and died last Month." On 11 April 1816, her twenty-first birthday, Equiano's surviving daughter, Joanna, inherited £950, the value of her father's estate clear of debts. Anna Maria had died on 21 July 1797.

APPENDIX G: NAMES OF SUBSCRIBERS ADDED AFTER THE FIRST EDITION

Second Edition (London, 24 December 1789)

His Royal Highness the Duke of Cumberland
Rev. Mr. Charles Adams
Miss Mary Adams
John Ady
Mrs. Ashman
Mr. Audley
Mr. Aufrere
Admiral George Balfour
Mr. Barton
Mr. J.P. Berthon
Mr. Harris[,] Bottisham
Alderman Boydell
Edward Burch, Esq., R.A.
Mr. Marcus Butcher
Mr. Joseph Chamberlain
Lord Bishop of Chester
Mr. Child
Mr. Thomas Cooper, Jun.
Mr. John Dalby
Mrs. M. Davey
John Delamain, Esq.
Mr. E.O. Donovan
Rev. Mr. William Dunn
Mr. John Elgar
Mrs. William Fielding
Mr. Richard George
Mr. Adam Graham
Mr. John Grant
Mr. Hafzelgrove
Mr. Benjamin Haigh
Charles Hamilton, Esq.
Thomas Hammersley, Esq.
Mr. Timothy Hansfield

Mrs. Harben
Mr. Thomas Hardy
Right Hon. Countess of Harrington
Mr. Hodgkinson
Mrs. Hogflesh
Mr. Abraham Horsfall
Mr. John Horsfall
Mr. Robert Hudson
Mr. Philip Hurlock, sen.
Mr. Hutson
Mr. George Hutton
Edward Ind, Esq.
Robert Ind, Esq.
Thomas Irving, Esq., 3 copies
Mr. James Jacobs
Mr. Thomas Jackson
Mr. Jefferys, Royal Navy
James Johnson, Esq.
Mr. James Jones
Rev. Dr. Jowett
James Karr, Esq.
Mr. Walter Lewis, Jun.
Mr. Samuel Lucas
Mr. P.M.
Mr. Matthews, 6 copies
The Reverend H. Michell
Mr. Musgrove
Mr. Thomas Musgrove
Henry Naylor, Esq.
Francis Noble, Esq.
Capt. Norman, Navy
Rev. Mr. J. Owen
Mr. M.P.

Mr. O. Parry
Rev. Dr. Peckard, of Cambridge
Rt. Hon. William Pickett, Esq.
  Lord Mayor of London
Mr. Samuel Purle
His Grace the Duke of
  Queensberry
Admiral Roddam
Mr. Sampson
Mr. Richard Shepherd
Mr. William Shill
Thomas Spalding
John Spratt
Mr. Charles Starkey
Mr. William Symonds
Dr. Thackeray
The Reverend Mr. Robert
  Thornton
Mr. Abraham Thorp
Mr. John Vaughan
Mr. William Watson
Mr. James Welch
Mr. George Wille
Mrs. Willmott
The Reverend Mr. Elhanan
  Winchester, 6 copies
Mr. Yeo, of Portsmouth

Third Edition (London, 30 October 1790)

Wm. Bliss, of Birmingham,
  12 copies
Dr. Brown, of Sheffield, 3 copies
Thomas Cooper, Esq., Manchester
Miss Susan Cullen
Alderman Curtis
Mr. Hall
William Hoyle
Thomas Irving, Esq., 4 copies
Mr. John Lowe, jun., of
  Manchester
Miss Mary Naw

William Shore, Esq., of Sheffield,
  12 copies
John James Smith
Mr. John Strickland
Robert Sutcliff
William Tuke, of York
Jonathan Walker, Esq., of Rother-
  ham, 4 copies
Joseph Walker, Esq., of Rotherham
Joshua Walker, Esq., of Rotherham
Samuel Walker, Esq., of
  Rotherham
Thomas Walker, Esq., of
  Manchester, 6 copies
Rev. James Wilkinson, of Sheffield,
  3 copies
Rev. Mr. Wraith, of
  Wolverhampton, 12 copies

Fourth Edition (Dublin, 20 May 1791)

Rev. Mr. Astley, of Chesterfield,
  3 copies
Mr. Law Atkinson, of Huddersfield,
  100 copies
Rev. Mr. Atkinson, of Leeds,
  12 copies
Mr. Beanson, of Doncaster
——Buxton, Esq., of Leicester,
  6 copies
Rev. Mr. Carlow, of Mansfield
Mrs. Chambers, of Derby, 3 copies
Tho. Clark, of Northampton,
  3 copies
John English Dolben, Esq.
Mary Ann Fothergill, of York
Dr. Hey, Leeds, 6 copies
Rev. Mr. Houseman, of Leicester.
Sir Egerton Leigh, of Northampton,
  2 copies
Charles and Sampson Loyd, esqs.,
  of Birmingham

Lindly Murry, of York
Pim Nevins, of Leeds, 18 copies
Rev. Robert Boucher Nickolls,
    dean of Middleham
John Plowes, Esq. Mayor of Leeds,
    6 copies
Rev. Mr. Robinson, of Dewsbery
Rev. Mr. George Walker, of
    Nottingham, 20 copies
Reverend Mr. Ward
Dr. White, Nottingham,
    6 copies

Irish Subscribers

A
His Grace the Archbishop of
    Dublin
Richard Abel, of Cork
Philip Abbott
William Adamson
Archdeacon Allen
Edward Neston Allen
John Allen, Esq.
Richard Allen
William Allen, 2 copies
Thomas Andrews, Esq.
William Armstrong
J.T. Ashenhurst, Esq.
Rev. Gilbart Austin

B
Right Hon. The Earl of Belvedere,
    10 copies
Mr. William Bardin
Mr. Thomas M. Bates, 7 copies
Luke Bernard
John Blachford, Esq., 1 copy
James Blacker
Mr. Mark Blair
Mr. Lyndon Bolton
Oliver Bond, Esq., 10 copies
Mr. W. Borillie
Henry Brooke, 1 copy
Robert Burton, Esq.

C
Right Rev. the Lord Bishop of
    Cork
Mr. Thomas Caddell
Mr. Ralph Carde
Joseph Chabiteau
James Christy of Lurgan
Matthew Church, Cork
Rev. Mr. Adam Clarke
John Dawson Coates, Esq.,
    6 copies
John Cowan
W.L. Cowan, Esq.
Cooper Crafford, Esq.
Edmond Cronyn
Thomas Crosbie
Hugh Crothers, Esq.
Montague Crothers, Esq.

D
James Dale, Esq.
Frederick Darley, 5 copies
Henry Darley
Richard Dillon
William Doolittle
James Doyle, Esq.
John Doyle, Esq.
Capt. Drough, of Mote
Nicholas Drumgoole, Esq.
Robert Dudley, of Clonmel
Thomas Dunn, Esq.

E
Rev. Dr. Ellison, of Kilkenny

F
Mr. John Farris
Mr. Samuel Fayle,
    2 copies
Fisher and Harvey, of
    Limerick
Capt. William Fitch
James Forbes
John Forbes

Mr. Samuel Forbes
Rev. Robert Fowler

G
Miss Sophia Gamble
John Garden, Esq.
Robert Gardiner, Esq.
Samuel Gardner
Mr. William Geary
William P. Gilburn
Mr. William Gladman
Edward Gleadowe, Esq.
Mr. James Grant
Mr. Jonathan Gray
Dr. William Gray
Joseph Greenwood
Mr. Richard Gregg

H
Thomas Hancocks, of Lisborn
Sir Henry Hays, of Cork
William Harkness
John Hart
James Hartley, Esq.
Joseph Henry, Esq.
John Hill, Esq.
Henry Hornton, of Catlow
The Right Hon. Henry How[i]son,
    Lord Mayor, 5 copies
Mr. Robert Hudson
William Humfrey, Esq.

I
Dr. Irving, of Lisborn

J
Henry Jackson, Esq., 5 copies
Alexander Jordan
Thomas Jordan, 2 copies

K
Mr. Adam Keith
Mr. William Kidd, of Mulingar,
    7 copies

Mr. Francis Kiernan
John King
Alexander Kirkpatrick, Esq., 5 copies
Francis Kirkpatrick, Esq.
William Kirkpatrick, Esq., 5 copies
Mrs. Kirkpatrick, 5 copies
Rev. Walter B. Kirwan, 2 copies
Francis Knox, Esq.

L
His Grace the Duke of Leinster
——Le Strange, Esq.
Mr. Michael Lewis
Lady Lough, of Drogheda
Gorges Lowther, jun. Esq.

M
The Right Rev. Lord Bishop of
    Meath
The Right Hon. The Earl of
    Miltown
Lady Miltown
Lady Moira
Mr. William Magrath
John Maiben, Esq.
Rev. Mr. W. Mann
Colin M'Kay, Esq., of Belfast
S. M'Guire, Esq.
Mrs. M'Kenny
John Mestayer
William Middleton
Mrs. D. Mills
Rev. Dean Morgan
William Myler, Esq.

N
Samuel Neal, of Corke
Sam Neilson, Esq., Belfast, 5 copies
John Nicolson
Mrs. Anna Maria Norris

O
Right Hon. Earl of Ormond
Right Hon. John O'Neal

Mr. Ogilby
M. O'Plunkett
Patrick O'Plunkett
Mrs. O'Reily

P
Matthew Parker
John Patrick, Esq.
Dr. Patten, of Tandragee
William Penrose, Esq., of
    Waterford
Mr. Pentland
Henry Pettigrew, Esq.
Patrick Plunket, M.D.
Mr. Thomas Prentice, of Armaugh
Mr. Richard Purcell, Esq., of Cork

R
T. Ramage
Thomas Reynolds
John Rice
Robert Roberts
William Robinson, Esq.
Sir Samuel Rowland, of Cork
Rev. Thomas Rutherford

S
Robert S. Sanders
Mr. Joseph Sandwich, 4 copies
Thomas Simmons
James Shaw
Ralph Shaw, Esq.
Thomas Simmons
Mrs. Singleton, 4 copies
Dr. F. Skelton, of Drogheda
Mr. William Sleater
Benjamin Smith, Esq., 45th
    Regiment
N. N. Smith, Esq., Inner Temple
William Smyth, Esq.,
    12 copies
Mr. William Sproule, of Athlone
Mr. Richard Stafford
Mr. William Staines

Jones Stevelly
Robert Stevelly, Esq.
Alexander Stewart, Esq., 2 copies
James Stewart, Esq., 20 copies
William Stewart
Amos Strettell

T
Right Hon. David La Touche,
    Esq., jun.
Lady Celia La Touche
——Talbott, Esq.
Ja[me]s. Napper Tandy, Esq.
William Tenwick
John Terry
Skeffington Thompson, Esq.,
    5 copies
Thomas Thompson, Esq.
Augustine Thwaites, Esq., 1 copy
Captain Tisdall
John Toler, Esq., Solicitor General
Lewis Tourtellote
Rev. Dr. Trail, of Lisborn

V
Philip Vegneaw
Richard Verschoyle, Esq.

W
William Walcott
John Walker, 6 copies
Joseph Walker, Printer
Joseph C. Walker, Esq.
Samuel Walker, Esq.
Solomon Walker
Robert Waller, Esq.
John Ward
Peter Warren
Richard Westenra, Esq.
Joseph Williams

FIFTH EDITION
(EDINBURGH, JUNE 1792)

——Atkinson, Esq.
Mr. Robert Kent, Soham

Scottish Subscribers

A

Hon. Lord Ankerville
Alexander Abercrombie, Esq., W. S.
Mr. Robert Ainslie, W.S.
Mr. William Alexander
Mr. Alexander Allison
Dr. J. Anderson, Leith
Mr. James Anderson, Leith
Mr. John Anderson
Professor Anderson, of Glasgow
Mr. William Anderson
Mr. Arrat, of Glasgow
Mr. Roger Ayton

B

Mr. Elphinston Balfour
Rev. Mr. Robert Balfour, of
   Glasgow
Mr. John Baxter
Mr. Andrew Blane, W.S.
Rev. Mr. Bogg, of Paisley
Messrs. Bogle & Scott
Mr. James Bonar
Mr. Braidwood
Messrs. Brash & Reid
Mr. Adam Brooks
Bailie Brown, Esq., Paisley
Mr. John Buchan, W.S.
Rev. Mr. Buchanan

C

Mr. John Campbell
Mr. John Campbell, W.S.
Mr. Horatius Cannon, W.S.
Mr. Cathcart, Advocate
Mr. David Cathcart, Esq., Advocate
Misses Chancellors

James Christie, Esq.
Mrs. Clark
Capt. Alexander Cochrane
Mr. John Cochrane, Paisley
Rev. Mr. John Colquhoun, of Leith
Mr. Robert Corbet, Esq., Advocate
Mr. Robert Craigie, Esq., Advocate
William Creech, Esq.
Mr. Andrew Crombie
Mr. John Crombie

D

David Dale, Esq.
Mr. William Dallas, W.S.
Mr. William Dalziel, W.S.
Mr. Dickson
Mr. Donaldson

E

Mr. John Elder
Col. Francis Erskine
Hon. Henry Erskine
Rev. Dr. John Erskine

F

Mr. Fletcher, W.S.
Sir William Forbes
Mr. Peter Forrester
Mr. Fowler

G

Capt. Gallia, of Greenock
Rev. Mr. Gilles, of Glasgow, D.D.
William Gillespie, Esq., of Glasgow
Mr. Adam Gillis, Esq., Advocate
Lord Adam Gordon
James Gordon, Esq., Advocate
Mr. John Gordon, Advocate
William Gordon, W.S.
Mr. Robert Graham, of Glasgow
Mr. Graham
Mr. Alexander Grant, W.S.
Miss Gray
Mr. John Gray

Rev. Mr. William Greenfield
Mr. John Guthrie

H
Mr. Haggart, W.S.
Sir James Hall
Rev. Mr. James Hall
Mr. Robert Hamilton, Esq.
Mr. William Handyside, W.S.
Mr. James Hay, junior, W.S.
Rev. Mr. Headrick
Mr. Henderson
Mr. Peter Hill
David Home, Esq.
Rev. Dr. Andrew Hunter
Mr. David Hutchinson

I
Mr. Henry David Inglis, Esq.
Mr. William Inglis, W.S.
Mrs. Irving
Mr. Irving, Advocate
Mr. Chalmers Izett
Dr. Jaffray, of Glasgow
Mr. Henry Jardine, W.S.

K
Rev. Mr. John Kemp
William Ker, Esq.
George Kinnear, Esq.

L
Mr. Laing, Advocate
J. Love, Esq., of Paisley

M
The Hon. Lord Monboddo
Mr. Colin M'Donald
Mr. Hector M'Donald
Mr. John M'Farquhar, W.S.
Mr. Andrew M'Kenzie
Mr. Colin M'Kenzie
Mr. Kenneth M'Kenzie
Mr. M'Laurin, Advocate

Mr. James M'Lean
Mr. Richard M'Lean
Mr. William M'Lean
Mr. William Mayne, of Glasgow
Mr. Hugh Mercer, W.S.
Mr. George Miller
Mrs. Mitchelson
Rev. Sir Henry Moncrieff-
    Welwood, baronet, D.D.
Mr. Montague, Advocate
John Monteith, Esq., of Glasgow
Mr. Montgomery, Advocate
Rev. Mr. William Moodie
John Morthland, Esq., Advocate
Mr. Christopher Moubray
Rev. Mr. James Moyse
Mr. Hugh Murray

N
Mr. Alexander Nairne, of Paisley
Mr. Adam Neal, of Glasgow

O
Mr. Will. Orhart, of Glasgow
Mr. Oswald, Advocate

P
John Pattison, Esq., of Glasgow
Pattison & Co.
Mr. Robert Plenderleath
Mr. Richard Prentice

R
Mr. William Rae, Esq.
Mr. David Ramsay
George Ramsay, Esq.
Mr. William Rae, Esq.
Mr. David Ramsay
George Ramsay, Esq.
Rev. Mr. Thomas Randall
Mr. Adam Rolland
Mr. Mathew Ross, Esq.

S
Hon. Lord Swinton
Francis Scott, Esq.
R. Scott-Moncrief, Esq., of
  Glasgow
Mr. Robertson Scott, Advocate
Sir John Sinclair, M.P.
Dr. Somerville, Edinburgh
Mr. Charles Stewart, W.S.
Dr. Charles Stewart
David Stewart, Esq.
Professor Dugald Stewart
Mr. G. Stewart, W.S.
Mr. John Swanston, of Glasgow
Mr. Swinton

T
Mr. Crawford Tait, W.S.
Mr. John Tawse, W.S.
Mr. Todd
John Trotter, Esq., of Glasgow
William Turnbull, printer

W
Mr. Wardlow, of Glasgow
Mr. John Watson
Mr. Wauchope, Advocate
Mr. Williamson, Advocate
Mr. Kirkpatrick Williamson

Y
Alexander Young, Esq.
Mr. Charles Young
Mr. Robert Young
Dr. Yuile

SIXTH EDITION, 1793
(LONDON, "TO THE
READER" DATED
30 DECEMBER 1792)

Rev. Mr. Burgess, of Durham
Thomas Digges, Esq. of America

Wm. Eddis, Esq., of Durham
Richard Fishwick, Esq., of New-
  castle
Wm. Green, Esq., of Newcastle
Dr. Grieve, of Newcastle
Capt. Hare, of Lincoln
William Hornsby, Esq., of
  Gainsborough
George Johnson, Esq., of Byker,
  100 copies
John Nelthorpe, Esq., of Lincoln
Mr. Deputy Nichols
Rev. Mr. Edward Parker, of
  Durham
Joseph Pease, Darlington
Rev. Isaac Richardson, of
  Newcastle
Thomas Richardson, of Sunderland
Mrs. M. Shaw
Dr. Trotter, of Newcastle

Hull Subscribers
A
Mr. George Adams
Dr. John Alderson, M.D.
Mr. Thomas Althorp
Captain Middlemore Antoine
Mr. Anthony Atkinson, 2 copies
Mr. Robert Atkinson

B
Mr. William Baker
The Rev. Mr. John Barker
Mr. William Barnes
Miss Ann Bateman
Mr. John Bayes
Dr. S. Stanhope Baynes, M.D.
Mr. Percival Bedill
William Johnson Bell, Esq.
Mr. John Belton
Dr. Alex. Bertram, M.D.
Miss Bine
Miss Bolton
Mr. William Bolton

Mr. William Bowden
Mr. John Boyd
Mr. Thomas Bramwell
Mr. Harrison Briggs
Mr. John Briggs
Mr. Richard Brigham
Mr. Charles Broadley, 2 copies
Mr. John Brookes
Mr. Eldred Brown
Mr. George William Brown
Mr. Jonas Brown
Captain Thomas Brown
Mr. Thomas Brown
Mr. William Brown
Mr. Thomas Buckton
Mr. Peter John Bulmer
Mrs. and Miss Burn
Mr. Isaac Burnett
Mr. John Burstale
Mr. Peter Buttery

C
Mr. Richard Capes
Mr. Robert Castle
Mr. John Cavieck
Mr. Edward Chapman
Mr. Joseph Chapman
Rev. Mr. Thomas Clark
Mr. Thomas Clay
Mr. Henry Coates
Mr. Joseph Cockerill
Mess. Cook and Walmsley,
    2 copies
Miss Rachael Ann Cook
Mr. William Coslass
Mr. E.F. Coulson
Mr. J.S. Crosley
Mr. J.N. Cross
Mr. Johnson Cotton
Mr. Thomas Cutsworth

D
Ralph Darling, Esq.
Mr. Robert Dear

Mr. James Delemain
Mr. John Delvitte
Mr. Joseph Denton
Mr. Joseph Dickinson
Major Ditmas
Mr. Dodsworth
The Rev. Mr. Thomas Dykes

E
Mr. Gardiner Egginton
Mr. Joseph Egginton
Mr. Joseph Eglin, 4 copies
Mr. Thomas Escrett

F
Mr. William Fea
Mr. George Fearley
Mr. John Fearn
Mr. John Fearnley
Mr. Henry Featherston
Mr. Thomas Fishwick
Mr. John Fox, 2 copies
Mr. George Fletcher
Mr. Thomas Fletcher
Mr. Edmund Foster
Mr. George Fowler
Captain James Frank
Mr. J. Frankish
Mr. Thomas Frost

G
The Rev. Edmund Garwood
Mr. John Gilder
Mr. John Givens
Mr. Lewis Gray
Mr. S. Gray
Mr. S.W. Green
Mr. William Green

H
Mr. Francis Hall
Mr. John Hall
Mr. Samuel Hall
Mr. Thomas Hall

Mr. John Hardy
Mr. John Harrap
Richard Acklom Harrison, Esq.,
  2 copies
Miss Harrison, 2 copies
Mr. Wm. Hawxwell
Mr. J.P. Hendry
Mr. M. Heseltine
Mr. Richard Hirst
Mrs. Holgate
Mr. Benjamin Holland
William Hornsby [Hornby], Esq.
Mr. John Horner, 2 copies
Mr. Richard Howard
Miss Howard, 5 copies
Mr. Joseph Howorth, jun.
Mr. Bachus Huntingdon
Mr. William Huntingdon
Mr. John Hutchinson
Mr. Robert Hyton, 3 copies

J
Mr. John Jackson
Mr. Robert Jackson
Mr. Thomas Jackson
John Jarret, Esq.
Mr. Robert Jennings
Mr. Joseph Jewett
Mr. William Johnson
Mr. Anthony Jones

K
Mr. James Keiro
Mr. Hugh Kerr
Mr. Robert Kinder
Mr. Samuel King, 2 copies
Mr. William Kirby
Mr. Frederick Kirsel, 2 copies
Mr. George Knowsley, 3 copies

L
The Rev. Mr. George Lambert
Mr. John B. Lambert
Mr. John Lawson

Mr. Thomas Lee
Mr. John Levett
Mr. Norrison Levett
Mr. William Levett

M
Mr. Bailey Marley
Mr. Godfrey Martin
Mr. Samuel Martin
Mr. Richard Matson
Mr. Thomas Matteson
John Melling, Esq.
Mr. Benjamin Metcalfe
Mr. Michael Metcalfe
The Rev. Mr. Joseph Milner, D.D.
Mr. W. Mitchinson
Mr. Joseph Monday
Mr. Richard Moxon, 2 copies
Mr. William Moxon
Mr. Thomas Mulcaster

N
Mr. John Newmarch
Mr. Norris

O
Mr. O'Kirkbride, 2 copies
Mr. John Orton
Robert Osbourne, Esq., 2 copies
William Osbourne, sen., Esq.
Mr. Benjamin Outram
Mr. Joseph Outram, Esq.
Mr. Thomas Outram

P
Mr. John Parker
Mr. William Parker
Mr. Thomas Parkinson
Miss Ann Pead, 2 copies
Joseph R. Pease, Esq., 2 copies
Mr. Robert C. Pease
Mr. Peter Peasegood
Mr. John Pickerd
Mr. Jonathan Pickwith

Isaac Pleasance, Esq.
Charles Pool, Esq.
Mr. John Popplewell
Mr. Josiah Prickett
Mr. William Proud, 2 copies
Mr. Benjamin Pullan
Mr. William Purdon

R

Mr. Edward Raisbeck
Mr. William Ramsden,
    6 copies
Miss Ann Ramsey
Mr. Joseph Randall
Mr. William Reest
Mr. Joseph Rennard
Mr. Richard Rennard
Mr. Josiah Rhodes, 6 copies
Mr. William Richmond
Mr. Edward Riddle
Mr. George Roberts
Rev. Mr. Arthur Robinson, D.D.
Mr. James Robinson
Mr. John Robinson
Mr. Thomas Robinson
Mr. Robinson
Mr. Charles Roe

S

Mr. Thomas Sanderson
Mr. Thomas Sargent
Mr. Thomas Scratcherd
Mr. William Sedgwick
Mr. William Shackles
Mr. John Simpson
Mr. Charles Smith
Mrs. Smith
Mr. John Spence, 3 copies
Mr. John Spouncer
Mr. Richard Stainton
Mr. Samuel Steekney
Mr. William Steeple
Mr. William Stickney
James Stoven, Esq.

Mr. John Swere
John Sykes, Esq., 2 copies

T

Mr. Richard Taylor, 2 copies
Mr. Thomas Taylor
Mr. Simon Teale
Mr. Thomas A. Terrington
Mr. William Terrington
Mr. Edward Terry
Mr. Richard Terry
Mr. Edward Thompson
Mr. John Thompson
Mr. Thomas Thompson, 2 copies
Mr. Christopher Thorley
Mr. William Thorp
Mr. Stephen Thorpe
Mr. John Todd
Mr. William Todd
Miss H. Travis
Mr. John Travis, 5 copies
William Travis
Mr. Charles Trevor
Doctor Nathaniel Tucker, M.D.
Mr. Thomas Turner

W

Mr. Jonathan Walker
Mr. George Wallis
Mr. William Waring
Mr. Thomas Wasney
Mr. William Wasney
Mr. J. Watson
Mr. Edward West
Mr. David Wharam
Mr. William Whitaker
Mrs. Whitaker
Mr. Thomas Whitehead
Messrs. Wilkinson and Dewitt,
    2 copies
William Williamson, Esq.
Mr. John Wilson
Mr. Isaac Womersley
Mr. Thomas Wood

Mr. George Woodhouse
Mr. John Wray
Mr. Benjamin Wright

V
Mr. John Voare

Seventh Edition (London, "To the Reader" dated August 1793)

William B. Crafton
Mrs. Dolben
David Priestman, of Malton
Stanley Pumphrey, of Worcester
Dan. Roberts, of Painswick
Rev. Mr. Townshend, of
  Cockermouth

List of Bristol Subscribers

A
Edward Ash
Samuel Atkins, 3 copies

B
Dan. Bailey
Mr. John Innes Baker
Joseph Baker
Martha Baker
Mr. A. Barber
Mr. Daniel Baynton
Mr. Thomas Baynton
Thomas Bonville
John Bradley
Rev. Mr. Samuel Bradburn, 2 copies
Mr. Robert Bruce
John Burt
Mr. George Bush

C
Robert Charlton
Fred. Cockworthy

E
George Eaton

F
Anthony Fletcher
Charles Fox, 2 copies
Dr. Fox, 5 copies
Arnee Frank
Cornelius Fry
Joseph Storrs Fry
Robert Fry

G
John Godwin, 2 copies
Mess. Granger and Cropper
Mr. Joseph Green

H
Henry Hale
Love Hammond
James Harford
Richard S. Harford
Mr. Job Harril
Edward Harwood, Esq.
Mr. Robert Hazel
Rev. Mr. John Hey
Joseph Hughes

I
William Impey
Rev. Mr. Robert Jacomb,
  2 copies
Mr. William James

L
Robert Lawson
Alice Ludlow
Mr. William Peter Lunall
John Lury, 6 copies
John Lury, jun.

M
Mr. Joseph Maurice, 2 copies
Jacob Merchant

Mr. William Moore, 2 copies
Mrs. More, of Minehead, 2 copies
Cath. Morgan
Mr. Thomas Morgan

N
George Napper
John Newman

P
Mr. William Painter, 2 copies
Henry Parsons
D.P. Peace
William Pink

R
Rev. Mr. Richardson, Bradford

S
W.T. Simpson
William Smith
William Stansell

T
Miss M. Thatcher
John Thomas, 2 copies
John Tuckett, 2 copies
P.D. Tuckett, 2 copies

W
John Waring, 3 copies
Edward Welmat
John Wills
Matthew Wright, 3 copies

Eighth Edition
(Norwich, March 1794;
"To the Reader" dated
"Edinburgh, June 1792")

Rev. Mr. James Dyer, Devizes
Rev. Mr. Kingsbury, Southhampton
William Langworthy, Esq.

Rev. Mr. Sloper, Devizes
Thomas Talford, Esq., Shrewsbury

Norwich Subscribers
A
John Addey, Esq.
Rev. Lancaster Adkin
Mrs. Aggs
Mr. John Annis
Mr. Hugh Alcock
Miss Amelia [later Opie] Alderson
James Alderson, M.D.
Mr. E. Amond, Wyndham
Mr. Atkins
Mr. William Atthill

B
Mr. James Back
Mrs. Mary Bacon
Mrs. Baldy
Mr. John Barnard
Mr. John Corsbie Barnard
Master Joseph Barnard
Mr. S.C. Barnard
Sam. Barnard, Esq., 5 copies
Mr. Thomas Barnard
Mr. William Barnard, 4 copies
Mr. William Barnard, Jr.
Mrs. Barnard
Mr. Isaac Barnes, Bungay
Mr. Edward Barrow
J[ohn]. G[reen]. Basely, Esq.
Mr. John Beckwith
Augustus Beevor, Esq.
Mr. John Bendeth
Mr. Berry
Mr. John Bidwell, 2 copies
Mr. Thomas Bidwell, Diss
Mr. Blunderfield
Mr. B[enjamin] Boardman
Rev. C[harles]. R[obert]. Bond
Mr. Samuel Bond
Mr. Edward Booth
Mr. John Bouzell

Mr. Robert Bowen
Miles Branthwaite, Esq.
Edward Bridgeman, Esq., Botesdale
Mr. John Bridges
Mr. Henry Brown, Diss
Mr. Browne, Coltishall
Mr. Brownsmith
Miss Buck, Bury
Mr. William Buck, Esq., Bury
John Buckle, Esq., Mayor
Mr. William Burt

C
E. Carver
Mr. T. Cattermoul, jun.
Mr. H. Catton, Elmham
Mr. Christian
Mr. Bernard Church
Mr. Joseph Clarke
Mr. Joseph Clover
Miss Coe
Mr. Coke
Mr. Wright Coldham
Mr. Sam. Cole, Sen.
Mr. John Coleman
Mr. Robert Colls
Mr. Cozens
Mr. Crane
Mr. Crickmore, Seething
Miss Crisp, Ipswich
Miss E.B. Crouse
Mr. Crouse
Mr. Cubitt, Ludham
Mr. John Cully
Mr. Cully, Taverham

D
Mr. Dairy
Mr. Dalrymple
Mr. Danser
Miss Day
Mr. E[lisha]. De Hague
[Brampton] G[urdon]. Dillingham,
    Esq.

Mrs. Dillingham
Mr. Dinmore
Mr. Ditchell, Cromer
Mr. Benjamin Dowson
Rev. Thomas Drake, Shelton
Mr. Thomas Dyson, Diss

E
Mr. J. Ebbets, Hellesdon
Mr. Ellington
William Enfield, LL.D.
Mr. Joseph English
Miss Eliza Errington, of Yarmouth
Miss Everett, Wyndham

F
Miss Fellows
Miss Firth
Mr. Firth
Mr. Fitch
Rev. Samuel Forster, D.D.
William Foster, jun., Esq.,
Mr. Freshfield, sen.
Mr. D[aniel]. Fromanteel
Miss Frost

G
Mrs. Gainsborough
Mr. Gardiner
Mrs. Goddard
Mr. Thomas Goff
Mr. F. Gostling, jun.
Mr. John Graves
Mrs. Gray
J. Grigby, Esq., Drinkstone, Suffolk
Bartlett Gurney, Esq.
Miss Gurney
Miss H. Gurney
Mr. Hudson Gurney
Mr. J. Gurney

H
Miss Hagon
Miss Hammond

Miss Hammont
Mr. William Hankes
Rev. Peter Hansell
Mr. Samuel Harmer
Mr. John Harper
Miss Hart
Miss Ann Harvey, Catton
J[ohn]. Harvey, Esq.
Mr. Wm. Harwin
Mr. Hawkins
Mr. James Hayward
Miss Headley
Mr. James Herring
Mr. John Herring
Robert Herring, Esq., 3 copies
William Herring, Esq., 3 copies
Rev. P[endlebury]. Houghton
James Hudson, Esq.

I
J. Ives, Esq.
Miss Jackson
Mr. Jagger
Miss Jarrold
Mr. T. Jeckell
Mr. J.L. Johnson

K
Henry Kett, Esq.

L
Mr. J[ames]. Landy
Mr. J. Langley, Long Melford
Mr. Robert Larke
Miss Lay
Mr. B. Lemon
Mr. Leyson Lewis
Rev. Mr. Lindley
Mr. John Lovick

M
Miss Maling, Bury
Mr. John March, 2 copies
Mr. Thomas Marks

Mr. Edward Marsh
Mr. David Martineau
Mr. Thomas Martineau
Mr. Matchett, Printer
Miss Mildred, Diss
Rev. Mr. Charles Millard
Mr. R. Mindham, jun., of Wells,
  2 copies
Mr. James Moore
Mr. Stephen Moore
Mr. Muskett

N
Mr. William Newson
Rev. Samuel Newton

O
Mr. Olier
Miss Olier
Mr. Edward Ollett
Mr. John Oxley

P
Mrs. Palmer
Joseph Parker, Esq., of Mettingham
Mr. Parkinson, Hellesdon
Robert Partridge, Esq.
Mr. J. Paul, Mettingham
Mr. Robert Paul, Starston
Mr. Thomas Paul
Mr. Robert Pearson
Mr. E[dmund]. Peckover
Mr. Pitchford, jun.
Mr. Plowman, Bungay
Miss Plumtree
Mr. Charles Potter
Mr. Prentice, Bungay
Mrs. Pullyn, Beccles

R
H. Raven, Esq., Bramerton
Mr. John Reymes
Mr. Richardson
Mr. Rigby

Mr. John Roach
Mr. W.T. Robberds, 4 copies
Mr. John Roberts
Rev. H[enry]. Robinson, Diss
Mr. James Robinson
Mrs. Rookes
Mr. James Rump
Mr. William Rye

S

Mr. John Scott, jun.
Mr. Sewell, sen., 2 books
Mr. Jacob Shalders
Mr. Sillis, jun.
Mr. J. Sims, 3 copies
Mr. J. Simpson
Mr. Simpson
Mr. W.W. Simpson, Diss
Miss E. Smith
Miss F. Smith
Mr. Jacob Smith
Rev. J.G. Smith
Mr. Edward Sparshall
Mr. Squire
Mr. Charles Starkey
Mr. Stevenson
Miss Stevenson
N. Styleman, Esq.
Robert Suffield, Esq.
Robert Suffield, jun.

T

Mr. John Taylor
Mr. John Taylor, sen.
Mr. J[ohn]. S[tuart]. Taylor
Mr. M. Taylor, Diss
Mr. William Taylor
Mr. Taylor, jun.
Mr. Thomas Theobald
Mr. J. Thompson
Mr. Thurgar, jun.
Mr. John Toll, sen.
Mr. Robert Tramplett

Mr. Charles Tuthill
Mr. John Tuthill, jun.

U

Mr. Unthank

W

Rev. John Walker
Mr. Robert Ward
Mr. John Waters
Mr. George Watson, 2 copies
Mr. Thomas Watson
Mr. John Webb
Rev. S. Westby, Diss
Mr. White, 2 copies
Mr. S. Wilkin
Mr. William Wilkins
Mr. Mark Wilks
Rev. Mr. [James] Willins
Mr. Peter Wilsea
Mr. Charles Winn
Mr. B. Wiseman, Diss
Mr. R[obert]. Woodhouse, 2 copies
Mr. Worth, sen.
Mr. John Wright
Mr. John Wright, Buxton

Y

Mess. Yarrington and Bacon, 2 copies
Mr. William Youngman

NINTH EDITION (LONDON, 1794)

Joseph Ainges, Yarmouth
Travel Fuller, Yarmouth
Rev. Mr. Ray, Sudbury
Rev. Dr. Temple, near Beccles

Lynn Subscribers
Mr. James Ayre
Mr. Thomas Ayre

Mr. Samuel Baker
Mr. Birkboek
Mr. William Cooper
Mr. James Coulton
Mr. William Currie
Mr. William Dunn, Docking
Rev. Mr. Edward Edwards
Mr. G. Edwards, 4 cop.
Mr. John Egleton
Mr. John Benson Friend
Mr. Michael Gage
Mr. T. Gales, 2 copies
Mr. Gamble
Mr. Harry Goodwin
Mr. Samuel Hadley
Rev. Mr. William Hardyman
Mr. J. Hedley, 4 copies
Mr. Michael Jackson
John Marshall, M.D.

Mr. Samuel Newham
Mr. Richard Newman
Josiah Packwood, M.D.
Mr. George Peeke
Mr. Henry Reggester
Rev. W. Richards, M.A.,
  2 copies
Mr. W.C. Tooke
Mr. R[obert]. Whincop

Wisbeach Subscribers
Mr. J. Clark, Gosberton
Mrs. Clarkson
Mrs. John Clarkson
Mr. John Cockett
Mr. William Fallows
Mr. William Friend
Elizabeth Heightholme
Mr. Jonathan Peckover, 2 copies